Mr. Justice Black and His Critics

Mr. Justice Black and His Critics

Tinsley E. Yarbrough

Duke University Press   Durham and London   1988

To my mother
Another strong-minded, granite-willed Alabamian

Contents

Preface

N his last opinion of his last term on the Supreme Court, Justice Hugo Lafayette Black reaffirmed his uncompromising commitment to an absolutist interpretation of the First Amendment. The occasion was the *Pentagon Papers Cases*, the words entirely familiar to anyone even vaguely aware of the Justice's jurisprudence. "I adhere to the view," Black asserted,

> that the Government's case against the Washington Post should have been dismissed and that the injunction against the New York Times should have been vacated without oral argument when the cases were first presented to this Court. I believe that every moment's continuance of the injunction against these newspapers amounts to a flagrant, indefensible, and continuing violation of the First Amendment. . . . In my view it is unfortunate that some of my Brethren are apparently willing to hold that the publication of news may sometimes be enjoined. Such a holding would make a shambles of the First Amendment.[1]

During that same final term of a distinguished 34 years' tenure, however, Hugo Black also came down on the side of government with what, for some, was astonishing regularity. In *Younger* v. *Harris*[2] he invoked "Our Federalism" in holding for the majority that federal district courts have no general power to enjoin "good faith" state criminal prosecutions, even those violative of First Amendment guarantees. Speaking for the Court in other cases, he upheld the submission of low-rent housing projects to community referendum,[3] sustained a statute favoring legitimate children over their illegitimate siblings,[4] affirmed Jackson, Mississippi's decision to close its municipal swimming pools rather than submit to court-ordered integration,[5] and denied Congress power to establish a minimum age for participation in state elections.[6] In conference discussion he rejected claims to a constitutionally guaranteed abortion right.[7] He also dissented from decisions overturning filing fee requirements for indigent couples seeking a divorce,[8] decisions holding that the Fourth Amendment grants a federal cause of action to the victims of illegal police searches,[9] and decisions prohibiting government from penalizing the mere public display of offensive epithets.[10] Sitting as circuit justice in *Karr* v. *Schmidt*,[11] moreover, he rejected claims that a school hair code raised constitutional implications. To the contention that the issue of school hair length regulations was becoming a national "crisis," he caustically retorted:

> The only thing about it that borders on the serious to me is the idea that anyone should think the Federal Constitution imposes on the United States courts the burden of supervising the length of hair that public school students should wear. . . . There can, of course, be honest differences of opinion as to whether any government, state or federal, should as a matter of public policy regulate the length of haircuts, but it would be difficult to prove by reason, logic, or common sense that the federal judiciary is more competent to deal with hair length than are the local school authorities and state legislatures of all our 50 states.[12]

Unlike those who measure a jurist purely in terms of his voting patterns, Justice Black could see little inconsistency in such seemingly eccentric responses to constitutional issues. To the extent humanly possible, he would insist, he had always been faithful to the Constitution's text and the intent of its framers. In certain cases that constitutional faith—a faith envisioning a ceiling as well as a floor for the Constitution's meaning—required decisions favoring government; in others, rulings for the individual. That had been his philosophy early as well as late in his career, Black argued, and it was the only approach to constitutional interpretation compatible with the democratic principle that legislators and Constitution makers, not judges, are the appropriate repositories of governmental policy.[13]

Naturally, such a jurisprudence is unacceptable to those who contend, with one of Black's critics, that constitutional judgments will survive only if "related to meaningful conceptions of justice."[14] Nor can it satisfy those who demand perfection in a judicial and constitutional philosophy or erroneously assume that Black believed in a self-interpreting Constitution. And Black's thinking was attacked on many other fronts as well. Early in his tenure, critics accused the "liberal-activist" Black of reading too much into the Constitution. During his last decade on the bench, when his voting patterns grew progressively, if not consistently, more conservative, critics of another persuasion complained he was reading too little into the nation's basic law. Others dismissed his interpretivist approach to constitutional construction as irrelevant to modern needs, or impossible to implement, and claimed that it produced "arbitrary" distinctions between what lay within and without the Constitution's perimeters. Still others challenged the Justice's claim to basic consistency over time, criticized the "perverse" results his constructions often yielded, and rejected his interpretations of significant constitutional provisions. Probably no other Justice's jurisprudence, in fact, has been subjected to such systematic and extensive criticism. Yet, to date, no study has attempted an assessment of the arguments raised by Black's many critics.

This book attempts such an evaluation as well as my own analysis of Justice Black's judicial and constitutional philosophy. Before beginning, however, I want to make clear the perspective from which I approach the Justice's jurisprudence and the thinking of his critics. Justice Black has been a research interest of mine for more than two decades. Over those years I have concluded that his conception of the judge's function in constitutional cases restricts judicial discretion to a greater degree than other approaches to the judicial function and offers a workable, if imperfect, alternative to noninterpretivist conceptions of the judicial role—to approaches, that is, which emphasize the open-ended nature of important constitutional provisions, exalting the desirability, or accepting the inevitability, of constitutional constructions bottomed not on text or history, but on moral, ethical, or social predilections. I am also convinced that, early as well as late in his career, Justice Black was essentially consistent in both his approach to the judge's role and construction of specific constitutional provisions and that his interpretations are generally well grounded in the Constitution's text and history. Even so, this study is no apologia for Justice Black's jurisprudence. Instead, I have simply subjected the contentions of Black's critics to the same sort of scrutiny they have long given the

Justice's jurisprudence. I hope that I have been fair; certainly, I have tried to be.

During the twenty years Justice Black has been one of my primary research interests, the insights of numerous students of public law generally, and of Justice Black's jurisprudence in particular, have been of tremendous benefit. I am especially grateful to Henry J. Abraham, Howard Ball, Gerald Dunne, A. E. Dick Howard, J. Woodford Howard, and M. Glenn Abernathy, as well as to several of the Black critics whose thinking is this book's core concern, including Wallace Mendelson, James Magee, and Sylvia Snowiss.

For critical financial support, I am indebted to the National Endowment for the Humanities, the Southern Regional Education Board, and the Research Committee of East Carolina University. My thanks go also to the staffs of the Manuscript Division of the Library of Congress, the Michigan Historical Collection at the University of Michigan, the Yale University Law Library, the Seeley G. Mudd Manuscript Library at Princeton University, the Supreme Court Library, and the Joyner Library at East Carolina University.

Finally, I am grateful to Julia Bloodworth, once again, for flawless typing; to Richard C. Rowson of Duke University Press for expertly shepherding the manuscript through the editorial and production process; and especially, as always, to Mary Alice, Sarah, and Cole for their tolerance and love.

One The Critics

HUGO Lafayette Black was a controversial figure all his public life and remains so in death. His membership in the Ku Klux Klan during the twenties was brief, pro forma, and, by Black's account, largely designed to enhance his ties with prospective Alabama jurors. But its revelation in the national press shocked the nation, casting a pall over his appointment to the Supreme Court. Anticipating southern segregationists by nearly two decades, one group condemned October 4, 1937, the Justice's first day on the high bench, as "Black Day," to be "so mourned each year as the *Blackest Day* in the history of American Justice."[1]

The liberal voting record Black soon forged largely allayed doubts that publicity about his Klan affiliation had aroused. But some never forgave him for that association or for his appeals to the racial and religious biases of Alabama jurors in a notorious murder case,[2] his rough treatment of Senate investigation targets,[3] and his opinion upholding World War II sanctions against Japanese-Americans in *Korematsu* v. *United States*.[4] Nor were such concerns alleviated by a 1967 newspaper interview with the Justice published following his death, wherein Black reaffirmed his *Korematsu* stance, emphasized the difficulty of separating loyal from disloyal Japanese, then remarked: "They all look alike to a person not a Jap."[5] In a review of Gerald Dunne's biography of the Justice, Professor John Noonan dredged up "the repulsive aspects" of Black's career, scoring "[t]his Birmingham trial lawyer, whose judicial experience consisted of a term in 1910 as a police court magistrate, this KKK-sponsored Senator who had gained national attention by his Mc-Carthyesque tactics as a senatorial investigator (Why is it McCarthyism and not Blackism?), this superpatriot who could never tell Americans of

Japanese descent apart from aliens."[6] Dunne, not his subject, Noonan concluded, was due admiration for his "accomplishment of charity in finding beneath Hugo Black's . . . practical failings a man . . . he can love."[7]

Noonan was not offended, however, merely by Justice Black's purported pre-Court insensitivities to civil rights or his *Korematsu* opinion. He also attacked the "intellectual disarray" he saw in elements of the Justice's judicial and constitutional philosophy.[8] And Noonan was hardly alone in that regard. Justice Black's contention that judges should stick to the Constitution's language and the intent of its framers, his claim that his interpretations squared with the document's "plain" meaning, and his insistence that conflicting constructions embodied mere personal policy preferences, as well as the often revolutionary meanings he perceived for specific constitutional provisions, generated considerable debate on and off the Court throughout his judicial career.[9] On the Court, moreover, the bulldog tenacity with which he advanced his positions probably fueled the controversy that the contours of his jurisprudence inherently aroused.

The Judicial Critics

Through most of their respective careers, of course, Felix Frankfurter was Black's principal jurisprudential antagonist on the Court— and, along with Robert H. Jackson, perhaps his major personal antagonist as well.[10] Black and Frankfurter denied stories of a long-running personal feud, but relations between the two were surely not entirely cordial. When Owen Roberts, who often had joined the Court's laissez-faire conservatives in invalidating early New Deal legislation, announced his retirement from the bench in 1945, Chief Justice Stone prepared the customary farewell letter for his colleagues' signatures. Justice Black, a harsh critic of the Old Court's repudiation of the Roosevelt recovery program, objected to a passage indicating the Justices' regret "that our association with you in the daily work of the Court must now come to an end," and to the observation that Roberts had "made fidelity to principle your guide to decision." To secure unanimity the Chief Justice agreed to Black's amendments. When Justice Frankfurter learned of the deletions, however, he persuaded Stone to circulate the original letter among their colleagues, with the passages to which

Black objected enclosed in brackets.[11] In addition, Frankfurter wrote his brethren a brief letter. He had no qualm, he informed them, about deletion of the first passage cited by Black. "But I cannot be party," he observed, "to the denial, under challenge, of what I believe to be the fundamental truth about Roberts, the Justice,—that he 'made fidelity to principle' his 'guide to decision.'" "My numerous and serious disagreements with Roberts," he pointedly added, "are, of course, beside the point."[12]

At times, moreover, Frankfurter sided with Justice Jackson in his protracted, well-publicized, and embarrassing battles with Justice Black. When Black was appointed to the bench, Jackson sent him a congratulatory letter expressing "high confidence" in Black's "capacity to translate into law our aspirations for a better social order" and "carry on a continuous tradition of liberalism."[13] After Jackson's appointment, however, philosophical differences, a clash of personalities, and abrasive competition for the leadership Chief Justice Stone had failed to provide the Court gradually took their toll;[14] and the Black-Jackson relationship became increasingly strained. With the *Jewell Ridge* coal company case,[15] their relations approached the breaking point.

In a suit between the Jewell Ridge Coal Corporation and a United Mine Workers local, a narrow majority, affirming a ruling of the Court of Appeals for the Fourth Circuit, held that provisions of the Fair Labor Standards Act covered the time spent by miners traveling underground between the portal of a bituminous coal mine and its working face, whatever the terms of any conflicting custom or contract. Justice Black joined the majority; Chief Justice Stone and Justices Roberts, Frankfurter, and Jackson dissented. Jackson circulated a lengthy dissent. Disputing the majority's reading of the Fair Labor Standards Act's legislative history, Jackson quoted remarks of then Senator Black, one of the bill's sponsors, which tended to support the coal company's claim that federal regulations did not reach "portal to face" travel covered by conflicting customs or contracts.[16]

Black was incensed. In a memorandum to his colleagues, he contended that his remarks were taken out of context and related to an "entirely different" bill than the version finally adopted. "If the dissent goes down as now printed," he asserted, "it will not be a fair representation of the true facts."[17] Albeit with some caution, Justice Frank Murphy's majority opinion in the case also rejected Jackson's reading of the legislative history as well as the dissent's use of Black's Senate remarks. But Jackson filed his dissent without deleting the offensive passages.

Nor was the battle nearly at an end. In the years since Justice Black's appointment, litigants had objected to his participation in cases reviewing the validity and meaning of statutes he had sponsored while a member of the Senate. In their petition for a rehearing, however, Jewell Ridge's counsel raised what to them was a more critical concern: Black had participated in the case even though his former law partner, Birmingham attorney Crampton Harris, had represented the union. Recusal is largely a matter of individual judgment over which a Justice's colleagues have no control. While agreeing that a rehearing should be denied, Chief Justice Stone suggested that the denial be accompanied by a statement indicating that the Court as a whole could not pass upon the propriety of a member's decision to participate in a given case. "If the *per curiam* goes down in this case," Justice Black quickly retorted, "please put the names of the Justices who agree to it, and leave mine out."[18] The Chief Justice next proposed that those dissenting from the original decision file such a statement[19] but soon withdrew that proposition as well. Justice Jackson was not so restrained. He concurred with the Court's denial of a rehearing. In a brief opinion which Justice Frankfurter joined, however, Jackson explained that Jewell Ridge's complaint "as to the qualification of one of the Justices to take part in" a decision could not "properly be addressed to the Court as a whole," adding: "Because of [a] lack of authoritative standards it appears always to have been considered the responsibility of each Justice to determine for himself the propriety of withdrawing in any particular circumstances. . . . There is no authority known to me under which the majority of this Court has power under any circumstances to exclude one of its duly commissioned Justices from sitting or voting in any case."[20]

The concurrence appeared on June 18, 1945. That same day Jackson departed for Nuremberg where he was to serve as American prosecutor of Nazi war criminals. Several days earlier Justice Frankfurter had written Black a conciliatory letter explaining why he had joined the Jackson opinion. He "greatly regret[ted] the whole incident," Frankfurter assured Black, and had "not the remotest foreknowledge" that Chief Justice Stone would raise the issue during conference discussion of the *Jewell Ridge* rehearing petition. Nor had he any "share in creating the situation whereby Bob felt it to be his duty to make clear the issue of qualification." At the same time he assumed all would "admit the correctness of what Bob says," and that once Jackson had acted, Frankfurter "could withhold joining only by suppressing my belief in the truth."[21]

Jackson's concurrence, of course, was more than an abstract discourse on recusal policy. In context it was a thinly veiled implication that Black should have refrained from participation in *Jewell Ridge*—and a particularly offensive implication in view of the fact that Black's recusal would not have affected the final outcome of the litigation. It thus is unlikely that Frankfurter's letter assuaged Justice Black's irritation at his colleagues' behavior.

Justice Jackson's absence provided a brief lull in the storm. By the spring of 1946, however, rumors of the feud were a frequent topic of Washington gossip, as were stories that Justice Frankfurter was promoting Jackson as a replacement for Chief Justice Stone, who had died in April. In May *Washington Star* columnist Doris Fleeson published an account of the friction afflicting the Court.[22] Justice Black, she reported, had reacted at Jackson's *Jewell Ridge* concurrence "with fiery storm to what he regarded as an open and gratuitous insult, a slur upon his personal and judicial honor. Nor did he bother to conceal his contempt. An already marked coolness, especially between Messrs. Black and Frankfurter, froze into impenetrable ice." President Truman, Fleeson added, was aware of the clash. "Black says," the President had reportedly confided to a senator, "he will resign if I make Jackson Chief Justice and tell the reasons why. Jackson says the same thing about Black."

For a time Justice Jackson, like Justice Black, declined public comment. But Jackson had long coveted the Court's center seat. And when President Truman nominated Fred M. Vinson to succeed Chief Justice Stone, Jackson's frustrations overwhelmed his judgment. On June 10, he dispatched a remarkable 1,500-word cablegram from Nuremberg to members of the House and Senate Judiciary Committees, copies of which he also provided the press.[23] In the cablegram Jackson bitterly denounced Justice Black, accusing him of "bullying" tactics, scoring his "publicized threats to the President," and implying that Black was the source of news reports suggesting that "offensive behavior on my part is responsible for the feud on the Court." While appointment of a Chief

Justice was pending, Jackson asserted, he had been unable to defend himself "without being in the position of pleading for the post." Now, he was free to respond "and chose to do so not by inspired innuendoes but over my signature." Relating his version of the *Jewell Ridge* affair, he insisted that his controversial concurring opinion was not part of any "personal vendetta," but instead was necessary to make clear that Justice Black's decision to sit in the case was his alone and that denial of a rehearing should in no way be construed as indicating the Court's approval of Black's decision. In the face of Black's conference threat of a "declaration of war" if any opinion were filed, Jackson added, his concurrence had also been his only way to maintain "self-respect."

At one point in the cablegram, Jackson denied saying that Black was "wrong" to sit; later, he rejected any inference that he considered Black's participation a reflection of a "lack of 'honor.'" But ultimately, he condemned "the employment of justices' ex-law partners to argue close cases," warning: "I wanted that practice stopped. If it is ever repeated while I am on the bench I will make my Jewell Ridge opinion look like a letter of recommendation by comparison."

The day the text of the cablegram appeared in the American press, a former law clerk wired Justice Black: "This outburst begins the final triumph. Congratulations on winning a real if bloody victory in the unmasking of a bad man."[24] The telegram was filed unanswered, and Justice Black continued to decline public comment, telling reporters: "I haven't made a statement of any kind to the press since coming up here. I don't expect to make any now."[25] As the telegram suggested, however, Jackson's cablegram was clearly more damaging to its author than to its target. One Republican senator demanded Black's resignation, while another hinted darkly at impeachment proceedings, and still other congressmen recommended a review of the recusal policy. But the chairman of the House Judiciary Committee dismissed an impeachment inquiry as a remote possibility,[26] and the Congress quickly lost interest in the allegations which, Justice Jackson had claimed, went "to the reputation of the Court for non-partisan and unbiased decision." President Truman informed newsmen, moreover, that he had attempted to dissuade Jackson from issuing the statement, at least until he had had an opportunity to discuss the matter with the Justice; and press reports noted Truman's "apparent" disapproval of Jackson's action.[27]

Jackson himself made no further public statements, and when he returned to the Court the following October, he and Black resumed outwardly cordial, if essentially aloof and formal, relations. But his feelings had hardly mellowed. At one point, apparently in 1949, he drafted another scathing attack.[28] His focus again was on the *Jewell Ridge* incident, but on this occasion his assault had a broader reach. As a senator, he wrote, Black had been "one of the most persistent patronage seekers" and a man whom "a subordinate better not cross and the heads of departments rarely offended for fear of reprisal." In Senate investigations his conduct had been "ruthless," reflecting "little regard for the constitutional rights of persons he was pursuing." And his appointment to the Court had been President Roosevelt's revenge against both the Court and the Congress.

> The president was angry at the Senate which had defeated his plan to reorganize the Court, and he was angry at the Court which had destroyed his favorite legislation. He could humiliate them both at a single stroke by naming Black. However distasteful to the Senate, it could not refuse to confirm him because of its tradition of Senatorial courtesy. . . . The Senate would have to swallow hard and approve. The Court would be humiliated by having to accept one of its more bitter and unfair critics and one completely alien to the judicial tradition. It was a choice which would get even with them both.

During Black's early years on the bench, the memorandum continued, Jackson, "[l]ike many other Americans, [had] felt a sense of relief that it was not as bad as had been expected. . . . [Black] never failed to support the Government in matters essential to its economic programs." When Jackson joined the Court, he knew that Black had opposed his appointment as Chief Justice, "quite naturally preferring [Stone,] an older man from whose appointment he could anticipate a vacancy." But he had anticipated no difficulty working with Black. He had soon found, though, that Black, who believed the conclusion of a "cheap" article that he was the Court's real leader and had "mastered philosophy in one summer," "cherished great resentment" whenever Jackson failed to vote with his senior colleague "with Party regularity."[29] Jackson was also "shocked to find," he wrote, "that Black was far to the left of anything that I had associated with in the New Deal. . . . [H]e embraced that form of collectivism which is so often confused with liberalism," his votes rarely going "against communist party lines."

Jackson's original draft was framed in the first person. Later, he crafted a different version.[30] Writing this time in the third person, he applauded his own record and attacked Black's, observing at one point, for example:

> Both Stone and Jackson had been among the liberal groups of the bar and of their respective parties; both had endangered their own interests by standing up for free speech, free press, and minority rights when Black was getting to the top of Alabama politics by joining the Klan and exploiting racial and religious bias. Now that he no longer found these serviceable but found them reacting to his injury, he had repudiated them and, with the zeal of a convert, outdid everybody in civil libertarianism.

A friend with whom Jackson shared his second draft was only guardedly sympathetic, suggesting that the Justice's references to Black's exploitation of "racial and religious bias" were "a little strong."[31] Perhaps for that reason Jackson decided against another public display of his feelings. He would go to his grave, however, resentful of Black and convinced that his colleague's opposition had denied him the chief justiceship.[32]

Justice Frankfurter's personal regard for Justice Black was apparently higher than Justice Jackson's. Frankfurter was also relatively assiduous in his efforts to maintain cordial relations with his colleague. When two Washington correspondents claimed in a gossipy 1950 account of the Truman administration that Frankfurter had fed Justice Jackson's growing irritation with Black, Frankfurter wrote Black a letter, complaining that the book was "so unqualifiedly unfounded in fact that I am greatly tempted to sue both the publishers and the authors for libel."[33] Black's response was soothing. Quoting Omar Khayyám, he assured Frankfurter that he had "neither seen nor read any part" of the book. "So far as I am concerned, it is the same as though it had never been written. For it too will pass away."[34]

Frankfurter's feelings for Black, however, were clearly complicated. Those corresponding with Frankfurter apparently had no inhibitions about referring to Black as a "skunk"[35] or in other disparaging terms. At times, moreover, Frankfurter carefully drafted and filed, for biographers no doubt, detailed and unflattering accounts of incidents in which Black was involved. One related to the plight of a defendant slated for execution in Alabama. As the late night hour of the scheduled execution approached, according to Frankfurter's account, his law clerk had visited his home "to tell me that Justice Black, in whose Circuit this matter lay, had made himself inaccessible all day so that he could not be reached [with petitions for a stay of execution], because he did not want to be involved in this case." When Frankfurter telephoned Black, he was told to "do what I pleased."[36] Frankfurter granted a stay, and the full Court later summarily reversed the defendant's conviction on the authority of *Chambers* v. *Florida*,[37] the 1940 decision in which the Court, through one of Justice Black's most moving opinions, had overturned the convictions of poor black defendants subjected to coercive police interrogation tactics.

Equally revealing, of its author more so perhaps than its subject, was Frankfurter's lengthy account of a conversation with Chief Justice Warren about their colleague. In late January 1961, Black had telephoned the Chief Justice, raising "very agitated" objections to Warren's decision to hold a conference in two First Amendment cases before Black returned to Washington from a Florida trip. Later, Warren visited Frankfurter's chambers, expressing dismay at Black's irritation. "I don't suppose these recesses of the Court," Frankfurter recorded himself telling the Chief Justice, "are meant as holidays for the members of the Court." "I agree with you entirely," Warren had replied, "they are not meant to be holidays in which men go off to do what they please." Frankfurter then observed that Black's reaction simply reflected "one of his deep traits" and illustrated his point with an anecdote involving Black's daughter Josephine when she was a child.

> She could not have been more than eight or nine years old when on one of our Conference days she turned up in my room just as I was about to go to the Conference room. I asked her to come along with me into the Conference room and she said that Daddy wouldn't like that. I said that if I wanted her to come along with me it would be all right, but she insisted, "Daddy wouldn't like it and so I can't come with you." "But," she added, "I wish you would do something for me." I told her I couldn't imagine that there was anything she might ask of me I wouldn't do for her, and she replied with fierce intensity, "I wish you would vote against Daddy, because he always has to have his way."

"I said to the Chief," Frankfurter added, " 'You know that is true,' and the Chief replied, 'Yes, I do.' "[38]

Justice Frankfurter's positions regarding elements of Justice Black's jurisprudence were not nearly so difficult to fathom, of course, as the essence of his personal feelings toward his colleague. Before Frankfurter's retirement from the Court, the Justices were confronted with the first of many sit-in cases challenging criminal prosecutions of civil rights demonstrators. In conference discussion of such cases, Justice Black had quickly made clear his view that the protesters had no constitutional right to remain on the premises of restaurants or other businesses against the owner's wishes, however racial his motives. After Frankfurter's retirement from the bench, he wrote Black a letter assuring him of his "esteem," applauding Black's sit-in stance, and urging him to file an opinion on the issue. "I am dead certain," he wrote,

> that if you could write a separate little piece setting forth the essentials of what you told all of us twice at Conference—that you would never consent to any decision which held that the Constitution of the United States compelled you to do business with whom you did not want to do business, subject of course to two qualifications, that "your" business was really wholly your own and neither in its origin nor in its maintenance drew directly or indirectly on State or Federal funds and because of that factor no racial discrimination was permissible, and secondly, provided a specific case does not violate the Due Process Clause in its procedural aspects. . . . Even a few words of moderation along the lines I have tried to recall would have a powerful educative effect not only on the Negroes but also on whites. You could of course include an expression of your credo on the subject of racism, but were you also to add a moderating note it would be one of the greatest services you could render the Nation and the Court.[39]

When Black's sit-in dissents in *Bell* v. *Maryland* and *Hamm* v. *City of Rock Hill* appeared in 1964, Frankfurter wrote again, praising his old adversary's "powerful" opinions.[40] Black soon responded. "More than a quarter of century's close association," he wrote, "has enabled both of us, I suspect, to anticipate with reasonable accuracy the basic position both are likely to take on questions that importantly involve the public welfare and tranquility. Our differences, which have been many, have rarely been over the ultimate end desired, but rather have related to the means that were most likely to achieve the end we both envisioned."[41]

Whether over "means" or "ends," the two Justices' philosophical differences were, as Black wrote, indeed numerous, their essential agreement on the sit-in issue hardly typical of their usual stances. Almost from the beginning of their respective careers on the bench, Justice Frankfurter questioned Black's assumption that the Constitution's provisions and the history underlying their adoption provided relatively clear guides for judges, if only they would heed them. At times Frankfurter suggested that Black's interpretivist approach to the meaning of constitutional provisions and statutes was largely a cloak concealing his colleague's political and social goals.

Consider, for example, Frankfurter's reaction to a Black dissent in a 1943 case involving the Interstate Commerce Commission.[42] The ICC had granted a railroad company request that the railroads be permitted to charge higher rates for the reshipment from Chicago of grain brought in by barge rather than by rail or lake steamer. The Court, per Justice Jackson, upheld the rate increase. In dissent, Justice Black contended that the sole issue in the case, albeit one hidden behind "a verbal camouflage of 'complexities and technicalities,'" was "whether the farmers and shippers of the middle west can be compelled by the Interstate Commerce Commission and the railroads to use high-priced rail instead of low-priced barge transportation for the shipment of grain to the east."[43] For Black, the answer was clear: congressional statutes prohibited differential rates for a kind of transportation shipped under substantially similar circumstances and conditions. But Frankfurter, siding with the majority, drafted, though he did not file, the following "concurrence":

> I greatly sympathize with the essential purpose of my Brother (former Senator) Black's dissent. His roundabout and turgid legal phraseology is an *en de coeur*. "Would I were back in the Senate," he means to say, "so that I could put on the statute books what really ought to be there. But here I am, cast by Fate into a den of judges devoid of the habits of legislators, simple fellows who feel that they must enforce the laws as Congress wrote them and not as they really should have been written, that the task which Congress has committed to the Interstate Commerce Commission should be left to that Commission even when it decides, as it did in this case, against the poor farmer of the Middle West."[44]

In correspondence and opinions, however, Frankfurter normally was not so blunt. Instead, he raised few questions about the sincerity of Black's commitment to interpretivism and challenged his colleague's approach on its own terms. In a significant December 15, 1939, letter, Frankfurter compared Black's thinking to that of the English utilitarian Jeremy Bentham. In the letter he recalled having referred to Black as a "Benthamite" during a recent conversation. He intended that label, he assured Black, to be "fundamentally" one "of praise," since he considered Bentham "the most fruitful law reformer of the Nineteenth Century." But he questioned extremes in Bentham's, and presumably Black's, thinking:

> [A]s is so often true of a reformer who seeks to get rid of the accumulated abuses of the past Bentham at times threw out the baby with the bath. In his rigorous and candid desire to rid the law of many far-reaching abuses introduced by judges, he was not unnaturally propelled to the opposite extreme of wishing all law to be formulated by legislation, deeming most that judges do a usurpation by incompetent men as to matters concerning which he believed them guilty of "judicial legislation."[45]

Frankfurter assured Black that he, too, was "opposed to judicial legislation in its invidious sense," but condemned as "equally mischievous—because founded on an untruth and an impossible aim—the notion that judges merely announce the law which they find and do not themselves inevitably have a share in the law-making," adding:

> Here, as elsewhere, the difficulty comes from arguing in terms of absolutes when the matter at hand is conditioned by circumstances, is contingent upon the everlasting problem of how far is too far and how much is too much. Judges, as you well know, cannot escape the responsibility of filling in gaps which the finitude of even the most imaginative legislation renders inevitable. And so it is that even in countries governed exclusively by codes and even in the best of all codes there are provisions saying in effect that when a controversy arises in court for which the code offers no provision the judges are not relieved of the duty of deciding the case but must themselves fashion the law appropriate to the situation.

When judges give the impression that they "only find the law and don't make it," Frankfurter concluded, they resort to a "very evil . . . lack of candor. By covering up the lawmaking function of judges, we miseducate the people and fail to bring out into the open the real responsibility of judges for what they do."

Nor, from the beginning, was Frankfurter willing to accept Black's contention that judicial discretion was a threat to democratic principles, allowing—indeed, forcing—judges to impose their personal moral, ethical, or policy predilections on the people and their elected representatives. In a November 13, 1943, letter to Black, Frankfurter agreed "that men who have power can exercise it—and too often do—to enforce their own will, to make their will, or if you like their notions of policy, the measure of what is right."[46] But he was also convinced that judges could exercise the discretion given them within a democratic context.

> I am . . . aware of the forces of tradition and the habits of discipline whereby men entrusted with power remain within the limited framework of their professed power. More particularly, the history of this Court emboldens me to believe that men need not be supermen to observe the conditions under which judicial review of political authority . . . is ultimately maintainable in a democratic society. When men who had such background and such relation to so-called property interests as did, for instance, Waite, Bradley, Moody, Holmes, Brandeis and Cardozo, showed how scrupulously they did not write their private notions of policy into the Constitution, then I am not prepared to say that all that a court does when it adjudicates in these constitutional controversies is an elaborate pretense, and that judges do in fact merely translate their private convictions into decisions and call it law and the Constitution.

For Frankfurter, in fact, "Hitler [was] the true prophet if there is no such thing as Law different from or beyond the individuals who gave it expression"; and judges were capable of discovering and applying such principles.

Although in less direct language, Frankfurter also raised such contentions in opinions challenging Black's stance in specific cases. In addition, of course, he became the leading critic on the Court of many of the more controversial elements of Black's constitutional jurisprudence, including his assertion that the Fourteenth Amendment incorporated the Bill of Rights, making its guarantees applicable against the states, and his construction of the First Amendment.

When Justice John Marshall Harlan replaced Justice Jackson on the Court in 1955, Frankfurter also moved quickly to secure Harlan as an ally in his jurisprudential battles with Black. Particularly when the language of a Harlan opinion would appear to accept, in some slight degree, Black's incorporation thesis, Frankfurter's reaction was prompt and predictable. In a minor 1957 state case, for example, Harlan circulated a draft opinion for the Court which included the statement, "It is indisputable that the right to counsel in criminal cases is fundamental to our jurisprudence."[47] Such language could have been construed to conflict with *Betts* v. *Brady*,[48] the 1942 case in which the Court had held, over Justice Black's dissent, that the Sixth Amendment guarantee of counsel was insufficiently "fundamental" to be generally required of states under the Fourteenth Amendment's due process clause. Frankfurter soon so reminded his colleague. "John, you can't use this phrase," he cautioned in a marginal notation on the Harlan draft. "I certainly cannot subscribe to it with *Betts* v. *Brady* on the books. It would be quoted at once as indicating an invitation to ask us to overrule" *Betts*.

Frankfurter's reaction to a Harlan draft of the Court's 1958 decision in *NAACP* v. *Alabama*,[49] protecting the anonymity of the organization's Alabama members, was even more extensive. In an early effort Harlan observed, "It is of course firmly established that the protection given by the First Amendment against federal invasion of such rights is afforded by the Due Process Clause of the Fourteenth Amendment against state action."[50] "Why in heaven's name," Frankfurter retorted, "must we, whenever some discussion under the Due Process Clause is involved, get off speeches about the First Amendment?"[51] In two lengthy letters and at least one conversation, Frankfurter defended his view that while the Fourteenth Amendment included within its meaning freedoms analogous to those in the Bill of Rights, the amendment's due process clause did not extend the First Amendment's terms, or construction in federal cases, to state legislation. He also expressed regret for any

> loose reference of mine years ago to the "First Amendment" as a shorthand for freedoms protected against state action by the Fourteenth Amendment. . . . Little did I dream in my early days when we were dealing with explicit curtailments of speech that loose rhetoric in the service of recently discovered doctrinaire views by members of the Court would be snowballed into a talismanic mouthing of "First Amendment" in dealing with state action. . . .
>
> . . . I have become strongly allergic to all this loose talk and the loose notions about "First Amendment" which will get this Court as sure as shooting into the same kind of dangerous controversy,

and from my point of view properly so, with the Congress and the Executive as it did in the prior period when it was riding high on "liberty [of] contract."[52]

The Fourteenth Amendment's "exact language" was the "only warrant" for the Court's interference with the action of states, Frankfurter asserted, urging Harlan to read his concurrence in *Adamson* v. *California* and other opinions on the amendment's meaning. The "liberty" protected by its due process clause was simply "my right," Frankfurter contended, "to do as I damn please, unless what I am doing is properly outlawable by the state in support of interests of the state, giving the state the broadest scope in asserting its interests and its means for safeguarding them."[53]

While entertaining "serious misgivings" about Frankfurter's "suggested approach,"[54] Harlan revised his draft, eliminating the offensive language. Now, however, Justice Black reacted. Albeit gently, with praise for a "magnificent job," and appreciation for Harlan's efforts to secure unanimity, Black challenged the recirculated opinion's "studious avoidance of any statement that might possibly imply a pertinency of the First Amendment," an omission leaving Black with the "impression . . . that that basic provision of our Bill of Rights might be as contaminating as the leprosy." By such an approach the Court would appear to be "repudiating the constitutional principles" of many earlier cases, and Black wanted no part of it. If a majority agreed to the amended draft, he would register a concurrence, stating his "belief . . . that the state has here violated the basic freedoms of press, speech and assembly, immunized from federal abridgement by the First Amendment, and made applica[ble] as a prohibition against the States by the Fourteenth Amendment."[55]

Ultimately, Harlan was able to craft an opinion agreeable to Black as well as Frankfurter. In his conception of the judicial function and approach to specific issues, however, Harlan was to be more regularly allied with Frankfurter. And after Frankfurter's retirement, he continued a strong defense of the elements of their jurisprudence, though giving the Fourteenth Amendment a somewhat more concrete meaning than Frankfurter perhaps preferred.

Especially during their last decade on the bench, Harlan and Justice Black apparently enjoyed a warm personal relationship. Black, a native of Harlan, Alabama, was convinced that Harlan—and thus

Harlan's grandfather, the first Justice Harlan, who had been the Court's earliest advocate of Fourteenth Amendment incorporation, and whose portrait hung in Black's chambers—was a distant relation.[56] Black also probably found Harlan's courtly, gracious manner appealing; and while Harlan, like Justice Frankfurter, possessed the prestigious academic credentials Black lacked, Harlan was not the condescending "professor" Frankfurter had often been. (Shortly after Black's appointment, Frankfurter had sent the new Justice a copy of his work on federal jurisdiction and procedure. And his lectures to Black even included an occasional spelling lesson. "Won't you please spell his name correctly," he pleaded at one point, "only one 'f,' viz CHAFEE.") Toward the end of their lives, moreover, Harlan and Black found themselves allied with growing frequency, particularly in opposition to the Court's expansive interpretations of equal protection, the scope of the "state" action which the Constitution reached, and, ironically, the First Amendment. Even so, Harlan was probably the most discerning and eloquent critic on the Court of the major elements of Black's jurisprudence—as was Black of Harlan's philosophy.[57]

The Scholarly Critics

While Frankfurter and Harlan, assisted occasionally by Jackson or another justice, produced the major judicial criticism of Justice Black's philosophy, scholarly criticism of his jurisprudence has moved through several stages. During Black's career Charles Fairman and Stanley Morrison produced their extensive challenges to his incorporation thesis,[58] and a number of commentators attacked his absolutist conception of the First Amendment. But University of Texas government professor Wallace Mendelson was Black's most persistent critic. Mendelson was an unabashed admirer of the Justice and his jurisprudence, even writing him once that a recent visit to Frankfurter's chambers had been "a 'green isle in this deep, dark sea of misery.' "[59] In a major book[60] and numerous articles[61] Mendelson largely embraced Frankfurter's conception of the judicial role and approach to specific constitutional claims, while attacking virtually every aspect of Black's thinking.

Toward the end of Black's tenure, when the Justice began assuming seemingly "conservative" stances in protest, privacy, and equal protection cases, Professor Mendelson conceded the possibility that, in the Justice's mind at least, Black had never been the "liberal-activist" Mendelson had long condemned.[62] When the Court, in the landmark *Gris-wold* v. *Connecticut*,[63] recognized a constitutional right of privacy, Justice Black vehemently dissented, rejecting Justice Douglas's contention that such a guarantee lay within the "penumbras" of the Bill of Rights, Justice Goldberg's reliance on the enigmatic Ninth Amendment, and the resort of Justices Harlan and White to substantive due process. Shortly thereafter Mendelson wrote of the Justice's apparent metamorphosis:

> Perhaps under the impact of his brother Goldberg's ultra-activism, Mr. Justice Black has changed his mind about the role of courts in a democracy. Perhaps, finding that the Court had gone too far, he now accepts the "old-fashioned" Holmes-Hand-Frankfurter view that keeping law abreast of life is primarily a legislative, not a judicial, function. Or is he convinced that—whatever friends and foes may think—he has always been an anti-activist, adhering to the plain mandates of the written law?[64]

Mendelson apparently remained convinced, however, that Black's commitment to liberal social goals, rather than to constitutional text and history, had been the key motivating factor through most of his career. In a 1963 article Charles Reich, who had clerked for Justice Black, suggested that the Justice was dedicated to the principle of a "living Constitution," adaptable by judges to changing social needs.[65] Later, another former clerk, A. E. Dick Howard, had defended Black's consistent dedication to the "rule of law."[66] "No doubt," Mendelson remarked, "Mr. Howard's analysis is quite compatible with the judge's *words*, just as Mr. Reich's view is quite compatible with the judge's *votes* (prior to the early 1960s)."[67]

Although Justice Black's stance in *Griswold*, protest cases, and certain other civil liberties contexts may have mellowed somewhat Professor Mendelson's impressions of his subject, Black's increasingly conservative voting patterns during the last half decade of his tenure frustrated scholarly admirers appalled at his apparent break with his "liberal-activist" past. Unable to accept the thesis that the issues, not the Justice, had changed, political scientist Glendon Schubert attributed what he saw as Black's growing conservatism to aging. Beginning with his dissents in the 1964 sit-in cases, Schubert argued, Black had begun "to backslide from what had been largely his public posture of staunch and outspoken and indeed activist support of both civil liberties and economic liberalism," so that, by the spring of 1969, his opinions remained "liberal" only with regard to "such orthodox aspects of political freedom as freedom of speech (literally construed), and to the occasional claims to religious freedom or to voting equality."[68] Why had Black become a spokesman for "orthodox conservative dogma," a dogma inconsistent with the Supreme Court's "proper role as an instrument for the facilitation of controllable change"?[69] For Schubert the answer was clear: Black had simply "become too old for the job."[70] Either "biological aging" or "cultural dissonance reflecting an unbridgeable void between the conceptual world of the elderly judge and that of the political actors who have generated the issues before him for decision"[71] had made Black's "present posture . . . a poor fit for the needs of our day."[72] Thus, according to Schubert, while the youthful, seventy-one-year-old Justice Douglas continued to speak of "policy goals appropriate to American life in the twenty-first century," his aging, eighty-three-year-old colleague had become preoccupied "with restricting the Court to the support of those human rights that were deemed important in the eighteenth century."[73]

As Gerald Dunne has noted, Schubert "stood almost as alone in conclusion as he did in vocabulary,"[74] but really only with respect to the biological underpinnings of his thesis. Others have also disputed Justice Black's contention that he remained essentially consistent over time and that his approach to constitutional issues was bottomed on an interpretivist conception of the judicial function rather than on his policy preferences. S. Sidney Ulmer has conceded his inability to disprove the proposition that Black was successful "in developing early in his career on the Court a philosophical orientation sufficient to enable him to decide consistently all cases coming before him in the period 1937–1971."[75] But Ulmer clearly seems convinced that Black was influenced in his voting by the goals of a "moderate liberal" and that his response to issues confronting the Court did change over time. He has simply concluded that the voluminous opinions Blacks' lengthy tenure had produced can be used to support "diverse viewpoints," that seemingly inconsistent positions can always be explained away as a factor of case uniqueness, and that Black was never the sort of "doctrinaire liberal" whose deviations could be readily established.[76]

The recent research of Burton M. Atkins and Terry Sloope led them to less tentative conclusions. Atkins and Sloope found no statistical support for the hypothesis that Justice Black's declining level of support for civil liberties was a reaction to the changing distribution of issues confronting the Supreme Court, or for the proposition that the change was the Justice's "temporary reaction" to the "liberal thrust of the Court in the mid-1960s." Rather, they concluded that changes in Black's voting behavior "appear[ed] to be part of an overall ideological change."[77]

Yet another line of commentary has accepted the Constitution's text and history as Justice Black's core decision-making guides, yet challenged that approach to the judicial function as well as significant elements in the Justice's response to specific constitutional claims. John Hart Ely, among others, has argued the "impossibility" of a clause-bound Constitution.[78] In the most thoroughgoing critique of Black's thinking to appear since the Justice's death, James Magee delivered a stinging indictment of Black's First Amendment absolutism and claim that he embraced absolutism early as well as late in his career.[79] Sylvia Snowiss has detailed what she considers to be the inherently "arbitrary" character of Black's jurisprudence,[80] and Jacob Landynski has critically reviewed his Fourth Amendment philosophy,[81] while Patrick McBride challenged Black's approach to the "speech-plus" and "symbolic speech" issues raised in political protest cases as well as the Justice's efforts to reconcile his stance with the broader contours of his First Amendment absolutism.[82] William Van Alstyne has probed Black's relatively narrow conception of the "state action" subject to the Constitution's coverage.[83] Others have addressed similar themes.

Confronted with Glendon Schubert's biological thesis, one is left largely to wonder how the aging process could affect a Justice's response to certain civil liberties issues while having no effect on his reaction to other claims—on, for instance, Justice Black's continued opposition to any governmental constraint of obscenity, libel, or slander. Given the crude case categorization methods inevitable in statistical research, methods obscuring important issue subtleties, the efforts of an Ulmer, Atkins, or Sloope are equally difficult to assess. The degree to which Justice Black should be held morally accountable, moreover, for insensitivities to civil liberties or for Court intrigues is more the concern of the biographer, psychohistorian, or theologian than the student of the Justice's judicial and constitutional philosophy. More promising, however, are the criticisms directed against Justice Black's jurisprudence by his colleagues and by scholarly evaluations of his thinking. The chapters which follow undertake an analysis of Black's philosophy and the contentions of his jurisprudential critics.

Two A Constitutional Faith

WITH a near-religious fervor, Justice Black repeatedly affirmed his constitutional faith. The Constitution was his "legal bible," its "plan of our government" his plan, its "destiny" his destiny. "I cherish every word of it, from the first to the last," he asserted in closing his 1968 Carpentier lectures at Columbia Law School, "and I personally deplore even the slightest deviation from its least important commands."[1] Unlike certain religious fundamentalists, Black did not question the commitment or sincerity of those brethren whose approach to the Constitution's meaning differed from his own. Like the fundamentalist, however, he did advocate complete fidelity to his legal bible's "literal" meaning, and he remained confident that his reading of the Constitution's provisions generally reflected the true intent of its framers.

Early in their Supreme Court careers, it will be recalled, Justice Frankfurter saw elements of the English legal reformer Jeremy Bentham in Justice Black's constitutional faith. Years later, Professor Paul Freund concurred in Frankfurter's assessment, concluding that "[t]here is more than a touch of Jeremy Bentham in Justice Black, a Bentham with an unmistakably American accent." Both, Freund explained, sought "to reform the laws, to cleanse away its excrescences, to look upon law as a clean instrument of popular will, not as the patina of judges' gloss," with Bentham railing against William Blackstone and other defenders of judge-made common law principles and Black attacking judicial excrescences on the U.S. Constitution.[2]

In my own initial research, I found strong similarities between Black's judicial and constitutional philosophy and the jurisprudence of Bentham's contemporaries, the early legal positivists, particularly John Austin.[3] I continue to embrace that interpretation of Black's jurisprudence, as well as the view that Black's positivist tenets, rather than his policy preferences, furnish the key to an understanding of his approach to specific constitutional issues, giving coherence and consistency to his judicial career. Shortly before his death, moreover, the Justice termed such an explanation of his approach to the judicial function "a statement closer to my views than any heretofore published."[4]

This chapter examines the contours of Black's positivism. It also considers reflections of the Justice's jurisprudence in constitutional areas not extensively treated in later chapters, including questions of congressional power over U.S. citizenship, the scope of presidential policymaking authority, judicial authority over state regulations of interstate commerce, and the nature of due process. Finally, the chapter evaluates the arguments of those who reject the feasibility or desirability of Black's approach to constitutional construction.

Black's Positivism

At one point or another in his lengthy career Justice Black was identified with each of the three main jurisprudential currents in the history of American law—natural law, positivism, and sociological jurisprudence.[5] Exponents of natural law contend that immutable moral principles should govern human relationships and that human law, to be true law and subject to obedience, must conform to these eternal principles. Especially when construing potentially open-ended constitutional clauses such as due process, the judge's task is clear: he should appeal to eternal verities in determining the meaning of human commands.

Like the natural lawyer, proponents of sociological jurisprudence also urge judicial resort to influences lying beyond the language of the law or the intent of its framers. As Justice Cardozo, one of the founders of sociological jurisprudence, once put it, to sociological jurisprudents, "the final cause of law is the welfare of society. . . . Logic and history and custom have their place. We [judges] will shape the law to conform to them when we may; but only within bounds. The end which the law serves will dominate them all."[6] For the sociological school, then, the judge is ultimately, and ideally, a "social engineer," adapting written law to the changing, judicially perceived needs of society.

A number of his critics and admirers have discovered elements of natural law philosophy or sociological jurisprudence in Justice Black's thinking. Wallace Mendelson has contended, for example, that, for Black, "law is largely an instrument in the service of his ideals," a tool "to insure achievement of his ideal Justice."[7] In her sympathetic 1950 study, Charlotte Williams concluded: "It is probable that Justice Black belongs to that school of thought which holds that every judge, consciously or unconsciously, writes into his opinions his own economic, social, and political ideas and that the notion of judicial impartiality is little more than a myth."[8] John Frank wrote in 1949 of the Justice for whom he had clerked that Black "sees the social point of a case, its implication to the lives of people, in a flash; and he has the energy and the ability to devise ways—new ways if need be—of serving what in his conception is the largest good."[9] As noted earlier, moreover, Black clerk Charles Reich has contended that Justice Black's philosophy of the judicial function permitted judicial "doctrine to keep pace with the times."[10] For Reich, apparently, Black's response to constitutional issues was preferable to that of the economic conservatives on the pre-1937 Court, not because his conception of the judicial function differed from theirs, but because of the results he favored. "Unlike Black," Reich declares, "they failed to give effect to [the Constitution] . . . as a living structure, and allowed outworn interpretations to strangle the nation's growth."[11]

A number of Justice Black's opinions evoke images of the judge as discoverer of eternal verities or evaluator of social need. In concluding his opinion for the Court in *Chambers* v. *Florida*,[12] for example, he observed: "No higher duty, no more solemn responsibility, rests upon this Court, than that of translating into living law and maintaining this constitutional shield deliberately planned and inscribed for the benefit of every human being subject to our Constitution—of whatever race, creed or persuasion."[13] During his 1968 cbs News interview, however, Black made clear his view that the Constitution itself, not judges via concepts beyond the Constitution, gave the document its "living" quality.[14] Throughout his career, moreover, he attacked natural law interpretations of due process and other constitutional provisions, as well as the notion that courts can adapt the Constitution's meaning to their perceptions of changing social need. Dissenting from the Court's 1965 recognition of a right of marital privacy, for example, he declared:

> I realize that many good and able men have eloquently spoken and written, sometimes in rhapsodical strains, about the duty of this

Court to keep the Constitution in tune with the times. The idea is that the Constitution must be changed from time to time and that this Court is charged with a duty to make those changes. For myself, I must with all deference reject that philosophy. The Constitution makers knew the need for change and provided for it. Amendments suggested by the people's elected representatives can be submitted to the people or their selected agents for ratification. That method of change was good for our Fathers, and being somewhat old-fashioned I must add it is good enough for me.[15]

What, then, of positivist tenets and Justice Black's judicial and constitutional philosophy? Positivists and students of legal positivism are not of one mind as to what positivist jurisprudence entails.[16] The position of positivists regarding the propriety of judicial lawmaking ranges, for example, from early positivist John Austin's hope that codification could reduce judicial legislation significantly[17] to the contention of John Chipman Gray, among other positivists, that, "in truth, all the law is judge-made law."[18] Any listing of basic positivist tenets is thus bound to be somewhat arbitrary. Several principles, however, are normally associated with positivist philosophy.

First, and fundamentally, positivists draw a distinction between legal and moral law. Obviously, they realize that moral concepts have significantly influenced legal systems and that law has played a profound role in the development of moral standards.[19] But for positivists, in the words of Roscoe Pound, "law [is] . . . for courts, morals [are] . . . for legislators."[20] They reject any notion that the legitimacy of an otherwise valid law should be measured by ethical or moral concepts. "[A]s long as the constitutional or institutional directives for the production of valid law are observed," Edgar Bodenheimer has written in summarizing positivist thinking, "law has authoritative force and must be applied and obeyed regardless of the reasonableness of the enacted measure."[21] The only alternative to this separation of law and morals, positivists contend, is anarchy or arbitrary rule.[22]

This "separation, in principle, of the law as it is, and the law as it ought to be," as another commentator has observed, "is the most fundamental philosophical assumption of legal positivism."[23] Positivists have also normally taken the related position, however, that lawmaking is a legislative, not a judicial, function. "Analytical positivism rests," one student of positivist jurisprudence has written, "on the command or imperative theory of law—that that is law which is laid down by duly constituted political authority— . . . and that only is law. From the command theory of law is derived a normative proposition that judges have no business making law, for that is the business of the legislature and it would be usurping the legislator's function for the judges to do so."[24] Positivists do not contend that judge-made law is not law. John Austin assumed, for example, "that judicial law-making is an existing, influential force."[25] Indeed, while he agreed that a "judiciary law" was inferior to a well-expressed statute, he preferred judicial legislation over "badly-expressed" legislative enactments.[26] Positivists obviously also accept the supremacy of constitutional limitations imposed by a sovereign electorate over the legislative will. As modern positivist H. L. A. Hart asserted,

> The difference between a legal system in which the ordinary legis-
> lature is free from legal limitations, and one where the legislature is
> subject to them, appears merely as a difference between the man-
> ner in which the sovereign electorate chooses to exercise its sov-
> ereign power. In England, on this theory, the only direct exercise
> made by the electorate of their share in the sovereignty consists in
> their election of representatives to sit in Parliament and the delega-
> tion to them of their sovereign power. . . . By contrast, in the
> United States, as in every democracy where the ordinary legislature
> is legally limited, the electoral body has not confined its exercise of
> sovereign power to the election of delegates, but has subjected
> them to legal restrictions. Here the electorate may be considered an
> "extraordinary and ulterior legislature" superior to the ordinary
> legislature which is legally "bound" to observe [constitutional re-
> strictions].[27]

But positivists stress the "evils" of judicial legislation, and Austin and other early positivists supported codification as a means of reducing the necessity—or opportunity—for judicial lawmaking.[28]

A third positivist tenet holds that judicial interpretation of statutes and constitutional provisions should be based, to the extent humanly possible, on the intent of their framers as indicated by the literal mean-ing of the words used or other indicia of intent. "Genuine interpreta-tion" of law, Austin maintained, "is the discovery of the intention with which [the lawgiver] constructed the statute, or of the sense which he attached to the words wherein the statute is expressed. The literal meaning of the words wherein the statute is expressed, is the primary index or clue to the intention or sense of its author."[29] For positivists, then, the judicial function was to be largely an exercise in logic, a mechanical application of the law to the facts of a given case. Positivists agree, of course, that it may not always be possible to determine the intent of a law's framers and that, in such "penumbral" situations, it is permissible to give a law the interpretation which has the greatest intrinsic merit. But they contend that such opportunities arise with relative rarity. "To be occupied with the penumbra is one thing," H. L. A. Hart has written; "to be preoccupied with it is another."[30]

Finally, positivists value clarity and consistency in the law, and they abhor the vague, shifting rules characteristic of judicial legislation. In his *Lectures on Jurisprudence* John Austin included among the "evils" of judiciary law its existence nowhere in fixed or determinate form, the haste with which it is developed, its "vague and inconsistent" character, and the uncertainty "that any judiciary rule is good or valid law, and will be followed by future judges in cases resembling the cases by which it has been established."[31] Such concerns and the support of early positivists for the codification movement reflect a desire for clarity and consistency in the law as well as grave doubt whether judge-made law is compatible with such goals.

Charles Reich could never bring himself to accept Justice Black's assertions that he had always sought to preserve the letter of the Constitution rather than his own conceptions of justice. "Justice Black," wrote Reich in a posthumous eulogy of the judge he had served, "often summed up a case which particularly outraged him by exclaiming: 'I don't think they have a right to *do* a man that way.' Today we increasingly need a guarantee that government will not 'do us that way.'"[32] Black, too, denied that his was a "logically pure" jurisprudence.[33] But reminded of Holmes's aphorism that "[t]he life of the law has not been logic; it has been experience," Black quickly retorted that "Justice Holmes was not there talking about the Constitution; he was talking about the evolving judge-made law of England and of some of our states whose judges are allowed to follow in the common law tradition."[34] Black was a "great admirer" of Jeremy Bentham,[35] moreover, and the elements of Black's judicial and constitutional philosophy bear a close resemblance to positivist theory. In fact, the Justice would appear to have been the preeminent positivist jurist.

For one thing, Justice Black drew the traditional positivist line between law and morals. Like other positivists he recognized the powerful influence of moral concepts on the law and of legal rules on moral values.[36] But he opposed constitutional interpretations empowering judges to declare laws and other governmental actions "unjust," "unfair," or "unreasonable." As one perceptive commentator has observed:

> It must not be concluded . . . that Justice Black opposed the concept of natural law as a jurisprudential theory. When he referred to the natural law theory as "degrad[ing] the constitutional safeguards of the Bill of Rights," he was referring to it as a principle of decisionmaking in specific cases, not as a philosophical theory of the sources of law. These two considerations are quite distinct, and it was consistent for Justice Black on the one hand to adhere to the natural law as a legal philosophy and, on the other, to reject the natural law theory as a methodology in coming to decisions in specific cases.[37]

Black's concern, frequently voiced during his last years on the bench, that political protest movements may degenerate into anarchy or repression is equally consistent with the positivist distinction between law and morals. Contrary, perhaps, to general belief, positivists do recognize a moral right to disobey unjust laws. They simply reject any "legal" justification for civil disobedience,[38] and fear of anarchy and support for an orderly society are important elements of positivist thought.[39] Justice Black also agreed that peaceful disobedience and even violent revolution may be necessary if government becomes "tyrannical."[40] However, he vigorously contended that where a legal system affords the means for peaceful change and the protection of individual freedom, those seeking relief from claimed injustice should resort to legal mechanisms available for such purposes.[41] An important tenet of his jurisprudence was thus, as one admiring former law clerk put it, belief in "a rule of law for the people at large: an appeal to channel grievances into lawful processes and not to take the law into their own hands, lest the undermining of order be the undoing of liberty."[42]

Second, of course, Black consistently maintained that lawmaking was a function for legislatures, not courts, and he condemned judicial lawmaking as an affront to majoritarian democracy and the concept of our written Constitution, a constitution intended to bind judges as much as other government officials. In his Carpentier lectures he repeatedly returned to this theme, observing at one point:

I assure you that in attempting to follow as best I can the Constitution as it appears to me to be written, and in attempting in all cases to resist reaching a result simply because I think it is desirable, I have been following a view of our government held by me at least as long as I have been a lawyer. This view is based on my belief that the Founders wrote into our Constitution their unending fear of granting too much power to judges. Such a fear is perhaps not so prevalent today in certain intellectual circles where the judiciary is generally held in high esteem for changes which it has made in our society which these people believe to be desirable. Many of these changes I believe were constitutionally required and thus I wholeheartedly support them. But there is a tendency now among some to look to the judiciary to make all the major policy decisions of our society under the guise of determining constitutionality. The belief is that the Supreme Court will reach a faster and more desirable resolution of our problems than the legislative or executive branches of the government. . . . I would much prefer to put my faith in the people and their elected representatives to choose the proper policies for our government to follow, leaving to the courts questions of constitutional interpretation and enforcement.[43]

While he was acquiring a rudimentary legal education at the University of Alabama, the Justice liked to recall, his professors had taught him "that legislators not judges should make the laws."[44] It was a lesson he was never to forget. In fact, he even opposed the arrangement by which Congress has largely delegated to the judiciary power to make rules governing federal court procedure, terming "[t]his kind of judicial lawmaking . . . wholly at odds with the philosophy of separation of powers contained in our Constitution."[45]

Third, Black's approach to the interpretation of constitutional provisions and statutes obviously paralleled the positivist model. A thoroughgoing literalist, he believed that language should be the first guide to construction. Where an examination of language proved fruitless, the judge was to consult the historical record. And only on the rare occasion when that effort failed to reveal the framers' intent was it proper to give a provision the interpretation believed to have the greatest merit.

For such a judge, long judicial acceptance of a particular legal interpretation did not alone establish its legitimacy. As Charles Reich has noted, Black was "notable in his willingness to overrule precedent, uproot established practice, . . . advocate novel constitutional doctrines, and acknowledge and correct his judicial mistakes."[46] Like his colleagues, he was reluctant to disturb existing interpretations of federal statutes, viewing the failure of Congress to enact clarifying legislation as confirmation of the judicial construction. "When the law has been settled by an earlier case," he observed in one opinion, "then any subsequent 'reinterpretation' of the statute is gratuitous and neither more nor less than an amendment; it is no different in effect from a judicial alteration of language that Congress itself placed in the statute."[47] Nor, of course, did he recognize any judicial power to abandon earlier constitutional interpretations on the ground that they were inconsistent with current social needs. However, he readily urged rejection of constructions which he found to conflict with the Constitution's text or the intent of its framers.

Black's departures from tradition in the First Amendment field and with regard to the relationship of the Bill of Rights to the Fourteenth Amendment are well known and given extensive treatment in later chapters. Early and late in his career, his literalism and emphasis on historical intent prompted challenges to prevailing doctrine in other constitutional areas as well. During his first term on the Court, for example, Black questioned the by then well-established assumption that certain portions of the Fourteenth Amendment include protection for the corporate as well as the natural "person." Dissenting from the Court's decision and opinion in *Connecticut General Life Ins. Co.* v. *Johnson*,[48] he declared that the doctrine of stare decisis "has only a limited application in the field of constitutional law" and argued that "[n]either the history nor the language of the Fourteenth Amendment justifies the belief that corporations are included within its protection."[49] His analysis was a classic and effective exercise in literalism laced with frequent references to the Fourteenth Amendment's primary historic purpose. The amendment, he asserted, guaranteed U.S. citizenship to "persons born or naturalized in the United States," yet a corporation "certainly" could not be naturalized. Earlier decisions had construed the amendment's due process clause to protect the "property" of corporations as well as natural persons, but the "life" and "liberty" of humans only. "In other words," Black caustically observed, "this clause is construed to mean as follows:" 'Nor shall any State deprive any *human being* of life, liberty or property without due process of law; nor shall any State deprive any corporation of property without due process of law.' "[50] He was similarly unimpressed with the judicial conclusion that the equal protection clause covered corporations:

> Both Congress and the people were familiar with the meaning of the word "corporation" at the time the Fourteenth Amendment was submitted and adopted. The judicial inclusion of the word "corporation" in the Fourteenth Amendment has had a revolutionary effect on our form of government. The states did not adopt the Amendment with knowledge of its sweeping meaning under its present construction. No section of the Amendment gave notice to the people that, if adopted, it would subject every state law and municipal ordinance affecting corporations (and all administrative actions under them) to censorship of the United States courts.[51]

If the people wished to deprive states of the power to regulate corporations, he added, "there is a way provided by the Constitution. . . . An Amendment having that purpose could be submitted by Congress as provided by the Constitution."[52]

Justice Black's *Connecticut General* stance fueled early concerns about his potential as a justice,[53] but his dissent was clearly compatible with his interpretivist approach to constitutional interpretation. So, too, was his earlier attack on directed jury verdicts. In *Galloway* v. *United States*,[54] a suit to recover benefits for an alleged war-related disability, a trial court had granted the government's motion for a directed verdict. The Supreme Court affirmed. The Seventh Amendment guarantees a jury trial in all suits at common law involving claims greater than twenty dollars and further provides: "no fact tried by a jury shall be otherwise re-examined in any Court of the United States, than according to the rules of the Common law." Justice Rutledge concluded for the *Galloway* majority that the Seventh Amendment did not reach disability suits against the United States, but also asserted that the amendment allowed a jury only "to make reasonable inferences from facts proven in evidence having a reasonable tendency to sustain them."[55] In a vehement dissent Justice Black accused the majority of usurping the jury function and argued "that a verdict should be directed, if at all, only when, without weighing the credibility of the witnesses, there is in the evidence no room whatever for honest difference of opinion over the factual issue in controversy."[56]

Justice Frankfurter was appalled at his colleague's challenge to tradition. In a letter to Justice Rutledge, Frankfurter objected to Rutledge's "full-dress discussion" of Black's contentions in a draft of the Court's *Galloway* opinion. "I am very happy indeed," wrote Frankfurter,

> that you adhere to your original conclusion regarding the intrinsic meaning of the jury trial guaranteed by the Seventh Amendment, namely, that there must be some solidity of evidence before the jury's function comes into play. As you say, our whole constitutional and judicial history is behind that conception of the institution of the jury. It is for this reason that I deplore that you should join issue at length on this question as though it still called for independent justification. There are things to which it ought to be enough to say that it is too late in the day to question them. I see nothing to be gained except confusion and unsettlement of things that certainly ought not to be unsettled to give respectability to a view which, on the grounds of reason as well as a matter of history, ought not to be treated as though it called for new and deep discussion. . . . [C]ertain attacks call for intelligent neglect.[57]

For Black, however, the Seventh Amendment's language, not long tradition, provided the ultimate key to the constitutional status of directed verdicts.

Other interpretations inconsistent with his view of the Constitution's literal meaning also drew a pointed Black response. In its second decision in *Williams* v. *North Carolina*,[58] the Court upheld the bigamy convictions of a North Carolina couple who had shed their previous spouses via Nevada divorces. Justice Frankfurter concluded for the majority that state courts have the power to determine for themselves, before recognizing the validity of an out-of-state divorce, whether residents of the state had established a bona fide domicile in the state granting the divorce. He thus saw no inconsistency between the bigamy convictions and the full faith and credit clause of Article IV. But Justice Black vigorously dissented, declaring, "never before today has this Court decided a case upon the assumption that men and women validly married under the laws of one state could be sent to jail by another state for conduct which involved nothing more than living together as husband and wife."[59] Again, for Black, the Constitution's text itself resolved the issue:

The Constitution provides that "Full Faith and Credit shall be given in each State to the public Acts, Records, and judicial Proceedings of every other State. And the Congress may by general Laws pre-scribe the Manner in which such Acts, Records and Proceedings shall be proved, and the *Effect thereof*." (Emphasis added.) Acting pursuant to this constitutional authority, Congress in 1790 declared what law should govern and what "Effect" should be given the judgments of state courts. That statute is still the law. Its command is that they "shall have such faith and credit given to them . . . as they have by law or usage in the Courts of the state from which they are taken." . . . If, as the Court today implies, divorce decrees should be given less effect than other Court judgments, Congress alone has the constitutional power to say so. We should not attempt to solve the "divorce problem" by constitutional interpretation.[60]

Nor did Black condone flexible interpretations of the Article I, Section 10, contract clause. During the Marshall era the Court had given that clause a broad and rigid interpretation, forbidding state interference even with contractual obligations bottomed on fraud.[61] In later years, however, the Court had modified its position, concluding, for example, in *Home Building & Loan Assn. v. Blaisdell* (1934)[62] that the prohibition against state impairment of contracts "is not an abso-lute one and is not to be read with literal exactness like a mathematical formula."[63] Giving the clause this sort of flexible reading, in 1965 a majority of the Justices upheld Texas's authority to modify the terms of contracts involved in the sale of public land.[64] Finding the modification at issue "a mild one indeed" and "hardly burdensome,"[65] Justice White ruled for the Court that the contract clause must be construed in har-mony with a state's power to protect the "vital interests" of its people. In dissent, Justice Black protested the "Court's balancing away" of a "plain [constitutional] guarantee."[66] Under the arrangement at issue the state in 1910 had sold some public land, provided forfeiture of the land in the event of nonpayment of interest, but allowed for forfeiting purchasers to reinstate their claims on payment of delinquent interest. In 1941 the applicable law was amended to limit reinstatement rights to five years from the forfeiture date. Black considered this "modification" a clear violation of the contract clause and ridiculed the majority's rationale for upholding the scheme, observing:

the Court says that since the State acts out of what this Court thinks are good motives, and has not repudiated its contract except in a way which this Court thinks is "reasonable," therefore the State will be allowed to ignore the Contract Clause of the Constitution. There follow[s] citation of one or two dicta from past cases and a bit of skillful "balancing," and the Court arrives at its conclusion: although the obligation of the contract has been impaired here, this impairment does not seem to the Court to be very serious or evil, and so therefore "The Contract Clause does not forbid such a measure."[67]

A final positivist characteristic clearly evident in Black's thinking was the preference for clear, consistent, relatively fixed constitutional standards. Black did not invariably opt for the constitutional interpretation which imposed the greatest restriction on the exercise of judicial discretion. He refused to accept an unconditional rule, for example, that all newly announced constitutional rules should be either purely retroactive or prospective in application, though his preference for retroactivity seemed clear (and most compatible with his approach to constitutional interpretation).[68] For Black, however, "flexible" legal standards were not standards at all, merely "mush."[69] He realized that certain constitutional provisions—most notably the Fourth Amendment's guarantee against "unreasonable" searches and seizures and the Fourteenth Amendment equal protection guarantee—obligate judges to make judgments on the reasonableness of official action. But he found few invitations to such decision making in the Constitution's text or historical record.[70]

Black's penchant for clarity extended to opinion writing. The recollections of his law clerks abound with anecdotes underscoring their Justice's preference for brevity and plain language. "For Justice Black," one former clerk has observed, "the object is simplicity. He dislikes a pretentious word where a simple one will do. His opinions are notably— and deliberately—free of Latin tags, those badges of erudition of which lawyers are so proud. He has been known to admonish a law clerk, in his own writing, 'to use, not the language of Oxford, but the language of your country forebears.' "[71] Recalls another:

Michaelangelo could not have been more careful with his sculpturing than Justice Black with his opinions. . . . All opinions were rewritten again and again, some more than a dozen times, with polishing and repolishing to clarify, to eliminate a word or phrase. Justice Black succeeded admirably in his judicial quest never to use two words if one would do, and to eliminate the "big" words unless they gave illumination. He rarely thought they did.[72]

But the Justice's instructions to yet another clerk perhaps best illustrated his position: omit "each word your barber can't understand."[73] Nor were Black's clerks the only ones aware or appreciative of the Justice's proclivity. Black occasionally urged his brethren to omit potentially confusing language from opinions. When Justice Rutledge used the word "polyglot" in his draft opinion for *Prince* v. *Massachusetts*, for example, Black praised the opinion's "clarity, force, and brevity," but suggested that "[t]he word 'polyglot' might possibly be misinterpreted and I should think it better not to use it. Someone might think it aimed at people who are recent immigrants."[74] During his first term on the high bench, moreover, a Nebraska lawyer who had served as Black's driver during a 1936 presidential campaign trip wrote the Justice: "I like your opinions. Their clearness, terseness, lucidity, and briefness commend them very much to the practitioner."[75]

Black and Constitutional Theory

Throughout his career each of the major positivist principles outlined in the previous section—a distinction between law and morals, a textbook conception of separation of powers limiting legitimate lawmaking largely to legislators rather than judges (or, for that matter, executives), constitutional interpretation bottomed on text and historical intent, and a preference for clear, relatively fixed legal standards—permeated Black's opinions and off-the-bench statements. In a number of issue areas, however, he appeared to base his interpretations of the Constitution more on what might be termed a political theory implicit in the document and the general history surrounding its adoption than on its specific provisions. Such thinking seemed to influence especially his position regarding the power of federal courts to intervene in state judicial proceedings, congressional control over the authority of state and local governments to enact legislation, and the constitutional status of malapportioned governmental bodies.

Consider first his stance regarding federal court interference in state court proceedings. Traditionally, the Supreme Court has been

extremely reluctant to uphold federal district courts which grant declaratory or injunctive relief against pending state court proceedings,
even when they are instituted under laws impinging upon the First
Amendment or other federal rights.[76] In *Dombrowski* v. *Pfister*,[77] a 1965
decision, the Court appeared to relax its opposition to such intervention, suggesting that federal courts could enjoin pending state criminal
proceedings instituted under overly broad or vague laws. Justice Black
did not participate in the *Dombrowski* decision. But when the Court in
1971 gave *Dombrowski* a narrow reading and reaffirmed its traditional
stance, Justice Black spoke for the majority. In the principal case,
Younger v. *Harris*,[78] a three-judge district court had enjoined a prosecution under California's Criminal Syndicalism Act. The California law
was virtually identical to an Ohio statute the Supreme Court had invalidated in 1969 essentially on overbreadth grounds.[79] Speaking for the
Younger majority, however, Black reversed the lower court; and in
Younger and companion cases[80] he held for the Court that only "special
circumstances," such as bad-faith enforcement of a law, would justify
declaratory or injunctive intervention in pending state prosecutions.
Interoffice correspondence among the Justices indicates, moreover, that
Black actively campaigned for the narrow construction of *Dombrowski*
and federal injunctive power that prevailed in *Younger*.[81]

Black based the Court's position on two grounds. The first was the
doctrine that equitable or declaratory relief should be denied when
adequate alternative remedies, such as the vindication of federal rights
in the state proceedings, are available. Lacking harassment or other
evidence of bad faith on the part of state judges, Justice Black asserted,
there was no reason to conclude that a state defendant's federal rights
would not be protected in the state court. The second consideration
underlying the Court's position was the doctrine of comity implicit in
"Our Federalism," which Black characterized "as a proper respect for
state functions, a recognition of the fact that the entire country is made
up of a Union of separate state governments, and a continuance of the
belief that the National Government will fare best if the States and their
institutions are left free to perform their separate functions in their
separate ways."[82] This policy, he added, required neither a "blind deference" to states' rights nor national control over every important public
issue. "What the concept does represent is a system in which there is
sensitivity to the legitimate interests of both State and National Governments, and in which the National Government, anxious though it

may be to vindicate and protect federal rights and federal interests, always endeavors to do so in ways that will not unduly interfere with legitimate activities of the States."[83]

Black made it clear, moreover, that the facial overbreadth or vagueness of a state law did not alone constitute a "special circumstance," despite "some statements in the *Dombrowski* opinion that would seem to support [such an] argument."[84] Indeed, he even questioned the very propriety of facial review "in the manner apparently contemplated by *Dombrowski*." Holding a statute void on its face and enjoining its further enforcement, he declared, were practices "fundamentally at odds with the function of the federal courts in our constitutional plan." Judges could not apply a statute inconsistent with the Constitution. But this did not mean that they had "an unlimited power to survey the statute books and pass judgment on laws before the Courts are called upon to enforce them." And even when a valid case or controversy arose,

> the task of analyzing a proposed statute, pinpointing its deficiencies, before the statute is put into effect, is rarely if ever an appropriate task for the judiciary. The combination of the relative remoteness of the controversy, the impact on the legislative process of the relief sought, and above all the speculative and amorphous nature of the required line-by-line analysis of detailed statutes . . . ordinarily results in a kind of case that is wholly unsatisfactory for deciding constitutional questions, whichever way they might be decided. In light of this fundamental conception of the Framers as to the proper place of the federal courts in the governmental processes of passing and enforcing laws, it can seldom be appropriate for these courts to exercise any such power of prior approval or veto over legislative process.[85]

Justice Black's opposition to facial review seemed compatible with his positivist conception of the judicial function, and his reading of the injunctive authority of federal courts appeared consistent with the traditional principle that the equity power should be used only to prevent irreparable injury to legal rights—a principle bottomed on common law and statute rather than constitutional construction. But his use of "Our Federalism" to reject federal court intervention in state prosecutions hardly squared with his usual insistence on fidelity to the Constitution's letter rather than its spirit. As Justice Douglas argued in

a *Younger* dissent, the Civil War amendments had fundamentally altered the nature of the federal system, giving the national government
an important role in the safeguarding of federal rights against state
interference. At least since the Civil Rights Act of 1871, moreover,
federal courts had been authorized to hear injunctive suits against state
officials charged with violating federal rights.[86] Yet, in *Younger*, Justice
Black employed general considerations of comity to obstruct such suits
where the interference at issue takes the form of state judicial proceedings.

Similar considerations prompted a partial Black dissent from the
Court's decision upholding provisions of the 1965 Voting Rights Act.[87]
Justice Black agreed that Congress's power to enforce the Fifteenth
Amendment authorized it to suspend literacy and related registration
tests in states and political subdivisions with a history of racial discrimination in voting. He also concurred in the Court's decision to uphold
provisions authorizing the Attorney General to appoint federal voter
examiners for such areas. He vigorously dissented, however, from the
portion of the decision upholding Section 5 of the law, which required
such areas to secure the permission of the Attorney General or the U.S.
District Court for the District of Columbia before adopting and enforcing new election laws. Black considered the provision unconstitutional
on "at least two grounds."[88] First, to the extent that it authorized
preclearance by the federal district court in Washington, he found it inconsistent with provisions of Article III limiting federal judicial power
to "cases or controversies." "[I]t is hard for me to believe," he asserted,
"that a justiciable controversy can arise in the constitutional sense
from a desire by the United States Government or some of its officials to
determine in advance what legislative provisions a State may enact or
what constitutional amendments it may adopt."[89] More fundamentally, he complained that the preclearance provision conflicted "with
the most basic principles of the Constitution," principles reflected in
the "distinction drawn in the Constitution between state and federal
power" and in the guaranty clause of Article IV.

> Certainly if all the provisions of our Constitution which limit the
> power of the Federal Government and reserve other power to the
> States are to mean anything, they mean at least that the States
> have power to pass laws and amend their constitutions without
> first sending their officials hundreds of miles away to beg federal

authorities to approve them. Moreover, it seems to me that § 5 which gives federal officials power to veto state laws they do not like is in direct conflict with the clear command of our Constitution that "The United States shall guarantee to every State in this Union a Republican Form of Government." I cannot help but believe that the inevitable effect of any such law which forces any one of the States to entreat federal authorities in far-away places for approval of local laws before they can become effective is to create the impression that the State or States treated in this way are little more than conquered provinces.[90]

In later cases he continued to condemn this "hat in hand" provision of federal law.[91] Here again, however, his position seemed based more on a philosophy of federalism than on specific constitutional language.

Of relevance also is Black's stance regarding malapportioned governmental bodies. The inherent vagueness of the equal protection clause is obviously troublesome to a jurist opposed to judicial lawmaking. Though he considered such developments inevitable, Black questioned the wisdom of judicial constructions which allowed the guarantee's reach to extend beyond its historic racial roots. Shortly before his death, in fact, he suggested that it might have been better had the clause never been adopted—not because he objected to the racial equality it was designed to protect, but because of its nebulous, open-ended language.[92] For that reason he attempted to limit strict judicial review of discriminatory laws largely to racial contexts. He generally opposed, for example, rigorous scrutiny in cases involving discriminatory voting regulations of a nonracial variety.[93] It was ironic, therefore, that he wrote or joined opinions imposing the "one person, one vote" standard in reapportionment cases. Speaking for the Court in *Wesberry* v. *Sanders*,[94] he based application of the principle to congressional districting on the requirement of Article I, Section 2, that members of the House of Representatives be elected "by the people," apparently viewing that provision as a more explicit underpinning for the Court's ruling than the vague contours of equal protection. In later cases, however, he was among those justices extending "one person, one vote" to state governmental bodies via the equal protection clause.[95] Years earlier, moreover, he had relied on the guarantee as well as on Article I, Section 2, in dissenting from a plurality's refusal to order reapportionment of the Illinois congressional districting scheme challenged in

Colegrove v. *Green.*[96] And shortly before his death he explained that the principle of popular sovereignty, on which all the nation's governmental systems are based, had profoundly influenced his stance in the reapportionment cases. For Black, raised in a state where malapportionment had meant years of political domination by "a small bloc of Whig planters," such apportionment schemes constituted as "irrational" a discrimination as any other action a state could take.[97]

Justice Black's support of the one person, one vote concept is consistent with his preference for clear, precise constitutional standards limiting the scope of judicial discretion and readily understandable to the people. For clearly that principle imposes a more precise requirement than, for example, the proposal of Justices Tom Clark and Potter Stewart that apportionment schemes be upheld so long as they were "rational" and did not permit "systematic frustration" of majority rule. Whatever the accuracy of his interpretation of Article I, Section 2, moreover, his use of that provision in extending "one person, one vote" to congressional districting is compatible with his positivist reliance on language and historical intent. But his appeals to popular sovereignty as a basis for applying the standard to state and local governmental bodies subject only to the requirements of equal protection are difficult to reconcile fully with the normal contours of his jurisprudence.[98]

However, one should resist any temptation to exaggerate the scope and frequency of Justice Black's departures from positivist principles. The Court's general opposition to federal court intervention in state judicial proceedings, reaffirmed in the *Younger* case, is firmly grounded in the traditional equity principle, embodied in statute as well as the common law, that a court should stay its hand where there is no special reason to believe that rights are not being adequately protected in other forums. Nor, arguably, can a judge be charged with undue creativity for merely finding among the reserved powers of state and local legislators authority to legislate without first securing permission from federal administrative or judicial officials. After all, the Constitution's framers themselves rejected the proposal of the Virginia delegates that Congress have a veto over proposed state laws.[99] In the main, moreover, Justice Black was faithful to a positivist conception of the judicial function, whatever one's assessment of the interpretations he gave constitutional provisions, and his judicial opinions offer ample evidence of his positivist commitment.

Positivist Responses to Constitutional Issues

In outlining the elements of Justice Black's jurisprudence, I have already touched on ways his positivism influenced his approach to a variety of constitutional issues. The positivist character of his judicial and constitutional philosophy can also be seen, however, in Black's reaction to assertions of presidential policymaking authority, congressional power over U.S. citizenship, and federal judicial power over state regulation of interstate commerce, as well as in his conception of due process, the element of his constitutional philosophy which perhaps most clearly embodied his positivist jurisprudence.

Justice Black's aversion to unauthorized lawmaking extended to the presidency. He clearly rejected the notion of "inherent" presidential policymaking power. In 1956, for example, he cited such concerns in objecting to a passage in a draft opinion Justice Harlan had written for *Cole* v. *Young*,[100] a case holding that federal employees with security-sensitive positions could be suspended without prior hearing. "I think the conditions for discharge are questions for Congress," he wrote Harlan, "and would regret to have the Executive view our opinion as an invitation to assert an 'inherent' power not subject to congressional control."[101] In rejecting President Nixon's attempted reliance upon an inherent executive power over national security in the *Pentagon Papers Cases*, moreover, Black asserted:

> The Government does not even attempt to rely on any act of Congress. Instead it makes the bold and dangerously far-reaching contention that the courts should take it upon themselves to "make" a law abridging freedom of the press in the name of equity, presidential power and national security. . . . To find that the President has "inherent power" to halt the publication of news by resort to the courts would wipe out the First Amendment and destroy the fundamental liberty and security of the very people the Government hopes to make "secure." . . .
>
> The word "security" is a broad, vague generality whose contours should not be invoked to abrogate the fundamental law embodied in the First Amendment.[102]

But the *Steel Seizure* litigation of 1952,[103] which raised fundamental questions about the nature and scope of presidential policy powers, provided the setting for the most clear-cut expression of Justice Black's position. The events leading to the Court's decision are familiar. Faced with a strike in the nation's steel mills at the height of the Korean War, President Truman ordered federal seizure of the mills to assure continued military production and avoid the inflationary pressures company acquiescence to union wage demands might generate. A six-three majority, in an opinion announced by Justice Black, overruled the president's order. But the three dissenters and all but two members of the majority either refused to take the position that the president had no "inherent" power to deal with "emergency" situations or chose not to articulate a position on the issue. Among the majority justices, for example, Justice Frankfurter asserted that long practice could confer legitimacy on an otherwise questionable exercise of executive power, but concluded that Congress had explicitly denied the president the power Truman had sought to exercise. Justice Jackson essentially agreed with Frankfurter, registering a lengthy and eloquent discourse on the complex nature of presidential policy power, and Justice Clark even reminded his brethren of President Lincoln's suggestion that strict adherence to the Constitution may jeopardize the safety of the Union. The three dissenters argued, moreover, that President Truman's action was supported by the practices of numerous predecessors, that he was simply attempting to protect national policies already part of law, and that he had agreed, in any event, to honor any congressional rejection of the seizure. They, too, stressed the complexities of presidential power.

To Black, however, the case was a simple one, involving application of firmly established principles of separation of powers embodied in the Constitution. In conference he had recalled his Senate opposition to the National Recovery Act and its delegation of lawmaking authority to the executive and private industries. He had also insisted that the president was not a legislator and that there was no congressional authorization for the seizure. Alluding no doubt to recent decisions upholding sanctions against Communists,[104] he apparently rejected, too, the president's assessment of the dangers the threatened work stoppages posed; the Court's decisions of the past two years, he pointedly observed, had constituted a greater threat to liberty than any threatened strike.[105]

His opinion largely tracked his conference remarks. In a brief, thirteen-paragraph opinion which cited few precedents, and none having a direct bearing on the central issue, Black asserted that the "President's power, if any, to issue the [steel seizure] order must stem either from an act of Congress or from the Constitution itself."[106] Congress had not authorized the seizure, nor could any justification be found in the Constitution. The president was commander in chief, and the government had cited cases upholding broad presidential war powers. But Justice Black was unimpressed: "Even though 'theater of war' be an expanding concept, we cannot with faithfulness to our constitutional system hold that the Commander in Chief of the Armed Forces has the ultimate power as such to take possession of private property in order to keep labor disputes from stopping production. This is a job for the Nation's lawmakers, not for its military authorities."[107]

Black gave equally abrupt treatment to the government's argument that the seizure order could be based on the president's constitutional powers as chief executive. "In the framework of our Constitution," he maintained,

> the President's power to see that the laws are faithfully executed refutes the idea that he is to be a lawmaker. The Constitution limits his functions in the lawmaking process to the recommending of laws he thinks wise and the vetoing of laws he thinks bad. And the Constitution is neither silent nor equivocal about who shall make laws which the President is to execute. The first section of the first article says that "All legislative Powers herein granted shall be vested in a Congress of the United States. . . . "[108]

The seizure order, he pointedly added, did "not direct that a congressional policy be executed in a manner prescribed by Congress—it directs that a presidential policy be executed in a manner prescribed by the President." And what of the force of past practice?

> It is said that other Presidents without congressional authority have taken possession of private business enterprises in order to settle labor disputes. But even if this be true, Congress has not thereby lost its exclusive constitutional authority to make laws necessary and proper to carry out the powers vested by the Constitution "in the Government of the United States, or any Department or Officer thereof."

> The Founders of this Nation entrusted the lawmaking power to the Congress alone in both good and bad times. It would do no good

to recall the historical events, the fears of power and the hopes for freedom that lay behind their choice. Such a review would but confirm our holding that this seizure order cannot stand.[109]

In a statement attached to Justice Black's opinion of the Court, Justice Frankfurter suggested that "the considerations relevant to the legal enforcement of the principle of separation of powers seem[ed] . . . more complicated and flexible than may appear from what MR. JUSTICE BLACK has written."[110] For Black, however, the president's usurpation of congressional lawmaking authority had been clear. He saw in congressional statutes providing for the expatriation of U.S. citizens, moreover, an equally clear violation of the Constitution—and one no more legitimized by long practice than President Truman's seizure order.

In *Perez* v. *Brownell*[111] the Court, per Justice Frankfurter, upheld a law providing for the involuntary expatriation of citizens who voted in a foreign election. Basing the statute at issue on congressional foreign affairs powers inherent in national sovereignty, Frankfurter held that Congress could reasonably have concluded that the law was necessary to prevent international embarrassment to the nation. Justice Black filed no opinion in the *Perez* case, but he did concur with the dissents of Chief Justice Warren and Justice Douglas. On the same day that *Perez* was decided, moreover, he helped form a majority which invalidated on cruel and unusual punishment grounds a statute mandating expatriation of citizens convicted of wartime military desertion.[112] He also joined later majorities striking down other expatriation provisions.[113] And when the Court, in *Afroyim* v. *Rusk*,[114] overruled *Perez*, Justice Black authored the majority opinion.

Black's *Afroyim* opinion, like his opinion in the *Steel Seizure* litigation, was a classic expression of his approach to constitutional interpretation. While agreeing that the historical record was susceptible to "conflicting inferences,"[115] he found little in that record to support any congressional power to expatriate U.S. citizens. He relied primarily, however, on the Constitution's language. The document conferred naturalization power on the Congress, and the Fourteenth Amendment endowed persons born or naturalized in the United States with citizenship. But neither the Fourteenth Amendment nor any other provision of the Constitution granted an express or implied power over expatriation. Nor was Black willing to find such power in national sovereignty. In *Perez* Justice Frankfurter had viewed expatriation as an "implied attribute of sovereignty possessed by all nations."[116] As the Court's spokesman in *Afroyim*, Justice Black did not specifically repudiate the traditional notion that foreign and military powers inhere in the nation's sovereignty. But he came close, asserting,

> Other nations are governed by their own constitutions, if any, and we can draw no support from theirs. In our country the people are sovereign and the Government cannot sever its relationship to the people by taking away their citizenship. Our Constitution governs us and we must never forget that our Constitution limits the Government to those powers specifically granted or those that are necessary and proper to carry out the specifically granted ones.[117]

During his last term on the Court, Justice Black, writing on this occasion in dissent, vigorously reaffirmed his view that Congress had no power whatever to strip persons of their U.S. citizenship. At issue in *Rogers* v. *Bellei*[118] was a federal law providing that persons who acquire citizenship by virtue of being born abroad of citizen parents could lose their citizenship if they did not satisfy a residency requirement between the ages of fourteen and twenty-eight. Speaking for a majority, Justice Blackmun distinguished *Afroyim* and upheld the law, concluding that such citizens were not "born or naturalized in the United States," that they were thus not citizens in the Fourteenth Amendment sense, and that Congress had power to impose conditions on their citizenship which were not "unreasonable" or "arbitrary." Citing Congress' authority under Article I, Section 8, to "establish an uniform Rule of Naturalization," the only constitutional provision specifically granting Congress power over citizenship, Justice Black rejected the majority's central premise, arguing that "[a]nyone acquiring citizenship solely under the exercise of this [naturalization] power is, constitutionally speaking, a naturalized citizen."[119] He also took a swipe at President Nixon, who had appointed Justice Blackmun and Chief Justice Burger, another member of the *Bellei* majority, and vowed to appoint "strict constructionists" to the Court. "Of course," Black caustically observed,

> the Court's construction of the Constitution is not a "strict" one. On the contrary, it proceeds on the premise that a majority of this Court can change the Constitution day by day, month by month, and year by year, according to its shifting notions of what is fair, reasonable, and right. There was little need for the founders to draft

a written constitution if this Court can say it is only binding when a majority finds it fair, reasonable, and right to make it so. That is the loosest construction that could be employed.[120]

In an *Afroyim* dissent joined by three other members of the Court, Justice Harlan had erected a reasonably effective rebuttal to Justice Black's reading of history and dismissed as "essentially . . . conclusory and quite unsubstantiated" Black's rejection of Justice Frankfurter's *Perez* rationale.[121] As Harlan undoubtedly realized, however, a recitation of pertinent constitutional language *was* conclusive for one of Black's positivist persuasion. The Constitution's language explicitly authorized Congress to confer citizenship but said nothing expressly or by implication about expatriation; in fact, Justice Frankfurter's *Perez* opinion had based expatriation on no particular constitutional provisions. And a Hugo Black could hardly have been expected to accept such a power—or, indeed, any power—drawn only from considerations of sovereignty.

Justice Black's generally solitary battle against judicial review of state laws impinging on interstate commerce was just as consistent with his positivist jurisprudence. Building largely on its 1852 decision in *Cooley v. Board of Wardens*,[122] the Supreme Court has developed a large body of case law empowering federal courts to invalidate, on commerce clause grounds, state laws and taxes held to constitute an "unreasonable" or discriminatory burden on interstate commerce. Mindful that the Constitution grants the commerce power to Congress, not the judiciary, the Court has recognized the ultimate power of Congress in this field, upholding congressional authority to permit state policies the Court has forbidden and to prohibit regulations the Court has approved. Within that stricture, however, the Court has assumed for the federal judiciary an authority to review the reasonableness of state controls over interstate commerce. And scholarly commentators as well as individual justices have cited the practical need for such an approach. Bernard Schwartz has observed, for example, that "as a practical matter" it is doubtful "whether the Congress could actually deal effectively with the myriad problems of state impediments to national trade," adding:

Even if we assume that an assembly so reflective of sectional interests could acquire the broad view and impartiality necessary to resolve these matters, it is hard to see where it would find the time, when it is now swamped by the pressures of its normal legislative tasks. And where is the legislative department to acquire the machinery and the personnel to operate it, which are required to deal speedily and effectively with cases of improper state action as they arise?[123]

Justice Douglas once observed, moreover, that "Congress, of course, could have removed [state] barriers [to interstate commerce] and probably would have done so. But the judiciary has moved with speed. As a result of the case by case approach, there has been no great lag between the creation of the forbidden barrier or burden and its removal by the judiciary."[124]

Even if he found them valid, of course, such pragmatic considerations could hardly have influenced Justice Black's approach to constitutional issues. Instead, the Constitution's language was again to be his guide. Black recognized that, under the supremacy clause, Congress could preempt a field of legislation exclusively for its own control. In *Hines* v. *Davidowitz*,[125] moreover, he held for the Court that Congress had implicitly preempted the field of alien regulation, leaving no room for state controls. Black insisted, however, that the power over interstate commerce had been delegated to Congress, not the courts, and that Congress alone could determine the reach of permissible state regulation. "Since the Constitution grants sole and exclusive power to Congress to regulate commerce among the States," he contended during his second term on the Court,

repeated assumption of this power by the courts—even over a long period of years—could not make this assumption of power constitutional. . . . State obedience to an unconstitutional assumption of power by the judicial branch of government, and inaction by the Congress, cannot [so] amend the Constitution. . . .

It is essential today, as at the time of the adoption of the Constitution, that commerce among the States and with foreign nations be left free from discriminatory and retaliatory burdens imposed by the States. It is of equal importance, however, that the judicial department of our government scrupulously observe its constitutional limitations and that Congress alone should adopt a broad national policy of regulation—if otherwise valid state laws combine to hamper the free flow of commerce . . . I would return to the rule that—except for state acts designed to impose discriminatory burdens on interstate commerce because it *is* interstate—Congress alone must "determine how far [interstate commerce] . . . shall be free and untrammelled, how far it shall be burdened by duties and imposts, and how far it shall be prohibited.[126]

Black was to stick to that position throughout his career. In *South Carolina Highway Dept.* v. *Barnwell Brothers*,[127] decided in 1938, the Court, speaking through Justice Stone, upheld a very burdensome state restriction on the weight and width of trucks and gave the federal judicial role in such cases a reading extremely deferential to state authority. Justice Black joined the Court's opinion and apparently also had a hand in pressing Stone toward the minimal judicial review of state regulations Stone's opinion appeared to embrace. After making revisions Black had suggested, for example, Stone had written his colleague a letter assuring him his *Barnwell Brothers* opinion now made clear that one cited precedent was "never to be taken as meaning that judges are to substitute their views of reasonableness for those of the legislature."[128] But *Barnwell Brothers* had merely come close to rejecting any supervisory role for the federal courts; while emphasizing the presumptive validity of state controls over interstate commerce, it had not adopted the unconditional hands-off policy Justice Black favored for all nondiscriminatory state regulations. And when, in subsequent cases, the Court invalidated such controls, Black registered biting dissents, attacking both what he considered to be a judicial usurpation of congressional power and his colleagues' evaluations of the reasonableness of challenged state controls—evaluations unduly restrictive, he almost invariably found, of state policymaking authority.

His dissent in *Southern Pacific Co.* v. *Arizona*,[129] a 1945 case, is a classic illustration of his approach. There, a majority, per Chief Justice Stone, distinguished *Barnwell Brothers* and struck down a state law severely limiting the length of trains. Counsel for Arizona defended the statute as a safety measure designed to reduce accidents caused by the "slack action" motion of long trains. But the Court was unpersuaded. The hazards created by the increased number of trains that compliance with the law could generate, the Chief Justice concluded, would more than offset any safety advantage it otherwise might have afforded; the serious burdens in time and expense which the regulation imposed on interstate rail transportation thus clearly outweighed any interest it was designed to serve.

For Justice Black the *Southern Pacific* majority's approach smacked of the "super-legislative" role the pre–1937 Court had assumed in economic cases—a role now long repudiated. The earlier decisions had merely "rested on the Due Process Clause while today's decision rests on the Commerce Clause."[130] Each line of decisions, in Black's judgment, was unconstitutional.

> [T]he determination of whether it is in the interest of society for the length of trains to be governmentally regulated is a matter of public policy. Someone must fix that policy—either the Congress, or the state, or the courts. A century and a half of constitutional history and government admonishes this Court to leave that choice to the elected legislative representatives of the people themselves, where it properly belongs both on democratic principles and the requirements of efficient government.[131]

Black had "no doubt whatever that many employees have been seriously injured and killed in the past, and that many more are likely to be so in the future, because of 'slack movement' in trains." But the relative safety advantages of short and long trains were not, in his view, matters for judicial determination. Instead, the "balancing of these probabilities" called for "legislative consideration."[132] And if national uniformity was to be imposed in this or any other field of interstate commerce, the decision was one for Congress, not the courts.

In *Morgan* v. *Virginia*,[133] decided the following year, Justice Black reaffirmed his position. He also announced, however, that "[s]o long as the Court remains committed to the 'undue burden on commerce formula,' I must make decisions under it,"[134] and agreed that the regulation at issue in *Morgan* violated the majority's "formula." But *Morgan* was hardly a harbinger of change, even in Black's voting patterns. For the statute *Morgan* held invalid required racial segregation in transportation, a policy soon to be held inconsistent with equal protection. And in later cases Black regularly voted to uphold challenged regulations, even those arguably having a discriminatory impact on interstate commerce.[135] He continued, moreover, to challenge the constitutional basis for the Court's approach. When in one case Justice Jackson rested the Court's role on the "great silences of the Constitution," Black sarcastically responded, "Maybe this Court would be a better guardian" of interstate trade than Congress, "but it may be doubted that authority

for the Court to undertake the task can be found in the Constitution—
even in its 'great silences.' "[136]

The Nature of Due Process

Justice Black, as noted earlier, saw little difference between the
Court's use of the commerce clause to invalidate "undue" state burdens
on interstate commerce and the pre–1937 Court's resort to due process as
a tool for ruling generally on the utility of economic legislation. In 1949,
for example, he observed:

> The judicially directed march of the due process philosophy as an
> emancipator of business from regulation appeared arrested a few
> years ago. That appearance was illusory. That philosophy con-
> tinues its march. The due process clause and commerce clause have
> been used like Siamese twins in a never-ending stream of challenges
> to government regulations. . . . The reach of one twin may appear
> to be longer than that of the other, but either can easily be turned to
> remedy this apparent handicap.
>
> Both the commerce and due process clauses serve high purposes
> when confined within their proper scope. But a stretching of either
> outside its sphere can paralyze the legislative process, rendering the
> people's legislative representatives impotent to perform their duty
> of providing appropriate rules to govern this dynamic civilization.
> Both clauses easily lend themselves to inordinate expansions of this
> Court's power at the expense of legislative power. For under the
> prevailing due process rule, appeals can be made to the "fundamen-
> tal principles of liberty and justice" which our "fathers" wished to
> preserve. In commerce clause cases reference can appropriately be
> made to the farseeing wisdom of the "fathers" in guarding against
> commercial and even shooting wars among the states. Such argu-
> ments have strong emotional appeals and when skillfully utilized
> they sometimes obscure the vision.[137]

While Black's rejection of the *Cooley–Southern Pacific* line of cases
was merely a major footnote to his jurisprudence, however, his strug-
gles against flexible conceptions of due process form perhaps the core of
his judicial and constitutional philosophy. Black did not favor an impo-
tent judiciary; indeed, he urged vigorous judicial protection for rights
he considered to be within the Constitution's language or the intent of

its framers. Moreover, when the Court upheld the power of circuit judicial councils to discipline federal judges, even stripping them of the authority to hear cases, he wrote a forceful, eloquent, and indignant dissent, exclaiming:

> While judges, like other people, can be tried, convicted, and pun-ished for crimes, no word, phrase, clause, sentence, or even the Constitution taken as a whole, gives any indication that any judge was ever to be partly disqualified or wholly removed from office except by the admittedly difficult method of impeachment by the House of Representatives and conviction by two-thirds of the Sen-ate. Such was the written guarantee in our Constitution of the independence of the judiciary, and such has always been the proud boast of our people.
>
> I am regrettably compelled in this case to say that the Court today, in my judgment, breaks faith with this grand constitutional principle. . . . This case must be viewed for what it is—a long history of harassment of Judge Chandler by other judges who some-how feel he is "unfit" to hold office. . . . What is involved here is simply a blatant effort on the part of the Council through concerted action to make Judge Chandler a "second-class judge," depriving him of the full power of his office and the right to share equally with all other federal judges in the privileges and responsibilities of the Federal Judiciary. . . .
>
>   .   .   .   .
>
> I fear that unless the actions taken by the Judicial Council in this case are in some way repudiated, the hope for an independent judiciary will prove to have been no more than an evanescent dream.[138]

But lacking clear authorization in the Constitution's language or his-tory, Black opposed constitutional constructions giving judges discre-tion to rule on the "fairness" or "reasonableness" of governmental ac-tions, and the gloss given the due process guarantee by "language-stretching" judges was the principal target of his concern.

In English law the guarantee of due process was originally consid-ered to be synonymous with the requirement, first recognized in the Magna Carta of 1215, that no man be deprived of his liberty or property except by the "law of the land."[130] Although the meaning of the law of the land guarantee was itself open to interpretation, its language suggested a relatively fixed standard obligating government to proceed against the individual according to law rather than whim. Especially in the hands of American judges, however, due process was to become a much more flexible and potentially limitless reservoir of rights explicitly stated only in the opinions of creative judges. Moreover, although its language appeared to impose purely procedural limitations on governmental power, American courts saw the guarantee as a source of substantive rights as well. And with the 1856 decision of the New York Court of Appeals in *Wynehamer* v. *New York*,[140] they began using substantive due process as a constitutional basis for ruling on the reasonableness of economic legislation. Initially, the Supreme Court declined invitations that it become a "super-legislature" in economic cases brought under the due process guarantee.[141] At least by 1905 and *Lochner* v. *New York*,[142] however, it too had fully embraced economic due process.

As a member of the Senate, Hugo Black had watched in horror as the Court employed due process and other devices to dismantle major portions of the Roosevelt New Deal and state economic legislation as well. And when President Roosevelt proposed legislation to enable him to pack the federal judiciary with judges unwilling to substitute their economic and social theories for those of elected lawmakers, Black became a major supporter of the court-packing plan. On the Senate floor and elsewhere, he attacked the due process clause as "wholly incapable of definition," caustically adding: "No one ever has marked its boundaries. It is as elastic as rubber."[143] He also voiced strong opposition to judicial legislation and constitutional amendment via judicial interpretation. In a national radio address defending the court-packing proposal, for example, he charged:

> Most of the framers believed in popular government by the people themselves. Like Jefferson, they were not willing to trust lifetime judges with omnipotent powers over governmental policies.
>
> · · · ·
>
> This prevailing dominant five-judge economic and social philosophy is becoming a part of our Constitution—not by amendments approved by our people but by the decisions of lifetime judges. With complete confidence in the integrity of the purposes of those dominant judges who are now following and expanding the economic philosophy of some of their predecessors in the Court, I believe with

Justice Holmes, and those other great Justices whose voices have been raised in protest, that their economic-social-constitutional philosophy is contrary to the letter and spirit of our Constitution. . . .

. . . A majority of our judges should not amend our Constitution according to their economic predilections every time they decide a case. By such action they block the orderly and necessary progress of the people and jeopardize our most sacred rights and liberties. Our democracy can work out its own problems within our Constitution if the rights of human beings as human beings are given first importance and if our Constitution is not so misinterpreted and altered as to shackle the democratic processes themselves. . . .

. . . Many of the mistakes of the past have not been because of our Constitution, but because of the alterations and amendments of that great charter by our judges. When our great charter is changed, the people should do it—not the courts.[144]

The court-packing plan failed to win approval in the Congress. While it was still pending, however, the Supreme Court began, in the early spring of 1937, what Washington wits quickly dubbed the "switch in time to save nine," consistently rejecting due process and other challenges to federal and state economic recovery legislation. When Justice Black won appointment to the bench later that year, he joined the majority in further repudiation of the Court's recent past. It soon became evident, however, that Black was bent on a more extreme restriction of judicial discretion than most, if not all, his colleagues were willing to embrace. Justice Holmes's dissents against the pre-1937 Court's use of substantive due process had not completely rejected the doctrine. Instead, Holmes had simply contended that judges should refrain from substituting their preferences for those of legislators with respect to any issue "upon which men reasonably might differ."[145] The dominant coalition beginning to develop on the Court at the time of Black's appointment was similarly inclined, favoring a substantial reduction in the substantive due process bite, but not total repudiation of the doctrine. Black, on the other hand, was committed to its complete dismantling.

In the Senate Black had conceded that "[m]ost men would be unable to change their natural bent of mind" on becoming judges, and he refused to question the integrity of presidents who sought to appoint judges whose economic and social attitudes paralleled their own, or of judges influenced by such attitudes in their decisionmaking.[146] Precisely because of this element of human nature, however, he preferred constitutional interpretations which severely restricted the scope of judicial discretion, and in the due process field he found such a construction in the guarantee's English roots. In a concurrence registered just six months after his appointment to the bench,[147] he maintained that due process had the same meaning as the provision of the Magna Carta forbidding governmental interference with the individual except by the "law of the land." When Justice Stone's draft opinion for the Court in *United States* v. *Carolene Products*[148] gave substantive due process a narrow reading but indicated that courts could invalidate economic laws lacking a "rational basis," Black made the ultimate implications of his own due process position abundantly clear. "As I read the opinion," he wrote Stone, "it approves the submission of proof to a jury or a court under certain circumstances to determine whether the legislature was justified in the policy it adopted. This is contrary to my conception of the extent of judicial power of review."[149] Stone was still uncertain whether he and Black were "in disagreement. . . . Would you ever hold any statute unconstitutional on grounds of substantive due process?" he asked his colleague. "If not, then of course you could not agree with the third [section] in the opinion in the *Carolene* case." Stone had his answer. When the decision was announced, Black declined to join its third section.[150]

In later cases he proved equally alert to substantive due process rhetoric in opinions he was expected to join. When, for example, Stone's draft opinion in the *Darby Lumber Co.* case[151] rejected due process challenges to the federal wage and hour legislation at issue there, noting, among other things, that no contention had been raised that the minimum wage fixed by the law was "unfair or oppressive," Justice Black quickly reacted. "The inference is left," he complained to Stone, "that had *we found* the wage rate 'unfair or oppressive,' we would hold the law offended the due process clause. I would not agree to such a conclusion were it announced. In fact, so far as the due process clause of the fifth amendment is concerned, I am unable to see its application to an act properly coming within the commerce power."[152] (On this occasion Stone accommodated his colleague's concerns, deleting the offensive passage.)

Black also regularly insisted that the Court's interpretations of

statutes be based on legislative intent, asserting in one pointed reference to a Frankfurter dissent that "for judges to rest their interpretation
of statutes on nothing but their own conceptions of 'morals' and 'ethics'
is, to say the least, dangerous business."[153] Where a congressional statute authorized an administrative agency to set "just and reasonable"
rates, he contended, moreover, that judicial review of such administrative judgments should be narrowly limited. "[T]he problem of ratemak-
ing," he asserted in one case, "is for the administrative experts, not the
courts, and . . . the *ex post facto* function previously performed by the
courts should be reduced to the barest minimum which is consistent
with the statutory mandate for judicial review."[154] And when a colleague even suggested the continued force of any pre-1937 economic
precedent, he raised vigorous protests, observing, for example, of a
Frankfurter citation to an 1890 case upholding judicial evaluations of
the reasonableness of rate regulations,

> That was the case in which a majority of this Court was finally
> induced to expand the meaning of "due process" so as to give courts
> power to block efforts of the state and national governments to
> regulate economic affairs. . . . We do not understand that Congress
> voluntarily has acquiesced in a Constitutional principle of govern-
> ment that courts, rather than legislative bodies, possess final au-
> thority over regulation of economic affairs. Even this Court has not
> always fully embraced that principle, and we wish to repeat that
> we have never acquiesced in it, and do not now.[155]

Since 1936 the Supreme Court has not invalidated a single economic control on substantive due process grounds, and the rationale of
the one case striking down an economic regulation on equal protection
grounds was later overruled.[156] Over his career, moreover, Justice Black
authored a number of opinions for the Court which appeared to be
complete repudiations of economic due process. In a 1949 case, for
example, he observed:

> This Court beginning at least as early as 1934 . . . has steadily
> rejected the due process philosophy enunciated in the *Adair-Cop-
> page* line of cases. In doing so it has consciously returned closer and
> closer to the earlier constitutional principle that states have power
> to legislate against what are found to be injurious practices in their
> internal commercial and business affairs, so long as their laws do

not run afoul of some specific federal constitutional prohibition, or of some valid federal law. . . . Under this constitutional doctrine the due process clause is no longer to be so broadly construed that the Congress and state legislatures are put in a strait jacket when they attempt to suppress business and industrial conditions which they regard as offensive to the public welfare.[157]

And in *Ferguson* v. *Skrupa*,[158] a 1963 case, he cited his 1949 opinion and other earlier precedents in exclaiming: "We refuse to sit as a 'super-legislature to weigh the wisdom of legislation.' . . . Whether the legislature takes for its textbook Adam Smith, Herbert Spencer, Lord Keynes, or some other is no concern of ours."[159]

As a close reading of *Skrupa* suggests, however, substantive due process was hardly dead, even, for certain justices, in economic cases. Justice Black's original *Skrupa* draft was a more clearcut rejection of the doctrine than that ultimately registered, and Justice Goldberg found some of the language in Black's "eloquent" original opinion disturbing. "By its many references to the idea that it is no longer this Court's function to pass upon the 'reasonableness' of a State's economic legislation," Goldberg wrote Black, "it implies resolution of some possible cases about which I am not at all sure and which, in any event, need not be reached in order to decide this case." Goldberg suggested modifications which would leave him "free to think in terms of 'unreasonableness' about the merits of conceivable extremes of state economic regulation when such cases arise."[160] In a notation scrawled at the bottom of Goldberg's letter Black indicated that he had "agreed to some of these changes with great regret but not to all." And he obviously realized their implications. "With these changes," he lamented, "we fail to administer the final fatal blow to the idea that this Court can overrule a legislature's belief of reasonableness."[161]

In the field of noneconomic legislation, moreover, substantive due process was not only still alive; it was on the verge of a modern reflowering. Black's harsh attacks on the "natural law" due process formula in early cases rejecting incorporation of Bill of Rights safeguards into the Fourteenth Amendment[162] had long made it clear that his distaste for flexible conceptions of due process was not confined to the economic sphere. To Black, due process was no more appropriate a vehicle for judicial recognition—or creation, as he would have termed it—of noneconomic rights than economic liberties. But on that issue he was to stand entirely alone, isolated even from Justice Douglas, who had appeared to reject economic due process with an absoluteness equaling Black's own.

Although principally concerned with property rights, the pre–1937 Court had used substantive due process to invalidate a number of laws impinging upon noneconomic interests. *Meyer* v. *Nebraska*,[163] decided in 1923, struck down, for example, a statute prohibiting the teaching of foreign languages to school students before their completion of the eighth grade. And in *Pierce* v. *Society of Sisters*,[164] decided two years later, the Court held a state law requiring all children to attend public rather than private schools inconsistent with the due process guarantee. Arguably, the Old Court also resorted to a form of substantive due process in beginning the incorporation of First Amendment guarantees into the Fourteenth Amendments' meaning.[165] The post–1937 Court completed that process, employing essentially the same approach.[166] Moreover, in *Skinner* v. *Oklahoma*,[167] a 1942 equal protection case invalidating a law providing for the selective sterilization of habitual criminals, the Court suggested that the Constitution guaranteed a "basic civil right" of procreation. For more than twenty years after *Skinner*, however, the Court had largely avoided resort to flexible conceptions of due process, at least outside the Fourteenth Amendment incorporation context.

But Justice Black's fear that substantive due process had not yet been given a "final fatal blow" was soon to prove prophetic. In 1964, the year after the Black-Goldberg exchange in *Skrupa*, the Court, per Goldberg, held in *Aptheker* v. *Secretary of State*[168] that a federal statute denying passports to Communists violated a right of international travel implicit in the Fifth Amendment due process clause. The following year, a seven-two majority, speaking through Justice Douglas, ruled in *Griswold* v. *Connecticut*[169] that a statute prohibiting the use of contraceptives, even in marital relationships, violated a right of privacy implied by several constitutional guarantees.

Justice Black considered the statute at issue in *Aptheker* a clear invasion of First Amendment freedoms, a bill of attainder, and a violation of due process, which meant for him that no governmental official could "deny people in this country their liberty to travel or their liberty to do anything else except in accordance with the 'law of the land' as declared by the Constitution or by valid laws made pursuant to it."[170] He was thus content to file a brief concurrence in which he summarized the statute's constitutional defects but rejected the majority's conclusion that due process, "standing alone, confers on all our people a constitutional liberty to travel abroad at will," adding, "Without reference to other constitutional provisions, Congress has, in my judgment, broad powers to regulate the issuance of passports under its specific powers to regulate commerce with foreign nations."[171] But the potentially far-reaching *Griswold* case was a different matter. Challenging the expansive implications of Justice Douglas's opinion for the Court and especially the concurring opinions of Justices Goldberg, Harlan, and White, Justice Black registered a lengthy and vehement *Griswold* dissent, then, when the decision was announced, delivered his brethren a stinging lecture from the bench.

The Connecticut law at issue in *Griswold* had been before the Court on two previous occasions, most recently in *Poe* v. *Ullman*,[172] a 1961 case in which a majority, per Justice Frankfurter, dismissed a challenge to its constitutionality by citing essentially the absence of a true case or controversy. In a *Poe* dissent Justice Douglas contended that Connecticut's broad ban on contraceptives infringed the Fourteenth Amendment due process clause. That clause, Douglas asserted, included within its meaning all the provisions of the first eight amendments, but its reach was not confined to those guarantees. It was also "a conception that sometimes gains content from the emanations of other specific guarantees . . . or from experience with the requirements of a free society."[173] The pre-1937 Court, he added, had not erred by "entertaining inquiries concerning the constitutionality of social legislation" under due process standards. Its error lay instead with the standards it applied and in its failure to recognize that a "free society needs room for vast experimentation. . . . [T]o say," Douglas continued, "that a legislature may do anything not within a specific guarantee of the Constitution [could] be as crippling to a free society as to allow it to override specific guarantees so long as what it does fails to shock the sensibilities of a majority of the Court."[174] Refusing to limit the Constitution to such specifics, Douglas concluded that one form of "liberty" guaranteed by the due process clause, though not specifically mentioned elsewhere in the Constitution, was the right to privacy, a right "implicit in a free society," and one which "emanates from the totality of the constitutional scheme under which we live."[175] The broad Connecticut ban on contraceptives interfered with that right and thus violated due process' substantive component.

Perhaps in a futile effort to secure Justice Black's concurrence, Justice Douglas avoided overt reliance in *Griswold* on the substantive due process concept he had embraced in *Poe*. In an initial *Griswold* draft, in fact, he had sought to rest a general right of marital privacy on the freedom of association which the Court—with Black's acquiescence—had held to be implicit in the First Amendment. But Justice Brennan doubted the wisdom of an opinion based entirely on the First Amendment and wrote Douglas a lengthy letter outlining a different approach. "Your opinion suggests, I think," wrote Brennan,

> a more fruitful approach, more closely tailored to the real interest at stake. You point out that, in creating a right of association, this Court has invoked the First Amendment to protect something not literally within its terminology of speech and assembly, because the interest protected is so closely related to speech and assembly. Instead of expanding the First Amendment right of association to include marriage, why not say that what has been done for the First Amendment can also be done for some of the other fundamental guarantees of the Bill of Rights? In other words, where fundamentals are concerned, the Bill of Rights guarantees are but expressions or examples of those rights, and do not preclude application or extensions of those rights to situations unanticipated by the Framers. Whether, in doing for other guarantees what has been done for speech and assembly in the First Amendment, we proceed by an expansive interpretation of those guarantees or by application of the Ninth Amendment that the enumeration of rights is not exhaustive, the result is the same. The guarantees of the Bill of Rights do not necessarily resist expansion to fill in the edges where the same fundamental interests are at stake.
>
> The Connecticut statute would, on this reasoning, run afoul of a right of privacy created out of the Fourth Amendment and the self-incrimination clause of the Fifth, together with the Third, in much the same way as the right to association has been created out of the First. Taken together, those amendments indicate a fundamental concern with the sanctity of the home and the right of the individual to be let alone. We need not say how far it would extend. . . . All that is necessary for the decision of this case is the recognition that, whatever the contours of a constitutional right to privacy, it would preclude application of the statute before us to married

couples. For it is plain that, in our civilization, the marital relationship above all else is endowed with privacy.

With this change of emphasis, an opinion resting on the persuasive precedent of the right of association for similar limited expansion of other specific guarantees of the Bill of Rights, would be most
attractive to me because it would require less departure from the
specific guarantees and because I think there is a better chance it
will command a Court.[176]

Justice Douglas had briefly alluded to such an approach in his *Poe*
dissent. But Brennan's letter had an undoubted influence. The opinion
Douglas ultimately filed largely tracked the "penumbra" rationale Brennan had outlined. The Court, Douglas soothed, had declined invitations
to use *Lochner* v. *New York* as its guide. "We do not sit as a super-
legislature to determine the wisdom, need, and propriety of laws that
touch economic problems, business affairs, or social conditions."[177]
But this did not mean that the constitutional guarantees courts were
charged with safeguarding were limited to specific rights. "[S]pecific
guarantees," wrote Douglas, "have penumbras, formed by emanations
from those guarantees that help give them life and substance."[178] Indeed, "without those peripheral rights the specific rights would be less
secure."[179] The Bill of Rights included protection for several specific
zones of privacy, and emanating from those guarantees was a general
right of marital privacy, a concept "older than the Bill of Rights—older
than our political parties, older than our school system."[180] Connecticut's ban on contraceptives, concluded Douglas, was an obvious and
sweeping infringement of that "noble" right of privacy.[181]

Despite broader language in his opinion, Douglas attempted to
draw strong parallels between the Court's recognition of a right of
privacy lying within the shadow of specific Bill of Rights safeguards and
the freedom of association and other rights the Court had held to be
implicit in the First Amendment. In fact, most of the precedents he
cited involved First Amendment freedoms, and he even attempted to
bottom two of the pre-1937 Court's decisions, *Meyer* v. *Nebraska* and
Pierce v. *Society of Sisters*, on the First Amendment, although both were
clearly based on substantive due process rhetoric.[182] But Justice Black
saw little semblance, ultimately, between the Court's approach in *Griswold* and the broad constructions given the First Amendment in earlier
cases. He seemed fully prepared to invalidate any prosecution under the

statute directed at speech alone. The physicians whose convictions for aiding and abetting a violation of the law were at issue in *Griswold*, however, were involved in more than mere speech. More fundamentally, he thought the Court's use of the penumbra concept in the case had gone beyond interpretation to a judicial rewriting of constitutional guarantees. "The Court talks about a constitutional 'right of privacy,' " he contended,

> as though there is some constitutional provision or provisions forbidding any law ever to be passed which might abridge the "privacy" of individuals. But there is not. . . . I get nowhere in this case by talk about a constitutional 'right of privacy' as an emanation from one or more constitutional provisions. I like my privacy as well as the next one, but I am nevertheless compelled to admit that government has a right to invade it unless prohibited by some specific constitutional provision.[183]

Black's reaction to the concurrence of Justices Goldberg, Harlan, and White was even harsher. In listing Bill of Rights safeguards purporting to create "zones of privacy," Justice Douglas merely quoted without comment the enigmatic assertion of the Ninth Amendment that "[t]he enumeration in the Constitution of certain rights, shall not be construed to deny or disparage others retained by the people." In his concurring opinion, however, Justice Goldberg cited the Ninth Amendment as evidence that the Constitution—and especially its due process guarantees—included protection for "fundamental" rights not specifically mentioned in the document's text. Justice Harlan, moreover, rested his objections to the Connecticut law on substantive due process, contending as he had in a *Poe* dissent and in other contexts that due process safeguards "basic values 'implicit in the concept of ordered liberty.' "[184] And in a separate concurrence, Justice White assumed a similar stance.

For Justice Black such rhetoric was nothing less than the "natural law" philosophy the pre-1937 Court had embraced. To him, the due process and Ninth Amendment arguments amounted to "the same thing—merely using different words to claim for this Court and the federal judiciary power to invalidate any legislative act which the judges find irrational, unreasonable or offensive."[185] The pre-1937 Court's resort to due process for such purposes had long been repudiated, and, in Black's judgment, "[t]hat formula . . . [was] no less dangerous when used to enforce this Court's views about personal rights than those about economic rights."[186] Nor was Goldberg's Ninth Amendment argument any more persuasive. The Ninth Amendment, Black asserted,

> was passed, not to broaden the powers of the Court or any other department of "the General Government," but, as every student of history knows, to assure the people that the Constitution in all its provisions was intended to limit the Federal Government to the powers granted expressly or by necessary implication. If any broad, unlimited power to hold laws unconstitutional because they offend what this Court conceives to be the "[collective] conscience of our people" is vested in this Court by the Ninth Amendment, the Fourteenth Amendment, or any other provision of the Constitution, it was not given by the Framers, but rather has been bestowed on the Court by the Court. This fact is perhaps responsible for the peculiar phenomenon that for a period of a century and a half no serious suggestion was ever made that the Ninth Amendment, enacted to protect state powers against federal invasion, could be used as a weapon of federal power to prevent state legislatures from passing laws they consider appropriate to govern local affairs. Use of any such broad, unbounded judicial authority would make of this Court's members a day-to-day constitutional convention.[187]

Despite Black's protests, of course, *Griswold* was not to be the Court's last or most overt exhumation of substantive due process. While Justice Douglas's opinion for the *Griswold* majority had attempted to tie the right of privacy to specific guarantees of the Bill of Rights, the Court was not so circumspect when it decided *Roe* v. *Wade*[188] in 1973. Like the *Griswold* majority, the *Roe* Court, speaking through Justice Blackmun, one of President Nixon's "strict constructionists," purported to disavow *Lochner* v. *New York*, then proceeded with the very sort of substantive due process analysis *Lochner* had epitomized, holding that a right of privacy implicit in the "liberty" safeguarded by due process was broad enough to encompass a woman's decision to abort an unwanted pregnancy. Justice Black had died in 1971. (Indeed, his absence from the Court may have been one reason for the Justices' uninhibited resort in *Roe* to the due process rationale their late colleague found so thoroughly offensive.) Before his death, however, Black had made clear in conference his view that the Constitution included no right of abortion.[189] During his last term, moreover, he spoke for the Court in rejecting a vagueness challenge to a District of Columbia abortion statute.[190]

Justice Black had made equally explicit before his death what had long been a clear implication of his incorporation opinions—that, in his judgment, due process was no more a repository for what judges consider to be "fundamental" requirements of "fair" procedure than for judicially created substantive liberties. In *United Gas Public Service Co. v. Texas*,[191] the 1938 case in which he first endorsed a "law of the land" construction of due process, he had quoted with apparent approval the following passage from the Court's 1877 opinion in *Davidson* v. *City of New Orleans*: "[I]t is not possible to hold that a party has without due process of law, been deprived of his property, when, as regards the issues affecting it, he has, by the laws of the State, a fair trial in a court of justice according to the modes of proceeding applicable to such a case."[192] Such language suggested that appellate courts could make judgments regarding the fairness of judicial proceedings. As the Court's spokesman in *Chambers* v. *Florida*,[193] moreover, Black construed due process to prohibit punishment of persons in criminal cases "until there had been a charge fairly made and fairly tried."[194] And speaking for the Court in a number of later cases he held due process to require convictions based only on a "charge fairly made and fairly tried" or on "a fair trial in a fair tribunal."[195] He also wrote or joined opinions articulating due process standards without reference to specific statutes or constitutional provisions. But certain of those rulings invoked standards which were merely restatements of Fifth and Sixth Amendment guarantees or closely related to such requirements.[196] Others imposed requirements compatible with his "law of the land" thesis. (He agreed, for example, that convictions based on vague statutes,[197] no evidence,[198] perjured testimony,[199] suppressed evidence,[200] or false evidence[201] violated due process.) And his use of "fair trial" rhetoric was extremely rare and confined largely to opinions authored for the Court.

Beyond the criminal law context, his conception of due process was even more restrictive. When the Court invalidated a wage garnishment scheme which included no provision for notice and prior hearing, he accused his brethren of "nothing more or less than an implicit adoption of a Natural Law concept which under our system leaves to judges alone the power to decide what the Natural Law means," then asked, "If the judges, in deciding whether laws are constitutional, are to be left only to the admonitions of their own consciences, why was it that the Founders gave us a written Constitution at all?"[202] When the Court required notice and hearing before termination of welfare benefits, he delivered a similar lecture, complaining that "[o]nce the verbiage is pared away it is obvious that this Court today adopts the views . . . 'that to cut off a welfare recipient in the face of . . . "brutal need" without a prior hearing of some sort is unconscionable,' and therefore, says the Court, unconstitutional."[203] And when a majority invoked due process to exempt indigent married couples from the burden of filing fees in divorce cases, he questioned whether the guarantee even applied to such civil proceedings, observing:

> In such cases the government is not usually involved as a party, and there is no deprivation of life, liberty, or property as punishment for crime. Our Federal Constitution, therefore, does not place such private disputes on the same high level as it places criminal trials and punishment. There is consequently no necessity, no reason, why government should in civil trials be hampered or handicapped by the strict and rigid due process rules the Constitution has provided to protect people charged with crime.[204]

Justice Black perhaps best summarized the ultimate procedural as well as substantive limits to his conception of due process, however, in a 1970 dissent filed for *In Re Winship*.[205] The *Winship* majority, per Justice Brennan, held that proof of guilt beyond a reasonable doubt was one of the "essentials of due process and fair treatment."[206] Black had joined earlier opinions which assumed such a standard of guilt to be a requisite of due process.[207] When the issue was placed squarely before the Court, however, he dissented, noting that no specific constitutional provision imposed the no-reasonable-doubt standard, rejecting the majority's "fundamental fairness" approach to due process, and contending once again that the guarantee required only that government proceed "according to written constitutional and statutory provisions as interpreted by court decisions."[208] For those, moreover, who considered such a conception of due process "a degrading and niggardly view of what is undoubtedly a fundamental part of our basic freedoms," Black offered a lesson in basic history.

> [T]hat criticism fails to note the historical importance of our Constitution and the virtual revolution in the history of the government of nations that was achieved by forming a government that from the beginning had its limits of power set forth in one written document that also made it abundantly clear that all governmen-

tal actions affecting life, liberty, and property were to be according to law. . . . [T]he struggle had not been simply to put all the constitutional law in one document, it was also to make certain that men would be governed by *law*, not the arbitrary fiat of the man or men in power. Our ancestors' ancestors had known the tyranny of the kings and the rule of man and it was, in my view, in order to insure against such actions that the Founders wrote into our Magna Carta the fundamental principle of the rule of law, as expressed in the historically meaningful phrase "due process of law." The many decisions of this Court that have found in that phrase a blanket authority to govern the country according to the views of at least five members of this institution have ignored the essential meaning of the very words they invoke. When this Court assumes for itself the power to declare any law—state or federal—unconstitutional because it offends the majority's own views of what is fundamental and decent in our society, our Nation ceases to be governed according to the "law of the land" and instead becomes one governed ultimately by the "law of the judges."[209]

The Desirability and Viability of a Clause-bound Constitution

Having examined the elements of Justice Black's positivist conception of the judicial role and their reflections in the Justice's approach to a variety of constitutional issues, we may now turn to critical assessments of the interpretivist jurisprudence he embraced. Some have agreed with Justice Harlan that " '[s]pecific' provisions of the Constitution . . . lend themselves as readily to 'personal' interpretations by judges" as due process and other general constitutional guarantees.[210] Others have contended that the language of due process and related guarantees suggests their framers' intent that they be given the sort of flexible, "fundamental fairness" interpretation Black detested. Ronald Dworkin argues, for example, that the vague terms of such provisions mean that they were designed to embody "the *concept* of fairness, not . . . any specific *conception* of fairness," and that "[i]f courts try to be faithful to the text of the Constitution, they will for that very reason be forced to decide between competing conceptions of political morality."[211] Still others, such as John Hart Ely, appear uncomfortable with noninterpretivism, yet have concluded that the language and history of certain of the Constitution's provisions support such an approach.[212] And many, of course, openly embrace noninterpretivism. Michael J. Perry has maintained, for example, that noninterpretivist review of the actions of government officials serves as a major vehicle for the continuing evaluation and evolution of political-moral values—a process in which courts articulate values and the political branches react, endorsing and enlarging upon judicially created standards through action of their own, doing nothing, or withdrawing the issue from further judicial scrutiny via jurisdictional controls.[213] Along similar lines, Thomas C. Grey has defended the Supreme Court's role as "the expounder of basic national ideals" and charged that the triumph of a "pure interpretivist model" of judicial review would require "an extraordinarily radical purge of established constitutional doctrine."[214]

Sylvia Snowiss has developed perhaps the most thoroughgoing critique, however, of Justice Black's conception of the judicial function. Black's First Amendment philosophy rejected "judgments about the quality of speech," and, in Snowiss's view, "his denigration of this kind of judgment" in every field of constitutional law was the "underlying problem"[215] with his entire jurisprudence for several reasons. First, she contends, Black failed to realize that the vitality and, indeed, the very survival of constitutional interpretation depend on the degree to which judicial decisions reflect "meaningful conceptions of justice" which the people accept and to which they are committed.

> For the constitutional guarantees to have genuine vitality there must first be a society willing to listen to its courts, and to the judicial resolution of a significant area of political conflict. This in turn rests on a general societal commitment to the principles of reasonableness, fairness, and justice, on the quality of debate in interpreting these commitments, and on the popular responsiveness to such debate.
>
> American courts, in the process of constitutional adjudication, play an enormous role in this debate, articulating and shaping basic values. In so doing they make as significant a contribution to a healthy society as they do in enforcing particular provisions of the Constitution.[216]

Second, according to Snowiss, Black's futile effort to find fixed constitutional rules in the Constitution's language and history—an effort based on fear that giving the judiciary authority to make qualitative judgments would endanger liberty—had given the false impression that the choice was between "unrestrained subjective judgments" or "absolute rules." Instead, the choice was between "better or worse standards for public life."

> No set of rules can provide in detail for the multiplicity of changing needs that must be judged as they arise. In addition to rules there must always be judgment. With respect to the necessarily broad rules of the Constitution, the need for judgment is even greater. That there is little likelihood of agreement on the worth of all judgments does not mean that no judgments are possible. Societies must continue to argue over and strive toward better judgments if they are not to succumb to the worst judgments. No judicial determination need end debate on the merit of a distinction that has been drawn. Public argument over alternative standards is far preferable to the denial of the possibility of defending any meaningful standard and the retreat to a legal objectivity and neutrality that is illusory.[217]

Finally, she argues, Black's interpretivism produced a number of "negative consequences," including "arbitrary" conclusions regarding the Constitution's meaning and judgments which failed to meet "all the needs of limited government." Black's failure to provide "satisfactory treatment" for privacy issues confronting the Court provided, in Snowiss's judgment, "major examples" of such "serious limitations" in his approach.[218]

To the extent that the foregoing criticisms reflect a preference for noninterpretivism over interpretivism on grounds of the former's greater intrinsic merit, they simply reveal, of course, not so much specific weaknesses in Black's thinking as a fundamental disagreement with the Justice over the proper role of moral, ethical, or utilitarian judgments in a legal system. Positivists such as Black, it will be recalled, do not reject the notion that considerations of "fairness," "reasonableness," and "justice" should have an impact on the law. They would merely limit the role of such concepts largely to the legislative arena, contending that judicial decisions should rest on noninterpretivist considerations only when the language of a law and the history underlying its adoption fail to provide the key to its meaning and application in specific cases. Black probably would also have argued that, in a representative democracy, a conception of the judicial function that would leave value judgments largely to elected lawmakers rather than to courts is more likely to engender respect for courts and their decisions than an approach recognizing for judges a major role in the "shaping" of "basic values." At the very least, moreover, one of Black's persuasion could be expected to contend that judicial decisions reflecting the value preferences of judges should be identified as such, not cloaked—as they invariably are—in what Black termed "catchwords and catch phrases"[219] designed to give them the aura of general principles and conceal their true character as personal policy choices. Because Justice Black termed the Constitution his "legal bible" and stressed his "faith" in its literal meaning, he has often been compared unfavorably to religious fundamentalists. With due respect, however, the appeals of his critics to "decencies of civilized conduct,"[220] to "some principle of justice so rooted in the traditions and conscience of our people as to be ranked as fundamental,"[221] to "those canons of decency and fairness which express the notions of justice of English-speaking people,"[222] and to related rhetoric seem decidedly more theological in nature than the approach Justice Black embraced.

Mindful of majoritarian democratic traditions, of course, most critics of Black's jurisprudence, or of interpretivism generally, do not rest their concerns solely on a belief in the inherent superiority of noninterpretivist jurisprudence. Instead, as indicated previously, they mix their preference for noninterpretivism—and its capacity for meeting "all the needs of limited government" through "satisfactory treatment" of constitutional issues—with the contention that, in any event, interpretivism is simply impossible to implement. The meaning of even the most "specific" constitutional provisions, it is argued, can rarely be drawn from their language or history. And the very language of due process and related open-ended guarantees virtually compels noninterpretive analysis. Indeed, their language suggests, as Ronald Dworkin has maintained, that this was their framers' intent.

Justice Black never argued, however, that even the Constitution's "specific" provisions were self-interpreting. He realized that language and history must themselves be construed, that different minds could reach different conclusions regarding a provision's literal or historically intended meaning, and that language and history would not always provide clear answers to constitutional questions. In his Carpentier lectures, for example, he observed: "Of course the Court's duty to strike down legislative enactments which violate the Constitution requires interpretation, and since words can have many meanings, interpretation obviously may sometimes result in contraction or extension of the original purpose of a constitutional provision, thereby affecting policy."[223] Black's differences with his critics over the meaning to be given "specific" provisions, therefore, were more of degree than kind. He merely found more clearcut meanings, and more frequently, in the Constitution's language and history than did his critics; at times, moreover, his conclusions regarding the document's literal or historically intended meaning simply differed from theirs. The relative merits of his constructions and those of his critics can be evaluated, and many are in later chapters. But their differences, in many instances, may not have been as fundamental as they appear.

Black's differences with his critics over the meaning of more general constitutional guarantees, on the other hand, are very basic and far-reaching in their implications. In a sense, of course, they too merely reflect different impressions of the Constitution's language and history and are differences in degree. They also embody, however, profoundly different visions of the proper scope of the judicial function. However susceptible to conflicting judicial interpretations the First Amendment freedoms, the Fourth Amendment, the Fifth Amendment's just compensation, double jeopardy, and self-incrimination guarantees, the procedural safeguards of the Sixth Amendment, or other specific constitutional provisions may be, their language imposes boundaries beyond which even the most creative judge arguably would not venture. And in many cases the boundaries are quite narrow. Not so the due process clauses, the Ninth Amendment, the Fourteenth Amendment privileges or immunities clause, and the equal protection guarantee. Acceptance of the contentions of Black's critics that the language and history of these clauses require judicial decisions bottomed on moral, ethical, or social considerations means endorsement of judicial authority to make such evaluations not only with regard to certain exercises of governmental power, but potentially over the entire range of public policy, practice, and procedure—authority for courts to act, in short, as "super-legislatures," however offensive judges embracing such an approach find that label. Acceptance, on the other hand, of Black's contention that the language and history of these clauses largely or entirely deny judges such power leaves the shaping—or discovery—of basic values primarily in the hands of elected policymakers.

The language and history of the Constitution's potentially open-ended guarantees provide conclusive support, of course, for neither

Justice Black's approach to the judicial function, nor that of his noninterpretivist counterparts. Arguably, however, majoritarian democratic
principles militate in favor of Black's position. Noninterpretivists are
obviously sensitive to the charge that their conception of the judicial
function conflicts with democratic principles and the genius of a written Constitution designed to restrain judges as well as other government officials. But they attempt to disarm such concerns by adapting
noninterpretivism to their version of democratic principles, by contending that life-appointed federal judges are, in any event, part of the
current majority, or by citing controls the political branches can wield
over the courts. John Hart Ely would invoke noninterpretivism, for
example, largely to clear the channels of political change and facilitate
effective minority representation in the political processes (in short, to
expand democratic participation), leaving the choice of substantive
policy values largely to those processes.[224] Michael Perry assures us,
moreover, that congressional power over the jurisdiction of federal
courts is an adequate safeguard against noninterpretivist threats to
majority will.[225]

Such efforts, however, are debatable at best. Ely to the contrary,
judicial creativity of an essentially procedural character would appear
as offensive to democratic principles as noninterpretive imposition of
substantive limitations on governmental power. Nor does history offer
much cause for confidence in Perry's remedy or related devices against
an unduly creative judiciary—devices whose activation is often seen,
ironically enough, as an affront to the rule of law (rather than the rule
of judges). And the idea that judicial lawmaking is somehow less objectionable to majoritarian principles because federal judges are appointed
by presidents indirectly elected by the voters is equally difficult to
accept. No, while judges may be better at shaping "basic values" than
legislators, the notion that due process and related constitutional guarantees clothe them with such authority over the entire range of public
policy—or even its procedural sphere alone—seems clearly inconsistent with democratic principles.

This inherent inconsistency, combined with the failure of constitutional language and history to provide conclusive support for either
Black's position or the views of his noninterpretivist counterparts, is
strong justification for endorsement of Black's relatively fixed constructions of due process and the Constitution's other potentially open-
ended guarantees over more flexible approaches. Of course, were the

Constitution's language and history to offer undeniable support for noninterpretivism, concerns about its conflict with democratic principles would be expected to yield to the demands of explicit law. But there is no such incontrovertible evidence in the Constitution's language and history. In fact, those sources offer very plausible support for Justice Black's position.

Consider, first, the language and history of the due process guarantee. The substantive due process concept—the idea, that is, that laws interfering with certain liberties violate due process, whatever the process employed to carry them out—flies in the face of the clause's very language. As Edward S. Corwin observed three-quarters of a century ago during the heyday of economic due process, substantive due process "is nothing less than the elimination of the very phrase under construction from the constitutional clause in which it occurs."[226] The history of the concept is no more impressive. Apparently no American court gave the guarantee a substantive due process interpretation until the New York Court of Appeals' *Wynehamer* decision of 1856; and, as Professor Corwin also concluded in writing of the status of due process prior to the Civil War,

> the *Wynehamer* decision found no place in the constitutional law that was generally recognized throughout the United States in the year 1856. Neither had it been foreshadowed by decisions in similar cases in other States, nor was it subsequently accepted in such cases. Also it met locally an immense amount of hostile criticism, both lay and professional. Altogether it must be considered an adversity, for the time being, to the derived doctrine of due process of law.[227]

Justice Black's total rejection of substantive due process thus hardly seems inconsistent with the Constitution's language or history, even if it does deny judges the opportunity to meet "all the needs of limited government."

The notion that due process requires government to follow not merely its own laws and procedures when depriving a person of life, liberty, or property, but also "fundamentally fair" procedures articulated by judges, does not seem obviously inconsistent with the clause's bare language. In 1856, the year *Wynehamer* was decided, the Court, per Justice Curtis, wrote of the Fifth Amendment due process clause in *Murray's Lessee* v. *Hoboken Land & Improvement Co.*:

The constitution contains no description of those processes which it was intended to allow or forbid. It does not even declare what principles are to be applied to ascertain whether it be due process. It is manifest that it was not left to the legislative power to enact any process which might be devised. The article is a restraint on the legislative as well as on the executive and judicial powers of the government, and cannot be so construed as to leave congress to make any process "due process of law," by its mere will. To what principles, then, are we to resort to ascertain whether this process, enacted by congress, is due process? To this the answer must be twofold. We must examine the constitution itself, to see whether this process be in conflict with any of its provisions. If not found to be so, we must look to those settled usages and modes of proceeding existing in the common and statute law of England, before the emigration of our ancestors, and which are shown not to have been unsuited to their civil and political condition by having been acted on by them after the settlement of this country.[228]

Later opinions employed more expansive language in summarizing the procedural content of the due process clause. In *Twining* v. *New Jersey* (1908),[229] for example, Justice Moody concluded that "consistently with the requirements of due process, no change in ancient procedure can be made which disregards those fundamental principles, to be ascertained from time to time by judicial action, which have relation to process by law and protect the citizen in his private right, and guard him against the arbitrary action of government."[230]

It should be remembered, however, that the Supreme Court's use of expansive language to describe due process' procedural content paralleled the Court's move toward acceptance of substantive due process, with the rhetoric for each line of cases virtually indistinguishable. It should also be recalled that, despite its use of language suggesting a flexible conception of procedural due process, the Court, at the time of the Fourteenth Amendment's adoption and for years thereafter, actually applied an interpretation that closely paralleled Justice Black's "law of the land" approach. In his *Twining* opinion, for example, Justice Moody employed seemingly expansive language, but then added:

The essential elements of due process of law [as a procedural requirement] . . . are singularly few, though of wide application and deep significance. . . . Due process requires that the court which assumes to determine the rights of parties shall have jurisdiction . . . and that there shall be notice and opportunity for a hearing given the parties. . . . Subject to those two fundamental conditions, which seem to be universally prescribed in all systems of law established by civilized countries, this Court has, up to this time, sustained all state laws . . . regulating procedure, evidence, and methods of trial, and held them to be consistent with due process of law.[231]

Remember, too, that even in modern cases the Court has rarely applied standards of procedural "fairness" which were not analogous or identical to specific Bill of Rights safeguards,[232] closely related to the requirement that government merely follow the "law of the land,"[233] or selective applications of specific Bill of Rights safeguards in juvenile hearings.[234] Justice Black's contention that due process largely obligates government simply to follow its own laws and procedures seems essentially compatible, therefore, with the Court's practice, if not its rhetoric. And the expansive linguistic gloss the Court has given the concept in procedural cases did not begin to develop until long after adoption of the Fifth Amendment's due process clause. Moreover, that development tracked, and to a great degree mirrored, development of a substantive due process doctrine which, though never entirely repudiated, was eventually discredited and remained so from 1937 to 1964, a period of nearly thirty years.

What of the Ninth Amendment as a basis for noninterpretivism? In his *Griswold* concurrence Justice Goldberg saw the amendment as evidence that there were other rights in the Constitution than those specifically mentioned in the document, rights courts were also sworn to protect. The district court in *Roe* v. *Wade*[235] invoked it in recognizing a constitutional right of abortion. A number of scholars[236] have given the amendment, and the history surrounding its adoption, a similar reading. John Hart Ely,[237] among others, has contended, moreover, that the amendment is a mere redundancy if it means no more than Justice Black construed it to mean—that the national government's authority is limited to delegated powers and powers reasonably implied from the delegated powers.[238] After all, Ely argues, the Tenth Amendment makes the delegated nature of national power abundantly clear.

The Ninth Amendment's language does seem, of course, an open invitation to judicial creativity. Moreover, although there is little legislative history relating to its meaning, Ely and others have used two statements by James Madison to support their contention that the amendment is a repository for unstated rights which courts can "recognize" and apply. In an October 1788 letter to Thomas Jefferson, Madison indicated reasons for his reluctance to press for adoption of a Bill of Rights:

> My own opinion has always been in favor of a bill of rights; provided it be so framed as not to imply powers not meant to be included in the enumeration. . . . I have not viewed it in an important light—1. because I conceive that in a certain degree . . . the rights in question are reserved by the manner in which the federal powers are granted. 2. because there is great reason to fear that a positive declaration of some of the most essential rights could not be obtained in the requisite latitude. I am sure that the rights of conscience in particular, if submitted to public definition would be narrowed much more than they are likely ever to be by an assumed power.[239]

Attempting to explain the Ninth Amendment on the floor of the Congress in June 1789, moreover, he remarked:

> It has been objected also against a bill of rights, that, by enumerating particular exceptions to the grant of power, it would disparage those rights which were not placed in that enumeration; and it might follow by implication, that those rights that were not placed in that enumeration, that those rights which were not singled out, were intended to be assigned into the hands of the General Government, and were consequently insecure. That is one of the most plausible arguments I have ever heard urged against the admission of a bill of rights into this system; but, I conceive, that it may be guarded against. I have attempted it, as gentlemen may see by turning to the last clause of the fourth resolution.[240]

With due respect, however, both these statements can be used—and much more easily, in my judgment—to support Justice Black's position. Traditionally, the Ninth Amendment has been construed to mean that the national government is limited to delegated powers and that if it goes beyond those powers, it violates the rights of the people, whether or not those rights are enumerated in the Constitution. So construed, the amendment is a safeguard against ultra vires actions of the national government, against any assumption that grants of national power over individual freedom are merely illustrative rather than inclusive, and against any notion that exercises of national power which invade no enumerated right are somehow within the scope of the Constitution. Madison's concern that an enumeration of rights might imply "that those rights which were not singled out, were intended to be assigned into the hands of the General Government," as well as other portions of his speech and letter, appears clearly compatible with the Ninth Amendment's traditionally accepted meaning, the construction to which Justice Black subscribed.

Nor does this interpretation make the Ninth Amendment a mere redundancy of the Tenth. The Tenth Amendment summarizes the relationship of national and state power under the Constitution; the Ninth clarifies the implications of the delegated powers concept for individual liberty. Of course, there is a marked parallel between the function Justice Goldberg, Professor Ely, and others might favor for the Ninth Amendment and the "dual federalism" interpretation the pre-1937 Court gave the Tenth. But judicial use of the Tenth Amendment to invalidate otherwise valid exercises of national power was repudiated long ago.[241] And to date a Supreme Court majority has never put the Ninth Amendment to similar use—a fact which itself may lend further support to Black's interpretation. The Ninth Amendment construction which Goldberg endorsed in his *Griswold* dissent is as potentially limitless, moreover, as flexible conceptions of due process—and thus as much a threat to democratic principles.

Critics of interpretivism also cite the Fourteenth Amendment's prohibition against state laws abridging the privileges or immunities of U.S. citizens, contending that this clause, too, suggests judicial power to declare rights not otherwise stated in the Constitution. John Hart Ely essentially agrees, for example, with Justice Black's contention that the clause was intended to incorporate specific Bill of Rights safeguards, but rejects what he considers to be "Black's *limitation*" of the clause's meaning to the Bill of Rights, adding: "the most plausible interpretation of the Privileges or Immunities Clause is, as it must be, the one suggested by its language—that it was a delegation to future constitution decision-makers to protect certain rights that the document neither lists, at least not exhaustively, nor even in any specific way gives directions for finding." When Black limited the privileges or immunities clause to Bill of Rights safeguards, Ely contends, he "rejected the counsel of text and historical purpose . . . turned to his own vision of what is right, . . . [and] began to engage in his own brand of noninterpretivism."[242]

Actually, Black never argued that the clause's meaning was limited entirely to the Bill of Rights guarantees. Largely because the clause has been a dead letter provision of the Constitution, used only once by the Supreme Court to invalidate a state law,[243] and in a precedent soon overturned,[244] Black was never obliged to state his views regarding its ultimate meaning, or his approach to determining the scope of the privileges it guarantees. In *Edwards* v. *California* (1941),[245] however, he joined a concurring opinion in which Justice Douglas included a right to interstate travel among the privileges of national citizenship. During conference discussion of *Edwards*, he also suggested that the privileges of national citizenship inhere in the nature of the union, for he based his contention that the privileges or immunities clause incorporated a right of interstate travel on the assumption that "we are a nation and that people can travel from place to place." Shortly before his death he reaffirmed his commitment to this position; moreover, some of the very remarks of Fourteenth Amendment sponsors which he used to defend his incorporation thesis also support the idea that the privileges or immunities clause was intended by them to guarantee other rights than those specified in the Bill of Rights.[246] Even so, *Edwards* was the only case in which he agreed that a right not within specifics of the Bill of Rights was one of the privileges of national citizenship protected by the Fourteenth Amendment. It is likely, therefore, that he limited the clause's scope to a narrow category of rights that "owe their existence to the Federal Government, its National character, its Constitution, or its laws,"[247] as the Court has, but included within that category of rights guarantees of the Bill of Rights, which the Court has not. Such an interpretation leaves room for judicial discretion, but clearly not the degree of latitude an essentially substantive due process construction of the clause would allow.

There remain, though, the contentions of Ely and others that remarks of the Fourteenth Amendment's sponsors support a "fundamental rights" or "natural rights" interpretation of the clause, a construction empowering judges to add indefinitely to the range of privileges the clause covers and invalidate "unreasonable," "unfair," or "unjust" invasions of those liberties.[248] Senator Jacob Howard and other Fourteenth Amendment sponsors gave a "fundamental rights" interpretation to the stipulation of Article IV, Section 2, that "The citizens of each State shall be entitled to all privileges and immunities of citizens in the several States," and further contended that the Fourteenth Amendment would include the "fundamental" rights of Article IV. In explaining the meaning of the proposed privileges or immunities clause during congressional debates over the Fourteenth Amendment's adoption, for example, Senator Howard indicated that the clause would embody the guarantees of Article IV, Section 2, observed that those privileges "are not and cannot be fully defined in their entire extent and precise nature," and referred to their "fundamental" character.[249] Citing such remarks, Ely contends[250] that those truly faithful to the history surrounding the Fourteenth Amendment's adoption—which Black, more than any other Justice, purported to be—will give the privileges or immunities clause a noninterpretivist interpretation.

However, a number of considerations militate against adoption of such a construction. Although many of the Fourteenth Amendment's backers obviously did believe that the privileges or immunities clause would include rights other than those explicitly mentioned elsewhere in the Constitution, "there was no consensus," as a recent exhaustive examination of the amendment's adoption asserts, "on what these rights were."[251] What does seem very clear, on the other hand, is that the amendment's supporters were referring to what to them were "eternal verities," to rights considered to exist at the time of the amendment's adoption and always. This sort of thinking is hardly parallel to Justice Frankfurter's steadily evolving due process clause, much less to the basic assumptions of modern noninterpretivism and its emphasis on judicial creativity. Particularly in view of the threat which noninterpretivism poses for democratic principles—a threat Professor Ely obviously recognizes—one arguably should hesitate to jump from the historical fact that many of the Fourteenth Amendment's supporters believed its provisions to embody rights not stated in the Constitution to the quite different notion that the amendment's framers embraced an evolving, dynamic conception of those rights and intended judges to have the primary role in their creation. The assumption of many of the amendment's backers that it would protect unstated rights is no brief for noninterpretivism. Instead, it is at most a call to judges and others charged with the amendment's construction and enforcement to probe the historical record in an effort to determine what, if any, consensus existed regarding the specific content of these unstated rights.

Finally, there is the equal protection clause. Inconsistencies and other weaknesses, real and apparent, in Justice Black's equal protection philosophy are the focus of a later chapter. As noted earlier, however, Black found the guarantee's open-ended language particularly troublesome and sought to limit its reach as a meaningful restriction on governmental power largely to racial contexts. Dissenting from the Court's decision invalidating the poll tax in *Harper* v. *Virginia State Board of Elections*,[252] for example, he cited economic cases[253] concluding that courts must uphold discriminatory laws so long as they are "not 'irrelevant,' 'unreasonable,' 'arbitrary,' or 'invidious.' "[254] He agreed that those terms were "vague and indefinite" and did not "provide a precise formula or an automatic mechanism for deciding cases."[255] He also acknowledged—with an eye toward the pre-1937 Court's substantive due process rhetoric—that in other contexts such semantics had "been used to expand the Court's power inordinately."[256] He concluded, however, that their "restrictive connotations" were "a plain recognition of the fact that under a proper interpretation of the Equal Protection Clause States are to have the broadest kind of leeway in areas where they have a general constitutional competence to act."[257] Noninterpretivists emphasize, on the other hand, that most governmental actions may be conceptualized in discrimination terms, that neither the clause's language nor the history surrounding its adoption establishes an intent to limit its meaningful reach solely to racial situations, and that it thus empowers judges to subject a potentially wide variety of discriminatory regulations to meaningful review.[258]

Here, again, in my judgment, although neither construction is incontrovertible, Justice Black's conception of equal protection is as consistent with the guarantee's language and history as the more flexible interpretation advanced by his critics, and one posing considerably less risk to democratic principles. Strict judicial review of racial and related forms of discrimination seems clearly compatible with the racial context of the guarantee's adoption. Indeed, given the guarantee's history, one can even consider such discriminations presumptively "unreasonable," as Black's *Harper* dissent seemed to suggest. The clause's language suggests a broader reach, as Black conceded, but neither its words nor the history surrounding its adoption makes clear, or even dimly so, its ultimate scope. Because of that vagueness noninterpretivists and critics of interpretivism see equal protection as yet another opportunity, or command, empowering—or obligating—judges to rule on the fairness, reasonableness, or justice underlying a virtually limitless variety of "discriminatory" laws. Given this nation's majoritarian democratic traditions, however, does vagueness in the language or history of a potentially open-ended constitutional guarantee justify such an approach? Or does it caution the more restrained construction Justice Black embraced? Regard for the concept of government through elected representatives suggests that the greater wisdom lies with the latter approach.

Noninterpretivists will counter, or course, that, carried to a logical conclusion, such thinking is nothing less than a repudiation of the entire doctrine of judicial review, since the Constitution's language and history provide conclusive answers to virtually no constitutional question. As noted earlier, however, the question is one of degree. Whatever the vagueness of the more or less specific constitutional provisions, their language ultimately does impose some restriction on their scope and the uses to which they can be put. Even the First Amendment is not so broadly worded that it can be used to extend constitutional protection to virtually every form of human activity. The same generalization simply cannot be made about equal protection or, for that matter, due process, the Ninth Amendment, or the privileges or immunities clause.

Finally, noninterpretivists also contend that a defense of Justice Black's jurisprudence bottomed on democratic principles, like the Justice's philosophy itself, misperceives the nature of judicial review. Leif H. Carter argues, for example, that "Black's appeal hides from us the nondemocratic character of judicial review. Worse, it turns the purpose of republican government on its head. It pretends that the Court's task is to promote democracy when it in fact should protect the few from the many."[259] But such criticisms are hardly fair. First, they ignore the fact that important elements of Justice Black's constitutional philosophy, such as his First Amendment views and incorporation stance, supported broad restrictions on the power of majoritarian institutions. Second, they assume that recognition of judicial review's nondemocratic nature is reason to extol that character, using it to defend broad judicial power over a potentially limitless array of official actions, when actually it is clearly a reason for caution. Justice Black obviously realized that judicial review is fundamentally a nondemocratic doctrine; indeed, in a sense his entire jurisprudence is bottomed on that recognition. It was precisely for that reason that he preferred constructions of constitutional provisions, especially the potentially open-ended guarantees, that would limit the range of judicial discretion in the exercise of this nondemocratic power. Such interpretations of the open-ended clauses can never be acceptable to those who believe, as Sylvia Snowiss put it with such admirable and revealing candor, that courts should provide for "all the needs of limited government." But, as I hope I have demonstrated, his interpretations were based on as plausible readings of language and history as more expansive constructions. And they did blunt judicial review's nondemocratic impact. For majoritarian democrats such an approach reflects regard for both the constitutional and the democratic character of the nation's political system.

Three The Bill of Rights and the States

HUGO Black assumed the supreme bench convinced that the "natural law" construction the Old Court had given due process in economic cases was an affront to the guarantee's original meaning and to the genius of a written Constitution. Very early in his judicial career—probably no later than 1939—he also concluded that the Fourteenth Amendment's framers intended its first section to incorporate within its meaning the entire Bill of Rights, making those great liberties, by their specific terms, fully binding on the states. Black considered his dissent in *Adamson v. California*, the 1947 case in which he first extensively advanced his incorporation thesis, his most significant opinion.[1] Certainly, it was among his most controversial. Scholarly and judicial critics derided the historical evidence he presented in support of his position, scorned what they saw as obvious inconsistencies between his position and the Fourteenth Amendment's language, and, depending on the critic, condemned his stance as unduly restrictive—or permissive—of governmental power.

This chapter examines the development and analytical contours of Justice Black's incorporation thesis as well as the contentions of his critics. It concludes that while the Justice's position regarding the relationship of the Bill of Rights to the states, like his conception of due process, can never be acceptable to those who see courts as repositories of basic values, his stance is consistent with the Fourteenth Amendment's history and language as well as with basic principles of majoritarian democracy.

Black's Incorporation Thesis: Early History and Contours

To the layperson unschooled in the intricacies of legal cant, the Fourteenth Amendment's ban on state laws abridging "the privileges or immunities of citizens of the United States" naturally evokes immediate images of the Bill of Rights. In its first confrontation with the amendment's language in the *Slaughter-House Cases* of 1873,[2] however, the Supreme Court limited the guarantees of national citizenship to a narrow category of privileges far removed from the basic liberties of the first eight amendments—a remarkable conclusion, particularly in view of the fact that, before the amendment's adoption, the Court had held that Congress already had power to protect such privileges and immunities from private as well as governmental interference.[3] Having thus relegated the privileges or immunities clause to the status of a constitutional dead letter, the Court then proceeded—albeit with initial reluctance—to convert due process into an instrument for the protection of propertied interests and to reject claims that the Fourteenth Amendment incorporated any or all of the Bill of Rights.

For the balance of the nineteenth century and well into the twentieth, in fact, only the first Justice Harlan embraced the incorporation thesis with any degree of consistency.[4] To a majority of justices, the privileges or immunities clause was an essentially meaningless guarantee, and due process, as Justice Moody put it in *Twining* v. *New Jersey*,[5] embodied only "immutable principle[s] of justice which [were] the inalienable possession of every citizen of a free government"[6] and were "to be ascertained from time to time by judicial action."[7] By the 1920s the Court had found within these "unchangeable principle[s] of universal justice"[8] only one guarantee analogous to a provision of the Bill of Rights—the right to just compensation for property seized by the state—and that right was held to be within the Fourteenth Amendment's meaning without any reference whatever to its Fifth Amendment counterpart.[9]

With *Gitlow* v. *New York*[10] in 1925, the Court began to suggest in dicta that freedoms comparable to those in the First Amendment were part of the "liberty" protected against state action by the Fourteenth. In *Powell* v. *Alabama* (1932),[11] the first of the Court's pronouncements in the notorious *Scottsboro Cases*, the Justices came close to concluding, moreover, that the Sixth Amendment guarantee to legal counsel was a "fundamental" right generally binding on the states via due process. But *Gitlow* and *Powell* were hardly harbingers of fundamental change in the Court's position on the incorporation question. Neither *Gitlow* nor its immediate progeny even suggested, much less held, that the freedoms of the First Amendment were identical in meaning to analogous freedoms of the Fourteenth Amendment. Instead, the Court seemed to be concluding only that something approximating the specific liberties of the First Amendment was implicit in the Fourteenth Amendment's due process clause. The *Gitlow* majority thus appeared to share the assessment of Justice Holmes, who observed in dissent that the freedom of speech guaranteed by the Fourteenth Amendment could "perhaps . . . be accepted with a somewhat larger latitude of interpretation than is allowed to Congress by the sweeping language [of the First Amendment] that governs or ought to govern the laws of the United States."[12] Furthermore, the *Powell* Court stopped short of establishing a per se right of counsel in state cases, concluding instead only that, under the circumstances of their case, denial of effective counsel to the *Scottsboro* defendants denied them the fundamental fairness mandated by the due process guarantee.

What a close reading of *Gitlow* and *Powell* makes reasonably evident the Court made clear with its 1937 decision and opinion in *Palko* v. *Connecticut*.[13] To Frank Palko's claim that the Fourteenth Amendment incorporated the right against double jeopardy and other guarantees of the Bill of Rights, Justice Cardozo replied: "There is no such general rule."[14] The *Palko* majority agreed that the amendment "absorbed" within its meaning rights "of the very essence of a scheme of ordered liberty,"[15] including guarantees analogous to those of the Bill of Rights. But the Court clearly rejected the incorporation thesis. Cardozo quoted with approval, for example, the following passage from Justice Moody's opinion in the *Twining* case: "It is possible that some of the personal rights safeguarded by the first eight Amendments against National action may also be safeguarded against state action, because a denial of them would be a denial of due process of law. . . . If this is so, it is not because those rights are enumerated in the first eight Amendments but because they are included in the conception of due process of law."[16] In determining whether the double jeopardy to which Frank Palko had been subjected was forbidden by the Fourteenth Amendment, moreover, Cardozo focused not on the general nature of the right against double jeopardy, but on the circumstances of Palko's treatment, asking: "Is that kind of double jeopardy to which the statute has subjected him a hardship so acute and shocking that our polity will not endure it? Does it violate those fundamental principles of liberty and justice which lie at the base of all our civil and political institutions. . . . The answer surely must be 'no.' "[17]

By the time *Palko* was decided, then, it was clear that the Court had begun to view due process as embodying freedoms analogous to those of the First Amendment—and perhaps the Sixth Amendment right to counsel as well, since Justice Cardozo's *Palko* opinion included that guarantee among the "fundamental principles of liberty and justice." Arguably, given its willingness to mention the specific language of the Bill of Rights in discussing the Fourteenth Amendment's content, the Court was also beginning to subject state action interfering with such rights to a more exacting scrutiny than that to which due process claims had generally been subjected, at least outside the economic sphere. The Justices obviously remained unwilling, however, to accept the incorporation thesis, or even to agree that all Bill of Rights safeguards "absorbed" within the Fourteenth Amendment's meaning were to be given the same force and effect as their counterparts in the first eight amendments.

When *Palko* was decided shortly after Justice Black's appointment, the Court's junior Justice joined the majority. Despite its citation and apparent approval of *Twining*, *Palko*, like *Gitlow* and its progeny, did seem to recognize a closer relation between the Bill of Rights and the Fourteenth Amendment—as well as a more concrete meaning for the amendment—than *Twining* and related earlier cases had appeared willing to accept. Since the *Palko* opinion was filled with the sort of "natural law" rhetoric Senator Black was already on record as abhoring, however, his position in the case is mildly perplexing. Black's law clerk at the time has written that the Justice joined the Cardozo opinion "with some difficulty" and out of admiration for its author.[18] John Frank attributed Black's stance to "plain inexperience or . . . insufficient opportunity in earlier life to study the subject matter" of the case.[19] Shortly before his death Justice Black concurred with Frank's assessment, explaining that it "takes time to get a legal opinion formulated" and that he had not "completely developed" his views regarding the Fourteenth Amendment when *Palko* was decided.[20] Throughout his career, moreover, he would emphasize contrasts in the *Palko* and *Twining* rationales as well as his preference for the former over the latter as an alternative to the total incorporation which he obviously preferred.[21]

Whatever the explanation for his decision to join *Palko*, however, Justice Black was soon to embrace the incorporation thesis *Palko* had rejected. In 1938 he refused to join the portion of Justice Stone's *Car-*

olene Products opinion which included Stone's Footnote Four suggestion that there might be a "narrower scope for operation of the presumption of constitutionality" for laws claimed to impinge on noneconomic liberties, including rights "within a specific prohibition of the Constitution, such as those of the first ten amendments, which are deemed equally specific when held to be embraced within the Fourteenth."[22] As indicated in the previous chapter, however, Justice Black objected to language in Stone's opinion suggesting that courts had power to overturn economic legislation lacking a "rational basis," and not, apparently, to Stone's reference to Bill of Rights safeguards embraced within the Fourteenth Amendment. In 1939, moreover, Black joined an opinion which Justice Roberts filed for *Hague* v. *CIO*,[23] wherein Roberts asserted that the First Amendment freedoms were among the privileges of national citizenship. His concurrence in the Roberts opinion suggests that Black was already beginning to consider the privileges or immunities clause, rather than due process, the vehicle for application of specific Bill of Rights safeguards in state cases.

A letter Justice Frankfurter wrote Black on October 31, 1939, offers the most convincing evidence, however, that very early in his Supreme Court career, Black's position on the incorporation issue was taking its final shape and that the well-known Frankfurter-Black debate on the question was already under way. "Perhaps you will let me say," Frankfurter wrote,

> quite simply and without any ulterior thought what I mean to say, and all I mean to say, regarding your position on the "Fourteenth Amendment" as an entirety.
>
> (1) I *can* understand that the Bill of Rights—to wit Amendments 1–9 inclusive—applies to state action and not merely U.S. action, and that *Barron* v. *Baltimore* was wrong. I think it was rightly decided.
>
> (2) What I am unable to appreciate is what are the criteria of selection as to the Amendments—which applies and which does not apply.[24]

Frankfurter's letter suggests that, even by this point, Black considered the Fourteenth Amendment's first section "as an entirety," rather than its due process clause alone, the vehicle of incorporation. The remaining portions of the letter leave unclear whether Black was by then contending for total incorporation or for merely an application of certain Bill of Rights safeguards in state cases, the first numbered paragraph suggesting the former proposition, the second paragraph the latter. Even after Black's preference for total incorporation had been made a matter of public record, however, Frankfurter would continue to press his colleague to indicate which provisions were incorporated and which were not.[25] It is thus probable that by 1939 Black was pressing for incorporation of "Amendments 1–9 inclusive," but Frankfurter had not yet grasped the full implications of his colleague's position.

In the years between the Frankfurter letter and the appearance of Justice Black's *Adamson* dissent, the Justice's support for incorporation became increasingly evident. Justice Murphy's biographer J. Woodford Howard[26] has suggested that the Frankfurter letter was occasioned by the Court's decision to review the coerced confession claims raised in *Chambers* v. *Florida*.[27] More than any of his other early pronouncements, Black's opinion for the *Chambers* Court, overturning the murder convictions and death sentences of four young blacks, based on confessions secured after more than five days of interrogation in an atmosphere of terror, established his credentials as a firm defender of civil liberties and helped to remove the doubts regarding his commitment to the Constitution his Klan membership had aroused.[28] Ironically, *Chambers* is an important symbol in the modern struggle for civil liberties not only because it involved the plight of humble black defendants. Its symbolic significance also rests on the simple, yet elegant, forceful language of Justice Black's opinion in the case—language which appears inconsistent with the relatively fixed construction of the Fourteenth Amendment he had begun to embrace as well as his distaste for flexible constitutional standards.

As Justice Black patiently but firmly sought to convince me shortly before his death,[29] however, a close reading of his *Chambers* opinion indicates that any inconsistency may be more apparent than real. The opinion does include language similar to that used in *Twining* and other earlier cases construing due process to require "fundamentally fair" state proceedings. At one point, for example, Justice Black asserted that due process prohibited criminal punishment "until there had been a charge fairly made and fairly tried in a public tribunal free of prejudice, passion, excitement, and tyrannical power."[30] And the opinion concluded, of course, with Black's oft-quoted reference to the Court's "solemn responsibility . . . of translating" constitutional commands "into living law."[31] But the Justice quoted neither *Twining* nor other flexible expressions of due process, and though, as the Court's spokesman, he was inhibited from giving free rein to his own position, his opinion contains much language consistent with both his "law of the land" conception of due process and his developing incorporation thesis. In defining due process he cited the constitutional prohibition against ex post facto laws and "the principle that criminal punishments could not be inflicted save for that which proper legislative action had already by 'the law of the land' forbidden when done."[32] Adding that "even more was needed," he also cited the "fundamental idea" of "a charge fairly made and fairly tried."[33] He made clear, however, that the Constitution's provisions, not abstract ethical concepts, were the source of procedural requirements necessary to assure a "fair" trial. "[A]s assurance against ancient evils," he wrote, "our country, in order to preserve 'the blessings of liberty,' wrote into its basic law the requirement, among others, that the forfeiture of the lives, liberties or properties of people accused of crime can only follow if procedural safeguards of due process have been obeyed."[34] In a footnote listing those safeguards he cited only specific constitutional provisions, including "The Bill of Rights (Amend. I to VIII)."[35] Elsewhere in the opinion, moreover, he wrote of the "current of opinion—which this court has declined to adopt in many previous cases—that the Fourteenth Amendment was intended to make secure against state invasion all the rights, privileges and immunities protected from federal violation by the Bill of Rights (Amendments I to VIII)."[36] Black's *Chambers* opinion thus stands in marked contrast to the rhetoric of *Twining* and the Frankfurter–Harlan II constructions of the Fourteenth Amendment's meaning. Finally, of course, the constitutional violations at issue in the case clearly fell within the scope of the Fifth Amendment's self-incrimination provisions—provisions Black by that point obviously considered within the Fourteenth Amendment's scope.

Although again as the Court's spokesman and no doubt inhibited by that status, Justice Black's opinion for the Court in *Bridges* v. *California* and *Times-Mirror Co.* v. *Superior Court of California*,[37] the important 1941 cases reversing state contempt-by-publication convictions, also included incorporationist language. Citing in a footnote earlier cases indicating that the First Amendment was secure against state abridgment by the Fourteenth,[38] Black clearly bottomed the Court's decision on First Amendment principles. As he was later to write, the tenor of the opinion was clearly to the effect that "the Fourteenth

Amendment literally and emphatically applied the First Amendment to the States in its very terms."[39] He noted at one point, for example, that the Court had not until the *Gitlow* case "recognize[d] in the Fourteenth Amendment the application to the states of the same standards of freedom of expression as, under the Fourteenth Amendment, are applicable to the federal government."[40]

Certainly, the incorporationist tone of Black's opinion was not lost on Justice Frankfurter—who initially had drafted a majority opinion upholding the convictions in the *Bridges* and *Times-Mirror* cases.[41] In a dissent directed as much, perhaps, at his colleague's growing insistence on literalism as the specifics of the incorporation thesis, Frankfurter questioned, as he would again on many subsequent occasions, whether incorporation, and its partial application in the cases at hand, could be squared with the amendment's language:

> We are not even vouchsafed reference to the specific provision of the Constitution which renders states powerless to insist upon trial by courts rather than trial by newspapers. . . . To say that the protection of freedom of speech of the First Amendment is absorbed by the Fourteenth does not say enough. Which one of the various limitations upon state power introduced by the Fourteenth Amendment absorbs the First? Some provisions of the Fourteenth Amendment apply only to citizens and one of the petitioners here is an alien; some of its provisions apply only to natural persons, and another petitioner here is a corporation. . . . Only the Due Process Clause assures constitutional protection of Civil liberties to aliens and corporations. Corporations cannot claim for themselves the "liberty" which the Due Process Clause guarantees. That clause protects only their property. . . . The majority opinion is strangely silent in failing to avow the specific constitutional provision upon which its decision rests.[42]

But *Betts* v. *Brady*,[43] decided the following year, was to provide the forum for the most extensive pre-*Adamson* debate between Frankfurter and Black over the incorporation issue. While Justice Sutherland's opinion for the Court in *Powell* v. *Alabama* had come close to holding that the right to counsel was a per se requirement of due process in state cases, *Powell* rested ultimately, it will be recalled, essentially on "fundamental fairness" grounds. Indeed, the Court did not even recognize a per se right of assigned counsel for indigent *federal* defendants until 1938 and Justice Black's opinion for the Court in *Johnson* v. *Zerbst*.[44] In *Betts* a majority, per Justice Roberts, again rejected the contention that the Fourteenth Amendment incorporated the Sixth Amendment right to counsel "as such,"[45] holding instead that counsel was required in state cases only where necessary to assure the accused "fundamental fairness." Due process, concluded Roberts,

> formulates a concept less rigid and more fluid than those envisaged in other specific and particular provisions of the Bill of Rights. Its application is less a matter of rule. Asserted denial is to be treated by an appraisal of the totality of facts in a given case. That which may, in one setting, constitute a denial of fundamental fairness, shocking to the universal sense of justice, may, in other circumstances, fall short of such denial. In the application of such a concept, there is always the danger of falling into the habit of formulating the guarantee into a set of hard and fast rules, the application of which in a given case may be to ignore the qualifying factors therein disclosed.[46]

Applying this standard "more fluid" and "less a matter of rule" than the specifics of the Bill of Rights to the petitioner's case, Roberts concluded that Betts—a repeat offender, after all, "not wholly unfamiliar with criminal procedure," who "was not helpless, but was a man forty-three years old, of ordinary intelligence"[47]—had suffered no denial of due process.

Justice Black vigorously disagreed with both the Court's formula and its application in the context at issue. In conference, according to Justice Murphy's notes,[48] he had contended that Betts was "entitled to a lawyer from [the] history of [the] 14th amendment," adding, "It was intended to make applicable to the States the Bill of Rights." The "prevailing doctrine" of due process, he charged, made "lawmakers" of judges. But even under that doctrine, state defendants were entitled to counsel. "How many times in your practice," he asked his colleagues, in effect answering his own question, "do you think that any man could [adequately] plan his defense, summon witnesses and otherwise conduct [a] trial in [the] face of organized opposition"? "[I]f I am to pass on what is fair and right," he asserted, with obvious vehemence, "I will say it makes me vomit to think men go to prison for a long time" without benefit of counsel.

By this point Justice Frankfurter's conference reaction to incorpora-

tion claims was as predictable as Justice Black's. The "14th Am.,"
Murphy recorded Frankfurter asserting, "did not incorporate the first 10.
If it did you would uproot all the structure of the states." Albeit confusing his fellow jurists, Chief Justice Stone essentially agreed, asserting
that "Brandeis" had met the issue wisely in the *Palko* case. "The practice of providing counsel is desirable," asserted Stone, "but [a] State
should not be compelled" to do so. Expressing, as he would in other
conferences, no feeling for the "sanctity of [the] 14th Amendment,"
which was enacted, in his judgment, during the "most scandalous and
lousy period in our history," Justice Jackson observed that, "for the time
being," he too would not uproot the Maryland policy for the assignment
of counsel at issue in *Betts*.

Ultimately, Justice Black, joined by Douglas and Murphy, dissented
from the *Betts* majority's decision and rationale. Black's dissent was
brief but foreshadowed the themes he was extensively to develop in
Adamson. First, he stated that the "Fourteenth Amendment"—not its
due process clause alone—"made the Sixth applicable to the states."[49]
Second, citing the research of Horace Flack, he concluded that "[d]is-
cussion of the Fourteenth Amendment by its sponsors in the Senate and
House shows their purpose to make secure against invasion by the states
the fundamental liberties and safeguards set out in the Bill of Rights,"
but added that since that position had "never been accepted by a majority of this Court . . . [a] statement of the grounds supporting it
[was] . . . unnecessary at this time."[50] Third, he termed the majority's
"universal sense of justice" conception of due process "a view which
gives this Court such vast supervisory power that I am not prepared to
accept it without grave doubts."[51] Finally, he reiterated his conference
position that, even under the Court's approach, indigent state defendants were entitled to appointed counsel, asserting:

> A practice cannot be reconciled with "common and fundamental
> ideas of fairness and right," which subjects innocent men to in-
> creased dangers of conviction merely because of their poverty.
> Whether a man is innocent cannot be determined from a trial in
> which, as here, denial of counsel has made it impossible to con-
> clude, with any satisfactory degree of certainty, that the defen-
> dant's case was adequately presented.
>   . . . [M]ost of the other States have shown their agreement by
> constitutional provisions, statutes, or established practice judi-

cially approved, which assure that no man shall be deprived of counsel merely because of his poverty. Any other practice seems to me to defeat the promise of our democratic society to provide equal justice under the law.[52]

After *Betts* the Black-Frankfurter debate continued, but for a time largely off the pages of judicial opinions. In his letter to Black of November 13, 1943, for example, Frankfurter again expressed skepticism about the incorporation thesis (as well as continued confusion regarding Black's position) and argued that judicial respect for political authority, not "specific" constitutional provisions, was the only adequate safeguard against the Court's abuse of its power. "As I understand it," Frankfurter wrote,

> you find restrictions against the exercise of unbridled power by fluctuating majorities on this Court, so far as the Fourteenth Amendment is concerned, in what you deem to be the specific provisions of the Bill of Rights. I should be very happy to be able to tie down [judges] by specific provisions that would bind them . . . assuming that what I call dialectics, namely the resourcefulness of interpretation, does not give room for the widest variants in the interpretation even of specific provisions. But I am truly eager for understanding on this matter, and therefore should be grateful to you if you will refer me to the materials which justify one in saying that the general language of the Fourteenth Amendment was in fact a compendious statement of some or all of the earlier first nine amendments. Are all nine so incorporated? Did the Fourteenth Amendment establish uniform systems of judicial procedure in all the states and freeze them for the future, both in criminal and in civil cases, to the extent that the Constitution does for federal courts? Is it conceivable that an amendment bringing about such a result would either have been submitted to the states, or, if submitted, would have been ratified by them? And if not all the nine Amendments, which of the prior nine Amendments are to be deemed incorporated and which left out?
>
> . . . Believe me that in writing this nothing is farther from my purpose than contention. I am merely trying to get light on a subject which has absorbed as much thought and energy of my mature life as anything that has concerned me. I ask you quite humbly to lead me to the materials that show that the Fourteenth Amendment

incorporated by reference the provisions—any or all—of the earlier nine Amendments. Needless to say there is no hurry about this. Whenever you feel inclined to help educate me, I shall be grateful.

For his part, Justice Black continued to argue in criminal procedure cases that specific Bill of Rights safeguards were within the Fourteenth Amendment's scope,[53] but for a time after *Betts* he advanced no elaborate defense of his position. In 1945, however, Black indicated that he would one day mount a challenge to his jurisprudential opponents' flexible conception of due process and rejection of incorporation. The occasion for his announcement was the Court's decision in *Malinski* v. *New York*,[54] a state coerced-confession case. Justice Frankfurter filed a separate *Malinski* opinion reiterating the arguments he had raised in the *Betts* conference. His predecessors on the Court, Frankfurter contended, had been wise in refusing to give the Fourteenth Amendment's due process clause a "rigid scope" or accept the claim that it was intended to be "a compendious expression of the original federal Bill of Rights (Amendments I to VIII)."[55] Due process, he asserted, possessed a "potency different from and independent of the specific provisions contained in the Bill of Rights."[56] It was "not a stagnant formulation of what has been achieved in the past but a standard for judgment in the progressive evolution of the institutions of a free society," incorporating within its scope the steadily evolving "notions of justice of English-speaking people" and "a demand for civilized standards of law."[57]

Justice Black had never suggested that the due process clause alone was the intended vehicle of incorporation, and by this point Justice Frankfurter surely must have been aware of this aspect of his colleague's thinking. Even so, Black's position was clearly the principal target of Frankfurter's opinion. In a memorandum to the Court, Black informed his colleagues that he would eventually answer the "natural law" theory implicit in Frankfurter's conception of due process. During the 1946 term he kept his promise.[58]

The *Adamson* Dissent

At least two petitions in the Court's 1946–47 caseload provided potential forums for an elaborate Black defense of incorporation and attack on the Frankfurter approach to due process. Initially, Black considered developing and defending his position in *Louisiana ex rel.*

Francis v. *Rewesber*,[59] the bizarre case in which counsel for convicted murderer Willie Francis sought to prevent further efforts to execute their client after Louisiana's portable electric chair malfunctioned during initial attempts. In an opinion announcing the Court's judgment, Justice Reed, joined by Chief Justice Vinson, Black, and Jackson, assumed, "without so deciding," that "principles" of the Fifth and Eighth Amendment guarantees against double jeopardy and cruel and unusual punishment were within the meaning of the Fourteenth Amendment due process clause, but rejected claims that Willie Francis's execution would violate those guarantees.[60] Justice Frankfurter filed a concurrence in the case, Justice Burton a dissent joined by Justices Douglas, Murphy, and Rutledge. Originally, Rutledge and Murphy also had written dissents, while Jackson and Black drafted concurrences.[61]

In his typewritten draft Justice Black had rejected the constitutional claims raised by Francis's counsel, asserting that "[t]he failure of the electrocution apparatus was purely accidental and not because of any desire of the State or any of its agents to prolong or aggravate the painful agonies which nearly always are associated with anticipation of imminent death." He also referred, however, to the "ample" historical support for incorporation; quoted remarks of Ohio Congressman John Bingham, the Fourteenth Amendment's principal sponsor in the House of Representatives, supportive of the incorporation thesis; construed earlier Fourteenth Amendment cases to have applied the First Amendment "literally and emphatically . . . to the States in its very terms"; and expressed wonder why "the process, heretofore followed, of selecting the provisions of the Bill of Rights to be applied to the States, should discriminate against the constitutional protections against cruel and unusual punishment and double jeopardy." In language later to appear in his *Adamson* dissent, moreover, he once again condemned the "standards of decency" and "fundamental principles" doctrine of due process as a "natural law concept" holding "that there is a higher law than the Constitution, a law which . . . courts alone can make, interpret and cause to be enforced." Rejecting that approach, he concluded:

> I share most of the sentiments of those members of the Court who have so feelingly argued that a defendant who has once been compelled to suffer the imminence of death by electrocution should not be put through [that experience] again. But I cannot agree with them that any provision of the Federal Constitution authorizes us

to rule that an accidental failure fairly to carry out a valid sentence of death on the first attempt bars execution of that sentence.

In an original draft opinion for the Court, Justice Reed had employed a "fair standards" approach to due process, as he termed it, citing *Twining* and related cases and concluding that Francis's execution would not "offend this nation's conception of justice." Confronted with Black's draft concurrence, Reed modified certain language in his opinion, including in its text the "assumption" that violation of the bans on double jeopardy and cruel and unusual punishment would also violate the Fourteenth Amendment. Black then joined Reed's opinion and withdrew his proposed concurrence. In a memorandum for the conference Frankfurter observed: "In order that there be an opinion of the Court, I had hoped to join brother Reed's opinion in addition to expressing my views. The reason I cannot do so, inter alia, is that I do not think we should decide the case even on the assumption that the Fifth Amendment as to double jeopardy is the measure of due process in the Fourteenth Amendment. . . . "[62]

For several tactical reasons Justice Black might have been wiser to employ *Francis* rather than *Adamson* as the forum for an elaborate defense of incorporation. In *Francis* he could have detailed his position in the context of a case upholding an exercise of state power. He thus could have emphasized the limits rather than the breadth of his stance's impact on state authority. A historical defense of incorporation could also have been more easily erected in *Francis* than in *Adamson*, for the Eighth Amendment guarantee against cruel and unusual punishments on which Willie Francis's claims were partly based was the only specific provision of the Bill of Rights which Representative Bingham mentioned during debate in the House of Representatives on the Fourteenth Amendment's adoption. Black perhaps opted for *Adamson* instead, however, because it involved procedures similar to those approved by the Court in the *Twining* case, which had rejected incorporation and embraced the flexible interpretation of due process Black so thoroughly detested. Another, even more basic consideration was undoubtedly also instrumental in his decision: Douglas, Murphy, and Rutledge, the only Justices he could hope to have join him on the incorporation issue, dissented in *Francis*, convinced that the defendant was being deprived of due process.

Adamson v. *California* upheld state procedures permitting judges and prosecutors to comment adversely on the failure of an accused to testify in his own behalf, thereby subjecting himself to cross-examination. Speaking for a five-man majority, Justice Reed assumed that the comment rule at issue would violate the Fifth Amendment safeguard against compulsory self-incrimination if allowed in federal cases, but rejected *Adamson's* contention that the Fifth Amendment, "to its full scope," fell within the ambit of the Fourteenth Amendment's privileges or immunities or due process clauses, as well as the claim that the appellant had been denied a "fair trial."[63] In a concurring opinion Justice Frankfurter, who had termed *Twining* "cloudless" in conference,[64] condemned both total and selective incorporation of the specific terms of the Bill of Rights into the Fourteenth Amendment, applauded *Twining's* anti-incorporation, "fundamental fairness" approach to due process, and warned that the triumph of the incorporation doctrine "would deprive the States of opportunity for reforms in legal process designed for extending the area of freedom."[65] Justices Black, Douglas, Murphy, and Rutledge dissented.

In conference, according to Justice Rutledge's notes, Justice Black had reaffirmed his view that the Fifth Amendment guarantee against self-incrimination applied to the states. He expressed uncertainty, however, whether California's comment rule offended the Fifth Amendment, and when the Justices were polled in conference, he passed.[66] Since Justice Reed's majority opinion merely assumed that adverse comment on an accused's failure to take the witness stand in his own defense would violate the Fifth Amendment, Black was relieved of any obligation to reach that issue in his *Adamson* dissent. Instead, he focused his attention on the incorporation question and on the flexible conception of due process which Frankfurter's concurrence and, to a less obvious degree, the majority opinion had embraced.

The dissent developed five basic themes. First, Black set forth more extensively than ever before his thesis that the Fourteenth Amendment's first section was intended to incorporate the Bill of Rights, observing: "My study of the historical events that culminated in the Fourteenth Amendment, and the expressions of those who sponsored and favored, as well as those who opposed its submission and passage, persuades me that one of the chief objects that the provisions of the Amendment's first section, separately, and as a whole, were intended to accommodate was to make the Bill of Rights, applicable to the states."[67] "With full knowledge," he added, "of the import" of *Barron* v. *Bal-*

timore, the 1833 decision rejecting the claim that the Bill of Rights applied directly to the states, "the framers and backers of the Fourteenth Amendment proclaimed its purpose to be to overturn the constitutional rule that case had announced."[68]

Second, Black charged that the Court had never given "full consideration" to evidence underlying the Fourteenth Amendment's "historical purpose."[69] Of cases relied on by the *Twining* Court to reject incorporation, he asserted, the briefs and opinions in only one had made "reference to the legislative and contemporary history . . . demonstrating that those who conceived, shaped, and brought about the adoption of the Fourteenth Amendment intended it to nullify" *Barron*.[70] In *Maxwell* v. *Dow*,[71] a 1900 case rejecting application of the Sixth Amendment right of jury trial in state cases, counsel for the appellant had cited a speech of Senator Jacob Howard of Michigan, one of the Fourteenth Amendment's sponsors, stating that the amendment was intended to apply the first eight amendments to the states. The *Maxwell* Court's opinion had acknowledged that reference, but then had concluded, "What individual Senators or Representatives may have urged in debate, in regard to the meaning to be given to a proposed constitutional amendment, or bill or resolution, does not furnish a firm ground for its proper construction, nor is it important as explanatory of the grounds upon which the members voted in adopting it."[72] Apart from *Maxwell*, no case cited in *Twining* had reviewed the historical evidence. Moreover, while the *Twining* Court had cited William D. Guthrie's 1898 study of the Fourteenth Amendment,[73] Guthrie devoted only a "few pages" to the amendment's legislative background and had not emphasized the speeches of Representative John Bingham who, wrote Black, "may, without extravagance be called the Madison of the first section of the Fourteenth Amendment."[74] On the basis of no more evidence than that, the *Twining* Court had concluded that the incorporation question was "no longer open" to consideration, though conceding that earlier cases "had resulted in giving 'much less effect to the Fourteenth Amendment than some of the public men active in framing it' had intended it to have," and observing that "Much might be said in favor of the view that the privilege [against self-incrimination] was guaranteed against state impairment as a privilege and immunity of National citizenship, but, as has been shown, the decisions of this court have foreclosed that view."[75] "Thus," wrote Black, the Court declined [in *Twining*], and again today declines, to appraise the relevant historical evidence of the intended scope of the first section of the Amendment. Instead it relied upon previous cases, none of which had analyzed the evidence showing that one purpose of those who framed, advocated, and adopted the Amendment had been to make the Bill of Rights applicable to the States. None of the cases relied upon by the Court today made such an analysis [either].[76]

Third, he condemned as a "natural law" formula and "incongruous excrescence on our Constitution"[77] the flexible conception of due process Frankfurter and, ultimately, the Court were embracing. In the *Slaughter-House Cases*, the first cases in which the Court construed the Fourteenth Amendment's meaning, the challengers presented no evidence of its framers' intent to incorporate the Bill of Rights. "Nor," Black asserted, "was there reason to do so. For the state law under consideration . . . was only challenged as one which authorized a monopoly, and the brief for the challenger properly conceded that there was 'no direct constitutional provision against a monopoly.' "[78] But the challengers had raised "natural law arguments . . . suggestive of the premises on which the present due process formula rests," observed Black, and the *Slaughter-House* majority "flatly rejected" those contentions, just as the Court rejected all such arguments for the first two decades after the Fourteenth Amendment's adoption.[79] The "natural law" philosophy which the Court later accepted, wrote Black, was a "second-thought interpretation" which amounted to an "about-face" from the *Slaughter-House* Court's approach.[80] It was also, he added, tracking many of his earlier opinions, an invitation for judges to ignore "clearly marked constitutional boundaries" and "roam at will in the limitless area of their own beliefs,"[81] "frustrat[ing] the great design of a written Constitution."[82]

Fourth, he challenged the majority's—and especially Justice Frankfurter's—reading of *Palko* and other earlier cases construing the relationship of the Bill of Rights to the Fourteenth Amendment. *Twining*, he agreed, had "broadly precluded reliance on the Bill of Rights to determine what is and what is not 'a fundamental' right" protected by the Fourteenth Amendment.[83] Later cases, however, had "through the Fourteenth Amendment literally and emphatically applied the First Amendment to the States in its very terms."[84] Arguably, other cases had similarly undermined the *Twining* doctrine. In answering the claim that all provisions of the Bill of Rights were incorporated into the Fourteenth Amendment, for example, the *Palko* Court had replied only that there was "no such general rule."

> Implicit in this statement, and in the cases decided in the interim between *Twining* and *Palko* and since, is the understanding that some of the eight amendments do apply by their very terms. Thus the Court said in the *Palko* case that the Fourteenth Amendment may make it unlawful for a state to abridge by its statutes the "freedom of speech which the First Amendment safeguards against encroachment by the Congress . . . or the like freedom of the press . . . or the free exercise of religion . . . , or the right of peaceable assembly . . . or the right of one accused of crime to the benefit of counsel. . . . In these and other situations immunities that are valid as against the federal government by force of the specific pledges of particular amendments have been found to be implicit in the concept of ordered liberty, and thus, through the Fourteenth Amendment, become valid as against the states." . . . In the *Twining* case fundamental liberties were things apart from the Bill of Rights. Now it appears that at least some of the provisions of the Bill of Rights in their very terms satisfy the Court as sound and meaningful expressions of fundamental liberty.[85]

Nor could Black understand why an "absorbed" right under the *Palko* doctrine should be applied to the states "in part but not in full." Although *Twining* made "clear" the Court's intent "to leave states free to compel confessions, so far as the Federal Constitution is concerned"[86] *Chambers* and other later cases had largely undermined *Twining*'s core premise, making "the principles of the Fifth Amendment . . . applicable to the States through the Fourteenth Amendment by one formula or another."[87] Yet the *Adamson* Court was asserting a prerogative to "apply part of an amendment's established meaning and discard that part which does not suit the current style of fundamentals."[88]

Finally, Justice Black challenged the contention that acceptance of total incorporation would "unwisely" enlarge national judicial power over state laws and proceedings. The *Twining* Court had termed the Bill of Rights an eighteenth-century "strait jacket," and Justice Frankfurter's concurrence had warned against "imprison[ing]" states "in what are merely legal forms even though they have the sanction of the Eighteenth Century."[89] Black vigorously disagreed, asserting:

> I cannot consider the Bill of Rights to be an outworn 18th Century "strait jacket" as the *Twining* opinion did. Its provisions may be thought outdated abstractions by some. And it is true that they were designed to meet ancient evils. But they are the same kind of human evils that have emerged from century to century wherever excessive power is sought by the few at the expense of the many. In my judgment the people of no nation can lose their liberty so long as a Bill of Rights like ours survives and its basic purposes are conscientiously interpreted, enforced and respected so as to afford continuous protection against old, as well as new, devices and practices which might thwart those purposes. I fear to see the consequences of the Court's practice of substituting its own concepts of decency and fundamental justice for the language of the Bill of Rights. . . .[90]

"The Federal Government," he added, had "not been harmfully burdened by the requirement" that it obey the Bill of Rights. "Who would advocate its repeal?"[91] True, as *Betts* v. *Brady* and other cases demonstrated, the "natural-law-due-process formula" could be used "to limit substantially" the Court's power to forbid state interference with the Bill of Rights. But, he warned, "this formula also has been used in the past, and can be used in the future, to license this Court, in considering regulatory legislation, to roam at large in the broad expanses of policy and morals and to trespass, all too freely, on the legislative domain of the States as well as the Federal Government."[92]

By the time *Adamson* reached the Court, Black had studied extensively the debates in the Thirty-ninth Congress over adoption of the Fourteenth Amendment. He had also compiled a massive collection of legal, judicial, and scholarly pronouncements regarding the nature of due process and other principles included within the amendment's language.[93] In a lengthy appendix to his *Adamson* dissent, he presented historical evidence purporting to support incorporation. His most significant evidence may be summarized as follows.

1. During House floor debate Representative Bingham, who was a key member of the Joint Committee on Reconstruction which produced

the Fourteenth Amendment as well as the congressman most responsible for its first section, said that an early version would empower Congress to protect the "immortal bill of rights" from state infringement.

2. When opponents of an early version charged that the amendment was unnecessary since the Bill of Rights already applied to the states, Bingham replied that the amendment was necessary to assure congressional enforcement authority.

3. After an early version of the amendment was rejected, Bingham opposed House enactment of a civil rights bill insofar as it protected Bill of Rights guarantees from state invasion; an amendment to the Constitution, he indicated, would be necessary to authorize such legislation.

4. When Representative Thaddeus Stevens of Pennsylvania, another member of the Joint Committee, introduced a House version of the amendment's first section, identical to the final draft except that it lacked a clause defining United States and state citizenship, Stevens explained that the Constitution limited only the national government and that the privileges or immunities clause of the proposed amendment—originally submitted to the Joint Committee by Representative Bingham—would remedy that defect. Presumably, his reference to the Constitution was to the guarantees of the Bill of Rights, which of course were not then applicable to the states.

5. When Jacob Howard, yet another key member of the Joint Committee, introduced the same proposal in the Senate, he said that its privileges or immunities clause included within its meaning the guarantees of the first eight amendments.

6. At the close of House debate on the measure, Bingham remarked that its first section would protect against state infliction of cruel and unusual punishments.

7. During the 1871 House debate on a bill to enforce the amendment, Bingham summarized his role in the amendment's adoption, asserted that the privileges and immunities of national citizenship were to be found primarily in the first eight amendments, then listed the specific guarantees of the Bill of Rights.

Black's opinion and appendix clearly demonstrate his preference for total incorporation. At one point in the opinion, for example, he agreed that "[i]f the choice must be between the selective process of the *Palko* decision applying some of the Bill of Rights to the States, or the *Twining* rule applying none of them, I would choose the *Palko* selective process," but then added: "rather than accept either of these choices, I would follow what I believe was the original purpose of the Fourteenth Amendment—to extend to all the people of the nation the complete protection of the Bill of Rights."[94] Elsewhere in his dissent, however, he observed: "Whether this Court ever will, or whether it now should, in the light of past decisions, give full effect to what the Amendment was intended to accomplish is not necessarily essential to a decision here."[95] Some[96] have construed this passage to reflect weakness in Black's commitment to total incorporation. When *Adamson* was decided, moreover, Justice Frankfurter gave Justice Rutledge's clerk the impression that, in Frankfurter's view, Black favored partial, rather than complete, incorporation. For in a memorandum to Rutledge written while *Adamson* was pending, the clerk indicated that Black, "contrary to Frankfurter's understanding, . . . does intend that all the First Eight Amendments apply to the states."[97]

Justice Douglas's reaction to a draft of Black's dissent makes clear, however, that the opinion's favorable references to selective incorporation were merely part of an ultimately futile campaign to secure the concurrence of Justices Murphy and Rutledge. Urging Rutledge to accept the *Palko* approach, Rutledge's clerk contended that "States, to some extent, though of course not as much as in the field of property rights, should be allowed to experiment in order that wiser and fairer systems of criminal justice may be devised," termed total incorporation "intolerable, at the present time," and concluded: "the privilege against self-incrimination should not be literally applied as against the states. I suggest to you that in the end non-rigidity in these matters may be the best protection for civil liberties. Like bones, when the Constitution becomes inflexible, it may break."[98] Initially, Justice Black may have believed that Rutledge and Murphy, too, opposed total incorporation. In a note to Black, Justice Douglas wrote that he "would prefer" that his colleague delete from his *Adamson* dissent reference to the "selective process" as an acceptable alternative to total incorporation, but added: "I appreciate that you may need it, however, to get the others in."[99]

As another likely element in his effort "to get the others in," Black also avoided mention in *Adamson* of his fixed, "law of the land" conception of due process, emphasizing instead perceived defects in the "fundamental fairness" approach. During an extensive campaign to persuade Rutledge and Murphy not to join Black's dissent, however, Rutledge's clerk had sought to make clear to the two Justices what was probably already apparent to them—that Black's construction of due process was much more limited in scope than their own. While *Adamson* was being considered, Justice Black had lunch with the law clerks, and they "subjected him to a cross-examination on his constitutional views. . . . [T]he results," Rutledge's clerk later wrote his Justice, "were a little surprising."

> [Black] stated, of course, that the bill of rights applies to the states, but he went further than that. He said that independent of the other provisions in the bill of rights the due process clause in the 5th Amendment, and I assume also in the 14th Amendment, had *no* meaning, except that of emphasis. In short, Black would never hold that a trial or other proceeding was bad solely for want of due process. He would have to find some violation of some other specific clause in the Constitution.[100]

Citing certain types of procedural unfairness which, in his judgment, Black's interpretation of due process would not forbid, the clerk added: "If this is the result of his views I want no part of them. And what is more important, I don't think that you do either." The Constitution, he wrote, "should be just what Black says it should not be, a sort of thermometer—always rising—for the civilized standards of the times." And if that view "be damned as 'natural law,' " the clerk did "not care." "It had proved a workable philosophy. . . . We are advancing gradually. Black's views, far from being an advance, I consider a retrogression in many respects, for he has destroyed due process which you described in Yamashita as 'that great absolute'."[101]

As noted earlier, Rutledge's clerk favored the *Palko* approach to the Fourteenth Amendment's meaning. At one point he recommended that Rutledge join Justice Frankfurter's *Adamson* concurrence, at least if Frankfurter agreed to remove certain objectionable language from his initial draft, including reference to the Bill of Rights as "parochial," and if Frankfurter's opinion were altered to state that "basic liberties essential to democracy—freedom of speech and press, for example—are subsumed in their full force in the 14th Amendment."[102] The clerk continued to oppose total incorporation. But when he learned that Justice Murphy was writing a separate dissent, he suggested to Murphy's clerk that if Murphy agreed with total incorporation, he at least "should reserve the question whether 'the due process clause is limited by the Bill of Rights,' for Murphy certainly believes, as witness his opinion in Yamashita . . . that due process is an absolute, independent of other provisions of the Bill of Rights."[103] Initially, Murphy had written Black a note indicating that he agreed with Black's opinion, though urging Black not to "be forced into a long discussion about" the *Twining* case and observing, "I think you go out of your way—as you always do—to strike down natural law."[104] Ultimately, however, Murphy decided to draft a dissent agreeing that the specifics of the Bill of Rights were fully binding on the states, but reserving the question whether a state proceeding might fall "so far short of conforming to fundamental standards of procedure as to warrant constitutional condemnation in terms of a lack of due process despite the absence of a specific provision in the Bill of Rights."[105]

When Murphy circulated his draft, Black objected to his colleague's implication that Black would limit procedural due process to "the specific prohibitions of the Bill of Rights," asserting: "I have not intended to say that in the Adamson opinion so far as *procedural* due process is concerned. In other words I have not attempted to tie procedural due process exclusively to the Bill of Rights. In fact there are other constitutional prohibitions relating to procedure which I think due process requires to be observed."[106] Even by that point, though, it was clear that Black was referring merely to specific guarantees in the original Constitution, not to standards of procedural "fairness" gleaned from due process itself. Murphy's draft quoted Black's observation in *Chambers* v. *Florida* that due process requires conformity "to fundamental standards of procedure." Quoted out of context, Black responded, the phrase seemed "to be a near approach to the 'fundamental justice' " language of *Twining* and *Hurtado* v. *California*,[107] another early case rejecting incorporation, and that appeared to be Murphy's implication. *Chambers*, Black insisted, did not support such an interpretation of due process. Now obviously aware of the implications—stated and unstated—of Black's opinion, Murphy deleted his citation of *Chambers*, but retained its language and filed his dissent, unwilling to join Black. Over his clerk's continued objections to total incorporation, Justice Rutledge concurred in Murphy's dissent.

Post-*Adamson* Refinements

As the Court's spokesman in a number of cases decided after 1947, Justice Black employed "fundamental fairness" language in applying particular Bill of Rights safeguards to state cases. In *In Re Oliver*,[108] decided the year after *Adamson*, for example, he made reference to Fifth and Sixth Amendment guarantees but held for the Court only that notice and a public trial were part of the "procedural due process" necessary to assure state defendants "a charge fairly made and fairly tried."[109] Speaking for the Court in *Gideon* v. *Wainwright*,[110] moreover, he employed the rhetoric of selective incorporation to overrule *Betts* v. *Brady* and apply the right to counsel to state cases. And in *Pointer* v. *Texas*[111] he concluded for the Court that the Sixth Amendment right of confrontation was "a fundamental right and is made obligatory on the States by the Fourteenth Amendment."[112] He also joined, of course, the other decisions of the 1960s employing various versions of selective incorporation to apply Bill of Rights safeguards to the states.[113]

There was no doubt, however, that Justice Black remained committed to total incorporation for the rest of his life. Black obviously took satisfaction in the Court's willingness during the 1960s to use the selective formula in applying most Bill of Rights provisions to the states, just as he did the Court's conclusion that all incorporated rights, not merely those of the First Amendment, were to be given identical application in state and federal cases[114]—a position to which the Justices, with one notable exception,[115] have remained essentially faithful since his death.

But Black's concurrence in the Court's resort to selective incorporation was purely tactical. Given his *Betts* dissent, it was especially appropriate that Black author the Court's *Gideon* opinion. As the Court's spokesman, though, he was obliged to use language acceptable to his selective incorporationist brethren. After writing an initial draft, he instructed his secretary Frances Lamb to have "the boys" look over it "to make sure about its words"—words, presumably, compatible with the jargon of selective incorporation. He also wrote Justice Brennan a note to accompany his copy of the opinion, assuring his colleague that "[t]here is no intimation in what I have written of an en masse application of the Bill of Rights to the States, something that can be made wholly clear if you wish, by a footnote or otherwise." Even in this context, however, Black and Douglas managed to include their views in the array of *Gideon* opinions. In a brief separate opinion Douglas conceded that "Unfortunately [total incorporation] has never commanded a Court," but added: "happily, all constitutional questions are always open. . . . And what we do today does not foreclose the matter." Douglas also emphasized that the Court did not accept the view that "rights protected against state invasion by the Due Process Clause of the Fourteenth Amendment [were] watered-down versions of what the Bill of Rights guarantees."[116] As the author of an opinion for the Court embracing selective incorporation, Justice Black could hardly join, formally, Douglas's opinion. But he undoubtedly shared most of its sentiments and probably had a hand in its final drafting. Before circulating an initial draft to other Justices, Douglas shared it with Black, asking, "Does this look Okay?"[117]

On several occasions after *Adamson*, moreover, Justice Black registered brief opinions reiterating his commitment to incorporation. Several were filed during the period before the 1960s when a coalition led by Justice Frankfurter was resisting further incorporation of Bill of Rights safeguards, by their terms, into the Fourteenth Amendment's meaning. Speaking for the Court in *Wolf* v. *Colorado*,[118] Justice Frankfurter agreed that "[t]he security of one's privacy against arbitrary intrusion by the police—which is at the core of the Fourth Amendment—is basic to a free society. It is therefore implicit in 'the concept of ordered liberty' and as such enforceable against the States through the Due process Clause."[119] But he rejected the claim that the exclusionary rule—applicable in federal cases since 1914[120]—was binding on the states or that due process was "shorthand for the first eight amendments of the Constitution and thereby incorporates them."[121] *Palko*, wrote Frankfurter, reaffirmed "a different but deeper and more pervasive conception of the Due Process Clause" than that reflected in the incorporation thesis.

> Due process of law . . . conveys neither formal nor fixed nor narrow requirements. It is the compendious expression for all those rights which the courts must enforce because they are basic to our free society. But basic rights do not become petrified as of any one time, even though, as a matter of human experience, some may not too rhetorically be called eternal verities. It is of the very nature of a free society to advance in its standards of what is deemed reasonable and right. Representing as it does a living principle, due process is not confined within a permanent catalogue of what may at a given time be deemed the limits or the essentials of fundamental rights.[122]

Not surprisingly, given his emphasis on literalism, Justice Black had difficulty finding an exclusionary rule within the Constitution; and his position on the issue, to be examined in a later chapter, varied greatly over the years. In a *Wolf* concurrence he concluded that the rule was not mandated by the Constitution. But he also reiterated his *Adamson* position, asserting: "I should be for reversal of this case if I thought the Fourth Amendment not only prohibited 'unreasonable searches and seizures,' but also, of itself, barred the use of evidence so unlawfully obtained."[123] And when Justice Frankfurter concluded for the Court in *Rochin* v. *California*[124] that use of a stomach pump to extract narcotics from a suspect was conduct "shocking to the conscience" and thus violative of due process, Justice Black condemned the "accordian-like qualities" of Frankfurter's approach to the Fourteenth Amendment, accused his colleague of "imperil[ing] the Bill of Rights," compared Frankfurter's conceptions of due process with the "evanescent standards" used by the Old Court in economic cases, wondered what "avenues of investigation" were available for discovering such "fundamental" principles, and concluded that the Fifth Amendment, made applicable to the states through the Fourteenth, was violated when "incriminating evidence is forcibly taken from [a suspect] by a contrivance of modern science."[125]

It was not until 1968 and the Court's decision of *Duncan* v. *Louisiana*,[126] however, that Justice Black again extensively developed his incorporation thesis in an opinion, on this occasion in a confrontation with Justice Harlan. In *Ohio ex rel. Eaton* v. *Price*,[127] a 1960 case foreshadowing the incorporation explosion of the sixties, Justice Brennan had registered an opinion, joined by Chief Justice Warren and Justices Black and Douglas, in which he indicated that he and the Chief Justice had "neither accepted nor rejected" total incorporation, but also asserted that the due process formula articulated in *Palko* was not "a license to the judiciary to administer a watered-down, subjective version" of the Bill of Rights in state cases.[128] In succeeding cases a majority extended most Bill of Rights safeguards to the states and indicated that incorporated rights were to have equal application in federal and state cases. To provide a semantic rationale for their rulings, moreover, the Justices replaced *Palko*'s conclusion that rights were to be applied to the states only if essential to any system of liberty and justice with the observation that, to be incorporated into the Fourteenth Amendment, rights need be basic only to the "American scheme of justice."[129] The *Duncan* majority found the Sixth Amendment right to a jury trial to be of that character—but only over Justice Harlan's vehement dissent.

After Justice Frankfurter's retirement from the bench in 1962, Justice Harlan had become the Court's leading critic of incorporation and proponent of the flexible due process formula Frankfurter had long espoused. In *Duncan* Harlan rejected the majority's conclusion that trial by jury was essential to due process and scorned the Court's selective incorporation approach as lacking even the "internal [logical] consistency" of Justice Black's position.[130] But Harlan also devoted much attention to Black's thesis, citing the "overwhelming historical evidence"[131] challenging his colleague's reading of the Fourteenth Amendment's legislative and judicial history and terming the "great words" of the amendment's first section "an exceedingly peculiar way to say that 'The rights heretofore guaranteed against federal intrusion by the first eight Amendments are henceforth guaranteed against state intrusion as well.' "[132]

In answering Harlan's contentions Justice Black clarified somewhat his own position. To Harlan's charge that the language of the Fourteenth Amendment was "an exceedingly peculiar way" to express an intent to incorporate the Bill of Rights, for example, Black retorted:

> I can say only that the words "No State shall make or enforce any law which shall abridge the privileges or immunities of citizens of the United States" seem to me an eminently reasonable way of expressing the idea that henceforth the Bill of Rights shall apply to the States. What more precious "privilege" of American citizenship could there be than that privilege to claim the protection of our great Bill of Rights? I suggest that any reading of "privileges or immunities of citizens of the United States" which excludes the Bill of Rights' safeguards renders the words of this section of the Fourteenth Amendment meaningless. . . . I conclude, contrary to my Brother HARLAN, that if anything, it is "exceedingly peculiar" to read the Fourteenth Amendment differently from the way I do.[133]

Black thus appeared in *Duncan* to be concluding that the privileges or immunities clause was intended to incorporate specific Bill of Rights safeguards, while the Fourteenth Amendment's due process clause was to have the same meaning as its Fifth Amendment counterpart.

In *Duncan*, *In Re Winship*,[134] and other cases decided during his last decade on the bench, Justice Black also elaborated upon his "law of the land" construction of due process, detailed in the previous chapter. Dissenting in *Cohen* v. *Hurley*,[135] decided in 1961, he asserted of due process and equal protection,

> I have always believed that those guarantees, taken together, mean at least as much as Daniel Webster told this Court was meant by due process of law, or the "law of the land," in his famous argument in the *Dartmouth College* case: "By the law of the land is most clearly intended the general law. . . . The meaning is, that every citizen shall hold his life, liberty, property, and immunities, under the protection of the general rules which govern society."[136]

His opinions in later cases, especially *Duncan* and *Winship*, made clear his view that due process largely required government merely to proceed according to the Constitution and other preexisting laws and procedures. On occasion, as indicated in the previous chapter, he did find within due process requirements not stated elsewhere in the Constitution, including safeguards against convictions based on no evidence or perjured testimony. In fact, when he drafted an opinion for the Court in *Thompson v. City of Louisville*,[137] voiding a state conviction on no-evidence grounds, Justice Harlan expressed concern about the opinion's potential breadth. In a letter to his colleague Harlan urged Black to emphasize that the record in the case was " 'completely devoid' of evidence . . . to fend against the future use of [Black's] opinion as a basis for due process attacks on grounds of mere 'insufficiency' of evidence."[138] Black found few independent procedural requirements within due process, however, and those he did find were largely approximations of Bill of Rights safeguards and other specific legal guarantees or essentially consistent with a "law of the land" conception of due process. Certainly, they reflected no willingness on the Justice's part to use due process as a device for ruling on the "reasonableness" or "fairness" of state laws and procedures. Finally, as also indicated in the previous chapter, although Justice Black reiterated shortly before his death his belief that the privileges or immunities clause included within its meaning a right of interstate travel, and presumably other rights not stated in the Bill of Rights as well, he never found any other particular rights within the clause's scope and obviously rejected the notion that it clothed judges with a general authority to add further "fundamental" rights to the Constitution's meaning.

Assessing the Critics

For the criticism it has attracted, Justice Black's incorporation thesis is neck and neck with his First Amendment jurisprudence. While obviously wide-ranging and frequently overlapping, attacks on his stance have fallen into one of essentially three categories: semantic, policy, and historical. Semantic criticisms are those directed at apparent inconsistencies between Black's position and the Fourteenth Amendment's language. Policy attacks raise questions bottomed on considerations of judicial self-restraint—or activism. And historical criticisms, of course, have rejected Black's reading of the history surrounding the Fourteenth Amendment's adoption and its early judicial construction.

Semantic Criticisms. When focusing on what they consider to be semantic difficulties with Black's position, the Justice's critics have often assumed due process to be his vehicle of incorporation. They have asserted, for example, that the Fourteenth Amendment's framers would never have intended that language from a part of the Bill of Rights—the due process clause of the Fifth Amendment—serve as shorthand for all the provisions of the first eight amendments. If, on the other hand, due process does embody the specific guarantees of the first eight amendments, those provisions were a redundancy. Finally, they argue, the judicial construction of due process before the Fourteenth Amendment's adoption flies in the face of any contention that the amendment's framers intended it to embody the Bill of Rights. For never before had the clause been given an interpretation compatible with anything approximating incorporation.[139]

Even had Justice Black based his incorporation thesis on due process alone, however, it is difficult to see how certain of his critics, most notably Frankfurter and Harlan, could raise such complaints, yet conclude that due process absorbed within its meaning rights approximating—or identical to—the specific safeguards of the Bill of Rights. Frankfurter and Harlan obviously never agreed that the due process clause embodies the Bill of Rights by its terms. But both clearly did assume due process to include within its scope substantive and procedural rights similar or equal in force to particular guarantees in the first eight amendments. In *Duncan* v. *Louisiana*, for example, Justice Harlan outlined his interpretation of due process as an evolving concept, then observed:

> The relationship of the Bill of Rights to this "gradual process" seems to me to be twofold. In the first place it has long been clear that the Due Process Clause imposes some restrictions on state action that

parallel Bill of Rights restrictions on federal action. Second, and more important than this accidental overlap, is the fact that the Bill of Rights is evidence, at various points, of the content Americans find in the term "liberty" and of American standards of fundamental fairness.[140]

Albeit less obviously, at least in his judicial opinions, Justice Frankfurter embraced the same notion. In an April 16, 1959, letter to Justice Brennan on the relationship of the Fourth Amendment to the Fourteenth, for example, Frankfurter wrote: "my mode of dealing with a question like this is to say that I derive the protection of privacy that the Fourteenth Amendment accords, not from the Fourth Amendment, but from the Fourteenth Amendment, though it turn out to be the same as that which for federal situations is covered by the Fourteenth Amendment."[141] How one could assume such a position, yet completely dismiss the notion of due process as a vehicle of incorporation, is difficult to comprehend.

But, of course, there is a much more fundamental and obvious response to such criticisms. Justice Black never contended that the Fourteenth Amendment's due process clause incorporated the Bill of Rights. Instead, he argued that "the provisions of the Amendment's first section, separately, and as a whole, were intended"[142] to apply the first eight amendments to the states. And he apparently assumed this position as early as 1939, for in his letter to Black of October 31 of that year, cited earlier, Justice Frankfurter referred to his colleague's "position on the 'Fourteenth Amendment' as an entirety." Although Black never actually embraced in so many words the view that the amendment's framers intended its privileges or immunities clause to incorporate the more specific guarantees of the Bill of Rights, while its due process clause would have the same meaning as its Fifth Amendment counterpart, that seems clearly to have been his position. In challenging Justice Harlan's assertion in *Duncan* that the language of the Fourteenth Amendment's first section was "an exceedingly peculiar way" to express an intent to incorporate the first eight amendments, for example, Justice Black cited the language of the privileges or immunities clause, then noted in a footnote: "My view has been and is that the Fourteenth Amendment, *as a whole*, makes the Bill of Rights applicable to the States. This would certainly include the language of the Privileges and Immunities Clause, as well as the Due Process Clause."[143]

Whatever may be said of due process, moreover, reference to "privileges or immunities of United States citizens" obviously evokes images of Bill of Rights guarantees in the minds of those unaware of—or unwilling to accept—the narrow construction the Supreme Court has given the privileges or immunities clause. Indeed, before Justice Frankfurter in *Adamson* concluded of the Fourteenth Amendment's language that "[i]t would be extraordinarily strange for a Constitution to convey such specific commands in such a roundabout and inexplicit way," he conveniently "put to one side the Privileges or Immunities Clause," not, obviously, because its language would also have been a "strange" way of indicating an intent to incorporate the Bill of Rights, but because, as he put it, of "the mischievous uses to which that clause would lend itself if its scope were not confined to that given it" in earlier cases.[144] Whether resurrection of the privileges or immunities clause could have been any more "mischievous" than Justice Frankfurter's flexible conception of due process is debatable at best. But there is no doubt, as Justice Black contended in *Duncan*, that the words of the privileges or immunities clause are an "eminently reasonable way of expressing" an intent to incorporate the Bill of Rights.

Justice Black's rejection of due process as the vehicle of incorporation does not answer, however, all semantic criticisms of his position. If the privileges or immunities clause was intended to embody the Bill of Rights rather than serve some other purpose, critics have asked, why did the framers also include in the Fourteenth Amendment's first section a due process clause virtually identical in language to a portion of the Bill of Rights? Why, too, would the framers have used a clause guaranteeing rights of United States citizens to apply against the states Bill of Rights safeguards which extended to all persons, not merely citizens?[145]

The first of these contentions seems more a makeweight than a serious argument. Although the historical record is silent on the question, it seems reasonable to conclude that the framers simply considered the privileges or immunities clause a shorthand expression for specific guarantees and due process a more general requirement identical to its equally general counterpart in the Bill of Rights. The second question, however, raises a much more serious issue. How could a literalist, such as Justice Black professed to be, consider a clause safeguarding, by its terms, rights of citizens a basis for obligating states to honor rights traditionally applicable to aliens as well? Only, according to Wallace Mendelson, by amalgamation of both the privileges or immunities and due process clauses. By asserting that the Fourteenth Amendment's first section, "separately, and as a whole," incorporated the Bill of Rights, Mendelson has observed: "In effect, Mr. Justice Black homogenized provisions. . . . To change the figure, the Justice treats the terms of the different clauses as interchangeable. Borrowing the privileges and immunities language as a reference to the Bill of Rights from one, and the word "persons" to get the desired breadth of coverage from another, he creates a new constitutional provision."[146] For Mendelson this was obviously a tortured construction of due process and one which also raised the question of how Black, who opposed due process and equal protection coverage for corporations, could employ the Fourteenth Amendment to protect the freedom of the press of newspaper companies in state cases.

Mendelson's is an interesting thesis. To my knowledge, however, Justice Black never indicated in any way that due process was designed to extend the rights of citizens to all persons. Instead, he seems simply to have recognized and accepted an anomaly prominent in the statements of the Fourteenth Amendment's chief sponsors, who included within the meaning of the privileges or immunities clause rights historically applied to citizens alone, as well as others extended to all persons—specifically, those of the Bill of Rights. Black argued, for example, that the safeguards of the Bill of Rights extended, via the Fourteenth Amendment, to all persons in state cases. However, in conference discussion of *Edwards* v. *California*[147] he indicated that interstate travel was a Fourteenth Amendment privilege extended only to citizens, not aliens.[148] As at least one writer has noted, the words of the clause were probably intended as "words of definition not of limitation."[149] After all, at the time of the Fourteenth Amendment's adoption, the distinction between citizens and aliens, at least apart from the question of the status of blacks, had not assumed the significance it would later have. At the time of the Civil War, only blacks were ineligible for citizenship, and other restrictions on eligibility for citizenship did not begin to emerge until the 1880s. It must be remembered, too, that according to Justice Black's reading of the history underlying the Fourteenth Amendment's adoption, its framers were bent on reversing *Barron* v. *Baltimore* and applying the provisions of the Bill of Rights—not merely some approximation of them—to the states; in addition, the incorporated rights were to have the same meaning—and breadth of application—in state cases that they were given in federal cases.

Similar considerations answer those who see inconsistencies between Black's opposition to due process or equal protection coverage for corporations, on the one hand, and his extension of freedom of the press to newspaper companies under the Fourteenth Amendment, on the other. As contended earlier, Black did not consider due process or, for that matter, equal protection vehicles for incorporation of specific Bill of Rights safeguards into the Fourteenth Amendment's meaning; nor did he use due process to extend citizenship rights to all persons. Moreover, the language of the First Amendment, which in Black's view was itself incorporated into the Fourteenth Amendment's meaning, does not limit its reach to natural persons.

Finally, of course, semantic criticisms of Black's incorporation thesis reject his contention that the words of the Bill of Rights impose a greater restriction on judicial discretion than the flexible conception of due process Justices Frankfurter and Harlan, among others, embraced. Recall, for example, Harlan's assertion, in his concurrence for *Griswold v. Connecticut*,[150] that "specific" constitutional provisions "lend themselves as readily to 'personal' interpretations by judges" as due process.[151] For Justice Black, however, the question was one of degree. The provisions of the first eight amendments simply imposed a greater degree of specificity, and thus greater restraint on judicial creativity, than the Frankfurter-Harlan due process formula. In my view his position is too obviously correct for argument. Indeed, his critics' own words essentially make Black's point for him. Consider the following passage from Justice Frankfurter's *Adamson* concurrence:

> And so, when as in a case like the present, a conviction in a State Court is here for review under a claim that a right protected by the Due Process Clause of the Fourteenth Amendment has been denied, the issue is not whether an infraction of one of the specific provisions of the first eight Amendments is disclosed by the record. The relevant question is whether the criminal proceedings which resulted in conviction deprived the accused of the due process of law to which the United States Constitution entitled him. Judicial review of that guaranty of the Fourteenth Amendment inescapably imposes upon this Court an exercise of judgment upon the whole course of the proceedings in order to ascertain whether they offend those canons of decency and fairness which express the notions of justice of English-speaking peoples even toward those charged with

the most heinous offenses. These standards of justice are not authoritatively formulated anywhere as though they were prescriptions in a pharmacopoeia. But neither does the application of the Due Process Clause imply that judges are wholly at large. The judicial judgment in applying the Due Process Clause must move within the limits of accepted notions of justice and is not to be based upon the idiosyncrasies of a merely personal judgment. The fact that judges among themselves may differ whether in a particular case a trial offends accepted notions of justice is not disproof that general rather than idiosyncratic standards are applied.[152]

Such rhetoric is eloquent; it frequently finds its way into judicial opinions. Ultimately, however, and with due respect to its authors, it is nothing more than a lofty expression of the fact that due process, as so construed, embodies the judge's personal predilections. Undoubtedly, the language of the first eight amendments also lends itself to judicial creativity, but not to the degree, arguably, that a flexible conception of due process does. Beyond a point, as asserted in the previous chapter, there is a limit to the contexts within which "freedom of speech," "impartial jury," "cruel and unusual punishments," "unreasonable searches and seizures," and other specifics of the Bill of Rights can be applied. That is simply not so with "liberty" and "due process."

Policy Criticisms. Critics of incorporation have also cited a number of policy considerations militating against its adoption. First, they argue that imprisoning states in the eighteenth-century "strait jacket" of the Bill of Rights unduly interferes with state autonomy and obstructs important objectives of the federal arrangement. In his *Adamson* concurrence, for example, Justice Frankfurter contended, it will be recalled, that incorporation would "tear up by the roots much of the fabric of law in the several States, and . . . deprive the States of opportunity for reforms in legal process designed for extending the area of freedom."[153] Elaborating on this theme in a later case, Justice Harlan expressed his

> firm conviction that "incorporation" distorts the "essentially federal nature of our national government," . . . one of whose basic virtues is to leave ample room for governmental and social experimentation in a society as diverse as ours, and which also reflects the view of the Framers that "the security of liberty in America rested

primarily upon the dispersion of governmental power across a federal system." . . . The Fourteenth Amendment tempered this basic philosophy but did not unstitch the basic federalist pattern woven into our constitutional fabric. The structure of our Government still embodies a philosophy that presupposes the diversity that engendered the federalist system.[154]

Second, critics maintain that incorporation may move judges mindful of the federal scheme to dilute the meaning of Bill of Rights safeguards in an effort to accommodate incorporation to principles of federalism, yet apply the same interpretations of the liberties involved in federal and state cases. Justice Harlan accused the majority of just such a course in *Williams* v. *Florida*,[155] decided in 1970. Two terms after applying the Sixth Amendment right of trial by jury to the states in the *Duncan* case, and despite numerous earlier opinions construing the Sixth Amendment jury to consist of twelve members,[156] the Court concluded that twelve-member juries were required in neither state nor federal criminal cases. In a separate opinion Justice Harlan pointedly observed:

> The decision envinces, I think, a recognition that the "incorporationist" view of the Due Process Clause of the Fourteenth Amendment . . . must be tempered to allow the States more elbow room in ordering their own criminal justice systems. With that much I agree. But to accomplish this by diluting constitutional protections within the federal system itself is something to which I cannot possibly subscribe. Tempering the rigor of *Duncan* should be done forthrightly, by facing up to the fact that at least in this area the "incorporation" doctrine does not fit well with our federal system, and by the same token that *Duncan* was wrongly decided.[157]

Elsewhere in the same opinion, moreover, Harlan expressed concern that " 'incorporation' would neutralize the potency of guarantees in federal courts in order to accommodate the diversity of our federal system."[158]

Third, proponents of both activism and self-restraint see Black's incorporation thesis, combined with his relatively fixed, "law of the land" construction of due process, as a serious obstacle to the efforts of courts to do justice. Justice Frankfurter charged in *Adamson* that Black's approach "leads inevitably to a warped construction of specific provisions of the Bill of Rights to bring within their scope conduct clearly condemned by due process but not easily fitting into the pigeon-holes of the specific provisions."[159] Echoing such sentiments in attacking the majority's use of constitutional "penumbras" to guarantee a right of privacy in the *Griswold* case, Justice Harlan observed: "what I find implicit in the Court's opinion is that the 'incorporation' doctrine may be used to *restrict* the reach of Fourteenth Amendment Due Process. For me this is just as unacceptable constitutional doctrine as is the use of the 'incorporation' approach to *impose* upon the States all the requirements of the Bill of Rights as found in the provisions of the first eight amendments and in the decisions of this Court interpreting them."[160] Clearly, similar thinking also underlay the Murphy-Rutledge dissent in *Adamson*, as well as the contentions of scholarly critics who have complained that Black's jurisprudence prevents courts from satisfying "all the needs of limited government."

Pure considerations of federalism, like the desire to clothe judges with authority to do "justice," would carry no weight, of course, with one of Justice Black's jurisprudential persuasion. Given his positivist view of the judicial role and reading of the Fourteenth Amendment's history, it would have been unthinkable for Black to yield to such concerns, rejecting incorporation and adopting a flexible conception of due process. And although his critics have suggested that both his conclusions regarding the intent of the amendment's framers and construction of due process were motivated by a policy predilection of his own—specifically, a desire to limit the range of judicial choice—those contentions are highly debatable. The first raises questions of integrity, which one should be reluctant to entertain lacking some direct evidence of a willful manipulation of historical records, or questions of unconscious motivation hardly susceptible to measurement. The second ignores the close parallels between Black's due process philosophy and the guarantee's original meaning, a meaning arguably accepted by the Supreme Court at the time of the Fourteenth Amendment's adoption and, in substance if not form, for many years thereafter, as contended in the previous chapter.

One may question as Black did, moreover, whether his stance, or that which Frankfurter and Harlan espoused, was a greater threat to state power. In *Adamson*, Black termed it "an illusory apprehension that literal application of some or all of the provisions of the Bill of Rights to the States would unwisely increase the sum total of the power of this Court to invalidate state legislation."[161] He also stressed the unlimited potential power with which the Frankfurter conception of due process clothed judges. His contention was obviously correct; whatever other objections can be raised against Black's interpretation of the Fourteenth Amendment, the potential it offered for federal judicial intrusion upon state power was much more limited than that inherent in opposing constructions.

Nor was the assertion that "jot-for-jot" incorporation would lead to a dilution of the meaning given Bill of Rights guarantees a fair prediction of Black's likely behavior in the field, whatever may be said of his colleagues. A need to reconcile incorporation and federalism may exert such an influence on certain judges; in fact, such factors may be having a hand in recent rulings weakening the reach of the exclusionary rule.[162] But they had no impact on Black. His conclusion in *Williams* v. *Florida* that twelve-member juries were not required under the Sixth or Fourteenth Amendment was a reflection of his emphasis on literalism, not his regard for federalism. The language of the Sixth Amendment, after all, requires an "impartial" jury, not one numbering twelve. Indeed, in *Baldwin* v. *New York*,[163] decided the same day as *Williams*, Black, joined by Justice Douglas, rejected a plurality's conclusion that juries are required only for cases involving more than six months' imprisonment. "The Constitution guarantees a right of [criminal] trial by jury in two separate places," he asserted, "but in neither does it hint of any difference between 'petty' offenses and 'serious' offenses."[164] The plurality's conclusion, he added, was thus "reached by weighing the advantages to the defendant against the administrative inconvenience to the State inherent in a jury trial and magically concluding that the scale tips at six months' imprisonment. Such constitutional adjudication, whether framed in terms of 'fundamental fairness,' 'balancing,' or 'shocking the conscience,' amounts in every case to little more than judicial mutilation of our written Constitution."[165]

Black's History. Although alleged semantic and policy weaknesses in Justice Black's incorporation thesis have been the object of frequent attack, critics of his position have focused primarily on his reading of the Fourteenth Amendment's history. Shortly after Black's *Adamson* dissent appeared, the *Stanford Law Review* published two articles which remain the most extensive critiques of his stance.

The first, authored by Professor Charles Fairman, vehemently challenged Black's conclusions regarding the intent of the Fourteenth Amendment's framers and accused the Justice of deliberately distorting the historical record.[166] Fairman was singularly unimpressed with Representative John Bingham, whom Black considered "the Madison of the first section of the Fourteenth Amendment." Initially at least, Fairman caustically observed, Bingham had erroneously thought that the safeguards of the Bill of Rights were already binding on the states and that an amendment was needed merely to clothe Congress with enforcement authority.[167] Fairman conceded that Bingham spoke often during the congressional debates of the "immortal bill of rights," but he rejected Black's assumption that Bingham's reference was to the first eight amendments and emphasized that Bingham specifically mentioned only one Bill of Rights guarantee—the Eighth Amendment ban on cruel and unusual punishments—as falling within the Fourteenth Amendment's ambit.[168] Indeed, Fairman added, only Senator Howard of the Amendment's supporters—and none of its congressional opponents—included most of the first eight amendments within the amendment's scope during debate over its passage. During the 1871 congressional debates over the amendment's meaning, Representative Bingham did itemize the first eight amendments. But, Fairman maintained, "[w]hat Bingham said in 1871 formed no part whatsoever of the facts that produced the Fourteenth Amendment. . . . He had made history, but his afterthought should not be allowed to remake it."[169]

For Fairman, moreover, the failure of the amendment's opponents in Congress, in the press, during political campaigns, or in the state legislative debates over its ratification to attack the amendment as an effort to bind the states to the Bill of Rights was "far more substantial" evidence of its meaning "than a few words uttered by Bingham and Howard in the debates of 1866."[170] Neither Congress, the state governments, nor the people, charged Fairman, would have tolerated so radical an alteration of the federal system, and had the Fourteenth Amendment been designed to implement such fundamental changes, its opponents would surely have turned that issue to their advantage. In Fairman's view the framers "had no clear idea as to the confines" of the privileges or immunities of national citizenship, and Justice Cardozo's *Palko* interpretation of due process probably came "as close as one can to catching the vague aspirations that were hung upon the privileges and immunities clause. This accommodates the fact that freedom of speech was mentioned in the discussion of 1866, and the conclusion that, according to contemporary understanding, surely the federal requirements as to juries were not included."[171] Whatever meaning the Amendment was intended to have, however, Fairman was convinced that "the record of history [was] overwhelmingly against" Black's thesis.[172]

In a companion article[173] Professor Stanley Morrison examined the Fourteenth Amendment's early history in the Supreme Court and condemned Justice Black's disregard for stare decisis, observing:

> [The incorporation theory] does not appear even to have been presented to that Court in the argument of counsel until 1887 [in *Spies* v. *Illinois*]. It did not receive the support of any Supreme Court judge until 1892 [in *O'Neil* v. *Vermont*]. Between 1868 and 1947, only three judges of the Court [the first Justice Harlan and Justices Field and Brewer] favored the doctrine, one of whom [Brewer] shortly recanted. On the other side are the large number of judges, many of them eminent, who listened to the argument and voted on the question. Some of these were mature men when the Fourteenth Amendment was adopted. The reaction of these men, as well as the failure of counsel in the earlier cases even to raise the question, affords ample proof that if the Amendment was designed to incorporate the Bill of Rights, this was not generally known to its contemporaries.[174]

Early Justices who embraced incorporation, Morrison further contended, appeared to base their positions, partially at least, not on perceived intentions of the Fourteenth Amendment's framers, but on the sort of "natural law" or "fundamental rights" thinking Black abhorred. Like Fairman, Morrison also questioned the quality of Black's research, concluding that a Supreme Court Justice simply did "not have the time for exhaustive historical" inquiry.[175] Finally, Morrison speculated that Black's historical findings may have been colored by his desire to eliminate the use of substantive due process as a tool for protecting economic interests from what he, as a New Deal liberal, would consider socially desirable state controls, while at the same time establishing an interpretation of the Fourteenth Amendment which would adequately protect noneconomic rights from state infringement. Incorporation, wrote Morrison, enabled Black "to have his cake and eat it too."[176]

The Fairman and Morrison studies have enjoyed enormous influence. Most scholars who have studied the issue in any depth have concluded that the Fourteenth Amendment's framers did intend to apply most or all the Bill of Rights to the states,[177] and even Professor Fairman appeared to accept the *Palko* version of selective incorporation. But the typical student of constitutional law has probably rejected Justice Black's understanding of original intent, and largely on the basis of an uncritical reading of the Fairman and Morrison articles. Indeed, Raoul Berger relied heavily on Fairman in his widely debated 1977 study rejecting incorporation and limiting the Fourteenth Amendment's meaning largely to the terms of the 1866 Civil Rights Act.[178]

As I attempted to demonstrate in a 1976 article, however,[179] it is possible to take issue with certain of the conclusions Fairman and Morrison reached even without undertaking an independent examination of the historical data on which they relied. First, even if Representative Bingham initially assumed, contrary to the *Barron* decision, that the Bill of Rights already placed a moral obligation on the states and that an amendment was needed merely to give Congress enforcement authority, he was still intent on enforcing the Bill of Rights against the states. As Justice Black's *Adamson* appendix indicates,[180] changes in the proposed amendment's language reflected growing attention to *Barron* and a need to recast the amendment in language compatible with the *Barron* ruling. The initial draft simply gave Congress civil rights enforcement power; a later version adopted the broader language eventually enacted—the privileges or immunities clause, which arguably calls to mind the first eight amendments.

Second, while only Senator Howard specifically listed many of the first eight amendments in congressional debates on the Fourteenth Amendment's adoption, no member of Congress rose to dispute his interpretation. Although Representative Bingham referred specifically only to the Eighth Amendment safeguard against cruel and unusual punishments, moreover, he and other proponents spoke often of the "bill of rights." And Professor Fairman's conclusion that their references were to something other than the guarantees of the first eight amendments flies in the face of the universal understanding that, whatever its ultimate reach, the phrase "bill of rights" includes within its meaning the Bill of Rights. Fairman apparently based his conclusion on statements of Fourteenth Amendment supporters including other rights than those within the first eight amendments within their conception of "bill of rights." But such statements suggest merely a conception broader than the first eight amendments, not that the amendment's sponsors—

contrary to all other persons before or since—excluded the Bill of Rights from the "bill of rights."

Third, although emphasizing the few occasions on which the Fourteenth Amendment's principal sponsors cited specific Bill of Rights safeguards in discussing the amendment's meaning, Professor Fairman appeared to agree that Bingham and Howard intended to apply the Bill of Rights to the states. He simply concluded that their "radical" views were not representative of the majority of the members of Congress or the state legislatures responsible for ratifying the proposed amendment. Assuming, however, that an inquiry into the intent of its framers is an appropriate means of discovering the construction to be given a constitutional provision—and surely it is—the statements of the Fourteenth Amendment's principal sponsors, on which Justice Black primarily based his incorporation thesis, would appear the most reliable indicator of original intent. In rejecting Fairman's findings, for example, Black observed in *Duncan*:

> I have read and studied [Fairman's] article extensively, including the historical references, but am compelled to add that in my view it has completely failed to refute the inferences and arguments that I suggested in my *Adamson* dissent. Professor Fairman's "history" relies very heavily on what was *not* said in the state legislatures that passed on the Fourteenth Amendment. Instead of relying on this kind of negative pregnant, my legislative experience has convinced me that it is far wiser to rely on what *was* said, and most importantly, said by the men who actually sponsored the Amendment in the Congress. I know from years in the United States Senate that it is to men like Congressman Bingham, who steered the Amendment through the House, and Senator Howard, who introduced it in the Senate, that members of Congress look when they seek the real meaning of what is being offered. And they vote for or against a bill based on what the sponsors of that bill and those who oppose it tell them it means.[181]

Fourth, while opponents of the Fourteenth Amendment did not specifically argue that it would shackle the states to the Bill of Rights, the statements of Bingham and Howard clearly afforded them the opportunity to make such a contention. The absence of such charges would thus appear to be evidence not that Justice Black was wrong, but that the amendment's opponents were unusually inept, did not appreciate the broader implications of incorporation, or perhaps even believed, in the abstract at least, that the guarantees of the Bill of Rights *should* apply to state, as well as federal, officials, and that the people would support incorporation.

Fifth, the contention that Black's reading of the Fourteenth Amendment's history may have been influenced by a desire to abolish substantive due process in economic cases, while extending the reach of judicial protection for noneconomic rights, ignores the significant limitations which Black's incorporation thesis imposes upon the power of judicial review. At the time Professor Morrison assessed Black's stance, the Justice was widely considered a doctrinaire liberal by admirers and critics alike. It is thus understandable that Morrison would evaluate Black's position in light of that liberal image. A discerning reading of the Justice's *Adamson* dissent, especially one juxtaposed with Justice Murphy's dissent in the case, makes clear, however, what Justice Rutledge's clerk quickly came to realize during the Court's review of *Adamson*—that, whatever his political leanings, Hugo Black was no judicial liberal in the mold of a Douglas, Rutledge, or Murphy.

Sixth, the Supreme Court's refusal to accept even selective incorporation for well over half a century after the Fourteenth Amendment's adoption is not necessarily an effective rebuttal to Justice Black's thesis. After all, there is little evidence that the contemporary Court was faithful to the wishes of the Reconstruction amendments' stronger supporters. In the *Slaughter-House Cases*, for example, the Court limited coverage of the privileges or immunities clause to rights which decisions antedating the Fourteenth Amendment had already recognized congressional authority to protect from state and, indeed, private interference. Surely, the amendment's framers intended more. By the latter part of the nineteenth century, moreover, the Court had converted the amendment into a tool principally for the protection of propertied interests despite an almost total absence of any evidence that the amendment's framers ever entertained such an intent. The limited constructions early decisions gave the Thirteenth Amendment and congressional power to enforce the Reconstruction amendments[182] hardly appear faithful to the desires of their principal backers. In fact, the Court's refusal to embrace incorporation, like its other narrow interpretations of the Reconstruction amendments, seems to have been based more on policy considerations—especially a regard for state autonomy, at least outside the economic arena—than on the history underlying their adoption. In the *Twining* case, for example, Justice Moody conceded "weighty arguments" supportive of incorporation, yet concluded for the Court that had the incorporation thesis prevailed, "it is easy to see how far the authority and independence of the states would have been diminished."[183]

More damaging to Justice Black's position, of course, is the apparent failure of counsel in early cases to advance a total incorporation construction of the Fourteenth Amendment before the courts. Even here, however, the evidence arguably is less substantial than it would first appear. *Twitchell* v. *Pennsylvania*[184] and *Justices* v. *Murray*[185] were the two pertinent cases which followed most closely the amendment's adoption. *Twitchell*, decided April 5, 1869, cited the *Barron* decision in refusing to overturn a state murder conviction on Fifth and Sixth Amendment grounds, Chief Justice Chase observing for the Court: "We are by no means prepared to say, that if it were an open question whether the 5th and 6th Amendments of the Constitution apply to the state governments, it would not be our duty to allow the writ applied for and hear argument on the question of repugnancy. We think, indeed, that it would. But the scope and application of these amendments are no longer subjects of discussion here."[186] Wallace Mendelson wondered why "[n]either counsel nor any member of the Court seemed aware of 'incorporation,' though it might have saved a man's life."[187] One should also wonder, however, why apparently no mention at all was made of the Fourteenth Amendment in the case. Whether one accepts incorporation, or the position of Mendelson or Fairman, the amendment's framers clearly intended it to impose some limitation on state proceedings. That no Fourteenth Amendment claim was raised at all suggests not that Black was wrong, but that Twitchell's counsel was unusually inept, or that a more thorough examination of the case is necessary before its role in the incorporation debate can be properly assessed.

The evidential value of *Justices* v. *Murray* is also doubtful. It first arose in the early 1860s, and while the *Murray* Court also reaffirmed *Barron*, the case actually involved the effect of the Seventh Amendment on the power of a *federal* appellate court. Moreover, intervening between *Murray* and the next case in which, according to Professor Morrison, an incorporation claim could have appropriately been raised were the *Slaughter-House Cases*, which emasculated the meaning of the privileges or immunities clause—the guarantee the Fourteenth Amendment's sponsors may have intended to incorporate the Bill of

Rights. The Court's decision in the *Slaughter-House Cases*, combined with the collapse of Reconstruction in the late 1870s and a general judicial undermining of the goals of the Fourteenth Amendment's most vigorous backers, may well have accounted for the failure of counsel to claim total incorporation before 1887.[188] It should be remembered too that well before 1887, litigants were claiming that particular Bill of Rights guarantees—those relevant to their specific cases and the only ones, presumably, which they would have been interested in asserting—were within the amendment's scope.[189]

The foregoing suggests that even without an independent examination of historical records, the contentions of those who challenge Justice Black's history can be drawn into serious question. Critics of Black's position now must also contend, however, with a recent, thoroughgoing study of the history surrounding the Fourteenth Amendment's adoption. In *No State Shall Abridge: The Fourteenth Amendment and the Bill of Rights*,[190] the most exhaustive historical analysis of the issue to date, Michael Kent Curtis has examined not only the congressional and state legislative debates over the amendment's adoption, but also records relating to passage of the Thirteenth Amendment and Reconstruction legislation, as well as the history and constitutional philosophy of the antislavery movement—important keys, as Curtis convincingly demonstrates, to an understanding of the thinking underlying the amendment's enactment. He concludes, as Justice Black did, that the amendment's framers did indeed intend to make the first eight amendments applicable to the states.

A thorough review of Curtis's impressive study should be required reading for every serious student of the incorporation issue and Hugo Black's jurisprudence. But a number of his more significant findings and conclusions may be briefly summarized.

1. Representative Bingham and other antislavery Republicans were aware of the *Barron* decision throughout the deliberations, just as they were familiar with *Dred Scott*; they simply considered both incorrect constructions of the Constitution.[191]

2. Republicans generally rejected the narrow, anti-discrimination construction of Article IV's privileges and immunities clause which the Supreme Court embraced. Instead, they believed that the clause was intended to protect "fundamental" rights, including those listed in the Bill of Rights, from state interference, and considered the Fourteenth

Amendment's privileges or immunities clause analogous in meaning to their construction of its Article IV counterpart.[192]

3. A broad range of Republicans, not merely "radicals," intended the amendment to incorporate the Bill of Rights.[193]

4. Although erroneous, the contention that the amendment's first section is no broader than the provisions of the 1866 Civil Rights Act is not inconsistent with incorporation. The act secured "the full and equal benefit of all laws and proceedings for the security of person and property," and Reconstruction Republicans, as well as "ordinary use of language," included the guarantees of the Bill of Rights among such "laws and proceedings."[194]

5. Debates in the Thirty-seventh, Thirty-eighth, and Thirty-ninth Congresses reveal that Republicans were extremely unhappy with the limited protection state governments had provided the speech, press, procedural, and related rights of abolitionists, and that the movement for the Fourteenth Amendment's adoption reflected such concerns.[195]

6. More than thirty statements of Republicans in the Thirty-eighth and Thirty-ninth Congresses indicated a belief that the Bill of Rights limited the states. Since a number of congressmen did not speak to the issue, the percentage of those who accepted the view that the Bill of Rights already limited the states was quite high.[196]

7. Although the records of state legislative debates on the Fourteenth Amendment's ratification are limited, certain statements indicated a belief that the amendment incorporated the Bill of Rights, or particular portions of the first eight amendments. Moreover, complaints "that the amendment would centralize power and allow federal courts to decide if citizens were being denied their rights were common refrains of opponents, North as well as South."[197]

8. As evidence contradicting incorporation, Professor Fairman cited Congress' decision to readmit certain southern states to the Union even though their constitutions included provisions inconsistent with the Bill of Rights. But Fairman found only one conflict (in the Georgia Constitution) which he considered clearcut, and even that claim was debatable. Moreover, he ignored an important political consideration accelerating the readmission process: congressional Republicans needed additional southern state ratifications of the Fourteenth Amendment— ratifications requisite to their readmission to the Union—to offset the defections of several northern legislatures which had repealed their own

ratifications after Democratic takeovers in the elections of 1866.[198] Presumably, the Republican desire to assure the amendment's adoption would have overwhelmed any inconsistencies they may have perceived between the southern states' constitutions and provisions of the Bill of Rights.

Nor is Curtis impressed with the contention that state legislators would never have "shackled" their governments to the first eight amendments. "This argument," asserts Curtis,

> ignores the realities of the political process. The campaign of 1866 dealt with gut issues: the rights of blacks, the political power of the rebellious southern states, racism, and protection for loyalists in the South. These were issues that could and did defeat politicians. No politician, then or since, is likely to be defeated for advocating grand juries, criminal juries of twelve, or the right to jury trial in civil cases where the damages exceed twenty dollars. The argument assumes that Republicans in state legislatures would allow the South a dramatic increase of political power by counting disenfranchised blacks for purposes of representation [a matter covered in Section 2 of the Amendment] rather than provide for jury trials in civil cases where the damages exceed twenty dollars. Politicians do not behave in this fashion.[199]

Some may contend that Curtis's findings are not entirely compatible with Justice Black's limitation of the reach of the Fourteenth Amendment's first section largely to the Bill of Rights or the Justice's opposition to noninterpretive review of state laws and procedures under the amendment's provisions. Curtis concludes that Representative Bingham probably intended to limit the scope of the privileges or immunities clause to constitutional rights. Like others who have examined the historical record, however, he also acknowledges that many of the amendment's backers believed the clause to include within its meaning rights not expressly mentioned in the Constitution.[200] Based on such data, some have given the amendment an incorporation-plus construction, contending that its framers intended it both to incorporate the first eight amendments and to protect other, unstated rights from state invasion, whether through the privileges or immunities clause or, as Justice Murphy's *Adamson* dissent recommended, via due process. A 1949 *Yale Law Journal* comment, for example, found "ample support" for Justice Black's contention that Representative Bingham intended incorporation, but also defended the idea of a "living" Constitution and concluded "that the intent which Justice Black imputes to Bingham is only one thread in a tangled skein."[201]

Curtis found no consensus among the amendment's supporters, however, regarding the content of these unstated rights.[202] And, as I argued in the previous chapter, the fact that many of the amendment's framers may have recognized the existence of such rights is a far cry from the contention that their content is to be found in a judge's own conceptions of ethics, morality, or social utility. Certainly, it is a flimsy historical basis for a defense of noninterpretivism, particularly given the dangers that approach to constitutional interpretation poses for democratic principles.

Whether or not the Fourteenth Amendment's framers intended to clothe judges with such powers, moreover, Curtis's work is a powerful defense of incorporation. Arguably, it demolishes the anti-incorporationists' position. Taken together with weaknesses in semantic and policy attacks on Justice Black's stance, it at the very least shifts the burden of proof decidedly to the anti-incorporationists and away from those who accept Justice Black's incorporation thesis as an accurate reflection of original intent.

Four Black's First Amendment

A S the Court's spokesman in *Bridges* v. *California*[1] and its companion, *Times-Mirror Co.* v. *Superior Court,* Justice Black reversed the contempt-by-publication convictions at issue in those celebrated 1941 cases, gave the clear and present danger test an extremely broad construction, observed that earlier cases invoking the test did "not purport to mark the furthermost constitutional boundaries of protected expression, nor do we here," then asserted: "[Those cases] do no more than recognize a minimum compulsion of the Bill of Rights. For the First Amendment does not speak equivocally. It prohibits any law 'abridging the freedom of speech, or of the press.' It must be taken as a command of the broadest scope that explicit language, read in the context of a liberty-loving society, will allow."[2] Initially, however, Justice Frankfurter had drafted a majority opinion upholding the convictions at issue in *Bridges* and *Times-Mirror.* While the cases were proceeding toward a final ruling, Frankfurter sent Justice Brandeis, then retired from the Court, a copy of his opinion. "Of course you have a unanimous Court for your opinion," Brandeis remarked when he next spoke with Frankfurter. "Hardly that," Frankfurter prophetically replied; "I am very doubtful whether I will keep a Court. Black has a fierce dissent." To that, Brandeis retorted, with vehemence by Frankfurter's account, "Black & Co. have gone mad on free speech!"[3]

Throughout his career and since his death Justice Black's First Amendment jurisprudence has often provoked such reactions, as well as much praise. With the possible exception of the amendment's religion clauses, Justice Frankfurter doubted whether its provisions—or certain of the amendment's constituents—were deserving of the judicial protection Black urged for the freedoms included within its scope.[4] As he once wrote Zechariah Chafee, Frankfurter believed that the Court "should be more exacting in observing the prohibition of unreasonable search and seizure," and presumably other rights as well, "than the requirement of freedom of speech, for the simple reason that the latter has strongly organized forces in its support—the press, the movie interests, publishers, etc., etc., while there is no such organized constituency on the alert against unreasonable search and seizure. On the contrary, the great weight of the police force and the fear of people about crime are easily enlisted against it."[5] In judicial opinions Frankfurter and Harlan, among others, vigorously challenged Justice Black's efforts to give the amendment a literal, absolutist construction, and in private exchanges Frankfurter's assessments were even more pointed. Of Black's dissent in two 1961 subversive-membership cases, for example, Frankfurter wrote Harlan: "I think I can make a good guess as to Holmes's comment on what Black, J. has written. . . . On far less provocation, he pithily disposed of writings by colleagues with, 'It makes me puke.' "[6]

Nor were Black's colleagues the only ones to deride the Justice's First Amendment philosophy. Through most of his career, scholarly critics charged him with reading too much into the amendment, assigning undue clarity to its history and "plain" language, and ignoring important countervailing social interests justifying restrictions on the amendment's reach. In a 1963 lecture, for example, Harvard Law Dean Erwin Griswold—whom, as solicitor general, Black was to gently chide in the *Pentagon Papers Cases*[7] for arguing "that 'no law' does not mean 'no law' "[8]—attacked the Justice's stance in *Engel* v. *Vitale*,[9] the school prayer case.[10] But Griswold focused attention primarily on Black's off-the-bench absolutist pronouncements, including his James Madison lecture at New York University, during which the Justice had observed: "It is my belief that there are 'absolutes' in our Bill of Rights, and that they were put there on purpose by men who knew what words mean, and meant their prohibitions to be 'absolutes.' "[11] Speaking on the theme "Absolute is in the Dark," Griswold took his cue from Black's observation, during a published interview with Edmond Cahn, that in his absolutist reading of the Constitution, he was not "far . . . from the Holy Scriptures."[12] Calling Black's a "Fundamentalist theological" approach to the Constitution's meaning, Griswold asserted:

If one thinks of the Constitution as a God-given text stating fixed law for all time, and then focuses on a single passage, or, indeed, on two words—"no law"—without recognizing all the other words in the whole document, and its relation to the society outside the document, one can find the answers very simple. " 'No law' means no law." No more thought is required. Earlier this month, I was in New Orleans, and saw a large illuminated sign outside a church there, which read: "God said it. We believe it. That's all there is to it." This seems a similar approach.

Griswold obviously did not accept such thinking.

[A]bsolutes are likely to be phantoms, eluding our grasp. Even if we think we have embraced them, they are likely to be misleading. If we start from absolute premises, we may find that we only over-simplify our problems and thus reach unsound results. It may well be that absolutes are the greatest hindrance to sound and useful thought—in law, as in other fields of human knowledge. . . . It provides its own anodyne for the pains of reasoning. It states the result with delusive finality. But it is, I think, a thoroughly un-satisfactory form of judging.

Instead, Griswold embraced a balancing approach to the First Amendment and other constitutional issues which Frankfurter and Harlan had long advanced on the Court, though Griswold preferred to call his formula a "comprehensive" or "integral" approach "since it involves looking to the text of all of the Constitution, and, indeed, in proper cases, to the 'unwritten Constitution.' " Asserted Griswold:

Instead of focusing on a few words, and ignoring all else, including the effect and meaning of those words, as distinguished from their apparent impact when isolated from everything else, as the absolu-tist or "Fundamentalist" approach does, the comprehensive or inte-gral approach accepts the task of the judge as one which involves the effect of all the provisions of the Constitution, not merely in a narrow literal sense, but in a living, organic sense, including the elaborate and complex governmental structure which the Consti-tution, through its words, has erected. Under the Fundamentalist approach, the judge puts on blinders. He looks at one phrase only; he blinds himself to everything else. Can this approach really be preferable or sounder than one under which the Court examines all Constitutional provisions in a living setting, and reaches its con-clusion in the light of all the relevant language and factors?

Philip Kurland had recently characterized further discussion of absolutism as tantamount "to thrashing a straw man."[13] Griswold hoped that Kurland was correct, but was doubtful of that prospect, given "the eminence of those who haven taken [the absolutist] position."

As in the incorporation field, moreover, certain scholars focused on inconsistencies between absolutism and the First Amendment's language. The philosopher Sidney Hook contended, for example, that a literal, absolutist application of the free exercise guarantee would constitutionalize a host of "morally objectionable practices ranging from polygamy to human sacrifices, all of which are forbidden by law."[14] Hook and others also complained of the disastrous consequences they saw flowing from general judicial acceptance of Black's position, Hook condemning on numerous occasions absolutism's "practical extremism" as well as its "intellectual simplicity," and observing:

> [T]he implications of Black's articulated philosophy are so terrifying that if it were to prevail, the entire structure of human freedom would be more seriously undermined than if the legislative measures he deplores were multiplied a thousand times over. For Justice Black would strip American citizens of any legal protection against every form of slander, libel and defamation, no matter how grave and irreparable the consequent damage to life, limb, property and reputation. The very foundations of civil society—and not merely of democratic society, whose vitality depends more than any other on certain standards of public virtue—would collapse if speech which falsely charged citizens with murder, theft, rape, arson and treason was regarded as public discussion and hence privileged under the law.[15]

Judges, Hook added, are typically "sensitive to the charge of absolutism, for an absolutist, like a fanatic, is one who refuses to test his principles in the light of reason and experience, and explore alternatives to what may be no more than arbitrary prejudices tricked out as self-evident axioms or convictions." Amazingly to Hook, however, Black was "proud" of his Bill of Rights absolutism.[16]

Scholarly criticism of Justice Black's First Amendment jurisprudence was not confined, however, to those who accused the Justice of reading too much into the amendment's provisions. Black's reaction to constitutional claims raised in civil rights and antiwar protest cases decided during his last decade on the bench[17] prompted concern that he was assigning the amendment an unduly restrictive construction. These critics saw his stance as further evidence that, toward the end of his career, the Justice had lost his "passionate concern"[18] for the "poor, the ignorant, the numerically weak, the friendless, and the powerless."[19] Like his earlier detractors, they also complained that his absolutism dictated "arbitrary" choices with unfortunate consequences, including absolute protection for "hardcore pornography," libel, and slander, and virtually none for the "much more deserving"[20] ideas of the protest movements. Some have contended, moreover, that Black's position in the protest cases was inconsistent with his stance in early labor picketing and handbill cases.[21] And at least one critic has argued that the Black of those earlier cases was an "undisguised" balancer,[22] that he embraced absolutism only after more than a decade on the bench, and that his approach in the protest cases of the 1960s was a "contrivance" designed to give an appearance of internal consistency—a fundamental premise of the Justice's philosophy—to an inconsistent record, "lest obvious inconsistency reduce his jurisprudence to a sham or a hoax."[23]

This chapter examines Justice Black's First Amendment philosophy, and the following chapter assesses criticisms of this significant element of his jurisprudence, especially charges directed at his literalist-absolutist reading of the amendment's provisions, treatment of the issues growing out of the protest cases of the sixties, and the claim to fundamental consistency in his approach to First Amendment cases early and late in his career. I conclude inter alia, (1) that Black had embraced absolutism at least by 1940–41, (2) that his stance in the later protest cases was remarkably similar to his response to early picketing and handbill claims, (3) that those who have questioned the tone of his later opinions largely confuse concern about the medium with contempt for the message or its messenger, and (4) that Black's position in the protest cases provided considerably more protection for demonstrative expression than his critics have assumed.

Absolutism: Scope, Limits, Basic Premises

Although Justice Black had concluded for the Court in the *Bridges* case that the clear and present danger test reflected only a "minimum compulsion" of the First Amendment, he did not first advance an absolutist construction of the amendment in published opinions until the early 1950s, when the Court began to condone a variety of regulations directed at members and former members of the Communist party. Dissenting from a majority's 1950 approval of federal regulations requiring "non-Communist" affidavits of labor union officials in *American Communications Ass'n, C.I.O.* v. *Douds*,[24] the Justice came close to a public declaration of his stance, asserting: "Whether religious, political, or both, test oaths are implacable foes of free thought. By approving their imposition, this Court has injected compromise into a field where the First Amendment forbids compromise."[25] In *Dennis* v. *United States* (1951)[26] he moved closer, quoting from his *Bridges* opinion to contend that, "[a]t least as to speech in the realm of public matters, I believe that the 'clear and present danger' test does not 'mark the furthermost constitutional boundaries of protected expression' but does 'no more than recognize a minimum compulsion of the Bill of Rights.' "[27] Interestingly, moreover, he did not join Justice Douglas's separate dissent or, presumably, Douglas's observation that "[t]he freedom of speech is not absolute; the teaching of methods of terror and other seditious conduct should be beyond the pale along with obscenity and immorality."[28] Then, in *Carlson* v. *Landon*,[29] decided the following term, Black specifically used absolutist language for the first time in a published opinion, declaring his belief "that the First Amendment grants an absolute right to believe in any governmental system, discuss all governmental affairs, and argue for desired changes in the existing order."[30]

But it was not until the month after the *Carlson* decision was announced that Black delivered the first extensive public exposition of his position. The occasion was the Court's decision of *Beauharnais* v. *Illinois*,[31] in which a majority, per Justice Frankfurter, upheld a state group libel law, but assured all that the freedoms of the Constitution were secure "[w]hile this Court sits."[32] In a vigorous dissent Justice Black objected to the Court's ruling, rationale, and basic premise.

> I do not agree that the Constitution leaves freedom of petition, assembly, speech, press or worship at the mercy of a case-by-case, day-by-day majority of this Court. I had supposed that our people could rely for their freedom on the Constitution's commands, rather than on the grace of this Court on an individual case basis. To say that a legislative body can, with this Court's approval, make it a crime to petition for and publicly discuss proposed legislation seems as farfetched to me as it would be to say that a valid law could be enacted to punish a candidate for President for telling the

people his views. I think the First Amendment, with the Fourteenth, "absolutely" forbids such laws without any "ifs" or "buts" or "whereases." Whatever the danger, if any, in such public discussion, it is a danger the Founders deemed outweighed by the danger incident to the stifling of thought and speech. The Court does not act on this view of the Founders. It calculates what it deems to be the danger of public discussion, holds the scales are tipped on the side of state suppression, and upholds state censorship. This method of decision offers little protection to First Amendment liberties "while this Court sits."[33]

Beauharnais was the leader of a white supremacist organization. He and his followers had circulated racist leaflets urging Chicago officials to "preserve and protect our white neighborhoods." "If there be minority groups who hail this holding as their victory," Black cautioned in concluding his dissent, "they might consider the possible relevancy of this ancient remark: 'Another such victory and I am undone.'"[34]

In later opinions and off-the-bench statements Black elaborated his position. First, he made clear its ultimately linguistic basis. His absolutism was obviously compatible with his positivist conception of the judicial function and preference for legal standards which would restrict the range of judicial discretion. His attacks on the clear and present danger, balancing, and related nonabsolutist approaches to the review of First Amendment claims clearly reflect such connections between the Justice's absolutism and his broader jurisprudence. In *Barenblatt v. United States*,[35] for example, he attacked the balancing doctrine's flexible character and application in Justice Harlan's opinion for the *Barenblatt* majority, declaring:

> To apply the Court's balancing test under such circumstances is to read the First Amendment to say "Congress shall pass no law abridging freedom of speech, press, assembly and petition, unless Congress and the Supreme Court reach the joint conclusion that on balance the interest of the Government in stifling these freedoms is greater than the interest of the people in having them exercised." This is closely akin to the notion that neither the First Amendment nor any other provision of the Bill of Rights should be enforced unless the Court believes it is *reasonable* to do so. . . . [T]his violate[s] the genius of our *written* Constitution.[36]

His discussions of the First Amendment's meaning also frequently in-cluded moving accounts of the historic circumstances underlying its adoption[37]—especially the persecution of political and religious dissi-dents—as well as repeated references to James Madison's injunction, on introducing the proposed Bill of Rights guarantees in Congress, that "If they are incorporated into the Constitution, independent tribunals of justice will consider themselves in a peculiar manner the guardians of those rights; they will be an impenetrable bulwark against *every* as-sumption of power in the Legislative or Executive; they will be natu-rally led to resist *every* encroachment upon rights expressly stipulated for in the Constitution by the declaration of rights."[38]

Black rested his absolutism primarily, however, on the First Amendment's words. It begins, "Congress shall make no law," and for Black, "no law" meant "No Law," even though others might have considered such an approach "rather old-fashioned" and evidence of a "slight naivete."[39] Explaining his position to Edmond Cahn, Black re-marked:

> I presume it could come to this, that I took an obligation to support and defend the Constitution as I understand it. And being a rather backward country fellow, I understand it to mean what the words say. Gesticulations apart, I know of no way in the world to commu-nicate ideas except by words. And if I were to talk at great length on the subject, I would still be saying . . . that I believe when our Founding Fathers, with their wisdom and patriotism, wrote this Amendment they knew what they were talking about. They knew what history was behind them and they wanted to ordain in this country that Congress, elected by the people, should not tell the people what religion they should have or what they should believe or say or publish, and that is about it. It says "no law," and that is what I believe it means.[40]

Second, Black rejected the thesis of the philosopher Alexander Meiklejohn[41] that the First Amendment reaches only political speech. He acknowledged that a desire to protect such expression was "no doubt a strong reason for the amendment's passage,"[42] and he remained doubt-ful to the end whether its guarantees to freedom of speech and press extended to other forms of expression.[43] He ultimately followed, how-ever, the amendment's language, which draws no distinctions among

types of speech. While emphasizing the First Amendment's role in safeguarding the discussion of "public affairs," moreover, he obviously did
not consider such expression the limit of the amendment's reach.

Third, he extended absolute First Amendment protection to two
forms of expression traditionally excluded from full coverage: libel, its
verbal counterpart slander, and obscenity. With its imposition of an
"actual malice" standard in *New York Times* v. *Sullivan*[44] and other
cases,[45] the Court established a potentially significant limitation on
civil and criminal libel actions growing out of comment about public
officials and "public figures." For Black, however, the Court had not
gone nearly far enough. "I base my vote to reverse," he asserted in a
concurrence, "on the belief that the First and Fourteenth Amendments
not merely 'delimit' a State's power to award damages to 'public officials against critics of their official conduct' but completely prohibit a
State from exercising such power."[46] "An unconditional right to say
what one pleases about public affairs," he added, "is what I consider to
be the minimum guarantee of the First Amendment."[47] And he obviously did not limit his position to comment about public officials or
public figures. In his view the "First Amendment was intended to leave
the press free from the harassment of libel judgments," and he placed no
conditions on that assertion. He assumed the same absolutist position
in the obscenity field,[48] even opposing laws forbidding the sale of erotica
to minors.[49] And when the Court, in *Stanley* v. *Georgia*,[50] rested a right
to possess obscenity on privacy considerations, then refused to extend
that right beyond the home,[51] he delivered one of the more humorous—
and devastating—salvos of his career. "[P]erhaps in the future," he
declared, *Stanley* "will be recognized as good law only when a man
writes salacious books in his attic, prints them in his basement, and
reads them in his living room."[52]

Black raised numerous objections to the Court's approach in each
field. He found the *New York Times* "actual malice" standard "an elu-
sive, abstract concept, hard to prove and hard to disprove," and thus "at
best an evanescent protection for the right critically to discuss public
affairs."[53] Under the malice formula, he contended, moreover, the
Court was obliged to "weigh the facts" of each case "and hold that all
papers and magazines guilty of gross writing or reporting are constitutionally liable, while they are not if the quality of the reporting is
approved by a majority of us." Such review of "factual questions in cases

decided by juries" was, in his judgment, a "flat violation of the Seventh Amendment."[54]

If anything, he had even less sympathy for prevailing obscenity law. He found the obscenity tests articulated by the Court and individual Justices "so vague and meaningless that they practically [left] the fate of a person charged with violating censorship statutes to the unbridled discretion, whim and caprice of the judge or jury which tries him."[55] The conclusion of a plurality, in *Memoirs* v. *Massachusetts*,[56] that, to be found obscene, erotic material must be "utterly without redeeming social value" prompted him, for example, to term that element of the plurality standard "as uncertain, if not even more uncertain, than is the unknown substance of the Milky Way."[57] And when the Court added a pandering factor to its litany of tests, holding that a distributor of erotic material who pandered to the prurient tastes of his prospective clients could be convicted on obscenity charges even though the product itself might not be obscene,[58] the Justice fairly exploded in dissent. The majority, he charged, had "in effect rewritten the federal obscenity statute," imposing "standards and criteria that Congress never thought about; or if it did think about them, certainly it did not adopt them."[59] Such a decision, he argued, was a clear violation of due process. He also considered censorship in any field, of course, "the deadly enemy of freedom and progress."[60]

His position obviously was not based on any special predilection for erotica, much less libel or slander. While he no doubt recognized the significance of sex as a fundamental human drive, he was almost Victorian in his artistic tastes. "I don't like it," he remarked of pornography on more than one occasion. "I don't use it, I never have; I've always detested it."[61] And he dismissed at least one critically acclaimed theatrical film which contained several sex scenes as "coarse and vulgar."[62] Unlike most of his brethren, however, he refused to impose his tastes on the rest of the country. He thus declined even to attend the Court's screenings of challenged films, writing Justice Harlan, who had scheduled one such session, "I cannot see that looking at the pictures would change my view that the First Amendment would be violated by barring the showing of these pictures. Consequently I shall not be present."[63] Nor would he take part in any other assessments of material claimed to be obscene. Instead, the First Amendment's words—not considerations of literary or artistic quality, truth or falsity, malice, care, or recklessness—were for him the ultimate key to the amendment's meaning and application. "That Amendment provides, in simple words," he observed in one obscenity case, "that 'Congress shall make no law . . . abridging the freedom of speech, or of the press.' I read 'no law . . . abridging' to mean *no law abridging*. The First Amendment, which is the supreme law of the land, has thus fixed its own value on freedom of speech and press by putting these freedoms wholly 'beyond the reach' of [governmental] power to abridge."[64]

Finally, along with emphasizing the linguistic foundations of his absolutism and willingness to include within the First Amendment's scope certain classes of expression traditionally excluded from protection, Black stressed the limits to his stance. He emphasized, for example, that the First Amendment protects "speech," not "conduct," and rejected direct and complete First Amendment protection for picketing and related forms of "speech-plus." In a 1964 labor picketing case he explained that picketing includes at least two elements—"speech," which is protected by the First Amendment, and "patrolling," which is not.[65] Since such activities, he later argued, involve "more than 'speech,' more than 'press,' more than 'assembly,' and more than 'petition,' as those terms are used in the First Amendment,"[66] government could subject them to regulations of time, place, and manner, or bar them completely.

Although he never specifically said so, he undoubtedly considered "symbolic speech," or communicative conduct, even less entitled to First Amendment protection. When a majority concluded in *Tinker* v. *Des Moines Independent Community School District* (1969),[67] for example, that the wearing of armbands by students as a symbol of protest was a form of protected expression "closely akin to 'pure speech,' "[68] he did not directly challenge the Court's conclusion. Instead, he observed, "Assuming that the Court is correct in holding that the conduct of wearing armbands for the purpose of conveying political ideas is protected by the First Amendment,"[69] then referred readers to a 1949 ruling, which he had authored, emphasizing the power of government over speech-related conduct.[70] In *Street* v. *New York*,[71] moreover, he found it beyond "belief that any thing in the Federal Constitution bars a State from making the deliberate burning of the American flag an offense," adding, "It is immaterial to me that words are spoken in connection with the burning. It is the *burning* of the flag that the State has set its face against."[72]

And while he spoke for the Court in *Schacht* v. *United States*,[73] overturning a federal regulation prohibiting the unauthorized wearing of a military uniform in theatrical productions tending to discredit the armed forces, he viewed the provision at issue as an infringement on "pure" speech. He agreed, for example, that Congress could constitutionally prohibit the unauthorized wearing of a military uniform but held that, under the challenged regulation, Congress had "in effect made it a crime for an actor wearing a military uniform to *say things* during his performance critical of the conduct or policies of the Armed Forces."[74]

Nor did Black's absolute First Amendment grant people a right to express views wherever they wished. He realized that the amendment guaranteed the right of peaceable assembly and petition, and he agreed that its provisions "would unquestionably appear to require" government to provide a place where petitions could be submitted.[75] But he argued that freedom of assembly may be constitutionally exercised only where people have a legal right of access and that government, not the individual, must determine where, when, and how petitions can be made. Just as government could protect private property, it could, in Black's judgment, exercise broad control over access to public property, even for purposes of expression. During his 1968 television interview, he observed:

> Now, the Constitution doesn't say that any man shall have a right to say anything he wishes, anywhere he wants to go. That's agreed, isn't it? Nothing in there says that. All right. It does not say people shall have a right to assemble to express views on other people's property. It just doesn't say it. It says they shall have a right to assemble, if they're peaceable, but it doesn't say how far you can go in using other people's property.

His interviewers were incredulous.

> AGRONSKY: You mean even government property—
> BLACK: Why, certainly, that's not theirs.
> SEVAREID: You can't assemble in mid-air.
> BLACK: That's not theirs.
> SEVAREID: Well, whose is it—is government property—
> BLACK: It belongs to the government as a whole. Just exactly as a corporation's property belongs to the corporation as a whole. And

just as an individual owns it. Now, the government would be in a bad fix, I think, if the Constitution provided that the Congress was without power to keep people from coming into the Library of Congress and spending the day there, demonstrating or singing because they wanted to protest the government. I don't think they could. They've got a right to talk where they have a right to be, under valid laws.[76]

Despite the restrictive contours of his position regarding regulations of speech-plus and symbolic speech, as well as access to public property, however, Black hardly considered them completely immune from judicial scrutiny. He was willing to invalidate such regulations on vagueness and overbreadth grounds. Thus, in *Edwards* v. *South Carolina*[77] he joined the majority in overturning the conviction of civil rights demonstrators under a common law breach-of-the-peace rule that South Carolina's Supreme Court had characterized as "not susceptible of exact definition."[78] And in *Gregory* v. *City of Chicago*[79] he concurred on vagueness and overbreadth grounds in the Court's decision to strike down the disorderly conduct convictions of protesters who had marched from the Chicago City Hall to the mayor's home in pressing school desegregation claims. The ordinance at issue, he asserted,

> was not . . . a narrowly drawn law, particularly designed to regulate certain kinds of conduct such as marching or picketing or demonstrating along the streets or highways. Nor does it regulate the times or places or manner of carrying on such activities. To the contrary, it might better be described as a meat-ax ordinance, gathering in one comprehensive definition of an offense a number of words which have a multiplicity of meanings, some of which would cover activity specifically protected by the First Amendment.[80]

The Justice subjected such regulations to other standards as well. He did not hesitate to invalidate controls which he found to be framed or applied in a discriminatory manner, terming them violations of both the First Amendment and equal protection.[81] Moreover, while he believed that nondiscriminatory regulations of speech-related conduct and access to public property imposed only "indirect" burdens on protected freedoms, rather than the "direct" interferences he viewed as absolutely forbidden, he was willing to subject such indirect burdens to review under a balancing test initially developed in early picketing and handbilling cases—balancing designed to assure "the complete protection of First Amendment freedoms even against purely incidental or inadvertent consequences."[82] Under that approach, such regulations would be struck down unless the governmental interests underlying them outweighed countervailing First Amendment interests, and no less restrictive means were available for promoting the state interests at issue in a particular case.

In a 1961 dissent from the Court's use of balancing in a context involving what Black considered to be a direct interference with the First Amendment, he summarized the origins and nature of the sort of balancing he was willing to accept. "The term came into use," he observed,

> chiefly as a result of cases in which the power of municipalities to keep their streets open for normal traffic was attacked by groups wishing to use those streets for religious or political purposes. When those cases came before this Court, we did not treat the issue posed by them as one primarily involving First Amendment rights. Recognizing instead that public streets are avenues of travel which must be kept open for that purpose, we upheld various city ordinances designed to prevent unnecessary noises and congestions that disrupt the normal and necessary flow of traffic. In doing so, however, we recognized that the enforcement of even these ordinances, which attempted no regulation at all of the content of speech and which were neither openly nor surreptitiously aimed at speech, could bring about an "incidental" abridgment of speech. So we went on to point out that even ordinances directed at and regulating only conduct might be invalidated if, after "weighing" the reasons for regulating the particular conduct, we found them insufficient to justify diminishing "the exercise of rights so vital to the maintenance of democratic institutions" as those of the First Amendment.[83]

He emphasized, however, that such balancing was inappropriate for cases in which government sought to have the views of "a person rightfully walking or riding along the streets and talking in a normal way . . . controlled, licensed or penalized in any way."[84]

As the foregoing suggests, Justice Black claimed that his speech-related conduct and direct-indirect distinctions guided his approach in early handbill and picketing cases. In later years, for example, he frequently quoted from his opinion for the Court in *Giboney* v. *Empire Storage & Ice Co.*, a labor picketing case, especially this observation: "It rarely has been suggested that the constitutional freedom for speech and press extends its immunity to speech or writing used as an integral part of conduct in violation of a valid criminal statute."[85] And this assertion as well:

> [I]t has never been deemed an abridgment of freedom of speech or press to make a course of conduct illegal merely because the conduct was in part initiated, evidenced, or carried out by means of language, either spoken, written, or printed. . . . Such an expansive interpretation of the constitutional guaranties of speech and press would make it practically impossible ever to enforce laws against agreements in restraint of trade as well as many other agreements and conspiracies deemed injurious to society.[86]

Arguably, the influence of these distinctions and related elements in this aspect of Justice Black's jurisprudence was also evident in his approach to other First Amendment claims. Black joined the Court's decision in *Valentine* v. *Chrestensen*,[87] the 1942 case recognizing a commercial-speech exception to protected speech. Although Justice Douglas also joined *Valentine*, he later regretted his decision. In 1958 Douglas wrote Justice Frankfurter that *Valentine* was "an ill-advised opinion on a very important constitutional question."[88] After Justice Black's death, Douglas registered his views in a dissent.[89] It is unlikely, however, that Black ever doubted the wisdom of his *Valentine* stance or considered it inconsistent with his absolute construction of the First Amendment. Instead, since commercial speech is inevitably part of a broader course of conduct—the attempted sale of a product or service— Black probably viewed regulations of advertising, early and late in his career, as part of valid governmental efforts to regulate conduct "in part initiated, evidenced, or carried out by means of language, either spoken, written, or printed."[90]

Similar considerations undoubtedly prompted him to agree, moreover, that antitrust laws could be applied to a wire-service combination. As the Court's spokesman in *Associated Press* v. *United States*,[91] Black argued that application of the Sherman Act to "a combination to restrain trade in news and views" would in fact enhance, rather than constrain, freedom of the press. The First Amendment, he declared, "rests on the assumption that the widest possible dissemination of information from diverse and antagonistic sources is essential to the welfare of the public, that a free press is a condition of a free society."[92] Black obviously embraced such sentiments. But since his First Amendment jurisprudence rested primarily on the amendment's language, rather than on values its protection was deemed to promote, the primary basis for his *Associated Press* position was probably more thoroughly reflected in his assertion that the amendment furnished no "shield for business publishers who engage in business practices."[93]

Justice Black never filed an opinion revealing his position with regard to the power of Congress over radio and television broadcasters. In *Red Lion Broadcasting Co. v. FCC*,[94] upholding the "fairness doctrine," the Court, per Justice White, asserted, as Black had in *Associated Press*, that the regulations at issue "enhance rather than abridge" freedom of expression.[95] White also suggested for the *Red Lion* Court, however, that the airwaves belong to the public, not individual licensees, and concluded that "nothing in the First Amendment . . . prevents the Government from requiring a licensee to share his frequency with others and to conduct himself as a proxy or fiduciary with obligations to present those views and voices which are representative of his community and which would otherwise, by necessity, be barred from the airwaves."[96] Black joined *Red Lion* and probably viewed the government's power to control the airwaves as comparable to its authority over other public property. Whether he also would have joined the Court's 1978 decision upholding the power of the Federal Communications Commission to sanction "offensive" broadcasts[97] is highly doubtful, but there is insufficient evidence for even informed speculation on that issue.

Given the distinctions Black drew between speech and conduct, however, reasonable speculation about his position is possible regarding the status of another form of speech-related conduct. While Justice Black deplored any law directly preventing or punishing the possession or distribution of sexual material, even in cases involving distribution to juveniles, he no doubt recognized broad authority for government to use such films and photographs as evidence in the prosecution—under rape and related statutes, not "obscenity" controls—of child rape and other criminal acts. In my judgment he also would have been willing to allow the prosecution of distributors, as accessories or in some other capacity warranted by the usual standards of criminal evidence.

Black's speech/conduct and direct/indirect dichotomies, as well as his views regarding governmental power over access to public property, were most clearly reflected, however, in the opinions which he registered for civil rights and antiwar protest cases of the 1960s, especially *Cox v. Louisiana*,[98] *Brown v. Louisiana*,[99] *Adderley v. Florida*,[100] and the *Tinker* case.[101] The *Cox* Court struck down convictions for breach of the peace, obstruction of public passages, and courthouse picketing intended to obstruct justice which arose out of a confrontation between civil rights demonstrators and police in Baton Rouge. Justice Black agreed that the portion of the Louisiana breach-of-peace statute invoked in the case was void for vagueness and overbreadth, since it was not narrowly drawn to "define the conditions upon which people who want to express views may be allowed to use the public streets and highways," leaving that decision instead to police discretion.[102] Because the breach-of-peace and obstruction-of-public-passages statutes exempted labor unions, he also found Cox's convictions under both "censorship in a most odious form," forbidden by the First Amendment and the equal protection guarantee.[103] But he had "no doubt about the general power of [the state] to bar all picketing on its streets and highways," subject only to a judicial balancing of competing interests.[104] "The First and Fourteenth Amendments," he contended,

> take away from government, state and federal, all power to restrict freedom of speech, press, and assembly *where people have a right to be for such purposes.* This does not mean, however, that these amendments also grant a constitutional right to engage in the conduct of picketing or patrolling, whether on publicly owned streets or on privately owned property. . . . Were the law otherwise, people on the streets, in their homes and anywhere else could be compelled to listen against their will to speakers they did not want to hear. Picketing, though it may be utilized to communicate ideas, is not speech, and therefore is not of itself protected by the First Amendment.[105]

Justice Brennan's notes indicate that Black had assumed the same position in conference debate on the issues raised in *Cox*.[106]

While Black joined the Court in overturning the first two counts of Cox's conviction, moreover, he vigorously dissented from its decision to reverse the appellant's conviction for picketing near a courthouse. The majority, per Justice Goldberg, had agreed that the statute on which that conviction was based was valid. But Baton Rouge police, according to Goldberg, had initially allowed Cox's group to gather across the street from the parish courthouse at which the incident occurred. Goldberg concluded for the Court that to uphold the appellant's conviction under such circumstances would be tantamount to condoning a form of entrapment forbidden by due process. Justice Black had difficulty understanding how the Court could "justify the reversal of this conviction because of a permission which could not have been authoritatively given anyway, and which even if given was soon afterwards revoked."[107] He also raised concerns which were becoming prominent themes of his opinions in such cases—specifically, regard for the rule of law, preference for political and social change through traditional channels, and a fear that peaceful mass protests can easily degenerate into violence and repression. "The streets are not now and never have been the proper place to administer justice," he warned, adding: "Use of the streets for such purposes has always proved disastrous to individual liberty in the long run, whatever fleeting benefits may have appeared to have been achieved."[108] He hoped that minorities and their leaders particularly would heed his counsel.

> [M]inority groups, I venture to suggest, are the ones who always have suffered and always will suffer most when street multitudes are allowed to substitute their pressures for the less clamorous but more dependable and temperate processes of the law. Experience demonstrates that it is not a far step from what to many seems the earnest, honest, patriotic, kind-spirited multitude of today, to the fanatical, threatening, lawless mob of tomorrow. And the crowds that press in the streets for noble goals today can be supplanted tomorrow by street mobs pressuring the courts for precisely opposite ends.[109]

In *Brown* v. *Louisiana*,[110] decided the following term, Black continued to press his position, on this occasion entirely in dissent. The *Brown* majority reversed the breach-of-peace convictions of five black youths who staged a sit-in in a small regional library to protest segregated library services. Speaking for a plurality, Justice Fortas concluded that there was no evidence to support a finding of breach of the peace and that, in any event, the convictions violated the petitioners' "right in a peaceable and orderly manner to protest by silent and reproachful presence, in a place where the protestant has every right to be, the unconstitutional segregation of public facilities."[111] Justice Brennan concurred in the judgment on the broad ground that the *Cox* decision had invalidated Louisiana's entire breach-of-peace statute on its face, while Justice White, casting the deciding vote, concluded that the petitioners' arrests and convictions had been racially motivated. The petitioners were in the library a total of ten to fifteen minutes before being arrested, and the sheriff and deputies who arrested them had come to the library without being called. For White such facts were decisive. He found it "difficult to believe that if this group had been white its members would have been asked to leave on such short notice, much less asked to leave by the sheriff and arrested, rather than merely escorted from the building, when reluctance to leave was demonstrated."[112]

In a dissent joined by Justices Clark, Harlan (who considered this one of Black's "best opinions"[113]), and Stewart, Justice Black challenged White's conclusion as well as the plurality's contention that the statute under which the petitioners had been prosecuted "was deliberately and purposefully applied solely to terminate the reasonable, orderly, and limited exercise of the right to protest the unconstitutional segregation of a public facility."[114] In a draft of his dissent he had suggested that his brethren were "apparently" influenced by the fact that "the arrests were made in the Deep South."[115] In his published dissent he pointed out that, although the library and a parish bookmobile service were segregated, the librarian had offered service to the petitioners and sought to provide them the service requested, objecting to their continued presence only after the petitioners asked for no additional service other than to inquire, "What about the Constitution?" "Whatever may have been the policy of the State of Louisiana in the past or may be the policy of that State at the present, at other places or in other circumstances," he asserted, "there simply was no racial discrimination practiced in this case. The petitioners were treated with every courtesy and granted every consideration to which they were entitled."[116]

Nor could Black accept Justice Brennan's assertion that Louisiana's entire breach-of-peace statute was facially void and had been so declared in *Cox*. The portion of the law on which the petitioners' convictions were based related to congregating in public buildings and ignoring orders to disperse. That provision, Black argued, was "in no way involved or discussed in *Cox*."[117] Brennan had objected to the statute's extension to various acts committed "with intent to provoke a breach of the peace, or under circumstances such that a breach of the peace may be occasioned thereby,"[118] and to the broad construction given that language by the Louisiana Supreme Court. Black contended, however, that the provision's vagueness and breadth must be evaluated in the context of each of the more than thirty offenses the statute covered. The "public buildings" portion of the statute, he argued, was not nearly so vulnerable to the "vice of discriminatory enforcement" as the "public streets" provision at issue in *Cox*. "In the public building, unlike the street, peace and quiet is a fast and necessary rule, and as a result there is much less room for peace officers to abuse their authority."[119]

Along similar lines Black attacked the plurality's finding that there was no evidence to support the petitioners' convictions. To reach such a conclusion, he contended, his brethren were measuring breaches of the peace in public buildings by standards appropriate to the streets. The plurality and Justice White seemed to assume, he wrote, that persons "who do not want library service" are guilty of a breach of the peace only if they

> stay there an unusually long time after being ordered to leave, make a big noise, use some bad language, engage in fighting, try to provoke a fight, or in some way become boisterous. The argument seems to be that without a blatant, loud manifestation of aggressive hostility or an exceedingly long "sit-in" or "sojourn" in a public library, there are no circumstances which could foreseeably occasion a breach of the peace.[120]

In his judgment such an approach violated "common sense and common understanding," and ignored the fact that "[p]ublic buildings such as libraries, schoolhouses, fire departments, courthouses, and executive mansions are maintained to perform certain specific and vital functions" requiring "[o]rder and tranquility of a sort entirely unknown to the public streets."[121] In that type of setting the petitioners' behavior clearly constituted breach of the peace, just as invasion of private property over the owner's protest was universally considered "one of the surest ways any person can pick out to disturb the peace."[122] The Louisiana courts had so concluded, and his brethren's substitution of their judgment for that of state officials conflicted with "settled doctrine" regarding federal court construction of state statutes.[123]

His most basic objection, however, was to the plurality's assumption that the petitioners had a constitutional right to remain in a library even though they did not wish to use its facilities "for library purposes." As in *Cox*, he rejected the view that the First Amendment guarantees people freedom "to use someone else's property, even that owned by government and dedicated to other purposes, as a stage to express dissident ideas."[124] He also expressed concern once again about what he considered to be the alarming implications of such thinking, declaring:

> It is an unhappy circumstance in my judgment that the group, which more than any other has needed a government of equal laws and equal justice, is now encouraged to believe that the best way for it to advance its cause, which is a worthy one, is by taking the law into its own hands from place to place and from time to time. Governments like ours were formed to substitute the rule of law for the rule of force. Illustrations may be given where crowds have gathered together peaceably by reason of extraordinarily good discipline reinforced by vigilant officers. . . . But I say once more that the crowd moved by noble ideals today can become the mob ruled by hate and passion and greed and violence tomorrow. If we ever doubted that, we know it now. The peaceful songs of love can become as stirring and provocative as the Marseillaise did in the days when a noble revolution gave way to rule by successive mobs until chaos set in. The holding in this case today makes it more necessary than ever that we stop and look more closely at where we are going.[125]

Several months after *Brown* was decided, Justice Black was able to command a narrow majority for a position approximating his own. *Brown* had been a five-four ruling with Justice White joining the majority, as noted earlier, on narrow grounds. In *Adderley* v. *Florida*[126] White joined another five-four ruling upholding, per Justice Black, the trespass convictions of more than a hundred demonstrators who had gathered on the grounds of a county jail to protest the arrest of other demonstrators, then ignored police orders to disperse. Justice Douglas, joined by Chief Justice Warren and Justices Brennan and Fortas, asserted in dissent that a jail was a seat of government subject to the right of petition, especially "when it houses political prisoners or those who many think are unjustly held."[127] Finding no evidence of interference with jail operations or security, Douglas charged that the petitioners were actually being prosecuted for the expression of unpopular ideas. "Today," he contended, "a trespass law is used to penalize people for exercising a constitutional right. Tomorrow a disorderly conduct statute, a breach-of-the-peace statute, a vagrancy statute will be put to the same end. It is said that the sheriff did not make the arrests because of the views espoused. That excuse is usually given."[128] Finally, he warned that the Court's acquiescence in the suppression of "orderly and civilized protests against injustice" would "increase the forces of frustration which the conditions of second-class citizenship are generating amongst us."[129]

Speaking for the majority, Justice Black rejected Douglas's assessment of the record and construction of the First Amendment. Emphasizing that "jails, built for security purposes," are traditionally closed to the public,[130] he disputed the contention that people have a right of access to such property. More broadly, he insisted that people have no right "to propagandize protests or views . . . whenever and however and wherever they please."[131] Nor could he accept the dissent's assumption of an effort to censor the expression of ideas. "There is not a shred of evidence in this record," he asserted,

> that this power was exercised, or that its exercise was sanctioned by the lower courts, because the sheriff objected to what was being sung or said by the demonstrators or because he disagreed with the objectives of their protest. The record reveals that he objected only to their presence on that part of the jail grounds reserved for jail use. There is no evidence at all that on any other occasion had similarly large groups of the public been permitted to gather on this portion of the jail grounds for any purpose.[132]

Justice Black's *Adderley* opinion painted with a broad brush, concluding with the assertion that "The United States Constitution does not forbid a State to control the use of its own property for its own lawful nondiscriminatory purpose."[133] But his personal position regarding the scope of governmental authority over speech-related conduct and access to public property was obviously broader and less flexible than that of all his brethren. His dissent in *Tinker* v. *Des Moines Independent Community School District*[134] made that contrast abundantly clear. The *Tinker* majority, speaking through Justice Fortas, ordered reinstatement of students suspended from school for wearing black armbands as symbols of protest against U.S. involvement in the Vietnam War. Fortas rejected the notion that students and teachers "shed" their constitutional rights "at the schoolhouse gate."[135] Instead, he declared, the First Amendment—which meant "what it says"—permitted only "reasonable regulation of speech-connected activities" in the school environment to protect against behavior that "materially disrupts classwork or involves substantial disorder or invasion of the rights of others."[136] The suspensions at issue were based at most on an "undifferentiated fear or apprehension of disturbance"[137] or, more likely, on the school officials' "urgent wish to avoid controversy."[138] Nor had school authorities banned "all symbols of political or controversial significance," added Fortas. Students wore campaign buttons and even the "Iron Cross, traditionally a symbol of Nazism." Only one particular symbol was "singled out for prohibition." And such a selective ban, "at least without evidence that it is necessary to avoid material and substantial interference with schoolwork or discipline, [was] not constitutionally permissible."[139]

Black and Justice Harlan were the only dissenters, and Harlan had no dispute with the Court's basic premise that the freedoms of expression and association extend to public school property. He would simply have given them a very narrow reading, placing the burden on plaintiffs to show that a particular regulation "was motivated by other than legitimate school concerns."[140]

Black's objections were much more fundamental. In *Brown* he had complained that the Court had "paralyzed" the ability of states to assure that their libraries would be used only "for library purposes," then added: "I suppose that inevitably the next step will be to paralyze the schools. Efforts to this effect have already been made all over the country."[141] Now, his words must have seemed prophetic to him, and he was deeply alarmed. None of the Court's precedents bore directly on the circumstances at issue in *Tinker*, and Black pointedly challenged the bearing of each of the cases Fortas cited in defense of the Court's position. Two 1923 cases on which Fortas relied perhaps most heavily—*Meyer* v. *Nebraska*[142] and *Bartels* v. *Iowa*[143]—had invoked substantive due process, and to Black the *Tinker* majority's approach smacked of the pre-1937 Court's use of due process to rule on the reasonableness of regulatory legislation. He wanted no part, of course, of such decision making. In his judgment the Court was no more appropriate a "national school board" than it had been a "super-legislature" in that discredited earlier era. He "wish[ed], therefore, wholly to disclaim any purpose on [his] part to hold that the Federal Constitution compels the teachers, parents, and elected school officials to surrender control of the American public school system to public school students."[144]

Even under the Court's formula, moreover, he was convinced that the challenged suspensions had been "reasonable." The record provided "ample" support for the conclusion that the armbands had distracted students from their studies and threatened school discipline. "But even if the record were silent," he declared,

> members of this Court, like all other citizens, know, without being told, that the disputes over the wisdom of the Vietnam War have disrupted and divided this country as few other issues ever have. Of course students, like other people, cannot concentrate on lesser issues when black armbands are being ostentatiously displayed in their presence to call attention to the wounded and dead of the war, some of the wounded and dead being their friends and neighbors. It was, of course, to distract the attention of other students that some students insisted up to the very point of their own suspension from school that they were determined to sit in school with their symbolic armbands.[145]

Tinker involved the claims of public school students. Justice Black would apparently have assumed the same general stance, however, with regard to the authority of government over expression on the campuses of public colleges and universities. In *Tinker*'s wake University of Texas law professor Charles Alan Wright wrote the Justice his impressions of the case. In his reply Black agreed that "the level of intelligence of college students would enable them to make mature judgments superior to that of high school students." He added, however, that he had not intended his *Tinker* dissent "to be limited to grade school or high school students." "As you probably gathered from my dissent," he observed in classic understatement, "I lean to the belief that it would be best for those in charge of the schools to establish the rules for the students to follow." His interpretation of the First Amendment posed no barrier to that preference or its extension to all levels of state-supported education.[146]

Justice Black's position regarding the meaning of the First Amendment's guarantees to freedom of expression may be summarized, then, as follows.

1. He believed that laws directly or primarily impinging on freedoms which he included within the amendment's scope were absolutely forbidden.

2. Although he had high regard for the values which the amend-

ment reflected and the historic considerations underlying its adoption, he based his absolutist position primarily on the amendment's language.

3. He favored a broad, liberal interpretation of the amendment's meaning. He agreed, for example, that freedom of assembly included a right of association,[147] and he favored absolute protection for libel, slander, and obscenity, forms of expression traditionally excluded from the amendment's coverage.

4. However, he rejected the notion that the amendment extended direct and full protection for all elements of picketing and related activities involving speech and other forms of conduct, and he probably denied any coverage whatever for "symbolic speech." Nor did he believe that the amendment granted people a right of access to public and private property.

5. He realized that controls over speech-related conduct would indirectly or incidentally infringe upon protected expression. He thus insisted that such regulations be nondiscriminatory, serve interests outweighing those underlying freedom of expression, promote interests not amenable to regulations less restrictive of protected rights, and be free of vagueness and overbreadth.

6. While he generally applied the same sorts of standards to controls over access to public property, he recognized broad power for government to determine what expression will be allowed in schools, libraries, and other facilities dedicated to special purposes. Thus, in *Tinker* he would have left to school authorities the decision whether campaign buttons and "symbol[s] of Nazism," as well as armbands, were to be allowed within school environs.

The Religion Clauses

Justice Black's position regarding the First Amendment's religion clauses was remarkably similar to the stance he assumed with respect to the amendment's guarantees to freedom of speech, press, and petition. As Black's critics like to point out,[148] the amendment's language forbids laws "prohibiting the free exercise" of religion, which literally would appear to include religiously based conduct. Black apparently reasoned, however, that the amendment's framers no more intended to protect all religious conduct than they meant to immunize all speech-related conduct from governmental interference or grant people a right to appropriate the property of others for purposes of expression. He thus construed the free exercise clause in the context of the amendment's other provisions, limiting its direct and full protection only to "religious speech"[149] and "belief,"[150] while subjecting governmental controls over religion-related conduct to a balancing of competing interests. In his Carpentier lectures,[151] for example, he spoke approvingly of the Court's 1878 decision in *Reynolds* v. *United States*,[152] which upheld a law of Utah territory forbidding polygamy, as applied to a member of the Mormon faith, and rejected Reynolds's claim that since his religion approved the practice of polygamy, his prosecution violated his rights under the free exercise guarantee. The *Reynolds* Court, Black observed in obvious agreement, concluded "that the First Amendment only protects the right to be a Mormon, to believe in and advocate its faith, but that a church cannot by giving conduct a religious approval bar government from making such conduct a crime. Thus the line was clearly drawn between freedom to believe in and advocate a doctrine and freedom to engage in conduct violative of the law."[153]

Black's decisional patterns on the Court reflected this distinction between religious conduct and religious speech and belief, as well as his willingness to balance competing interests in ruling on governmental regulation of conduct in which people wish to engage, or refrain from engaging, for religious reasons. Thus, he joined the Court's 1961 use of balancing in upholding Sunday closing laws against the free exercise claims of Orthodox Jews[154] and its 1963 ruling overturning South Carolina's refusal to grant unemployment compensation to a Seventh-Day Adventist unable to find employment not requiring Saturday work.[155] And while he joined the Court's decision in *West Virginia Board of Education* v. *Barnette*,[156] overturning compulsory flag programs in the public schools, he had initially joined the 1940 *Gobitis* ruling[157] upholding such programs. In *Barnette*, moreover, he explained that his earlier vote reflected a "[r]eluctance to make the Federal Constitution a rigid bar against state regulation of conduct thought inimical to the public welfare," and also condemned the compulsory "physical position" and repetition of "the words of a patriotic formula" as a "test oath," which had "always been abhorrent in the United States."[158]

His position regarding the First Amendment's guarantee of "no law respecting an establishment of religion" generally tracked that of the Court during his tenure. He seemed to agree, that is, that laws affecting religious institutions were beyond the establishment clause's reach if they had a "secular purpose" and a "primary effect" neither advancing nor harming religion.[159] At times, however, he disagreed vehemently with his brethren's application of those standards in specific contexts.

While Black authored several opinions involving the free speech claims of religious dissidents,[160] he wrote no opinion dealing with free exercise claims per se. Indeed, the Court itself decided few such cases during his tenure. He did register a number of significant establishment opinions, however, both as the Court's spokesman and in dissent. A number of his opinions for the Court aroused little dispute, at least among his colleagues. Of those participating, for example, only Justice Stewart dissented from his opinion invalidating the state-written prayer at issue in *Engel* v. *Vitale*.[161] And although Justices Frankfurter and Harlan concurred only in the result when Black held for the Court that Maryland's religious test oath for public officeholders violated the First and Fourteenth Amendments,[162] no Justice dissented or filed a separate opinion.

In a number of other issue areas, however, his position differed markedly from that of a majority or significant number of his brethren. Most controversial, perhaps, was his ruling for a majority in *Everson* v. *Board of Education*,[163] rejecting establishment and other challenges to state reimbursement of school transportation expenses to parents of children attending nonprofit private as well as public facilities. His *Everson* opinion included, of course, his now classic statement of "wall of separation" doctrine, Black observing for the Court:

> The "establishment of religion" clause of the First Amendment means at least this: Neither a state nor the Federal Government can set up a church. Neither can pass laws which aid one religion, aid all religions, or prefer one religion over another. Neither can force nor influence a person to go to or to remain away from church against his will or force him to profess a belief or disbelief in any religion. No person can be punished for entertaining or professing religious beliefs or disbeliefs, for church attendance or nonattendance. No tax in any amount, large or small, can be levied to support any religious activities or institutions, whatever they may be called, or whatever form they may adopt to teach or practice religion. Neither a state nor the Federal Government can, openly or secretly, participate in the affairs of any religious organizations or groups and *vice versa*. In the words of Jefferson, the clause against

establishment of religion by law was intended to erect "a wall of separation between church and State."[164]

He also agreed that the New Jersey reimbursement plan approached the "verge" of permissible state power.[165]

To the consternation of four colleagues, however, he rejected the contention that the challenged program violated the establishment clause. The program, he concluded, obviously helped parents send their children to parochial schools. "There [was] even a possibility that some of the children might not be sent to the church schools" without such assistance.[166] But he ultimately saw no appreciable difference between the challenged program and state provision of police, fire, sewage, and other secular services "separate and . . . indisputably marked off from the religious function."[167] To conclude that such services violate the establishment clause would go beyond the First Amendment's command that the state be "neutral in its relations with groups of religious believers and non-believers" and "require the state to be their adversary." "The First Amendment," he concluded, "has erected a wall between church and state. That wall must be kept high and impregnable. We could not approve the slightest breach. New Jersey has not breached it here."[168]

The four dissenters vehemently disagreed. Justice Jackson, joined by Justice Frankfurter, challenged Black's analogy of the reimbursement plan to programs relating to a "child's safety or expedition in traffic."[169] More fundamentally, Jackson read the program to allow reimbursement only to the parents of children attending public or Catholic schools, not "private secular schools or private religious schools of other faiths."[170] To him, such a scheme little resembled the provision of police and fire protection.

> Could we sustain an Act that said the police shall protect pupils on the way to or from public schools and Catholic schools but not while going to and coming from other schools, and firemen shall extinguish a blaze in public or Catholic school buildings but shall not put out a blaze in Protestant church schools or private schools operated for profit? That is the true analogy to the case we have before us.[171]

Justice Rutledge, joined by Frankfurter, Jackson, and Burton, also saw no parallel between the challenged reimbursement plan and the provision of services traditionally considered "matters of common right."[172] Like Jackson, moreover, Rutledge concluded that Catholic parents were being given a special benefit not extended to the parents of children attending other private schools. But Rutledge did not base his position on that relatively narrow ground alone. Instead, he viewed the reimbursement scheme as tantamount to a government subsidy of parochial schools, absolutely forbidden by the Constitution.

Rutledge's conclusion—and, presumably, Jackson's also—that the challenged reimbursements were available only to parents of children attending Catholic schools was based on pertinent school board minutes referring only to public and Catholic schools. "There is no showing," asserted Rutledge, "that there are no other private or religious schools in this populous district. I do not think it can be assumed there were none."[173] The New Jersey statute providing for the reimbursements did not limit coverage, however, only to public and Catholic schools. Its language included all nonprofit private schools. Had the parents of children attending such schools been excluded from the program, moreover, surely the taxpayer challenging it would have given that fact prominent play in his suit. A significant inference Justice Jackson drew from the statute's exclusion of for-profit schools is also difficult to accept. Jackson found "[r]efusal to reimburse those who attend such schools . . . understandable only in the light of a purpose to aid the schools, because the state might well abstain from aiding a profit-making enterprise."[174] That inference led him, in turn, to suggest that the program was designed to aid Catholic schools alone. State legislators could just have easily reasoned, however, that the parents of children attending private schools operated for profit would generally be better able to endure the financial burdens of school transportation than other parents, then tailored the reimbursement system to that assumption, just as other public benefit programs are often tied to assumed as well as established need. As Justice Rutledge indicated, police protection and fire protection, among other municipal services, are normally extended to all persons and property within a community's jurisdiction. That does not mean, though, that a state cannot limit certain services to those believed most needy.

Despite such arguable weaknesses in their perception of the issues raised, the *Everson* dissenters remained firm in their opposition, just as Justice Black remained resolute in his commitment to the decision and its rationale. In 1948 the Court voted, in *McCollum* v. *Board of Educa-*

tion,[175] to invalidate "released-time" religious instruction in the Champaign, Illinois, public schools. Justice Frankfurter, who had joined the *Everson* dissents, suggested that opinions filed for *McCollum* make no mention of the earlier ruling. Justice Black soon circulated a biting rejoinder, declaring, "I will not agree to any opinion in the *McCollum* case which does not make reference to the *Everson* case. Time has confirmed my conviction that the decision in the *Everson* case was right."[176] Ultimately, Black, joined by two *Everson* dissenters (Rutledge and Burton), authored an opinion for the *McCollum* Court which quoted from both his *Everson* opinion and Rutledge's dissent, then concluded that the Illinois program was barred under "the views expressed both by the majority and minority in the *Everson* case."[177] In a separate opinion Justice Frankfurter, joined by Justice Jackson, as well as Rutledge and Burton, observed, with an obvious eye toward *Everson*, that "the mere formulation of a relevant Constitutional principle is the beginning of the solution of a problem, not its answer."[178]

In *Zorach* v. *Clauson*,[179] upholding released-time programs conducted off school property, Justice Black again "reaffirm[ed his] faith in the fundamental philosophy" of *Everson* as well as *McCollum*.[180] On this occasion, however, he spoke in dissent from the opinion that Justice Douglas, a member of the *Everson* Court, registered for the *Zorach* majority, and Justices Frankfurter and Jackson concurred in Black's vote, if not his rationale. Emphasizing that "We are a religious people whose institutions presuppose a Supreme Being,"[181] Douglas found in the off-campus setting of the *Zorach* program a meaningful distinction between it and the scheme invalidated in *McCollum*. Extending *McCollum* to such off-campus programs would mean, asserted Douglas, "that public institutions can make no adjustments of their schedules to accommodate the religious needs of the people. We cannot read into the Bill of Rights such a philosophy of hostility to religion."[182] Black, on the other hand, saw no "significant" difference in the two programs. In both, he contended, "school authorities release some of the children on the condition that they attend religious classes, get reports on whether they attend, and hold the other children in the school building until the religious hour is over."[183]

Somewhat ironically, given his *Zorach* stance, Justice Douglas later repudiated *Everson*.[184] Justice Black never did. As his *Zorach* vote and opinion made clear, however, Black's *Everson* posture was no harbinger of a flexible position regarding the establishment clause's reach. On rare occasions after *Everson*, he joined decisions upholding governmental policies defended as promoting secular objectives while also burdening religious institutions.[185] He consistently refused, however, to condone aid to parochial schools, their students and parents, even that claimed to be secular in nature.[186] When the Court construed *Everson* to allow the loan of textbooks to parochial school students, for example, he vigorously dissented, declaring that judicial approval of

> a State's power to pay bus or streetcar fares for school children cannot provide support for the validity of a state law using tax-raised funds to buy school books for a religious school. The First Amendment's bar to establishment of religion must preclude a State from using funds levied from all of its citizens to purchase books for use by sectarian schools, which, although "secular," realistically will in some way inevitably tend to propagate the religious views of the favored sect. Books are the most essential tool of education since they contain the resources of knowledge which the educational process is designed to exploit. In this sense it is not difficult to distinguish books, which are the heart of any school, from bus fares, which provide a convenient and helpful general public transportation service. With respect to the former, state financial support actively and directly assists the teaching and propagation of sectarian religious viewpoints in clear conflict with the First Amendment's establishment bar; with respect to the latter, the State merely provides a general and nondiscriminatory transportation service in no way related to substantive religious views and beliefs.[187]

In one area in which he and the Court ultimately avoided a constitutional ruling, moreover, Black initially found another establishment violation. The Selective Service Act granted conscientious objector status only to those who opposed all war on grounds of "religious training and belief." In *United States* v. *Seeger*[188] and other Vietnam-era cases, the Court broadly construed this provision to include not only members of traditional pacifist faiths but also anyone whose opposition to war was based on a "sincere and meaningful belief which occupies in the life of its possessor a place parallel to that filled by the God of those admittedly qualifying for the exemption."[189] By following that approach and thus authorizing extension of the exemption to a wide variety of draft resisters, the Court avoided deciding whether Congress could constitutionally grant conscientious objector status to religious pacifists, while denying it to their nonreligious counterparts. Justice Black joined such decisions. In fact, he authored an opinion announcing the Court's judgment in *Welsh* v. *United States*,[190] which extended the exemption to a pacifist who, originally at least, had insisted that his opposition to war was based on "history and sociology" rather than "religious belief."[191]

According to Justice Brennan's *Seeger* notes,[192] however, Justice Black had initially argued in conference that while the government could "compel everyone to go to war whether for or against war," it would deny "equal protection" if it attempted to separate objectors on the basis of belief. He assumed essentially the same position in a *Seeger* draft concurrence[193] in which he concluded that the federal law at issue violated the First Amendment both by distinguishing between theistic and nontheistic beliefs and "by choosing between conscientious beliefs which are religious and those which are not." He had no doubt, he asserted, about the congressional power to draft "men to fight for their country whatever their views may be." But that did not mean that Congress could "run roughshod over the First Amendment by selecting the soldiers who must do the dangerous fighting on the basis of whether or not they are religious persons."

Even Black's establishment position reflected, however, his support of broad governmental authority over the use of public property. Consider especially his concurrence in *Epperson* v. *Arkansas*,[194] the 1968 case striking down a state law forbidding the teaching of evolution in the public schools. The Court, per Justice Fortas, held that the statute's "sole" purpose was exclusion from the school curriculum of an account of the origins of man deemed to conflict with the fundamentalist religious version. Black concurred in the Court's decision, but reluctantly and only on the ground that the Arkansas "monkey law" was unconstitutionally vague. He was doubtful that the suit, a declaratory judgment action brought by a Little Rock teacher, presented a "genuinely justiciable case or controversy," especially since the state had never attempted to enforce it and a biology text adopted for the Little Rock schools devoted an entire chapter to evolution.

Foreshadowing his *Tinker* dissent, he also raised more fundamental concerns about "federal intrusion into state powers" over public school curricula. Questioning Fortas's conclusion that the challenged statute was designed to assure "that the Book of Genesis must be the exclusive source of doctrine as to the origin of man,"[195] Black pointed out that Arkansas's highest court had not given the law that interpretation, then asserted that the state may simply have wished to remove an "emotional and controversial subject" entirely from the curriculum of its public schools.[196] He had no doubt of the state's power to take such action.

> It is plain that a state law prohibiting all teaching of human development or biology is constitutionally quite different from a law that compels a teacher to teach as true only one theory of a given doctrine. It would be difficult to make a First Amendment case out of a state law eliminating the subject of higher mathematics, or astronomy, or biology from its curriculum. And . . . this particular Act may prohibit that and nothing else. This Court, however, treats the Arkansas Act as though it made it a misdemeanor to teach or to use a book that teaches that evolution is true.[197]

Since there was "no indication" that the Genesis account of man's origins was being taught in the Arkansas schools, the bar against the teaching of evolution, suggested Black, simply placed "the State in a neutral position toward these supposedly competing religious and anti-religious doctrines."[198] Before finding an impermissible intent behind the law, he added, the Court should remand the case to the state courts for clarification or limit its ruling to the vagueness issue.

Finally, as he was to make clear the following year in *Tinker*, Black was "not ready to hold that a person hired to teach school children takes with him into the classroom a constitutional right to teach . . . subjects that the school's managers do not want discussed."[199] Nor, despite the Court's assumption, could he agree that "academic freedom" permitted such a breach of a teacher's contract, or that the Court could so intrude upon school policy. "However wise this Court may be or may become hereafter," he asserted, "it is doubtful that, sitting in Washington, it can successfully supervise and censor the curriculum of every public school in every hamlet and city in the United States. I doubt that our wisdom is so nearly infallible."[200]

Five Black's First Amendment Critics

JUSTICE Black's interpretation of the religion clauses has been subjected to little critical analysis not forming part of attacks on his broader First Amendment jurisprudence. That broader philosophy, however, has drawn extensive critical comment, to which we now turn.

The Consistency of Black's Position

One theme of such critiques is the charge that the Justice was not consistent in his First Amendment philosophy or its application. Certain critics have contrasted the tone and substance of his stance in the protest cases of the 1960s with his position and opinions in earlier cases, especially those involving picketing, handbilling, and other forms of speech-related conduct. At least one of Black's more systematic critics has gone further. In the most thorough critique of the Justice's First Amendment thinking yet to appear,[1] Professor James Magee has argued (1) that Black did not embrace an absolutist interpretation of the First Amendment for more than a decade after his appointment to the bench, (2) that he initially was a balancer, even in cases involving what he later would call "direct" and absolutely forbidden abridgments of First Amendment freedoms, (3) that the dichotomies (speech/conduct, direct/indirect burdens) so prominent in his opinions in the later protest cases were part of an effort to accommodate his latter-day absolutism to issues not amenable to absolutist review, thereby giving an appearance of internal and longitudinal consistency to his First Amendment jurisprudence, and (4) that such dichotomies were not truly evident in his approach to earlier cases involving speech-related conduct.

Directed at a Justice who prided himself—with ample justification, some would say—on the consistency of his jurisprudence, Professor Magee's charges are extremely serious, amounting almost to an assertion that Black was a liar, and a manipulative, calculating liar at that. They thus must be subjected to close scrutiny. To assess them as well as more general claims of inconsistency in the Justice's earlier and later positions regarding speech-related conduct and the power of government over public property, I shall first examine what I consider to be conclusive evidence of Black's early absolutism, evidence Magee overlooked, then review the evidence Magee presents in support of his position, and finally assess the more general claims of Magee and others that, whatever the nature of Black's First Amendment jurisprudence early and late in his career, the tone and substance of the Justice's position regarding speech-related conduct changed over time.

The evidence of the Justice's early absolutism which Magee failed to consider is the "fierce dissent," as Justice Frankfurter termed it,[2] which Black originally drafted for *Bridges* v. *California*. Speaking ultimately for a majority in the case, it will be recalled, Black invoked a broad reading of the clear and present danger doctrine to overturn the contemptuous publication convictions at issue there and in *Times-Mirror*. But he also asserted that earlier cases applying the clear and present danger test did "not purport to mark the furthermost constitutional boundaries of protected expression, nor do we here," and that the earlier cases reflected only "a minimum compulsion of the Bill of Rights," adding: "[T]he First Amendment does not speak equivocally. It prohibits any law 'abridging the freedom of speech, or of the press.' It must be taken as a command of the broadest scope that explicit language, read in the context of a liberty-loving society, will allow."[3] As he began publicly to reject the clear and present danger standard and overtly embrace absolutism, Black cited this language.[4] Particularly in view of his status as the Court's spokesman in *Bridges*, it is reasonably strong, if indirect, evidence that, even by the time *Bridges* was decided, Black had already begun to give the First Amendment an absolutist meaning.

But the *Bridges* and *Times-Mirror* dissent Black originally drafted, when Justice Frankfurter had a narrow majority for rejecting the First Amendment claims at issue there, conclusively demonstrates, in my judgment, that Black had already embraced absolutism when *Bridges* and *Times-Mirror* were decided.[5] In his excellent analysis of the "constitutional faiths" of Black and Frankfurter, Mark Silverstein concludes that "[a]lthough Black did not characterize the First Amendment as an absolute in his *Bridges* dissent, that conclusion pervades the entire opinion."[6] Indeed it does. In fact, the opinion is overwhelmingly absolutist in tone. At one point, for example, Black observed:

> [T]he First Amendment was written in the form of a command so clear, so unequivocal, and so pervasive in its expressions and implications that it is impossible to deny that those who drafted it intended to mark off an inviolable area and dedicate it to the liberties there enumerated. It may be true that there are no such things as absolute liberties. It may be true that newspapers and others take undue and mischievous advantage of the privileges granted them by the Constitution. But even if the newspapers were guilty of all the offenses to which they have sometimes been accused, it was the theory of those responsible for our Bill of Rights that in the last analysis the solution would lie in censorship by public opinion rather than in censorship by a court of law.

The fundamentally absolutist thrust of this passage is unmistakable: any limitation on the freedoms granted by the First Amendment could constitutionally be imposed only by "public opinion," not by government.

Even though Black apparently circulated his dissent in an effort to break the Frankfurter coalition which initially prevailed, the opinion abounds with other such statements. One passage is particularly significant given Black's later use, as the Court's spokesman, of the clear and present danger test to overrule the convictions at issue in *Bridges* and *Times-Mirror*. "[S]ince the Court [had] held that the states do have the power to abridge freedom of expression in matters which relate to causes pending in courts," he urged that such power be allowed "only when hedged about and safeguarded to the utmost extent consistent with the permitted abridgement." Earlier cases had concluded that publications could be cited for contempt if they had a "tendency" to interfere with the administration of justice. Citing "the value of the constitutional liberties that are abridged," Black pressed his brethren to rule instead "that state courts should never punish for contempt in such cases unless there was found to be a clear and present danger of an immediate interference which could not be averted without the imposition of punishment." Black ultimately persuaded a majority to apply such a standard and reverse the state courts. As his draft dissent indicates, however, he embraced the clear and present danger test only because his colleagues were convinced "that the states do have the power to abridge freedom of expression."

In defending his thesis Magee cites Black's reliance on the clear and present danger doctrine in *Bridges* as well as subsequent contempt-by-publication cases the Justice joined.[7] Particularly in light of Black's draft *Bridges* dissent, such cases would appear of dubious value as evidence that the early Black was no absolutist. Instead, they most likely indicate only that Black was willing to submerge his own doctrinal preferences, especially those shared entirely by no other Justice, so long as an approach more appealing to his colleagues led the majority to the same result his absolutist jurisprudence would require. Had Black voted even once for the government in such cases, a different interpretation might be in order. But Black, of course, invariably voted to uphold the rights of the press against citations for contemptuous publication.

Magee's other evidence is also vulnerable to challenge. One of his citations seems to ignore what Magee obviously realized—though the Justice's widow apparently concluded he did not[8]—that Black considered only certain provisions of the Constitution, not all of them, to embody absolute commands. Magee contends that the Court's decision in the *Korematsu* case,[9] upholding, per Black, military sanctions imposed against Japanese-Americans, "evolved through judicial reasoning which could hardly be that of a judge preoccupied with the conviction that his official duty demands the absolute protection of civil rights."[10] *Korematsu* obviously did not reflect absolutist thinking. But neither did any of Black's other equal protection opinions, early or late in his career. Outside the field of racial discrimination, in fact, Justice Black was generally very deferential to government in equal protection cases, as the concluding chapter to this book amply demonstrates. Moreover, the Justice never assumed an absolutist construction of the equal protection guarantee even in racial cases. Magee's references to *Korematsu* thus misperceive both the scope of Black's absolutism and the nature of his equal protection philosophy. During his 1968 television interview, Black reiterated his belief that "there are 'absolutes' in our Bill of Rights," but emphasized that he had never said "that our entire Bill of Rights is an absolute."[11] Certainly, he did not consider the entire Constitution—or especially its equal protection clause—an absolute.

Magee's use of the Justice's stance in two citizenship cases as evidence that the early Black did not embrace absolutism is equally unpersuasive. Black's conception of Congress's power over U.S. citizenship could in a sense be termed absolutist. Speaking for the Court in *Afroyim* v. *Rusk* (1967),[12] it will be recalled, he concluded that Congress had no power to expatriate a citizen. During his last term, moreover, he dissented when a majority, in *Rogers* v. *Bellei*,[13] distinguished *Afroyim* and upheld a provision of federal naturalization law providing that persons who acquire citizenship by virtue of having been born abroad of citizen parents "shall lose" that citizenship by failing to comply with a residency requirement. "[T]he Fourteenth Amendment," he asserted, "has put citizenship, once conferred, beyond the power of Congress to revoke."[14]

Magee contrasts Black's *Bellei* dissent with the Justice's stance in *Knauer* v. *United States*,[15] a 1946 decision upholding cancellation of the citizenship papers of an enemy spy who had obtained them through fraud.[16] In a *Knauer* concurrence Black cited "the dangers inherent in denaturalizations," but was "unable to say that Congress is without constitutional power to authorize courts, after fair trials like this one, to cancel citizenship obtained by the methods and for the purposes shown by this record."[17] Magee agrees that "*Knauer* and *Bellei* are fundamentally different cases," that the "difference is substantial," and "Justice Black's vote in *Knauer* . . . justifiable and not unpersuasive."[18] He contends, however, that *Knauer* lacked the "absolutist language" on which Black's "reasoning and denunciation of the majority opinion" in *Bellei* was based, adding, "[Black's] willingness to make an exception [in *Knauer*], even though in the case of one who fraudulently acquires his citizenship, stands to refute the view that he was an absolutist. An absolutist makes no exception, even in times of national peril."[19]

Justice Black's two-paragraph *Knauer* concurrence does indeed recognize national authority to "cancel citizenship obtained" by fraud. Viewed in the context of the *Knauer* case and the law at issue there, however, the Justice's opinion is entirely compatible with what Magee terms the "absolutist" position he assumed in *Afroyim* and *Bellei*. One who seeks to obtain citizenship by fraud in truth never acquires that citizenship, just as nothing is ever legally acquired by fraud. Knauer was thus not being stripped of his citizenship. The courts were simply concluding that he had never legally acquired it. The language of the law at issue in *Knauer* makes clear the case's true nature, for it authorized judicial proceedings "for the purpose of revoking and setting aside the order admitting such person to citizenship and canceling the certificate of naturalization on the ground of fraud or on the ground that such order and certificate of naturalization were illegally procured."[20] In short, citizenship papers were being set aside, not Knauer's citizenship—a citizenship he never legally had and thus never had. Black's joining such a decision, therefore, is hardly inconsistent with his contention in *Bellei* that citizenship, "once conferred," cannot be withdrawn. Under the regulation at issue in *Bellei*, on the other hand, persons acquiring citizenship by virtue of their parent's citizenship were citizens from birth, the law providing merely that they would "lose" that citizenship if they failed to meet the residency requirement.

Of course, in one sense *Knauer* does have some bearing on Justice Black's First Amendment views. Had the judgment against Knauer rested on the petitioner's "mere philosophical or political beliefs," Black asserted in his concurrence in the case, the Justice would not have voted as he did. He was convinced, however, that the government's action was based on Knauer's "conduct."[21]

Magee also finds inconsistencies between Black's absolutism and his willingness to join early opinions recognizing exceptions to protected expression.[22] Obviously, the Justice did join such opinions, but their weight as support for Magee's position is more apparent than real. Nearest to Magee's point is *Chaplinsky* v. *New Hampshire*,[23] the 1942 case upholding state power to punish face-to-face verbal assaults. Black joined *Chaplinsky*, in which Justice Murphy observed for a unanimous Court:

> Allowing the broadest scope to the language and purpose of the Fourteenth Amendment [making the First applicable to state governments], it is well understood that the right of free speech is not absolute at all times and under all circumstances. There are certain well-defined and narrowly limited classes of speech, the prevention and punishment of which have never been thought to raise any Constitutional problem. These include the lewd and the obscene, the profane, the libelous, and the insulting or "fighting" words— those which by their very utterance inflict injury or tend to incite an immediate breach of the peace. It has been well observed that such utterances are no essential part of any exposition of ideas, and

are of such slight social value as a step to truth that any benefit that may be derived from them is clearly outweighed by the social interest in order and morality.[24]

Such broad language was obviously unnecessary, however, to the Court's decision. *Chaplinsky* upheld a statute prohibiting verbal assaults with offensive, derisive, or annoying words, but the New Hampshire Supreme Court had construed it to reach only words "likely to provoke the average person to retaliation," and the case involved a face-to-face verbal assault. In fact, Justice Jackson wrote of *Chaplinsky* at the time, "The Constitution does not include a right to brawl and that's about all that seems to be involved."[25]

Black plainly viewed *Chaplinsky* in that narrow light. He wrote on a draft of Murphy's opinion in the case, "I agree and think you have shown much wisdom in deciding the case with such restraint."[26] Shortly before his death, however, he said that he had not fully formulated his First Amendment views when *Chaplinsky* was decided and that, in any event, he had joined the decision because he saw the case as one in which the speech in question was merely part of a course of conduct. He also noted the obvious—that, like other judges, he did not necessarily subscribe to all the language in every opinion he joined or, at least as the Court's spokesman, wrote.[27] Even during the period when Magee would consider him an absolutist, moreover, the Justice did not repudiate *Chaplinsky*. In fact, during his last term on the Court, he joined a dissent in which Justice Blackmun cited *Chaplinsky* as support for the proposition that government had power to penalize behavior which "was mainly conduct and little speech." The occasion was the Court's decision of *Cohen* v. *California*,[28] in which a majority overturned the breach-of-peace conviction of a young man who carried a jacket bearing an offensive slogan into the corridor of a courtroom. I view Black's *Cohen* stance as more consistent with his treatment of the breach-of-peace issue in *Brown* v. *Louisiana*, the library sit-in case, than with *Chaplinsky*. But the fact that Professor Magee's latter-day absolutist Black would continue to embrace *Chaplinsky* is hardly helpful to the case's status as evidence that the early Justice was not an absolutist. It simply raises questions about the nature and limits of the Justice's absolutism, early and late in his career.

Except for Justice Murphy's reference to the "social interest in . . . morality," his allusions in *Chaplinsky* to types of expression excluded from the First Amendment's protection could be limited to the case's specific context—face-to-face verbal assaults, which can take the form, after all, of "the lewd and the obscene, the profane, [and] the libelous," as well as the "insulting or 'fighting' words." But Black also joined later opinions assuming governmental authority to penalize obscenity and libel. Citing such cases, Magee asserts:

> The absolutist Justice Black of the 1950s and 1960s hardly ever joined the Court's opinions in libel and obscenity cases: instead, he characteristically wrote a separate opinion in each case—even when he agreed with the Court's result—spelling out his interpretation of the First Amendment. In the 1940s Justice Black is found agreeing—at least by silent consent—that libel and obscenity are not protected forms of expression.[29]

To what cases, however, does Magee refer? One held that the postmaster general had no statutory power to prescribe standards for the literature or art which a mailable (that is, non-obscene) periodical disseminates, or to determine whether the periodical's contents meet some standard of the public good or public welfare.[30] Another struck down as unconstitutionally vague a state statute penalizing the distribution of magazines tending to incite violent crimes.[31] The third was *Pennekamp* v. *Florida*,[32] in which the Court reversed yet another post-*Bridges* contempt-by-publication conviction, but explained that a judge who is the victim of a defamation can seek civil damages. In none of these cases did the Court uphold the government regulation at issue or even discuss what sorts of publications could constitutionally be penalized as "obscene" or "libelous." When the Court first upheld a libel law in *Beauharnais* v. *Illinois*, Black immediately cited the First Amendment as an absolute bar against such legislation.[33] When the Court began to define obscenity and uphold obscenity controls, he promptly took the same course in that field,[34] just as he did when the Court began to uphold Smith Act prosecutions of Communist advocacy and membership,[35] as well as other "direct" interferences with First Amendment freedoms. Without citing his source, Magee asserts that the nonabsolutist Black of the 1940s "was among the majority who denied certiorari" in *Dunne* v. *United States*[36] "and thereby upheld the provisions of the Smith Act,"[37] in marked contrast to his later absolutist dissent in the *Dennis* case. In his autobiography, however, Justice Douglas stated that "Black voted to grant" certiorari in the *Dunne* case.[38]

Magee does refer to two cases from the 1940s in which Black voted to uphold government controls over publications. In *Donaldson* v. *Read Magazine*[39] the Court, per Black, upheld a fraud order of the postmaster general directing that mail sent to *Facts Magazine* from participants in a "puzzle contest" be returned to the sender marked "Fraudulent" and that postal money orders sent to the magazine in connection with the contest also be returned to participants. *Valentine* v. *Chrestensen*,[40] as noted earlier, recognized the commercial-speech exception to protected expression. Magee considers each case further evidence that the Justice eschewed absolutism through the forties. Each clearly fits, however, within the contours of Black's assertion, early and late in his judicial career, that speech which is an integral part of other, unprotected conduct enjoys no direct First Amendment protection. Published descriptions of the "contest" at issue in *Read Magazine* were found to be intentionally deceptive.

> First, . . . prospective contestants were falsely led to believe that they might be eligible to win prizes upon payment of $3 as a maximum sum when in reality the minimum requirement was $9, and as it later developed they were finally called on to pay as much as $42 to be eligible for increased prize offers. Second, . . . it was not [actually] a puzzle contest; . . . respondents knew from experience that the puzzles were so easy that many people would solve all the "puzzles" and that prizes would be awarded only as a result of a tie-breaking letter-essay contest; and . . . contestants were deliberately misled concerning all these facts by artfully composed advertisements.[41]

Citing such findings, Black found not "the slightest support" for the contention that the First Amendment included "complete freedom, uncontrollable by Congress, to use the mails for perpetration of swindling schemes."[42] Commercial advertisements of the sort at issue in *Valentine* are also invariably part of what advertisers hope, at least, will be a course of conduct culminating in an exchange of money.

The Court upheld the order at issue in *Read Magazine*, it should be added, only after reargument and the government's limitation of the order purely to mail and money orders relating to the fraudulent puzzle contest. Justice Black's concern about the breadth of the order's language, moreover, was apparently the principal catalyst behind the decision to order reargument. After initial argument and a conference vote upholding the order, Black was assigned to write the Court's opinion. Instead, he wrote Chief Justice Vinson a lengthy letter.[43] "The only question discussed at Conference and in the Government brief," he noted, "was whether there was sufficient evidence to support the Postmaster General's finding that respondent had been using the mails to obtain money by fraudulent practices or representations." That question obviously had given Black no difficulty. But he had now decided that the order, "as written," raised First Amendment and related constitutional problems, and he recommended that Vinson schedule additional argument on that issue. Only after reargument and assurance that the order's scope was limited purely to the magazine's "swindling scheme" did Black reaffirm his original vote in the case.

Professor Magee also sees a fundamental inconsistency between Black's willingness in *Read Magazine* to uphold regulations penalizing "deception of the public" through publications and the Justice's opposition to all governmental controls over "calculated falsehoods designed to ruin reputations."[44] The issues were different, however, not the Justice's position. A libelous statement obviously may result in serious damage to its victim. But one who commits a libel inflicts injury only by words. Where words are part of an attempt to commit a fraud, as they almost invariably are, those words are simply part of a broader attempted course of conduct—specifically, an effort to secure money or some other thing of value under false pretenses, as in *Read Magazine*. The same thing is inevitably true of the usual commercial advertisement and, for that matter, of conspiracies to commit murder. Those involved may get no further than words, or they may actually secure money or engage in other conduct, as the *Read Magazine* respondents did. Unlike those who commit libel or slander, however, persons seeking to commit a fraud or sell a product through advertising are involved in a broader anticipated or executed course of conduct than the mere recitation of words. For one of Justice Black's jurisprudential persuasion, early and late in his tenure, this was the constitutionally crucial distinction between activities of the sort sanctioned in a *Read Magazine* or *Valentine* and the attacks of one who commits a libel or slander—even though, in any given case, the latter may cause significantly greater injury than the former. A *Read Magazine* or *Valentine* would be more analogous to a libel or slander suit were those involved simply to publish an advertisement, but neither seek nor accept money. But that, of course, never occurs in such situations. The words used are inevitably mere incidents of a broader course of conduct.

Finally, there is Professor Magee's assertion that the clear-cut speech/conduct, direct/indirect dichotomies Justice Black drew in the later protest cases were part of an effort to accommodate his latter-day absolutist philosophy to issues not susceptible to such analysis and were not truly evident in his votes and opinions in earlier cases involving labor picketing, handbilling, and similar forms of speech-related conduct. As indicated previously, Black cited these earlier cases as evidence that he had long drawn such dichotomies and was willing to balance competing interests in litigation challenging indirect burdens on First Amendment liberties, including controls over speech-related conduct and access to public property. Magee argues, however, that Black did not really recognize the speech/conduct, direct/indirect distinctions in the earlier cases and that he pursued a balancing approach in such cases even when the regulation at issue imposed what the Justice considered to be "direct" burdens on protected expression. Magee writes:

> [Black's] undisguised [early] record as a balancer who had protected some forms of symbolic expression (especially labor picketing), his later desire at least to seem consistent with his past, and the practical need to restrict the reaches of his absolutism are all factors that help to explain why in the 1960s Justice Black sought refuge in the hidden meaning of his unarticulated dichotomies. They were created to set practical limits to his newly acquired absolutist stance on First Amendment issues; they were concepts devised to manipulate and manage this absolutism through a web of unanticipated problems and also to establish some basis for the belief that his doctrinal approach to free speech cases had never changed.[45]

Magee further asserts that, "[s]trangely enough," I acknowledged "as much" in a 1974 article examining Justice Black's stance in speech-plus and symbolic speech cases.[46] My study concluded that, except in tone, Black's position in such cases was remarkably consistent early and late in his career. It would thus have been strange indeed for me to accept an assessment of Black's position at all comparable to Professor Magee's. Magee bases his assumption on my observation that the dichotomies Black drew reflected "the only position that he could have adopted and still remain faithful to his absolutist first amendment philosophy."[47] He also notes the italicized portion of my further assertion that "Black balanced interests in cases involving what he viewed as indirect burdens on first amendment freedoms in order to retain *absolutism in certain first amendment contexts*, to allow states ample power to control speech-related conduct, and to insure 'the complete protection of First Amendment freedoms even against purely incidental or inadvertent consequences.'"[48] But these statements contain not the slightest hint of a suggestion that the Justice developed and applied such dichotomies *only late* in his career, much less the view that they were part of an effort "to manipulate and manage [his] absolutism through a web of unanticipated problems" and provide "some basis" for his claim to doctrinal consistency. In fact, the whole thrust of the article was entirely in the contrary direction. Nor could I have ever agreed that Black's dichotomies were a desperate afterthought. A judge as longheaded as Hugo Black could never have developed an absolutist interpretation of the First Amendment—at whatever stage of his career—without anticipating the sorts of rather obvious problems the later protest cases would raise. Except in degree and frequency after all, such problems confronted the Court throughout his tenure, including the period in which Magee believes that the Justice was developing his absolutist philosophy.

Magee's reading of Justice Black's position in early First Amendment cases is almost as dubious. As already noted, the absolutist dissent the Justice initially drafted in *Bridges* deals a serious—in my view, fatal—blow to Magee's basic premise that the early Black was not an absolutist. A close reading of the Justice's opinions and conference remarks in the early picketing and handbill cases demonstrates that Black also embraced, early as well as late in his career, his speech/conduct and direct/indirect dichotomies Magee largely finds only in the Justice's reactions to the sixties protest cases. Admittedly, the distinctions were not as obviously drawn in the early years. Black's more distinctive delineation of them in the later protest cases arguably reflects, however, not a basic change in his First Amendment jurisprudence, but rather the growing urgency of the Justice's concern, in an era of mass protest movements, that the people understand the amendment's limits as well as its reach—a concern which, if entertained at all, he could hardly have considered pressing in earlier years, when the Court's speech-plus caseload was confined mainly to isolated labor picketing and handbilling cases.

Apart from this difference in emphasis, Black's dichotomies are clearly evident in the earlier cases. He did join Justice Murphy's opinion in *Thornhill* v. *Alabama*,[49] the 1940 case which broadly assimilated picketing to free speech. But a jurist obviously does not necessarily subscribe to every part of any opinion from which he chooses not to register an objection. As Murphy's biographer has pointed out, moreover, "[t]he *Thornhill* opinion contained something for everyone."[50] In later years Black would emphasize the overbreadth of the statute at issue in the case,[51] and when *Thornhill* was under review, he underlined on his copy of Murphy's opinion the following passage from the law at issue: "Any . . . who, without just cause or legal excuse . . . go near to . . . for the purpose or with the intent of influencing, or inducing other persons not to . . . be employed by such persons. . . . "[52] Furthermore, the language and approach of his own opinions were quite similar to his stance in the later protest cases. In *Carpenters Union* v. *Ritter's Cafe* (1942)[53] for example, he observed in dissent:

> It is one thing for a state to regulate the use of its streets and highways so as to keep them open and available for movement of people and property. . . ; or to pass general regulations as to their use in the interest of public safety, peace, comfort, or convenience . . . , or to protect its citizens from violence and breaches of the peace by those who are upon them. . . . It is quite another thing, however, to "abridge the constitutional liberty of one rightfully upon the street to impart information through speech or the distribution of literature. . . . " . . . The court below did not rest the restraints imposed on these petitioners upon the state's exercise of its permissible powers to regulate the use of its streets or the conduct of those rightfully upon them. Instead, it barred the petitioners from using the streets to convey information to the public, because of the particular type of information they wished to convey. In so doing, it directly restricted the petitioners' rights to express themselves publicly concerning an issue which we recognized in the *Thornhill* case to be of public importance. It imposed the restriction for the reason that the public's response to such information would result in injury to a particular person's business, a reason we said in the *Thornhill* case was insufficient to justify curtailment of free expression.[54]

Professor Magee cites the latter portion of this passage as evidence that the early Black was willing to balance competing interests even in cases involving a "direct" burden on protected expression. When Magee wrote, however, he was unaware of the absolutist dissent Black had initially drafted in the *Bridges* case. That dissent and Black's later willingness to invoke the clear and present danger doctrine as the Court's spokesman in *Bridges* indicate that, by the time *Ritter's Cafe* was decided, Black had made a tactical decision to postpone a public avowal of his absolutist philosophy. Nor is the likely basis for that decision difficult to fathom. Absolutism, after all, was a doctrine no other Justice entirely accepted. Black could hardly have felt pressed to pursue such a controversial position, moreover, in an era in which his side in First Amendment cases prevailed much more frequently than it was to in the 1950s, when he often wrote in solitary or near-solitary dissent and a public espousal of his absolutist philosophy had little impact on the outcome of particular cases or the maintenance of voting coalitions.

For one mindful of the *Bridges* dissent, the Justice's *Ritter's Cafe* opinion seems very compatible with those he was to register in the later protest cases. In it he recognizes the power of states to control the use of public property, but concludes that the injunction at issue in the case was granted because of the views the picketers were expressing rather than out of concern for free movement on the public streets and walkways. At one point, in fact, he asserted that the injunction "was granted not because of any law directly aimed at picketing—Texas has no statute against picketing as such—nor to prevent violence, breach of the peace, or congestion of the streets."[55] In conference, according to Justice Murphy's notes, Black had assumed the same stance. Noting that a state has a "right to preserve order" and citing the "great difference between a narrow[ly] drawn statute aimed directly at an evil" and an injunction "that violates free speech," he observed, "If Texas had a statute narrowly drawn, aimed at suppression of picketing I would not have this difficulty. I think there is [a] difference between law [the injunction] that fits [a] particular case and a general policy which covers everybody."[56]

Since the injunction was selective, directed only at certain picketers, rather than a general ban on the obstruction of public passages, Black found it a "direct" interference with the First Amendment, just as he would condemn the selective ban at issue years later in *Cox v. Louisiana*. As Magee has noted, Black did not then declare that such burdens are absolutely forbidden. Instead, he concluded that the injunction was based on "a reason which we said in the *Thornhill* case was insufficient to justify curtailment of free expression."[57] To consider this isolated statement evidence that the early Black was no absolutist even in cases involving "direct" abridgments of protected expression requires one, however, to ignore the Justice's *Bridges* dissent, the obvious fact that an effective dissenter in a close (five-four) case would seek to bottom his vote on precedent rather than on a philosophy unacceptable to any colleague, and the equally obvious fact that Douglas and Murphy—neither of whom embraced absolutism—joined Black's dissent. It must again be noted, of course, that in *Ritter's Cafe*, as in every other early case in which the Justice found a "direct" infringement of the First Amendment, Black voted against the government. Had Magee been able to cite even one case to the contrary, one could more easily accept his basic thesis. But he found none.

Black's 1941 dissent in *Milk Wagon Drivers Union* v. *Meadowmoor Dairies, Inc.*[58] also reflected the dichotomies he was to emphasize in the later protest cases. There, the dairy had secured an injunction against further picketing of its facilities by union members and others involved in a labor dispute which had been permeated with beatings, window smashings, bombings, and arson. The trial court enjoined only acts of violence, but the state supreme court had substantially enlarged the decree's scope, prohibiting the defendants from "interfering, hindering or otherwise discouraging or diverting, or attempting to interfere with, hinder, discourage or divert persons desirous of or contemplating purchasing milk and creams or other products, including the use of . . . signs, banners or placards, and walking up and down in front of said stores. . . , and further preventing the deliveries to said stores of other articles which said stores sell through retail; [or] from threatening in any manner to do the foregoing acts." In a dissent from a decision upholding the injunction, Black, joined by Douglas as in *Ritter's Cafe*, found this language fatally overbroad, potentially forbidding those enjoined to "speak, write or publish anything anywhere or at any time which the Illinois court . . . might conclude would result in discouraging people from buying milk products of the complaining dairy."[59] Applying the clear and present danger variation of the balancing test, he also concluded that, despite the violent aspects of the labor dispute, the picketing at issue had been peaceful, creating no imminent danger sufficient to justify "an abridgment of the rights of freedom of speech and the press."[60] Clearly, however, he was not broadly incorporating picketing or a right of access to public property into the First Amendment's meaning. In language foreshadowing his opinions in the protest cases of the sixties, he agreed that "a state has the power to adopt laws of general application to provide that the streets shall be used for the purpose for which they primarily exist, and because the preservation of peace and order is one of the first duties of government."[61] He was simply emphasizing, as he would in the later protest cases, "that local laws ostensibly passed pursuant to this admittedly possessed general power could not be enforced in such a way as to amount to a prior censorship on freedom of expression, or to abridge that freedom as to those rightfully and lawfully on the streets."[62]

Black took the same position in *Bakery & Pastry Drivers and Helpers* v. *Wohl*,[63] decided the following term. The *Wohl* Court overturned an antipicketing injunction which a trial court had based on the theory that the picketing at issue involved no "labor dispute"—and thus no constitutional rights which the injunction could infringe. With an eye obviously toward the trial court's rationale, Black contended in conference that the challenged injunction was "not aimed at picketing as such," but at "freedom of speech."[64] Later he joined a concurrence in which Justice Douglas condemned the trial court's censorial approach but also observed that "Picketing by an organized group is more than free speech, since it involves patrol of a particular locality and since the very presence of a picket may induce action of one kind or another, quite irrespective of the nature of the ideas which are being disseminated. . . . [T]hose aspects of picketing make it the subject of restrictive regulation."[65]

An unfiled concurring opinion the Justice drafted for *Cox* v. *New Hampshire*[66] bears mentioning as well. In *Cox* the Court upheld an ordinance requiring those who wished to conduct assemblies, parades, or processions to secure a permit. Chief Justice Hughes's original opinion for the Court stressed the reasonableness of the permit system. Concerned about Hughes's basic premise that the Court could rule on the reasonableness of statutes, Black drafted a concurrence bottoming his vote on the "literal language of the First Amendment." That language, he asserted, was "clear, unambiguous and unequivocal," and it did not forbid a state to regulate access to public property. In his judgment the Court should announce that judgment and go no further.

I hesitate to enter into a discussion as to what our course should be if there had been a denial or abridgment of these rights but only to the extent that we believe reasonable or warranted. And upon the same basis I hesitate to discuss the reasonableness of a state's exertion of power in connection with a subject admitted to be within its province—to regulate public parades on the street. Fully realizing the difficulties involved in enforcing observance of these constitutional privileges in instances where they apparently clashed with other exertions of power, I am still not persuaded that invocation of the word "reasonable" offers a solution to the problem. Standards of reasonableness vary according to individual views. The broad and I might say limitless range within the area of differing concepts of the word "reasonable" cause[s] me to fear its use in relation to the cherished privileges intended to be guaranteed by the First Amendment.[67]

Black also shared his concerns in a letter to the Chief Justice. "If your opinion were amended so as to eliminate discussion as to reasonableness," he wrote, "I can agree. Otherwise it will be necessary for me to write a special concurrence."[68] Acknowledging that he had "used the word 'reasonable'" in his opinion "out of abundant caution," Hughes readily agreed to delete the language Black found offensive and the draft concurrence was never circulated.[69]

In agreeing to the deletions Black had recommended, Justice Frankfurter expressed amusement that the revised version of the Court's opinion recognized "a broader power . . . [for] states to make inroads on 'civil liberties' than" Hughes's original draft would have allowed—a stricture Frankfurter was very happy to accept.[70] Although a perceptive policy assessment, Frankfurter's observation suggests an erroneous assumption that Black's First Amendment jurisprudence flowed ultimately from his colleague's liberalism rather than his interpretivist commitment to the amendment's language—a commitment Black embraced early as well as late in his career. What Black's stance in *Cox* does clearly indicate is that the early Black, like the later Justice, did not include a right to parade or obtain access to public property within the First Amendment's direct meaning. In cases decided before and after *Cox*, he did agree that the indirect burdens on protected expression such regulations impose may be subjected to a balancing of competing interests. Balancing, like the clear and present danger doctrine, is simply a reasonableness approach cloaked in other language. The Justice's draft *Cox* concurrence thus seems inconsistent with his acceptance of balancing in other cases contemporary with *Cox*, as well as in the later protest cases. But his *Cox* concurrence hardly suggests that the early Black was less likely to draw clearcut distinctions between protected speech and unprotected conduct than was the later Justice.

Black also drew such distinctions, as noted previously, in early handbill cases. In *Schneider* v. *Irvington*[71] and other such cases, the Court struck down permit schemes that gave police discretion "to determine, as a censor, what literature may be distributed . . . and who may distribute it,"[72] while subjecting absolute bans on handbilling to a balancing test. In *Schneider*, for example, the Court concluded that First Amendment interests affected by a ban on the distribution of handbills outweighed the interest in the prevention of litter the state had advanced in the ordinance's defense. Black's opinions in handbill cases followed closely the balancing approach utilized in *Schneider*. Speaking for the Court in *Martin* v. *Struthers*,[73] for example, he overturned the conviction of a Jehovah's Witness who violated an ordinance forbidding door-to-door distributors of handbills to ring doorbells, knock on doors, or otherwise summon residents. Balancing asserted community interests against the appellant's interest in freedom of expression and the individual householder's right to decide whether to receive a message, Black stressed that "[d]oor to door distribution of circulars is essential to the poorly financed causes of little people."[74]

Although some of Black's language in the handbill cases seems to conflict with his support in the later protest cases of broad governmental power over the use of property, close analysis suggests that any inconsistency is more apparent than real. In *Jamison* v. *Texas*,[75] for example, the Justice appeared to reject a city's contention "that its power over its streets is not limited to the making of reasonable regulations for the control of traffic and the maintenance of order, but that it has the power absolutely to prohibit the use of the streets for the communication of ideas."[76] Elsewhere in his opinion, however, he made it clear that he was referring only to the "communication of ideas by handbills . . . literature [and] the spoken word." More significantly, he stated that the freedom to communicate ideas in public was limited to "one who is rightfully on a street which the state has left open to the public."[77]

But there is even more compelling evidence from the handbill cases that the early Black distinguished protected speech from unprotected conduct, direct from indirect burdens on protected expression, and controls over speech from controls over access to public and private property and its use. Originally, Black had drafted an opinion for a five-four majority upholding the handbilling ordinance ultimately invalidated in *Martin* v. *Struthers*, even though the householders the state was seeking to protect could easily have posted signs denying solicitors access to their property. Not until the second circulation of the draft, in fact, did he change his vote and the case's outcome.

In his original opinion[78] Black emphasized that the First Amendment did "not grant an unrestrained liberty to engage . . . in conduct which may seriously jeopardize the rights of others." A regulation of conduct "which to some extent limits the dissemination of knowledge" was valid, he wrote, if it furthered legitimate and substantial community interests, and the ordinance at issue met that test because it served to "control conduct leading to substantial social evils which a city may find it necessary to restrain," including interference with the peace and quiet of the home, burglary, and door-to-door canvassing for purposes of fraud.

Consider, too, a two-page draft of suggestions Black prepared for an unidentified handbilling case of the same period. In *Hague* v. *CIO*,[79] a 1939 case, the Court had overturned a parade permit ordinance which left issuance of permits to the discretion of a local official. In a *Hague* concurrence, which Black joined, Justice Roberts observed that "Wherever the title of streets and parks may rest, they have immemorially been held in trust for the use of the public and, time out of mind, have been used for purposes of assembly, communicating thoughts between citizens, and discussing public questions."[80] In his draft for the later case,[81] however, Justice Black clarified his views regarding state power over such property, observing:

> [T]he municipality in the Hague case could have closed all parks and constructed public buildings or housing projects thereon; or people could have been permitted in the parks, but assemblies of persons forbidden by an ordinance declaring an epidemic of contagious disease, a regulation in the "interest of all" within the meaning of the Hague case. There is a manifest distinction between legislation which stops all communication of ideas at a place over which the legislative authority has complete control to act in the

> public interest . . . and legislation which does not end all com-
> munication of ideas at a traditional scene of communication, but
> merely provides for administrative censorship of the quality, type
> or desirability of ideas there communicated. As in the Hague case
> the disputed legislation did not seek to close the parks to all assem-
> blies . . . but instead provided for administrative determination of
> the character of assemblies to be permitted.

Surely even Professor Magee would concede that this language bears a
strong resemblance to Black's assertions in the later protest cases of "no
doubt about the general power of [a state] . . . to bar all picketing on its
streets and highways,"[82] or otherwise control access to public property,
as well as his opposition to selective controls of that character.

Of early cases, however, Justice Black perhaps quoted most frequently from *Giboney* v. *Empire Storage & Ice Co.*[83] in tying the dichotomies he drew in the sixties protest cases to his—and the Court's—past.
Giboney involved the constitutionality of a Missouri injunction to halt
picketing by members of a Kansas City coal and ice handlers' union.
Hoping to pressure nonunion peddlers into joining the union, union
officials sought agreements from wholesale ice distributors not to sell to
nonunion peddlers. All distributors except Empire agreed to the union's
demands. When Empire refused to yield, union members began picketing its facilities. When the company's business immediately dropped
by 85 percent, Empire secured an injunction and Missouri's highest court
affirmed, concurring in the trial court's findings that the union's conduct "was pursuant to a local transportation combination"[84] forbidden
by the state's anti-restraint-of-trade statute. A unanimous Supreme
Court upheld the state courts, rejecting the union's First Amendment
claims.

Justice Black's opinion for the *Giboney* Court, it will be recalled,
paralleled in many respects the language and analysis of his 1960s'
opinions. He emphasized, for example, that "picketing may include
conduct other than speech, conduct which can be made the subject
of restrictive legislation."[85] He rejected any construction of the First
Amendment that would deem it "an abridgment of freedom of speech or
press to make a course of conduct illegal merely because the conduct
was in part initiated, evidenced, or carried out by means of language,
either spoken, written, or printed," and added that "[s]uch an expansive interpretation . . . would make it practically impossible ever to

enforce laws against agreements in restraint of trade as well as many other agreements and conspiracies deemed injurious to society."[86] He concluded that since the union's activities "constituted a single and integrated course of conduct" violative of state law, the injunction "did no more than enjoin . . . a felony."[87] And he insisted that although a state could not abridge the freedoms of speech and press "to obviate slight inconveniences or annoyances" otherwise within its power to control, Missouri's interest in preventing restraints of trade outweighed any First Amendment interest which the challenged injunction burdened.[88]

An earlier draft of the Justice's opinion, moreover, had included language perhaps even closer to his pronouncements in later cases— language his status as the Court's spokesman may have obliged him to remove.[89] Noting at one point that the union had "impliedly concede[d] that states may bar picketing carried on en masse, by violence, or by threats of violence," he observed, "The contention seems to assume . . . that these are the only circumstances that would justify regulation of picketing by a state. We cannot agree that the Federal Constitution so drastically limits a state's power." He also asserted that a state could "regulate use of its highways and streets . . . in the interest of their primary purpose, and this includes the power to regulate such things as standing, patrolling, and parading along the streets and highways." Most tellingly, he discussed the elements of picketing and concluded: "Whatever its scope, the undoubted power of states to regulate the use of their highways and streets illustrates the inaccuracy of treating a 'right to picket' as identical with a 'right to freedom of speech and press.' Whatever constitutional right to picket may be thought to exist flows from its association at times with the constitutional guaranty of freedom of speech and press."

Since Professor Magee did not examine Justice Black's papers, he overlooked this draft, just as he neglected to examine Black's draft *Bridges* dissent. Magee cites the Justice's opinion for the Court in *Giboney* as further evidence that the early Black was a balancer even in cases involving direct infringements on First Amendment freedoms. The only "'conduct' at which the injunction was aimed," Magee reasons, "was not the picketing element apart from speech, but the consequences of the continuation of the union's 'publicizing,' consequences that eventually would have produced a violation of Missouri's anti-trade-restraint law."[90] Since the injunction was aimed solely at the

message the picketers were advancing, it "had the direct effect of suppressing the content of the placards—the speech itself—state action
that Justice Black would later argue was absolutely forbidden."[91] In
Magee's judgment the *Giboney* rationale could thus be used to repudiate Black's claim of absolute First Amendment protection for those who
inflict "injurious lies" upon "the innocent."

> Surely a state has a legitimate and valid interest in protecting its
> citizens against the calculated destruction of their privacy, reputa-
> tion, liberty, and even their lives, resulting from defamatory false-
> hoods—a state interest indisputably as great as that sanctioned in
> *Giboney*. And certainly the free speech interest in lies is less than
> that in knowing the truthful facts about a labor dispute.[92]

Giboney apparently did give Justice Black considerable difficulty,
for he originally voted to overturn the injunction at issue there.[93] It is
grossly inaccurate, however, to compare *Giboney* to a libel case. As
noted earlier, one who commits a libel may by that libelous statement
cause serious injury. But utterance of the libel itself is the sole activity
involved and against which any sanction is directed. In *Giboney*, by
contrast, the appellants were not simply displaying words on a placard.
Instead, the union was attempting to pressure Empire into an illegal
commercial arrangement. Had the company yielded, it would have
been obliged to sell ice only to the union's members. The injunction, it
is true, enjoined only the picketing. About 85 percent of the truck
drivers working for Empire's customers were members of unions, however, and any who crossed the picket line were subject to fine or imprisonment by the unions to which they belonged. For those truckers
the picketing certainly involved more than words on a placard. The
injunction was clearly directed at an illegal conspiracy, not at the bare
words of the picketers' message. As Justice Black emphasized, the picketing could not be viewed "in isolation." It was simply part of a broader
effort to violate Missouri's law against restraint of trade—a course, or
attempted course, of conduct "initiated, evidenced, or carried out by
means of language, either spoken, written, or printed." A criminal
prosecution or damage suit, with the picketing used merely as evidence
of the conspiracy, would have posed fewer First Amendment problems,
and use of an injunction to attack the combination may explain Black's
initial position in the case. But likening the picketing in *Giboney* to a

libel is analogous to comparing a libelous newspaper column to a stock swindle involving only the exchange of printed stock certificates.

Professor Magee, of course, has not been the only scholar to contend that Justice Black's position in the later protest cases was inconsistent with his stance in earlier cases involving speech-related conduct. Patrick McBride apparently takes no issue with Black's claim to general doctrinal consistency. But he has suggested that the Justice's position in *Feiner* v. *New York*[94] and *Kovacs* v. *Cooper*,[95] as well as in the early handbill cases, shows more toleration for demonstrative speech than his position in the protest cases of the 1960s.[96] Black's stance in *Feiner* and *Kovacs*, however, is arguably compatible with his later pronouncements. The *Feiner* majority used imminent danger rhetoric to uphold the disorderly conduct conviction of a university student who delivered a vitriolic street-corner political harangue and ignored police orders to stop when his speech provoked "angry mutterings" and threats from a crowd of onlookers. Justice Black vigorously dissented, charging that Feiner was being punished for his "unpopular views." Had Feiner been prosecuted under a narrowly drawn, nondiscriminatory statute controlling access to the streets, his position probably would have been different. But Feiner was lawfully on the street, and no law protecting the free flow of pedestrian and vehicular traffic forbade street-corner speechmaking. Feiner was convicted because he failed to heed a police judgment that his speech could no longer continue, and, according to Black's reading of the record, police made no attempt to protect him. Nothing in Black's later opinions indicates that he would have voted then to uphold convictions imposed under such circumstances, or that he no longer agreed with his contention in *Feiner* that, "if, in the name of preserving order, [police] ever can interfere with a *lawful* public speaker, they first must make all reasonable efforts to protect him."[97]

In *Kovacs* the Court upheld a conviction under a statute prohibiting use on the public streets of sound trucks or other amplifiers emitting "loud and raucous" noises. Black argued convincingly in dissent, however, that the appellant was neither charged nor convicted for operating a "loud or raucous" amplifier, that instead he was convicted merely for operating a sound truck. His conviction, in Black's judgment, thus violated due process.[98] More broadly, the ordinance, as construed to allow Kovacs's conviction, imposed an "absolute prohibition of all uses of an amplifier" on the public streets. It thus suppressed one instrument of communication and potentially gave "an overpowering influence to views of owners of legally favored instruments"—an advantage forbidden by the Constitution.[99]

Black's *Kovacs* dissent does appear to display a greater sensitivity to the "poorly financed causes" and modes of communication "of little people" than that evident in the later cases. In *Kovacs*, however, the Justice termed the challenged ordinance an "invidious prohibition against the dissemination of ideas by speaking"[100] and clearly viewed amplifier equipment as simply a technological advancement in the realm of speech and press. Even at the time *Kovacs* was decided, therefore, he would not have placed parades, picketing, and sit-ins in the same category as amplified speech. In *Kovacs*, moreover, he recognized broad power for government to regulate even amplified speaking, declaring:

> I would agree without reservation to the sentiment that "unrestrained use throughout a municipality of all sound amplifying devices would be intolerable." And of course cities may restrict or absolutely ban the use of amplifiers on busy streets in the business area. A city ordinance that reasonably restricts the volume of sound, or the hours during which an amplifier may be used, does not, in my mind, infringe the constitutionally protected area of free speech. It is because this ordinance does none of these things, but is instead an absolute prohibition of all uses of an amplifier on any of the streets of Trenton at any time that I must dissent.[101]

Finally, of course, certain of Black's critics claim that the general tone of his opinions in demonstrative speech cases changed over time. Sylvia Snowiss concedes, for example, that "[i]t is hard to find a single case where Justice Black did not satisfactorily explain his vote," but contends that "his later opinions . . . deviated from his earlier work in emphasis and implication . . . form[ing] the single greatest inconsistency of his judicial career."[102] Prominent in the later protest opinions, writes Snowiss, are a fear of mob violence and deep concern for "public order and institutional integrity" not evident in his reaction to earlier claims, while missing from them is a "concern for the role of picketing as a means of communication by the poor, or the use of trespass laws to suppress unpopular demonstrations."[103] In the later cases, adds Snowiss, the Justice also began to disparage protest groups and their leaders. "Earlier," she writes, "Justice Black studiously avoided making negative references to even the most offensive causes. Later, he deprecated groups as 'clamorous and demanding,' who 'think they have been mistreated or . . . have actually been mistreated.' "[104] She finds the depth of this hostility difficult to explain and wonders "why contemporary advocacy is likely to degenerate into mob violence and a subversion of democracy, while analogous fears about labor organizing, racial agitation, or the consequences of Communist party activities were not worth serious attention."[105]

For Snowiss the answer apparently lay in the Justice' conviction that "the New Deal and the postwar years [were] successful in taking government out of the hands of the few and putting it in the service of the many."[106] In her judgment Black was convinced that American institutions had become responsive to the needs of the many. He thus had little sympathy with protest movements which, in effect, challenged the effectiveness of those institutions as viable instruments of reform.

> Protection of individual rights was always, for Justice Black, intimately linked with populist notions of the few and the many and the opportunity to foster needed political reform. There was always a presumption that the dissident in need of constitutional protection was acting on behalf of "the people" and that other dissidents could be safely endured, as they would lose out in the market place of ideas. The individualism associated with Justice Black's conception of individual rights was a community centered, patriotic individualism, grounded not in individual differences but in shared moral virtues of hard work and self-denial.
>
> . . . . .
>
> Justice Black's long-standing concern for the poor, the weak, the heretic, and the dissenter always rested on a clear conception of moral virtue and its connection with the political good. With that conception shaken, there was bound to be some change in his work, even though he was able to maintain an internal, technical consistency.[107]

The tone of Justice Black's opinions in demonstrative speech cases undoubtedly did change during his last years on the bench. Arguably, however, the harsher tone of his later protest opinions was directed more at the medium and its broader context than at the message and its messengers. As I already have attempted to demonstrate, Black's

First Amendment jurisprudence rested ultimately on the amendment's words, as the Justice insisted, not on his conception of democracy, as Professor Snowiss suggests, or, for that matter, on his admittedly high regard for the liberties he believed the amendment to contain, or any other element of his political, as opposed to his judicial and constitutional, philosophy. In my judgment, moreover, the harsh tone of the Justice's later opinions can be traced to several factors unrelated to his conception of democracy or any basic change in his First Amendment jurisprudence.

First, whether as a lawyer, a congressional inquisitor, or a Supreme Court Justice, Hugo Black was extremely combative, willing to attack with little hesitation those whose positions he opposed as well as the positions themselves. A good defense attorney attempts to convince the jury that his client's alleged victim deserved his fate. A reading of Justice Black's opinions in a variety of fields reveals that Black was not above such a ploy, even when it meant attacking "language-stretching" judges and his rhetoric, as in *Tinker* and *Brown* v. *Louisiana*, appeared to do his cause more harm than good.

Second, and much more fundamentally, the harsh tone of Black's opinions undoubtedly reflected the depth of his alarm at the far-reaching implications of the First Amendment claims raised in the later cases. Professor Snowiss is surprised that the early Black apparently entertained few "fears about labor organizing, racial agitation, or the consequences of Communist party activities."[108] But the Communist "activities" Black sought to protect fell clearly within the ambit of freedoms directly and absolutely protected by his First Amendment jurisprudence—a jurisprudence which opposed the balancing of public fears against individual rights. The "racial agitation" at issue in the *Beauharnais* case was of the same nature. And while Feiner's street-corner harangue included racial appeals and provoked bystanders, he was not prosecuted under a general law controlling access to public property. Instead, he was a lawful public speaker whom police chose to silence rather than protect. The isolated incidents of labor picketing the Court confronted during Black's early years, moreover, were hardly comparable in frequency, general size, and burdens on government resources to the protest movements of the sixties. Nor should Black's critics forget that the First Amendment claims raised in the later cases were not limited to the streets, but extended to schools, libraries, jail grounds, and other property over which government had traditionally been recognized to possess broad authority—authority now limited to the sort of indefinite, case-to-case, judicially created standards of "reasonableness" the Justice detested. In such settings the tone of Black's opinions seems readily understandable.

Finally, the Justice's later opinions may have flowed not merely from a fear of mob violence but also from concern that public distaste for the techniques of demonstrative expression might ultimately threaten the "worthy" goals (as Black described them) that the protests were designed to advance, and perhaps general public toleration of free speech as well. Certainly, opinion polls of the era provided a basis for such concerns. In a nationwide survey conducted in the summer of 1961, 66 percent of those polled approved of judicial decisions outlawing segregated trains, buses, and terminals. But 64 percent disapproved of the freedom riders' tactics and 57 percent believed direct action protests would harm the chances for racial integration. Sixty-three percent of a 1963 survey voiced unfavorable attitudes about the civil rights march on Washington. In a 1965 survey, only 10 percent of respondents indicated that they had "ever felt the urge to organize or join a public demonstration about something." And a 1969 survey of reactions to antiwar protests produced unfavorable comments which outweighed favorable responses three to one. Among the objections frequently mentioned by those who disapproved of the demonstrations was the assertion that "other approaches are better."[109]

These statistics may contain a valuable lesson, as may the general direction of American politics during and since the protest movements of the sixties. Whatever the basis for the tone of Justice Black's later protest opinions, moreover, his votes in such cases arguably reflected the acceptance of broad governmental power over property and conduct which was evident in his earlier opinions. Nor, arguably, were his votes in the later cases any more affected by distaste for protesters than his continued opposition to obscenity controls and coerced confessions reflected any appreciation for pornographers and their wares, or special sympathy for the criminal defendant.

Black's Dichotomies

Justice Black's critics have attacked not only the consistency of his position in First Amendment cases but also what they consider weaknesses in his efforts to distinguish protected speech from unprotected conduct and direct from indirect burdens on freedoms the amendment guarantees. Certain of his critics have contended with regard to his speech/conduct dichotomy, for example, that the clearcut distinction he appeared to draw between speech and conduct cannot be squared with the amendment's language, especially its guarantee to peaceably assembly and the free exercise of religion.[110] Others point out the enormous conceptual problems seemingly inevitable in any attempt to distinguish speech from conduct. One student of Black's First Amendment jurisprudence has remarked: "[T]he Justice's opinions seem to suggest that the line between 'speech' and 'conduct' is intuitively obvious. It is not."[111] Consider, too, Professor Harry Kalven's suggestion "that all speech is necessarily 'speech plus.' If it is oral, it is noise and may interrupt someone else; if it is written, it may be litter."[112]

On their face such complaints seem eminently sound. When the distinction Black drew between "speech" and "conduct" is placed in perspective, however, his critics' contentions lose much of their force. While at times Black did contend that the First Amendment protects "speech," not "conduct," he was simply answering those who, instead of sticking to the amendment's words, were characterizing picketing and related activities as "speech-plus" and asserting that the Constitution directly protects such activities. Black was merely trying to emphasize that the amendment's language protects "speech," not "speech-plus." He never argued in the abstract that the amendment protects no forms of conduct. In fact, he sometimes entirely circumvented the semantic difficulties of the speech/conduct dichotomy by characterizing all activity as conduct and asking only whether the Constitution protected the conduct at issue. In a separate opinion registered for *Coates* v. *Cincinnati*,[113] for example, he framed the First Amendment issue raised by a law prohibiting "annoying" conduct solely in terms of protected and unprotected conduct. He did limit the free exercise clause's reach to religious "speech" and "belief." But that construction was, after all, compatible with the First Amendment's general emphasis and based on the logical assumption that the amendment's framers surely did not intend to insulate all religiously motivated conduct from governmental regulations. He never claimed, moreover, that freedom of assembly and petition did not involve conduct; he simply contended that government had broad power to control the location of such activities, just as it possessed authority generally over access to public property. Arguably, then, Black resorted to the speech/conduct semantic only as a shorthand way of separating his First Amendment views from the stance of those who contended that the amendment protected a larger number of activities than he was willing to concede, and not because he had an "insufficient appreciation of the fuzziness of the boundaries between speech and conduct."[14]

Criticism of Black's direct/indirect dichotomy is equally vulnerable to rebuttal. In his highly perceptive analysis of the Justice's conception of the judicial function, Paul Freund observed: "In the hands of a less sensitive judge than Justice Black the test could yield results that by his standards would be quite perverse."[115] Others have also voiced skepticism about the dichotomy's application in specific contexts, and Patrick McBride has suggested that it invites inappropriate inquiries into judicial motivation. For Black, writes McBride, "the term direct . . . refer[red] not to the order of impact of a law, nor even to its ostensible purpose of regulation of conduct, but rather to what he observe[d] to be the real and overriding purpose of punishing belief in and expression of hated ideas."[16] Such "judicial probing of the inner motives of legislatures and other governmental bodies," McBride contends, "is a touchy business which requires judges to speculate about intentions that may be lost in a fog of legislative rhetoric."[117]

Obviously, judges and others can easily disagree over whether a challenged regulation imposes a direct or indirect burden on First Amendment freedoms. At least in the context of his epic battle with Justices Frankfurter and Harlan over the balancing doctrine, however, Black's disputes with other Justices probably related more to fundamentally different conceptions of the direct/indirect principle than to conflicting conclusions over application of a uniformly perceived doctrine in specific cases.[118] Frankfurter and Harlan apparently believed that the First Amendment burden at issue in a given case was indirect, and thus amenable to a balancing of competing interests, whenever a law was applied ultimately not to control speech but to fulfill an overriding governmental objective (for example, national security) unrelated to the expression of ideas—even if the sole immediate effect of the regulation was to burden freedom of expression. Black, on the other hand, included within the category of indirect burdens on expression only those regulations that by their terms reached matters clearly within the state's power to control, such as controls over access to public property, prosecution of fraud, control of monopolistic business practices, and other regulations directed at activities which may include elements of speech. If such conceptual differences could be resolved, the difficulties claimed to be inherent in application of the direct/indirect dichotomy in specific cases arguably would substantially disappear.

Nor, in Black's hands, was the dichotomy really vulnerable to the complaint that its application required improper inquiries into judicial motivation. Justice Black did contend that regulations ostensibly directed at conduct within the state's power to control were nonetheless direct abridgments of the First Amendment if "openly [or] *surreptitiously* aimed at speech."[119] But Black clearly recognized the dangers of judicial decision making bottomed on conclusions regarding legislative motivation.[120] He concluded that a regulation ostensibly aimed at conduct was really directed at protected expression, moreover, only where the challenged law was framed or applied in a discriminatory manner, terming such selective controls "censorship in a most odious form."[21] He thus was much less vulnerable to charges of improper probing into governmental motivation than certain of his colleagues. In upholding the trespass convictions arising from the jailground demonstration at issue in *Adderley* v. *Florida*,[122] for example, he found no evidence of discrimination and refused to conclude that trespass prosecutions of civil rights protesters in segregated communities are per se racially motivated. Not so inhibited, Justice Douglas and the other *Adderley* dissenters readily assumed discriminatory intent. Political realists may applaud Douglas's perception. His position rested, however, on judgments about the motives of public officials that courts normally avoid.

Black and Balancing

Black's critics are not concerned solely with the Justice's dichotomies and their viability as devices for distinguishing protected from unprotected expression. They claim, too, that the dichotomies' application affords inadequate protection for speech-related conduct and against "indirect" burdens on protected expression. While a vehement critic of balancing in cases involving "direct" interferences with First Amendment rights, Black, it will be recalled, was willing to apply a balancing test to laws regulating speech-related conduct or otherwise imposing "indirect" burdens on protected freedoms in order to assure "the complete protection of First Amendment freedoms even against purely incidental or inadvertent consequences."[123] Patrick McBride, among others, contends, however, that in the protest cases of the 1960s

Black "applie[d] the [balancing] test—if he applie[d] it at all—in a nebulous way which seem[ed] to foredoom the forms of demonstrative speech."[124] The Justice failed, asserts McBride, to set forth precisely the competing interests to be balanced and gave an exaggerated weight to property and other social interests advanced to justify controls over demonstrative speech.

I doubt, however, whether Black really embraced case-to-case balancing as a means of resolving constitutional issues of the sort raised in the sixties protest cases. Instead, he confined actual application of case-by-case or ad hoc balancing largely to cases in which individuals lawfully upon the streets and highways were forbidden to distribute handbills, approach private households for such purposes, or use amplifiers to enhance the range of their speech. In cases involving picketing, parades, sit-ins, and assemblies, on the other hand, he attempted, in my judgment, to provide an alternative to the ad hoc balancing implicit in the Court's position. Under the prevailing doctrine during his last years on the bench, groups wishing to engage in such activities could be denied all access to certain property; beyond that, however, government could impose only "reasonable" regulations of time, place, and manner—or regulations serving "substantial" governmental interests, which amounts to the same thing. Since reasonable minds can differ about the "reasonableness" of specific controls, the majority's approach left government officials, and the people generally, uncertain what activities were and were not protected on what type of property. Justice Black's jurisprudence recoiled at such vague, shifting, judicially created standards.[125] He apparently believed, moreover, that society's interest in avoiding the expense, traffic problems, and potential for violence that picketing, parades, sit-ins, and assemblies created was inherently more compelling than any free expression interests raised in their defense. For he put no conditions in the later protest opinions on his assertion that "[t]he State, no less than a private owner of property, has power to preserve the property under its control for the use to which it is lawfully dedicated,"[126] or on his contention that there could be "no doubt about the general power of [a state] to bar all picketing on its streets and highways."[127] Nor, as indicated earlier, did he in conference remarks and unpublished drafts for picketing cases decided before his public avowal of absolutism. He recited the balancing formula but apparently applied a per se balancing standard in cases involving picketing and related forms of speech-related conduct. Given the important interests inherently underlying them, controls over access to public and private property, as well as regulations of demonstrative speech, were valid per se, so long as they were nondiscriminatory and free of the vices of vagueness and overbreadth.

Indeed, I am not entirely certain that Black even resolved the issues raised by the handbilling cases in balancing terms. The distribution of handbills by individuals walking along streets and knocking on doors is closely analogous, after all, to people talking to passersby and house-holders—activities not reached by handbill bans. Black thus may have viewed the ordinances forbidding handbill distribution, like the pro-hibitions of amplifier equipment at issue in *Kovacs*, as a selective and "invidious prohibition against the dissemination of ideas by speaking."

My reading of the Justice's approach to balancing may help to explain Black's "nebulous" application of the doctrine in the later pro-test cases. It does not answer the more basic contention that, whatever his method, he largely ignored the social interests served by speech-plus. For a Justice whose First Amendment jurisprudence turned on language rather than on an evaluation of the interests a particular construction of the Constitution might serve, such complaints would carry no weight. There can be, moreover, no value-neutral response to them. But at least two arguments bearing on the issue should be cited in Black's defense.

First, picketing, mass assemblies, and related forms of demonstra-tive speech clearly do present law enforcement officials with a variety of problems that may seriously strain manpower and other governmen-tal resources. Under the Court's rulings, federal, state, and municipal authorities apparently are constitutionally compelled to leave streets, sidewalks, and most other public property open for such activities, subject only to "reasonable" controls. Justice Black, on the other hand, would have given governments an option: They could have banned all parades, picketing, and mass assemblies, thereby avoiding the strains on governmental resources such activities pose. Or they could attempt to cope with them through regulations of time, place, and manner.

Second, as indicated previously, Black insisted that any regulation or ban of speech-related activities on property generally open to the public be nondiscriminatory. Governments could ban picketing and parades. But if they chose that route, they would be obliged to ban all such activities, not merely those scheduled by groups espousing un-popular ideas. James Magee finds the constitutional protection afforded by such a requirement illusory. For Black, contends Magee, "the constitutional right of assembly was reduced to a privilege which, subject only to restraints of writing clear, specific, nondiscriminatory laws, government may withhold, extend, or withdraw. . . . What could be more irrelevant, a more meaningless constitutional guarantee, than an absolute right to assemble, but only in midair?"[128]

But is such a requirement a meaningless gesture? As Professor Kalven wisely observed, "Everyone at some time or other loves a parade whatever its effect on traffic and other uses of public streets."[129] Governments are thus generally reluctant to ban all such activities. In fact, even though the Supreme Court has never squarely ruled that a flat ban on picketing and related activities is unconstitutional, few, if any, communities have attempted to exclude such activities from property open to general public access. Justice Black clearly appreciated the protection a requirement of nondiscrimination extended to unpopular groups and their messages. Shortly before his death, I asked him whether he would approve a law denying general public access to the U.S. Capitol and surrounding grounds for expression or other purposes. While reluctant to indulge in hypotheticals, he agreed that such a regulation would be constitutional. "But," he added with a smile, "they [members of Congress] won't do it."[130] He realized, in short, that equal protection may require parades for thoughts we hate. If governments wanted to avoid the obvious traffic, protective, and related burdens of demonstrative speech, they could ban them. For Black, though, it was imperative that such regulations reach all parades. And he realized that few, if any, government officials were willing to take that politically risky step.

Assessing Absolutism

For Black's critics, of course, the most fundamental weakness in the Justice's First Amendment jurisprudence was his absolutist construction of its provisions. Absolutism, they contend, is inconsistent with the history surrounding the amendment's adoption, with its language, with common sense, and with what they consider to be a proper balance of competing societal and individual interests. Citing the conclusions of various scholars,[131] Professor Magee reminds us, for example, that the First Amendment revealed by the historical record is "strikingly short" of Black's interpretation.[132] Magee readily concedes that both history and the amendment's language support Black's contention that "no

law" means "No Law," and he faults Wallace Mendelson, Erwin Griswold, and others whose attacks on Black's thinking appear to challenge
the amendment's very words. Magee argues, however, that the amendment's language and history leave unclear what freedoms its provisions
absolutely protect from government regulation.[133]

Early critics of Black's jurisprudence did challenge the notion that
the First Amendment is, in any sense, an absolute. And they persisted
in that position. Recall, for example, Erwin Griswold's assertion, to
Black's amusement, in the *Pentagon Papers Cases* that " 'no law' does
not mean 'no law.' "[134] They probably embraced, however, essentially
the same sort of approach to the amendment's meaning that Magee has
more recently advanced. Certainly, their jurisprudential mentor Felix
Frankfurter recognized that any effective attack on Black's absolutism
should turn on his colleague's equation of "freedom of speech" with
"speech" rather than on any quixotic assertion that "no law" does not
mean "no law." After Black's Madison lecture on the Bill of Rights, for
example, Frankfurter wrote Justice Harlan: "Should I formally advise
Mr. Justice Black that when liberties are 'admittedly covered by the Bill
of Rights' they cannot be abridged by any 'superior public interest.' "[135]
But whether Black's critics challenge his contention that "no law"
means "No Law," or his assumption that "speech" and "freedom of
speech" amount to the same thing, their attacks lead ultimately to the
same conclusion: language and history are imprecise guides to the
amendment's meaning; its reach must thus be determined by a balancing of competing interests.

Black's critics also find the Justice's assumption "that the First
Amendment absolutely protects every utterance . . . an obviously absurd and impossible standard in a free and ordered society."[136] "The
most stringent protection of free speech," they remind us, bringing
down the aura of Justice Holmes on Black's head, "would not protect a
man in falsely shouting fire in a theater and causing a panic."[137] Other
situations equally belying the viability of the Justice's stance, they
assure us, abound.

Along similar lines Black's critics also contend that his absolutism,
like his interpretivist philosophy generally, drew "arbitrary" lines between protected and unprotected behavior—lines "provid[ing] less protection for earnest expression of important views [via demonstrative
speech] than some of his nonabsolutist brothers would want to guarantee . . . [yet] complete safety for some kinds of expression (defamation,

invasion of privacy, trial publicity) which probably do not deserve immunity from all official interference."[138] Professor Snowiss has stated the position with her usual revealing candor. Were Black's "equation of all speech and . . . strident refusal to make judgments on the content of speech" adopted, she warns, it would be constitutionally impossible to "distinguish honest inquiry . . . from such attacks on meaningful public discussion as demagoguery, calculated slander, or systematic subversion." Under such a regime, it was, in her judgment, "at least as likely that 'bad speech' . . . would drive out honest discourse" as it was that the latter would prevail. Snowiss wants no part of such a jurisprudence. "First Amendment problems would . . . be easier to handle," she writes, "if there were more acceptance of the legitimacy of judgments about the quality of speech and if there were overt assessments of the threat of particular speech to other interests, such as fair trial, public peace, or institutional integrity."[139] While certain of Black's critics might state their positions more narrowly, or at least with greater caution, presumably all would accept Snowiss' basic assertion that absolutism produces undesirable consequences as well as her central premise that the separation of "honest inquiry" from "demagoguery" is an appropriate subject for judicial resolution. Certain of Black's critics would simply support greater judicial deference to government than would others.

Taking these various charges in order, what first of the contention that absolutism is inconsistent with the First Amendment's history and language? I have already responded to the claim that the amendment's references to assembly and the free exercise of religion refute an absolutist reading of its provisions. There remain, however, the assertions that Black's interpretation was based on slender historical evidence and confused "speech" with "freedom of speech." As Professor Magee and many others have pointed out, the historical record provides an inadequate basis for a defense of Black's position. But history provides even less a basis for distinguishing "speech" from "freedom of speech" or for the further assertion of Black's critics that the amendment's scope is to be determined by a balancing of competing interests or application of other tests empowering judges to rule on the reasonableness of governmental action. While the Justice did refer often to the history surrounding the First Amendment's adoption, moreover, his absolutism was based ultimately on the amendment's words. As a positivist, he sought the Constitution's meaning first in its language, looking to the historical record only to supplement evidence furnished by the document's text or when, as in the case of due process and equal protection, for example, language alone afforded no clear direction. He realized that his reading of the Constitution's language, like his reading of its history, was imperfect. But he found his approach more compatible with the document's language and the concept of a written Constitution than one which holds that "'no law' does not mean 'no law,'" or to a distinction between "speech" and "freedom of speech" which ultimately amounts, as applied, to the same thing. Dissenting in *Barenblatt* v. *United States*,[140] it will be recalled, Black recast the First Amendment for those who appeared to agree that "no law" does not mean "no law."[141] Had he directly confronted the distinction his critics have drawn between "speech" and "freedom of speech," he might have been tempted to suggest that, under such a view, the amendment is rewritten to read: "Congress shall make no law . . . abridging any right which courts find to reflect a reasonable accommodation of societal and individual interests and thus to be part of 'freedom of speech.'"

Next, we come to the argument that absolutism is an "obviously absurd and impossible standard" because it would provide absolute protection for behavior no society can tolerate, including false fire alarms in crowded theaters. Criminal prosecution of those who shout "Fire!" falsely in crowded theaters is perfectly compatible, however, with Justice Black's repeated assertion that the absolute freedom to speak exists only in a place where a person has a right to be for that purpose. An absolute right of speech was not, for Black, a right to appropriate the property of others, even the public's property held in trust by its government, for purposes of expression. A person who enters a theater is thus subject, according to Black's thinking, to whatever rules have been established for the facility's use, including regulations relating to speech, disturbance of the peace, and the like. In my judgment, moreover, the Justice's acceptance of governmental authority over demonstrative conduct, speech which is an integral part of a course of conduct, and access to public property resolves every conceivable related contextual challenge to absolutism's feasibility as an approach to the First Amendment's application.

Ultimately, however, the critics' objections to absolutism appear to turn less on the feasibility of Black's approach to the First Amendment's meaning than on the undesirable consequences its adoption would produce—on the contention, in short, that under an absolutist regime, "bad" speech might too often triumph, while much "good" speech would be "foredoomed." I have already attempted to answer such charges in the context of Black's reaction to demonstrative speech claims. But two bits of evidence used to bolster his critics' position require comment.

First, there is Black's extension of absolute First Amendment protection to libel and slander. "The very foundation of civil society . . . would collapse," Sidney Hook, it will be recalled, predicted, "if speech which falsely charged citizens with murder, theft, rape, arson and treason was . . . privileged under law."[142] Black's response to such concerns, of course, was a predictable reference to the Constitution's amending article. If the people find libel, slander, obscenity, or any other form of speech intolerable, they can amend the Constitution to allow government suppression of such material. The judiciary, Black contended, simply should not be allowed to make that value judgment. Even if there were no provision for constitutional amendment, however, Hook and other critics of Black's thinking surely exaggerate the importance of libel suits as a safeguard against defamation.[143] Do Black's critics really believe that reputable newspaper staffs are driven to accuracy only or primarily out of fear of libel suits, rather than by a desire for peer and public respect and confidence as well as the professional and material success they help to promote? Do they really believe that the lies and half-truths of supermarket tabloids and other disreputable publications do frequent and serious harm to an individual's reputation? Do they really believe that the "knowing" or "reckless" falsehood standard provides anything more than an appearance of an intelligible basis for distinguishing protected falsehoods from unprotected lies? Most fundamentally, perhaps, do they believe that the defamation most common and damaging in the lives of most of us—the unprinted lies of gossip-mongers circulated within the victim's immediate community—are really amenable to control through libel actions? Those who object to absolutism largely because of its extension to libel and slander would do well to examine the basic premises on which their concerns rest.

Second, critics cite *Sheppard* v. *Maxwell*.[144] Black dissented without opinion from the *Sheppard* Court's 1966 decision reversing a conviction held to be tainted by prejudicial media coverage, a carnival-like atmosphere in the courtroom, and the trial judge's failure to take appropriate "remedial" action. Black's critics see his *Sheppard* dissent as a further reflection of the extremes to which absolutism can lead, as evidence, in Professor Magee's words, of the Justice's commitment "to following a dogma . . . no matter how unfair or absurd the consequences."[145] But *Sheppard* involved absolutely no asserted violation of a First Amendment right; the Court's decision did no more than reverse a criminal conviction. The *Sheppard* majority did recite the usual devices for coping with prejudicial publicity, but the Justices essentially rejected use of the contempt power against the press, as Justice Black consistently had. And the techniques suggested directly restricted the activities of newsmen only in the courtroom—an area to which Justice Black's absolute First Amendment most assuredly did not extend. Black's vote in the case thus had no bearing on his First Amendment views; his was not a vote for protection of one absolute right over another guarantee. He simply rejected the petitioner's due process claims, principally assertions that Sheppard had been denied a "fair trial" and impartial jury. Given Black's "law of the land" conception of due process, the Justice obviously would not have accepted a "fair trial" claim. He did believe, of course, that the Sixth Amendment right to an impartial jury was binding on the states via the Fourteenth Amendment. But he apparently rejected Sheppard's claim that he had been denied such a jury—perhaps because the record contained no direct evidence that any particular juror was biased and Black, unlike his brethren, refused to speculate that juror prejudice was inevitable in such cases. His assessment of these procedural claims can be questioned—just as can, for that matter, his votes to *uphold* prejudicial publicity claims in other cases.[146] His stance in such cases is hardly evidence, however, of the "unfair" and "absurd" consequences of *absolutism*.

Of course, whether complaints that the triumph of absolutism would produce unsatisfactory results come from critics who consider the First Amendment largely admonitory, or from those who accused Black of reading both too much and too little into the amendment's meaning, such charges are essentially simply another line of attack on the Justice's interpretivist conception of the judicial function. Black believed that the First Amendment's meaning should be limited as nearly as possible to its "clear—unequivocal" language, as he indicated in his draft *Bridges* dissent. Unencumbered by esoteric distinctions between "speech" and "freedom of speech"—distinctions definable, after all, only in terms of the same sort of judicially created standards of reasonableness the Justice condemned in other constitutional fields—he pursued such a positivist approach to the amendment throughout his career. As in other fields, his approach produced a mixture of policy results—results fully satisfying neither those who view the amendment largely as an admonition to government nor more recent critics confident that the judiciary must meet "all the needs of limited government." His critics also condemn the "arrogance" of a judge who could claim to know the amendment's "plain" meaning. Arguably, however, Black's absolutist philosophy, like his interpretations of other constitutional provisions, narrowed the range of judicial discretion to a greater degree than did competing constructions. It is at least debatable, moreover, who is the more "arrogant"—the judge who attempts to anchor his jurisprudence to the Constitution's language, however imperfect his judgments may be, or one who "humbly" recognizes the imperfectibility of such efforts, then uses the amendment as yet another tool for open-ended rulings on the reasonableness of challenged legislation.

Six The Flexible Clauses

THE language and history of most of the Constitution's provisions enabled Justice Black to ascribe to them a relatively fixed meaning which narrowed considerably the permissible range of judicial choice in constitutional cases. Many of the criminal procedure safeguards in the Bill of Rights are of that character. The Fourth Amendment's ban on "unreasonable searches and seizures" imposes on judges, however, a continuing duty to rule on the reasonableness of police investigative tactics. Its enforcement thus requires the sort of case-to-case, ad hoc rule-making Black generally abhorred as an affront to the notion of a written Constitution binding upon all officials, including judges. The Fourteenth Amendment's equal protection clause poses a similar problem for one of Black's jurisprudential persuasion. Since classification is the essence of government through laws of broad, general application, it is obvious that the amendment's framers did not intend its equal protection clause to require identical treatment of all persons. That guarantee thus also appears to invite judicial evaluations of the reasonableness of legislation.

Ultimately, of course, Black gave both the Fourth Amendment and the equal protection clause constructions which substantially limited the scope of judicial choice in cases involving such claims. Since the Fourth Amendment forbids only the "unreasonable" search and seizure, he refused to read what he considered an extremely flexible standard as a stringent restriction on governmental power. In assessing the equally nebulous "probable cause" standard of the warrant clause, moreover, he largely deferred to the assessments of trial courts. Nor was he willing to convert the amendment's protection of the individual's person, "houses, papers, and effects" into a more general safeguard against eavesdropping and related intrusions upon personal privacy. In discrimination cases he followed a similar approach, confining meaningful application of the equal protection bite largely to its historic racial context while extending virtually unlimited discretion to government in most other fields.

Black's critics have devoted much less attention to the Justice's Fourth Amendment jurisprudence than to his First Amendment philosophy, incorporation thesis, and positivist conception of the judicial function. Jacob W. Landynski, a leading authority on the law of search and seizure,[1] has subjected Black's construction of the Fourth Amendment, however, to thoughtful and thorough scrutiny.[2] Among other asserted weaknesses in the Justice's stance, Landynski has scored Black's erratic position regarding the exclusionary rule, his rejection of the amendment's extension to eavesdropping, and his refusal to construe its guarantee against "unreasonable" search and seizure in the context of the "stringent" requirements of its warrant clause. Black's equal protection philosophy has been the subject of even less systematic critical scholarship. Relying largely on the conference notes of Justice Harold Burton, however, S. Sidney Ulmer has raised questions regarding Black's stance in *Brown* v. *Board of Education*[3]—questions which cemented the Justice's resolve to destroy his own conference notes.[4] William Van Alstyne has critically evaluated, moreover, Black's relatively narrow conception of the "state action" doctrine in racial discrimination and other cases.[5] This chapter assesses such concerns in the context of an examination of Black's criminal procedure and equal protection jurisprudence.

Literalism and Procedural Guarantees

Justice Black's preference for "liberal," yet "literal" or historically based, constructions of the Constitution's provisions is amply reflected in his reaction to criminal procedure claims. So too are the mixed policy results his interpretivism produced in other constitutional fields. In certain areas his interpretivist approach to questions of criminal procedure called for significant restrictions on governmental authority and abrupt breaks with long tradition. In others it prompted what many viewed as extreme and undue deference to that authority.

While the "liberal" element of Black's criminal procedure jurisprudence is perhaps most evident in his approach to certain specific guarantees, it is also reflected in the limits he sought to impose on the jurisprudence of military tribunals, in his opposition to summary citations for criminal contempt, in his position regarding application of the Bill of Rights to juvenile proceedings, and in his broad reading of the "criminal prosecutions" to which the safeguards of the Sixth Amendment extend. The Fifth Amendment's grand jury provision exempts from its coverage "cases arising in the land or naval forces, or in the militia, when in actual service in time of war or public danger." And most other Bill of Rights safeguards have long been assumed to extend only to civilian proceedings.[6] In my judgment Justice Black never publicly challenged this assumption. Since the Constitution specifically exempts the grand jury alone, however, he probably believed that only that right could be denied servicemen. In 1949 he did hold for the Court that a temporary delay, relocation, and reorganization of a court-martial proceeding did not amount to double jeopardy. But he in no way suggested that the double jeopardy guarantee was inapplicable to military courts. He simply rejected the notion that it was violated "every time a defendant is put to trial before a competent tribunal . . . [and] the trial fails to end in a final judgment."[7] Throughout his career, moreover, he sought to limit the scope of military jurisdiction. In 1955, for example, he spoke for the Court in rejecting military trial of discharged servicemen, even for offenses committed during their tour of duty.[8] Two years later he held for a plurality that military tribunals have no authority to try civilian dependents of military personnel.[9] And in 1969 he joined the Court in limiting military jurisdiction over the crimes of servicemen themselves to "service-connected" offenses.[10] Congress's authority over the armed forces, he asserted, did not empower it "to deprive people of trials under Bill of Rights safeguards, and we are not willing to hold that power to circumvent those safeguards should be inferred through the Necessary and Proper Clause."[11]

Nor, despite long tradition, was Black willing to accept summary citation of criminal contempts. He recognized a judge's broad summary power to secure compliance with court orders. Dissenting from a majority's 1958 refusal to require a jury trial in criminal contempt cases, for example, he emphasized that the contempt citations at issue were "not at all concerned with the power of courts to impose conditional imprisonment for the purpose of compelling a person to obey a valid order. Such coercion, where the defendant carries the keys to freedom in his willingness to comply with the court's directive, is essentially a civil remedy designed for the benefit of other parties and has quite properly been exercised for centuries to secure compliance with judicial decrees."[12] Speaking for the Court in a 1970 case, he also upheld a judge's power to order an unruly defendant bound and gagged, or removed from the courtroom, as appropriate means of maintaining order and preventing obstruction of the judicial process.[13]

As he indicated in a 1952 contempt case growing out of the *Dennis* case, however, the Justice considered the summary contempt power proper only to "preserve order and decorum and compel obedience to valid court orders."[14] Even in that context, moreover, he would accept only summary civil action, in which the defendant held the "keys to freedom," not criminal punishment through a fixed jail term. During his last term the Court, per Justice Douglas, held that criminal contempts involving verbal abuse of a judge must be heard by another judge unless the original judge "instantly acted, holding petitioner in contempt, or excluding him from the courtroom, or otherwise insulating his vulgarity from the courtroom."[15] "As you know," Black wrote Douglas after reviewing a draft of his colleague's opinion in the case, "I would prefer to have your opinion say that Mayberry was entitled to a jury trial. This, of course, would mean that he could not have been instantaneously held guilty of contempt."[16] When Douglas did not delete the language to which Black objected, the Justice concurred "in the judgment and with all of the opinion except that part which indicates that the judge, without a jury, could have convicted Mayberry of contempt instantaneously with the outburst."[17]

For Black, as he had stressed years before, there was a "crucial" distinction between "conditional confinement to compel future performance and unconditional imprisonment designed to punish past transgressions."[18] The latter was a "criminal prosecution" and thus subject to all the Sixth Amendment's requirements, including jury trial. Since the amendment's language reached "all" criminal prosecutions, moreover, Black concurred in the Court's decisions, late in his career, requiring trial by jury in criminal contempt cases, but rejected its restriction of the ruling to cases involving more than six months' imprisonment.[19] The Sixth Amendment's language drew no distinctions between "serious" and "petty" cases and neither would he.

At the same time he was unwilling to give the amendment's reference only to criminal prosecutions what he considered an unduly narrow and artificial reading. Especially since the fate of juvenile offenders was often as harsh as, or harsher than, that which befell convicted felons, he refused to indulge in efforts to distinguish juvenile proceedings from criminal prosecutions. "Where a person, infant or adult, can be seized by the State, charged and convicted for violating a state criminal law, and then ordered by the State to be confined for six years," he asserted in the *Gault* case, "the Constitution requires that he be tried in accordance with the guarantees of all the provisions of the Bill of Rights made applicable to the States by the Fourteenth Amendment."[20]

Chief Justice Burger was unable to dissuade him from the view, moreover, that a preliminary hearing is part of a "criminal prosecution" and thus subject to the Sixth Amendment's guarantee to the assistance of counsel. In *Coleman* v. *Alabama*[21] the Court had initially voted— over the dissents of Black, Douglas, and Harlan—to reject that claim. Black had drafted a dissenting opinion,[22] and he and the other original dissenters eventually won Justices Brennan and Marshall to their side. But not the Chief Justice. The Sixth Amendment also obligates government to inform a defendant of the nature and cause of the accusation. If applicable only at the time of the accused's trial, this right would be meaningless. Any attempt to limit the Sixth Amendment's guarantees to trials alone thus flies in the face of the notice requirement. In a memorandum to the conference, however, Chief Justice Burger found no "language, nor even a hint, that the authors [of the Bill of Rights] thought they were commanding counsel at the preliminary hearing . . . which is confined to the narrow question whether a person is to be held for further inquiry, [and] simply is not 'a criminal prosecution' under the Constitution."[23] In a letter to Burger, Black argued that the amendment did "not divide up into details the prosecution against the defendant" and contended that it "would disregard reality to say that a preliminary trial is not an important part of a prosecution under which the State is preparing to punish a man either by taking his life or his liberty away from him."[24] In a later letter he elaborated upon his position.

> If not a "criminal prosecution", what is it when a person is taken before a judge in a state court on the charge that he has committed a murder at which trial he can be acquitted or he can be held over for further action leading to a final verdict? . . . What is called a "preliminary trial" [in Alabama] is no more than a beginning of the "criminal prosecution" in which a defendant desperately needs the

"Assistance of counsel for his defense" which the Sixth Amendment guarantees. At least that is the way I read the actual, literal language of the Constitution itself.[25]

Burger was not convinced. "A release following a preliminary hearing is not an 'acquittal,'" he retorted. Nor was it "the beginning of a criminal prosecution." Instead, it was "an exploration to determine" whether a prosecution should begin.[26] But Black was not dissuaded either. In a brief concurrence he agreed that counsel was required in preliminary hearings, not because the Constitution requires a "fair trial," but because "the plain language of the Sixth Amendment requires" it.[27]

Black's commitment to "plain language" led him to "broad and liberal" readings of other specific Bill of Rights safeguards as well. The Fifth Amendment protects the individual from being "compelled in any criminal case to be a witness against himself." Those words do not exempt the coerced fruits of police interrogation, and while Black was willing in early cases, as the Court's spokesman, to overturn coerced confessions on general due process grounds,[28] he obviously considered them a violation of the Fifth Amendment's specific ban on compulsory self-incrimination. For he joined the *Miranda* decision and spoke for the Court in later emphasizing that *Miranda* applied to all custodial interrogation, not merely the station house variety.[29] In fact, during conference discussion of *Miranda*, he argued that since arrest itself is "coercive," police had "no right" to question suspects, or even to subject them to booking procedures. He would, he asserted, "put an end to [such] interrogation." "The kind of warning" suspects should be given was thus "not important."[30]

Nor, given the Fifth Amendment's language, was he willing to join the Court's repeated holdings that the guarantee against self-incrimination forbids compulsion only of "testimonial" evidence, not blood samples and other "physical" evidence. "To reach the conclusion that compelling a person to give his blood to help the State convict him is not equivalent to compelling him to be a witness against himself," he asserted in one case, "strikes me as quite an extraordinary feat."[31] He took the same position with regard to the compulsion of handwriting exemplars,[32] voice samples,[33] and witness identifications secured through compulsory lineup procedures.[34]

Black agreed, of course, that an individual could waive the right against compelled self-incrimination, just as other guarantees can be knowingly and voluntarily waived. But he insisted on clear evidence of such waivers to assure that the individual was not "compelled . . . to be a witness against himself." When a divided Court held in 1951 that a witness who voluntarily answers certain questions implicitly waives the right to refuse to answer subsequent related questions, Black, joined by Douglas, vehemently dissented. "Some people," he wrote,

> are hostile to the Fifth Amendment's provision unequivocally commanding that no United States official shall compel a person to be a witness against himself. They consider the provision as an outmoded relic of past fears generated by ancient inquisitorial practices that could not possibly happen here. For this reason the privilege to be silent is sometimes accepted as being more or less of a constitutional nuisance which the courts should abate whenever and however possible.[35]

He wanted no part of any effort to invoke a "broad construction of the doctrine of 'waiver' " as a device for eliminating that "nuisance."

> Apparently, the Court's holding is that at some uncertain point in petitioner's testimony, regardless of her intention, admission of associations with the Communist Party automatically effected a "waiver" of her constitutional protection as to all related questions. To adopt such a rule for the privilege against self-incrimination, when other constitutional safeguards must be knowingly waived, relegates the Fifth Amendment's privilege to a second-rate position.[36]

Similar reasoning appeared to underlie his opposition to immunity statutes. In *Feldman* v. *United States* (1944)[37] he vigorously dissented from the Court's decision, per Justice Frankfurter, upholding use in a federal criminal prosecution of incriminating statements compelled by state officers under a state immunity statute. Especially given his incorporation position and the obvious fact that Feldman was being convicted on the basis, as Black put it, of "words he was forced to speak,"[38] the Justice's stance was hardly surprising. In *Ullmann* v. *United States*,[39] however, he joined Justice Douglas in challenging the constitutionality of a federal statute which granted complete or "transactional" immunity to suspected felons. An argument can be made that a statute compelling a suspect to submit to interrogation about a crime is compatible with the Fifth Amendment if the suspect is completely immunized from prosecution for that crime. It can even be argued, as the post-Black Supreme Court has held,[40] that a statute compelling responses to otherwise incriminating questions is valid if the fruits of that interrogation cannot be used against the suspect. In such situations, after all, the suspect is compelled to answer questions, but his responses are not used in a criminal prosecution. Black and Douglas contended, however, that immunity statutes are based on an unduly narrow reading of the Fifth Amendment. Noting in *Ullman* that the statute at issue there did not necessarily immunize a suspect from all government-imposed disabilities, Douglas emphasized that the amendment's language was not limited to situations in which a criminal conviction, or even a prosecution, might result. "Wisely or not," asserted Douglas, "the Fifth Amendment protects against the compulsory self-accusation of crime without exception or qualification,"[41] placing "the right of silence . . . beyond the reach of Congress."[42]

Just as he was unwilling to accept dilution of the guarantee against compulsory self-incrimination via immunity statutes and notions of implied and involuntary "waiver," Black also refused to condition the Fifth Amendment's safeguard against double jeopardy on considerations of federalism stated nowhere in the Constitution's text. In *Bartkus* v. *Illinois*[43] a majority, speaking through Justice Frankfurter, upheld the state conviction of a defendant who had been acquitted of the same offense in the federal courts. Black dissented.

> The Court apparently takes the position that a second trial for the same act is somehow less offensive if one of the trials is conducted by the Federal Government and the other by a State. Looked at from the standpoint of the individual who is being prosecuted, this notion is too subtle for me to grasp. If double punishment is what is feared, it hurts no less for two "Sovereigns" to inflict it than for one. If danger to the innocent is emphasized, that danger is surely no less when the power of State and Federal Governments is brought to bear on one man in two trials, than when one of those "Sovereigns" proceeds alone. In each case, inescapably, a man is forced to face danger twice for the same conduct. . . . We should . . . be suspicious of any supposed "requirements" of "federalism" which result in obliterating ancient safeguards.[44]

When *Bartkus* was decided, the double jeopardy guarantee had not yet been extended to the states. Even after its incorporation into the

Fourteenth Amendment's meaning, however, the Court reaffirmed its "separate sovereignties" doctrine, though refusing to extend it to state-local contexts, while Justice Black reiterated his commitment to his *Bartkus* dissent.[45]

As in the First Amendment area and other civil liberties fields, however, Black's literal approach to the Constitution's criminal procedure guarantees did not inevitably lead him to "liberal" results. He refused, as noted earlier, to go beyond the language of the double jeopardy guarantee, for example, to hold that continuation of a trial after delay, relocation, or even reorganization of the court was a per se violation of the guarantee.[46] Neither would he agree that imposition of a heavier sentence following retrial violated the Constitution without a showing of special reasons for the increase in sentence. In a partial dissent from the Court's decision laying down such a standard in *North Carolina* v. *Pearce*,[47] he agreed that a state obviously could not "punish" a defendant for exercising a right of appeal provided in the state's own laws. Such a scheme would be unconstitutional, he asserted, not because it was "unfair," but because it would be analogous to two conflicting laws, "one encouraging and granting appeals and another making it a crime to win an appeal"—laws which "would create doubt, ambiguity, and uncertainty, making it impossible for citizens to know which one to follow."[48] At the same time he had no constitutional objection to a system in which "a State makes no provision for re-evaluation of sentences generally but permits the penalty set after retrials to be whatever penalty the trial judge finds to be appropriate whether it be higher or lower than the sentence originally set."[49] A stiffer sentence imposed for punitive reasons could not stand. But that did not mean "that '[i]n order to assure the absence of such a motivation,' [the] Court could, as a matter of constitutional law, direct all trial judges to spell out in detail their reasons for setting a particular sentence, making their reasons 'affirmatively appear,' and basing these reasons on 'objective information concerning identifiable conduct.' "[50] For Black such a requirement was "pure legislation if there ever was legislation."[51]

His literal interpretation of the Sixth Amendment's guarantee to trial by an impartial jury did not invariably lead Black to liberal results either. He insisted that the jury provision, like other Bill of Rights safeguards, was binding on the states[52] and refused to limit its application to "serious" cases alone.[53] But he also rejected claims that a twelve-member jury was required by the Constitution[54] and would probably have dissented from the Court's 1972 reaffirmation of a requirement of unanimous verdicts in federal cases, as well as from the rationale for the Court's decision not to require unanimity in state cases.[55] He opposed, moreover, directed verdicts[56] and other attempts to denigrate the jury's role in civil and criminal cases, even when such efforts were designed to assure "fair" proceedings.

In *Jackson* v. *Denno*,[57] for example, he dissented when the Court held that the voluntariness of a confession must be determined by a judge before its submission to the jury and overturned a New York arrangement under which the jury considered issues of voluntariness, disregarding confessions found to be the product of coercion and weighing the reliability of voluntary statements. Black agreed, of course, that judges could ultimately review and reject a jury's findings. But he could see no constitutional defect in the New York practice.

> The reasons given by the Court for this downgrading of trial by jury appear to me to challenge the soundness of the Founders' great faith in jury trials. Implicit in these constitutional requirements of jury trial is a belief that juries can be trusted to decide factual issues. Stating the obvious fact that "it is only a *reliable* determination on the voluntariness issue which satisfies the constitutional rights of the defendant. . . " [;] the Court concludes, however, that a jury's finding on this question is tainted by inherent unreliability. In making this judgment about the unreliability of juries, the Court, I believe, overlooks the fact that the Constitution itself long ago made the decision that juries *are* to be trusted.[58]

He conceded the possibility that a jury could find a confession coerced, yet ignore the judge's instructions to disregard it "because it may also believe the confession is true, the defendant is guilty, and a guilty person ought not be allowed to escape punishment." He emphasized, however, that such a possibility was "inherent in any confession fact-finding by human fact-finders" as well as one "present perhaps as much in judges as in jurors."[59] For him the crucial factor in the case was the absence of any constitutional provision forbidding the submission of such questions to jurors.[60]

Along similar lines he dissented when the Court overturned on impartial jury grounds a state law forbidding changes of venue in misdemeanor cases. "[T]he right to trial by jury," he declared, "can be protected in many ways. . . . But it simply cannot be said that the right to trial by an impartial jury must necessarily include a right to change of venue."[61] Where, as in *Rideau* v. *Louisiana*,[62] a state provided for change of venue, a trial court's failure to grant such a motion despite extensive prejudicial publicity would amount to a denial of due process. Any defendant, moreover, who fell victim to jury bias was entitled to a new trial. But the right to trial by an impartial jury was not, in Black's view, a right to have the site of the trial relocated.

Black's reaction to issues of criminal procedure was most deferential to government, however, in cases involving rights cast in what the Justice viewed as very flexible language. One such guarantee was the Eighth Amendment's ban on "cruel and unusual punishments." Although the occasions on which the Supreme Court has invoked that nebulous standard have been extremely rare, the provision has long been considered an evolving concept not limited in reach to forms of punishment its framers would have found cruel and unusual. Black, on the other hand, refused to invalidate forms of punishment common at the time of the Bill of Rights' adoption, and he reserved its application for only the most extreme situations. In *Robinson* v. *California*,[63] for example, he joined the Court in holding that the imposition of criminal punishment for the mere status of narcotics addiction was cruel and unusual. When Robinson's petition initially came before the Court, however, he had voted to deny certiorari and later to affirm Robinson's conviction on the merits.[64] When a majority temporarily construed *Robinson* to forbid criminal punishment of any offense committed under the compulsion of a "disease," moreover, he drafted a vigorous dissent.[65] The occasion was *Powell* v. *Texas*,[66] involving a challenge to the public drunkenness conviction of a chronic alcoholic. In his draft dissent Black agreed that the criminal punishment of a status rather than conduct, condemned in *Robinson*, was "particularly obnoxious" and could "reasonably be called cruel and unusual, because it involves punishment for a mere propensity, a desire to commit an offense. . . . This is a situation universally sought to be avoided in our criminal law." But he "refuse[d] to plunge from the concrete and almost universally recognized premises of *Robinson* into the murky problems raised by" the Court's approach in *Powell*. The *Powell* Court's premise was "that it is cruel and unusual to punish a person who is not morally blameworthy." Black was "sympathetic" to the moral and ethical considerations underlying such thinking. "But the question here," he reminded his colleagues, was "one of constitutional law. The legislatures have always been allowed wide freedom to determine the extent to which moral culpability should be a prerequisite to conviction of a crime." And Black vehemently opposed use of the Eighth Amendment as a tool for converting the insanity defense and other issues of criminal responsibility into constitutional questions.

Ultimately, of course, Black's *Powell* position prevailed. His stance regarding capital punishment would not. His unfiled concurrence in the *Francis* case had made clear his early opposition to the claim that the death penalty is per se a form of cruel and unusual punishment. During his last term he reiterated his stance and emphasized its interpretive basis, observing:

> The Eighth Amendment forbids "cruel and unusual punishments." In my view, these words cannot be read to outlaw capital punishment because that penalty was in common use and authorized by law here and in the countries from which our ancestors came at the time the Amendment was adopted. It is inconceivable to me that the framers intended to end capital punishment by the Amendment. Although some people have urged that this Court should amend the Constitution by interpretation to keep it abreast of modern ideas, I have never believed that lifetime judges in our system have any such legislative power.[67]

Nor was his acceptance of capital punishment limited to murder cases, the offense for which Willie Francis was convicted. He once recommended, for example, that a cruel and unusual punishment challenge to the death penalty for common-law robbery be rejected as "frivolous."[68] When the Court upheld provisions leaving imposition of capital punishment to the jury's unfettered discretion—a position the Court would reject less than a year after the Justice's death[69]—he vigorously concurred.[70] And when, several years earlier, a majority rejected exclusion of jurors with scruples against capital punishment from death penalty cases, he chided his colleagues for both their conception of an "impartial" jury and indirect assault on capital punishment. "With all due deference," he declared, "it seems to me that one might much more appropriately charge that this Court has today written the law in such a way that the States are being forced to try their murder cases with biased juries. If this Court is to hold capital punishment unconstitutional, I think it should do so forthrightly, not by making it impossible for States to get juries that will enforce the death penalty."[71]

The Fourth Amendment

Justice Black's Fourth Amendment jurisprudence, however, was perhaps even more deferential to government than his Eighth Amendment stance. He insisted that the Fourth Amendment prohibited only "unreasonable," not warrantless, searches and seizures, even though it also imposed standards for the issuance of warrants. Since the amendment's ban on "unreasonable searches and seizures" indicated only that a search or seizure be based on reasonable grounds, moreover, he believed that the Court should be deferential to law officers and local judges in deciding what police tactics comport with that flexible command, that determinations of reasonableness should turn on the circumstances of each case, and that the Court should thus avoid resort to per se rules in the Fourth Amendment field.

His dissent in *Vale* v. *Louisiana*,[72] a 1970 case, well reflects his position. There, police officers possessing warrants for Vale's arrest were watching his mother's house, where he resided. During their surveillance they observed an automobile arrive, sound its horn, back into a parking place, and again sound its horn. Shortly thereafter Vale, who had been arrested twice the previous month and was then under indictment for a narcotics offense, came out of the house and spoke with the driver of the car. At the conclusion of their conversation, Vale looked up and down the street, then returned to the house. When he reappeared, he again looked up and down the street before walking to the car and leaning inside. His behavior convinced the police that an exchange of narcotics was taking place, and they drove down the street toward the suspect and the parked car. When they approached within a few car lengths of the two men, Vale spotted them and began to walk quickly back to the house while the driver of the car attempted to pull away from the curb. The officers stopped both Vale and the driver and also observed the driver, whom they recognized as a known addict, place something in his mouth and apparently swallow it. The police then placed both men under arrest and searched the house, discovering narcotics in a bedroom.

A majority had little difficulty overturning the seizure of narcotics and Vale's conviction. In *Chimel* v. *California*,[73] decided the previous year, Justice Stewart had held for the Court that, with a few exceptions involving "exigent circumstances," warrantless searches were absolutely forbidden. A limited search incident to a valid arrest was one such exception. But such searches, Stewart insisted, must be truly "incidental" to the arrest, extending only to the person arrested and the area within his reach. The search of Chimel's entire three-bedroom house at the time of his arrest, Stewart held, thus exceeded permissible constitutional limits. Writing for the *Vale* majority, Stewart assumed the same position. Even if *Chimel* were not retroactive, he held, the search of Vale's residence could be upheld as an incident of his arrest only if the arrest occurred *inside* the house.

In a *Chimel* dissent Justice White had argued that the search of Chimel's home was "reasonable" whether or not viewed as incidental to his arrest, because Chimel's wife or someone else aware of his arrest could have removed the coins he was arrested for stealing while officers sought a warrant. Justice Black joined White's *Chimel* dissent and assumed a similar stance in *Vale*. He did not "suggest that all arrests necessarily provide the basis for a search of the arrestee's house."[74] He insisted, however, that the search which led to Vale's conviction was reasonable and, like White in *Chimel*, found it "unnecessary to determine whether the search was valid as incident to . . . arrest."[75] When the officers arrested Vale in full view of his mother's house, they had reason to believe that the house contained a supply of narcotics which they could reasonably have feared Vale's mother or someone else would destroy or remove were a search warrant sought. When the officers undertook a quick initial search of the house, they discovered no one there. At that point, however, Vale's mother and brother arrived. "Now what had been a suspicion," Black asserted, "became a certainty: Vale's relatives were in possession and knew of his arrest. To have abandoned the search at this point and left the house with Vale, would not have been the action of reasonable police officers."[76]

Nor was it of any consequence, in Black's view, that the officers had earlier secured warrants for Vale's arrest. Justice Stewart had reasoned for the majority that since the officers had already obtained arrest warrants, there was "no reason . . . to suppose that it was impractical for them to obtain a search warrant as well."[77] Black pointed out, however, that the arrest warrants were not issued because of "any present misconduct" on Vale's part.

[T]hey were issued because the bond had been increased for an earlier narcotics charge then pending against Vale. When the police came to arrest Vale, they knew only that his bond had been increased. There is nothing in the record to indicate that, absent the increased bond, there would have been probable cause for an arrest, much less a search. Probable cause for the search arose for the first time when the police observed the activity of Vale and Saucier [the person in the car] in and around the house.[78]

Black was equally deferential to government in his approach to the warrant clause. That provision requires "probable cause" for the issuance of warrants. In *Aguilar* v. *Texas*[79] the Court overturned a warrant issued on the basis of information supplied by an informant where the affidavit given by the officers seeking the warrant contained no information regarding the underlying circumstances on which the informant based his tip or the officers' reasons for concluding that the informant was creditable and his information reliable. In a dissent Justice Clark pointed out that the challenged affidavit was also based on a week's police surveillance of the suspect's residence. Justice Black joined Clark's dissent, as did Justice Stewart.

Initially, however, Black had also drafted a separate dissent[80] emphasizing that the Fourth Amendment "uses words which have patently flexible meanings." In determining what is "reasonable" and what constitutes "probable cause," he asserted, "the Court should recall that each Fourth Amendment case rests on its peculiar facts." He doubted, moreover, whether the Court was "any more qualified to upset the factual findings of local magistrates as to what constitutes probable cause than it is to review a jury's resolution of disputed facts."

> In the case of probable cause, as in other situations where there are facts from which conflicting inferences can be drawn, we should, at least in the absence of exceptional circumstances, leave it to the magistrate to draw the inferences, especially since the magistrate is on the scene, has an intimate and firsthand knowledge of the locality, is asked repeatedly by the same police department to issue warrants, knows something of the character and reliability of the officers who come before him, and therefore is best placed to know the reliability of the information given him.

In his view a local magistrate's findings of probable cause were entitled to the "same respect" the Court had extended to the decisions of grand juries despite claims that they were based on "incompetent" or hearsay evidence.

In published opinions Black advanced similar themes, accusing the majority at times of equating the probable-cause proceeding with a "little trial" in which "the magistrate is to sit as a judge and weigh the evidence and practically determine guilt or innocence before issuing a warrant."[81] In *Spinelli* v. *United States*,[82] for example, he again dissented when the Court, citing *Aguilar*, overturned a search warrant based on what a majority considered an inadequate statement of the circumstances on which an informant based his tip. Wrote Black:

> The existence of probable cause is a factual matter that calls for the determination of a factual question. While no statistics are immediately available, questions of probable cause to issue search warrants and to make arrests are doubtless involved in many thousands of cases in state courts. All of those probable-cause state cases are now potentially reviewable by this Court. It is, of course, physically impossible for this Court to review the evidence in all or even a substantial percentage of those cases. Consequently, whether desirable or not, we must inevitably accept most of the fact findings of the state courts, particularly when, as here in a federal cause, both the trial and appellate courts have decided the facts the same way. It cannot be said that the trial judge and six members of the Court of Appeals committed flagrant error in finding from evidence that the magistrate had probable cause to issue the search warrant here. It seems to me that this Court would best serve itself and the administration of justice by accepting the judgment of the two courts below. After all, they too are lawyers and judges, and much closer to the practical, everyday affairs of life than we are.[83]

Black refused, moreover, to read into the Fourth Amendment any particular description of those authorized to issue warrants. In *Coolidge* v. *New Hampshire*,[84] for example, he dissented when the Court overturned a warrant issued by an attorney general acting as a justice of the peace, who had also assumed charge of the investigation and was later the chief prosecutor at the petitioner's trial. Emphasizing the overwhelming evidence underlying the attorney general's finding of probable cause to support issuance of the warrant, Black asserted: "[T]here is no language in the Fourth Amendment which provides any basis for the disqualification of the state attorney general to act as a magistrate. He is a state official of high office. The Fourth Amendment does not indicate that his position of authority over state law enforcement renders him ineligible to issue warrants upon a showing of probable cause supported by oath or affirmation."[85] Had the evidence on which the warrant was based been marginal, Black no doubt would have considered the attorney general's status a signal for closer scrutiny of the probable-cause decision than he normally favored. But he refused to reject a finding of probable cause on a theory that the Fourth Amendment by implication forbids certain officials to make such findings.

Neither was it surprising, given his literal approach to constitutional interpretation, that he was unwilling to hold that the Fourth Amendment reaches police eavesdrop practices. Early in his career he joined the Court[86] in reaffirming *Olmstead* v. *United States*,[87] the 1928 decision limiting the Fourth Amendment's application to cases involving physical trespass and the search and seizure of tangible items. And when the Court seriously undermined *Olmstead* in *Berger* v. *New York*,[88] then effectively overruled it in *Katz* v. *United States*,[89] he vehemently dissented. "I do not believe," he asserted in *Katz*, "that the words of the Amendment will bear the meaning given them by today's decision" or that it was "the proper role of [the] Court to rewrite the Amendment in order 'to bring it into harmony with the times' and thus reach a result that many people believe to be desirable."[90] The amendment's language, he asserted, was "the crucial place to look in construing a written document such as [the] Constitution."[91] The amendment's first clause protected "persons, houses, papers, and effects." Those words "connot[ed] the idea of tangible things with size, form, and weight, things capable of being searched, seized, or both," with qualities that conversations "overheard by eavesdropping whether by plain snooping or wiretapping," did not possess.[92] In his judgment the warrant clause "further establishe[d] the Framers' purpose to limit its protection to tangible things," for it required that warrants "particularly" describe "the place to be searched, and the persons or things to be seized." "How," he asked,

> can one "describe" a future conversation and, if one cannot, how can a magistrate issue a warrant to eavesdrop one in the future? It is argued that information showing what is expected to be said is sufficient to limit the boundaries of what later can be admitted into evidence; but does such general information really meet the specific language of the Amendment which says "particularly describing"? Rather than using language in a completely artificial

way, I must conclude that the Fourth Amendment simply does not apply to eavesdropping.[93]

In his view the Fourth Amendment simply did not embody a "broad, abstract and ambiguous concept' of 'privacy' " through which the Court was given "unlimited power to hold unconstitutional everything which affects privacy." Instead, it "protect[ed] privacy only to the extent that it prohibit[ed] unreasonable searches and seizures of 'persons, houses, papers, and effects.' "[94]

Along similar lines he dissented when the court held in 1971 that the amendment itself created a cause of action under which victims of unlawful search and seizure could sue federal agents for damages. The Justice had no doubt that Congress had power to create such a basis for suit, just as it already had against officials acting under color of state law. For the Court to create such a right, however, amounted for him to "an exercise of power that the Constitution [did] not give."[95]

Finally, Black's literal approach to constitutional interpretation, as well as his penchant for clear legal standards, prompted considerable ambivalence on his part with respect to the nature and scope of the exclusionary rule in Fourth Amendment contexts. In 1948 he dissented from what he later would term the Court's "unarticulated premise" in *Trupiano* v. *United States*[96] "that the Fourth Amendment of itself barred the use of evidence obtained by what the Court considered an 'unreasonable' search."[97] Speaking for the Court a year later, he rejected extension of the rule to the subpoena process in civil cases.[98] And when the Court, per Justice Frankfurter, held in *Wolf* v. *Colorado*[99] that something approximating the Fourth Amendment was applicable to the states via the Fourteenth Amendment's due process clause, yet rejected application of the exclusionary rule in state cases, Black concurred. He agreed, of course, that the Fourth Amendment was fully binding on the states. But he also concurred in the majority's "plain implication" that the federal exclusionary rule, first established in *Weeks* v. *United States* (1914),[100] was "not a command of the Fourth Amendment but is a judicially created rule of evidence which Congress might negate."[101] Then, after more than a decade in which the Court reaffirmed *Wolf* while reviewing state evidence claims on general due process, "fundamental fairness," "shock-the-conscience" grounds in *Rochin* v. *California*[102] and other highly controversial decisions of the 1950s,[103] he joined the Court's decision in *Mapp* v. *Ohio*,[104] overruling *Wolf* and applying the exclusionary rule per se to the states. He still did not agree that the Fourth Amendment alone embodied the rule. Largely tracking Justice Bradley's opinion for the Court in *Boyd* v. *United States* (1887),[105] however, he asserted that the Fourth Amendment and the Fifth Amendment's guarantee against compulsory self-incrimination were entitled to "a liberal rather than a niggardly interpretation" and that when "considered together . . . a constitutional basis emerge[d] which not only justifie[d] but actually require[d] the exclusionary rule."[106]

A variety of considerations probably pushed Black to the position he assumed in *Mapp*. Not surprisingly, given his preference for clear legal standards, one factor undoubtedly at work was the confusion created by the *Rochin* approach to state search and seizure claims—a formula under which certain fruits of illegal search were excluded, others were not, and the outcome of each case turned purely on the degree to which five Justices were revolted by challenged police tactics. In his *Mapp* concurrence he expressed satisfaction that "[f]inally, today we clear up that uncertainty," adding: "we . . . reject the confusing 'shock-the-conscience' standard of the *Wolf* and *Rochin* cases and, instead, set aside this state conviction in reliance upon the precise, intelligible and more predictable constitutional doctrine enunciated in the *Boyd* case."[107]

He seems clearly to have been influenced too by the close analogy between compulsion of a person's words or physical evidence taken from a person's body, which he believed the Fifth Amendment also reached, and the forcible extraction of reading materials from a person's home, at issue in *Mapp*, and unlawful seizure of papers challenged in *Boyd*. Indeed, he may have intended to limit his *Mapp* concurrence to such situations. While resting the exclusionary rule on both the Fourth and Fifth Amendments in *Mapp*, he devoted a considerable portion of his *Mapp* concurrence to similarities between *Mapp* and *Rochin*. In the latter, it will be recalled, a majority found use of a stomach pump to extract morphine capsules from a suspect "shocking" conduct and thus violative of due process. Black concurred in the Court's decision on Fifth Amendment grounds, asserting: "I think a person is compelled to be a witness against himself not only when he is compelled to testify, but also when as here, incriminating evidence is forcibly taken from him by a contrivance of modern science."[108] In discussing *Rochin* in his *Mapp* concurrence, he again argued that the Fifth Amendment "barred the introduction of . . . 'capsule' evidence just as much as it would have forbidden the use of words Rochin might have been coerced to speak."[109] And he seemed clearly to view the forcible extraction of evidence from Mapp's house as analogous to the extraction of evidence at issue in *Rochin*. While he rested his *Mapp* concurrence on both the Fourth and Fifth Amendments, therefore, he appeared to view the Fourth Amendment as simply support for an interpretation of the Fifth which would cover the forcible extraction of evidence not involving the sort of intrusion upon a person's body challenged in *Rochin*. Indeed, during his last term on the Court he asserted that the Fifth Amendment alone commanded an exclusionary rule and argued that "[t]he evidence seized by breaking into Mrs. Mapp's house and the search of all her possessions, was excluded from evidence, not by the Fourth Amendment which contains no exclusionary rule, but by the Fifth Amendment which does. The introduction of such evidence compels a man to be a witness against himself."[110]

Whatever the motivation for his *Mapp* concurrence or the ultimate nature and reach of the exclusionary rule he embraced there, Black supported its full retroactive application[111] and continued to accept it for the remainder of his career. He was never comfortable with it, however. In *Mapp* he agreed that the rule was "perhaps not required by the express language of the Constitution strictly construed"[112]—a major concession for one of his jurisprudence. Toward the end, moreover, his attacks on what he condemned as unduly expansive constructions of the Fourth Amendment's substantive meaning frequently included expressions of strong misgiving about the exclusionary rule as well. Such concerns apparently influenced him also to endorse the "harmless error" rule in search and seizure cases[113]—though apparently not in other procedural contexts[114]—and to favor limitations on collateral review of Fourth Amendment claims.[115]

For one who sees in Justice Black's opinions and voting patterns a remarkable internal and longitudinal consistency, his pronouncements regarding the exclusionary rule make for frustrating reading. During his career, as indicated previously, he seemed to conclude that the rule was required by the Fourth and Fifth Amendments, required by the Fifth alone, or not required at all by the Constitution. His impression of Justice Bradley's recognition in the *Boyd* case of a rule bottomed on the Fourth and Fifth Amendments ranged, moreover, from acceptance to near-ridicule. His interpretations of the bases for the Court's decisions in *Weeks*, *Mapp*, and other major cases involving the rule appear equally inconsistent over time.[116] One can thus find little to fault in Jacob Landynski's devastating, if at times overdrawn, assessment of conflicts in Black's position—even if the difficulties the rule created for the Justice are understandable, given his jurisprudence. Certain aspects of Landynski's critique of Black's Fourth Amendment jurisprudence, however, are vulnerable to serious question.

1. Landynski challenges Black's failure to construe the amendment's ban on unreasonable searches and seizures in light of its warrant clause and what Landynski sees as the lessons of the history underlying the amendment's adoption. The "main object" behind the amendment's enactment, Landynski asserts, "was to prevent the recurrence of the detested general warrant," which was "in effect a lifetime hunting license in the hands of the officer, requiring neither probable cause nor particularity of description of persons or premises, nor even judicial approval of the search."[117] Surely, he contends, the Fourth Amendment's framers would not have imposed "stringent warrant requirements"[118] to protect against general warrants, yet have intended the reasonableness of individual searches and seizures to be evaluated without reference to that clause. Under such an approach the term "unreasonable" in the first clause "becomes in effect a free-floating standard unrelated to the specific requirements in the second clause (or to the amendment's history) and depends for its meaning on whatever content the judges will pour into its shapeless form."[119] An approach more consistent with "common sense and the amendment's antecedent history," in Landynski's judgment, is one which "treat[s] the two clauses conjunctively so that the reasonableness required by the first clause is defined in terms of the standards set forth in the second clause." When the Fourth Amendment is so construed, he asserts, "a reasonable search is one conducted pursuant to a judicially authorized warrant, an unreasonable search is one that is not. Only in the event of exigent circumstances, where the warrant standard is inappropriate because pressures of time do not permit the issuance of a warrant . . . would different standards of reasonableness need to be fashioned and applied, as indeed they have been."[120] In short, Landynski favors the approach the Court articulated most clearly in *Chimel* v. *California*.

There is, as Landynski argues, a rich historical record relevant to the Fourth Amendment's adoption. It is by no means certain, however, that history supports the construction for which he contends. The framers could just as logically have meant to ban the general warrant and impose standards for the issuance of warrants without intending at the same time to require warrants for most searches. A desire to ban a "lifetime hunting license" is a far cry, after all, from an intent to mandate warrants for most searches. And, in my judgment, it is perfectly plausible to conclude that the framers wished to forbid the general warrant and other similarly abusive search and seizure techniques, but would have seen little similarity between the purposes they envisioned for the Fourth Amendment and the expansive construction given it in *Chimel* and certain other modern cases. Given the Fourth Amendment's language, moreover, Landynski's thesis would logically require warrants for most arrests as well as most searches. Yet he appears to accept warrantless arrests as the rule rather than the exception, citing common law practice as support for his own inconsistency despite the fact that general warrants were also condoned at common law.[121] As for his assertion that "the term 'unreasonable' . . . depends for its meaning on whatever content the judges will pour into its shapeless form," the same observation can be made of "probable cause" and other elements of the warrant clause, not to mention the "exigent circumstances" under which, in Landynski's judgment, warrantless searches should be permitted. Under Black's approach, or Landynski's, judges are obliged to construe and apply the flexible standards inherent in the amendment's language.

2. Landynski sees an "irreconcilable" inconsistency between Black's absolutism and his flexible construction of the Fourth Amendment. "If, as Black maintained, the framers were indeed animated by the intention of reducing judicial discretion in the field of individual liberties to the extent of 'absolutizing' the guarantees in the remainder of the Bill of Rights," Landynski asks, "would they have singled out the one amendment that is at the heart of the individual's security against the totalitarian 'knock at the door' for a grant of virtually unfettered discretion to the judiciary as to its definition and application?"[122] Black never contended, though, that every Bill of Rights safeguard embodies an absolute command, and the Fourth Amendment's language flies in the face of an absolutist approach to its meaning except in the obvious sense that an "unreasonable" search, as Black put it, "is absolutely prohibited."[123] Black obviously did oppose interpretations empowering judges to rule on the "reasonableness" of governmental action. But the

Fourth Amendment's words impose such an obligation. As construed earlier, moreover, Landynski's approach really vests judges with no less "unfettered discretion" than Black's.

3. Landynski questions how Black could have little difficulty assimilating motion pictures and related modern forms of communication to freedom of speech and press, yet reject extension of the Fourth Amendment to eavesdropping. The issue, of course, is one of degree. But motion pictures do reproduce speech and visual images just as newspapers, books, and magazines do. The seizure of words, on the other hand, clearly does not amount to the seizure of "persons, houses, papers, and effects," against which the Fourth Amendment's language protects. Moreover, even if the amendment's protection of "persons" is read to forbid eavesdropping and all other "unreasonable" intrusions upon personal "privacy"—a truly "unfettering" construction Black repeatedly rejected—it is difficult to answer the Justice's contention that it is impossible to "particularly" describe a conversation that has not yet taken place, indeed may never occur, especially if the warrant clause is given the "stringent" construction Landynski favors.

4. In dissenting from the Court's extension of the Fourth Amendment to eavesdropping, Justice Black readily conceded that wiretapping and related modern forms of electronic surveillance were "an unknown possibility" at the time of the amendment's adoption. He insisted, however, that eavesdropping was "an ancient practice" condemned as a nuisance at common law, "that the Framers were aware of this practice, and if they had desired to outlaw or restrict the use of evidence obtained by eavesdropping, . . . they would have used the appropriate language to do so in the Fourth Amendment. They certainly would not have left such a task to the ingenuity of language-stretching judges."[124] Landynski maintains that Black's "contention will scarcely stand the light of day," adding:

> The type of eavesdropping the framers were familiar with, which was carried out by the unaided human ear, was even further removed from the sophisticated electronic devices in use today than was the ox cart from the airplane. It took no great ingenuity, only reasonable precautions, for one to be on guard against the human eavesdropper, whereas the ordinary citizen is virtually defenseless against the resources available to the mechanical eavesdropper.[125]

On its face, however, Landynski's assertion supports rather than challenges Black's basic premise that the amendment's framers did not consider the sort of eavesdropping familiar to them worthy of constitutional scrutiny and thus included no restrictions on eavesdropping within the amendment's scope. Landynski seems to be contending, in other words, not that the framers included protection against eavesdropping in the amendment, but that they would have had they anticipated modern technology, and that judges should thus adapt the amendment's meaning to problems its framers did not foresee. Black, of course, would have no part of such an approach to the Constitution's meaning.

5. Landynski contends that Black's rejection of the Fourth Amendment's application to eavesdropping conflicts with the Justice's position regarding the constitutional status of administrative searches. In *Frank v. Maryland* (1959)[126] Black joined Justice Douglas's dissent from the Court's refusal to require a warrant for such searches. In 1967 he helped form a Court to overrule *Frank*.[127] Landynski reads Douglas's *Frank* dissent to hold that "the specific abuses which were responsible for bringing the fourth amendment into being should not be confused with the idea of a broader right of privacy from governmental intrusion which . . . the framers wished to secure for the citizen."[128] Then he asserts that "this [right of privacy] is the very value which according to Black's eavesdropping opinions is not the concern of the fourth amendment except in the context of an eighteenth century search."[129] Douglas did accuse the *Frank* majority of "greatly dilut[ing] the right of privacy which every homeowner had the right to believe was part of our American heritage."[130] A reading of Douglas's opinion makes clear, however, that his reference was to the privacy language that Justice Frankfurter, author of the *Frank* majority opinion, had employed the previous month in *Wolf* v. *Colorado* to apply the Fourth Amendment to the states and was in no way intended as a shorthand substitute for an interpretation of the amendment based on its words and the "specific abuses" leading to its adoption. The major thrust of Douglas's dissent, in fact, was the contention that the Fourth Amendment was intended to reach beyond "searches for evidence to be used in criminal prosecutions"[131] and that the history relating to the amendment's adoption, like the language of its first clause, supported such a construction of its scope. Douglas was arguing, in short, that the "specific abuses" which led to the amend-

ment's adoption went beyond outrages growing out of criminal investigations and included those arising from administrative searches. In
Griswold v. *Connecticut*[132] and other later cases, of course, Douglas
would join those finding a general right of privacy within various Bill of
Rights safeguards. But his *Frank* dissent was not part of that odyssey. Had
it been, Black would surely have condemned it, just as he vehemently
dissented from the approach Douglas and company pursued in *Griswold*.

Nor, despite Landynski's contention to the contrary, is the literal
construction of the Fourth Amendment on which Black's position on
eavesdropping relied inconsistent with the Justice's extension of the
amendment's coverage to administrative searches. "Even if an inspec-
tion can be considered a 'search' in the literal sense," Landynski argues,
"it does not give rise to a 'seizure.' Yet Black clearly read the two words
in conjunction where eavesdropping was concerned: only such a search
as could result in a seizure was forbidden by the amendment."[133] But did
he? In *Katz*, as noted earlier, Black contended that the Fourth Amendment's "words connote the idea of tangible things . . . capable of being
searched, seized, *or* both."[134] Administrative inspections may rarely
involve "both" a search and a seizure; but they clearly constitute a
search, and nothing in Black's opinions on eavesdropping suggests that
"searches" of "houses" somehow cease to be searches subject to the
Fourth Amendment's controls unless seizures are also contemplated.

6. Landynski asserts that, toward the end of the Justice's career,
"[t]he guilt of defendants began to color Black's fourth amendment
opinions in a sustained fashion."[135] His implication appears to be that
such considerations began to influence the Justice's votes as well. As
part of his assaults on what he considered unduly expansive constructions of the Fourth Amendment and the exclusionary rule, Black
did register detailed and graphic descriptions of the crimes involved in
search and seizure cases brought before the Court as well as the often
overwhelming evidence of the defendant's guilt.[136] To suggest that a
defendant's guilt would influence Black's resolution of Fourth Amendment issues raised in that defendant's case ignores, however, the fact
that such factors obviously continued to have absolutely no impact on
the Justice's reaction to self-incrimination, counsel, and other procedural claims raised by petitioners whose guilt often seemed equally
obvious. In *California* v. *Byers*,[137] decided May 17, 1971, just four
months before his retirement, Black dissented from a decision upholding a state statute which required motorists involved in automobile

accidents to stop at the scene and give their names and addresses, as well as from a plurality's conclusion that the challenged regulation created no "substantial risk of self-incrimination" or compulsion of "testimonial" evidence. Interestingly, in light of Landynski's thesis, Black concluded his *Byers* dissent with the following observation.

> I can only assume that the unarticulated premise of the decision is that there is so much crime abroad in this country at present that Bill of Rights' safeguards against arbitrary government must not be completely enforced. I can agree that there is too much crime in the land for us to treat criminals with favor. But I can never agree that we should depart in the slightest way from the Bill of Rights' guarantees that gave this country its high place among the free nations of the world.[138]

Justice Black's reaction to the cases Landynski discusses in elaborating his thesis seems entirely compatible, moreover, with the flexible, case-by-case, "reasonableness" construction of the Fourth Amendment he had always embraced, as well as with his continuing uncertainty regarding the exclusionary rule and his literal approach to constitutional interpretation. Consider, for example, *Bumper v. North Carolina*.[139] In *Bumper*, Landynski observes, Black dissented when the Court "reversed the conviction of an obviously guilty and incredibly brutal rapist because his grandmother, with whom he lived, had been tricked into consenting to the search which yielded the evidence."[40] Police had told the petitioner's grandmother they had a warrant though they did not. But Black emphasized in dissent that her "*immediate response*" at the time, "without mentioning anything about a warrant or asking to see it or read it or have it read to her, was to tell the deputy 'to come on in.'" His study of the record convinced him that "she actually wanted the officers to search her house—to prove to them that she had nothing to hide." The grandmother's trial testimony provided direct support for that conclusion. At one point, she observed:

> He did tell me he had a search warrant. I don't know if Sheriff Stockard was with him. I was not paying much attention. I told Mr. Stockard to go ahead and look all over the house. I had no objection to them making a search of my house. I was willing to let them look in any room or drawer in my house they wanted to. Nobody threatened me with anything. Nobody told me they would give me any

money if I would let them search. I let them search, and it was all my own free will.[141]

At another point she explained that she gave the officers "a free will to look because I felt like the boy wasn't guilty."[142] Surely, had the decision to allow a search been prompted by the police reference to a warrant, she would have so testified. At the very least she would not have insisted in court that her decision was the product of her "own free will." For one of Justice Black's Fourth Amendment jurisprudence to find such a search reasonable is hardly surprising. Nor, arguably, would he have been any less likely to assume such a position had other evidence of Bumper's guilt not been overwhelming.

7. In rejecting Black's contention that any exclusionary rule must be bottomed ultimately on the Fifth Amendment rather than the Fourth, Landynski argues that

> the fifth amendment says no more concerning the use which may be made in court of compelled evidence than the fourth amendment does of evidence obtained through unreasonable search. To the extent that incriminating evidence might be extracted from a defendant in the courtroom under judicial process, to forbid its extraction is, of course, tantamount to forbidding its use. But what of forced incrimination at the hands of grand juries, prosecutors, and policemen? Black himself once explained the matter this way: "And if the Federal Government does extract incriminating testimony . . . the immunity provided . . . should at the very least prevent the use of such testimony in any court. . . . " Certainly this reasoning can be applied with equal force to evidence taken in violation of the fourth amendment.[143]

Can it? The issue, of course, is one of degree. The Fifth Amendment provides, however, that "[n]o person . . . shall be compelled in any criminal case to be a witness against himself." How else can a person be "a witness against himself in any criminal case" except by providing testimony or, in Black's view, other evidence which is then used against him in court? The amendment's language does not limit the forbidden compulsion, moreover, to the courtroom. Where a person is "compelled . . . to be a witness against himself" is irrelevant, so long as the compulsion takes place in the context of a "criminal case." The Fourth Amendment, on the other hand, merely forbids unreasonable searches and seizures. It makes no reference whatever to the relation of such searches and seizures to "any criminal case."

8. Finally, Landynski rejects the notion that Black's Fourth Amendment stance can be explained entirely in terms of his interpretivist jurisprudence, yet fails to suggest a generally applicable alternative explanation. Citing Charles Reich's assertion that the Justice's jurisprudence was responsive to social change[144] and Black's own stated preference for a "broad, liberal interpretation"[145] of Bill of Rights safeguards, Landynski suggests that, "for all Black's incessant emphasis on literalism," the Justice "perceived the judicial task to be, in some measure, creative rather than mechanical."[146] Landynski wonders why Black's Fourth Amendment jurisprudence was so literal and so devoid of considerations of social need. He is perplexed, too, that a Justice who considered both " 'language *and* history' . . . the 'crucial factors' influencing his exposition of the Constitution" could emphasize only "the naked text of the [fourth] amendment to the deliberate exclusion of its history and purpose," thereby "obliterat[ing] the accumulated meaning concealed within its words."[147] Landynski suggests that Black's "deep and overriding concern" about the Court's growing recognition of a right of privacy might explain his "strident" later opinions, especially in eavesdropping cases.[148] He concedes, however, that such an explanation should not be "overstated," since "[a]t no time during his years on the Court did Black's fidelity to the guarantees in the fourth amendment match his devotion to other provisions in the Bill of Rights." Thus, he concludes, Black's relegation of the Fourth Amendment "to a secondary position in the hierarchy of constitutional safeguards" must await "full exploration" and may never be satisfactorily explained.[149]

In my judgment, however, Black's Fourth Amendment jurisprudence is thoroughly consistent with his interpretivist, positivist approach to constitutional interpretation. The Justice did believe that both language and history should be the primary determinants of the Constitution's meaning. As I have already contended, however, Professor Landynski arguably reads entirely too much into the Fourth Amendment's words and the history underlying its adoption. His own reading of its history indicates that the amendment's framers were primarily bent on eliminating the general warrant. History provides little, if any, direct evidence of other purposes it was expected to serve—certainly little to support the expansive construction given it by Landynski or in *Chimel* and other modern cases. The amendment's language, moreover, forbids only "unreasonable" searches and seizures. That standard, like its requirement that warrants be bottomed on "probable cause," is, as Black contended, a flexible one. When confronted with such standards, Black was always reluctant to substitute his judgment for that of local officials, especially trial judges in the best position to evaluate the circumstances underlying a challenged search or seizure. Since the Fourth Amendment's language and history obviously embody no specific reference to an exclusionary rule, his interpretivist's frustration with the rule is equally understandable. So, too, given the amendment's reference only to the search and seizure of tangible items and requirement that warrants "particularly" describe the things to be seized, is his rejection of its extension to eavesdropping. In short, the Justice's relegation of the amendment to "a secondary position in the hierarchy of constitutional safeguards" seems clearly based on the fact that the amendment speaks in flexible, nonabsolutist language, while the First Amendment and certain other Bill of Rights safeguards do not. Black did favor, of course, "broad, liberal" constructions of constitutional guarantees. He insisted, however, that they be rooted in language and history. That was as true, incidentally, of his construction of the First Amendment as it was of the Fourth.

Equal Protection

Of Fourth Amendment issues, only the exclusionary rule appeared to pose serious problems for Black and his interpretivist approach to constitutional construction. The Fourteenth Amendment's equal protection clause was a different matter. Its language defies a literal interpretation, yet appears to reach beyond its historic racial context. Characteristically, Black never publicly revealed the concern the guarantee caused him. Shortly before his death, however, he agreed, as noted in Chapter Two, that the clause should perhaps have been left out of the Constitution altogether, stated in more explicit terms, or at least not allowed to extend beyond race. His equal protection philosophy largely reflects such frustration. In logical consistency it is also the least satisfying element of his jurisprudence. He attempted to give the guarantee a clear, precise, internally consistent construction. But the clause's vague phrasing and history, as well as conflicting elements in the Justice's judicial philosophy, obstructed his efforts, often leaving him open to the very charge of judicial creativity he so frequently directed at others.[150]

Confronted with a clause that appeared potentially open-ended in meaning, Black elected to confine the guarantee's scope as a meaningful limitation on government largely to the core of its historical context, subjecting racial classifications to strict scrutiny while according most other forms of discrimination extreme deference. In fact, on at least one occasion he expressed doubt whether equal protection should be invoked at all for review of the reasonableness of economic controls, and presumably other nonracial classifications as well. In *Daniel* v. *Family Security Life Ins. Co.*,[151] decided in 1949, the Court, per Justice Murphy, upheld a South Carolina statute regulating the funeral business. In a draft of his opinion Murphy observed, "We cannot say that the South Carolina statute does not seek to correct real evils. Nor can we say that the measure has no relation to the elimination of these evils. There our inquiry must stop." Between "There" and "our inquiry" on his copy of the draft, Black inserted "if not before," adding in the margin, "I do not think that we can strike down a state statute because we are unable to say that the remedy has a 'relation' to 'real evils.' At most, I suppose such action would follow only if there is no conceivable state of facts that would justify [a finding] of evil and relationship of it to the remedy. *I regret to become involved at all in this formula useful only to invalidate state laws objectionable to the Court.*"[152]

In economic cases such as *Family Security*, Black was consistently deferential to governmental power. He dissented from the sole modern Supreme Court ruling invalidating economic legislation on equal protection grounds,[153] and the only case in which he dissented from a decision upholding such controls involved a regulation which had First Amendment undertones and seemed completely irrational.[154] This is not to suggest that he had no difficulty with economic classifications. He found the scheme at issue in *Kotch* v. *Pilot Commissioners*,[155] for example, one of the most troublesome of his career.[156] The *Kotch* Court reviewed a Louisiana system for the appointment of waterway pilots. The governor made the appointments, but they were limited to candidates who had served a six months' apprenticeship with a licensed pilot, and critics complained that incumbent pilots generally selected only relatives and friends as apprentices. In a dissent joined by Justices Reed, Douglas, and Murphy, Justice Rutledge charged that, under the scheme, "[b]lood [was], in effect, made the crux of selection" and found no difference "in effects" between a classification "founded on blood relationship" and one based on race.[157] Black thought Rutledge's rationale persuasive and agonized over a decision. Ultimately, however, he assumed his traditional stance, invoking rational-basis rhetoric to uphold the challenged arrangement as one relevant to the selection of well-trained pilots.

Black's approach to economic classifications was thus compatible with the lower level of the two-tiered equal protection formula developed on the Court during his tenure. He also wrote or joined opinions invoking the upper tier and holding that discriminatory laws which were based on "suspect categories" of classification or abridged "fundamental rights" were to be subject to strict judicial scrutiny and upheld only if found to be the least restrictive means for promoting a legitimate and compelling governmental interest. The "fundamental rights" branch of that "new" equal protection philosophy had its roots in *Skinner* v. *Oklahoma*,[158] the 1942 case in which the Court, per Justice Douglas, overturned a law providing for the selective sterilization of habitual criminals and indicated that laws impinging on "basic civil rights of man" were to be strictly scrutinized.[159] Justice Black joined *Skinner* and provided an important semantic basis for "suspect-categories" doctrine with his observation for the Court in the *Korematsu* case that "all legal restrictions which curtail the civil rights of a single racial group are immediately suspect" and "courts must subject them to the most rigid scrutiny."[160] Over the years, moreover, he wrote or joined opinions indicating that discrimination based upon national origin and alienage should be accorded strict scrutiny.[161] And in 1968 he authored a textbook illustration of Warren era "new" equal protection rhetoric. *Williams* v. *Rhodes*[162] invalidated state regulations restricting party access to the ballot. Such regulations, Black asserted for the *Williams* Court, burdened voting and associational rights—rights which "rank among our most precious freedoms." The state, he added, had "failed to show 'any compelling interest' which justifies imposing such burdens on the right to vote and to associate."[163]

Black's stance in such cases is hardly proof, however, that he personally embraced the expansive model of equal protection which germinated in *Skinner* and *Korematsu*, then flowered during the Warren years. The sterilization statute at issue in *Skinner* was vulnerable to challenge even under relatively lenient standards of review, and Black's characterization of racial classifications as "suspect" in *Korematsu*— like his later agreement that those based on national origin and alienage are also suspect—seems compatible with a traditional, historical conception of the Fourteenth Amendment. *Williams* v. *Rhodes* can be conceptualized, moreover, as a First–Fourteenth Amendment case involving the sort of indirect burdens on association Black had long been willing to subject to a balancing test. When asked about his use of modern equal protection rhetoric there, he smiled and responded: "Sometimes I have to use words to hold my Court. They're just semantics. They mean nothing to me."[164] Most significantly, perhaps, his original drafts for both *Williams* and *Korematsu* included no such rhetoric.[165] Those passages were added later, apparently at a colleague's suggestion. And in the most extensive public expression of his equal protection philosophy, his dissent for *Harper* v. *Virginia State Board of Elections*,[166] he insisted, it will be recalled, that strict scrutiny be limited to racial classifications. Strict review of racially discriminatory laws, he argued, was "compelled by the purpose of the Framers of the Thirteenth, Fourteenth, and Fifteenth Amendments completely to outlaw discrimination against people because of their race or color."[167] In other areas states were "to have the broadest kind of leeway."[168]

Throughout his career Black was generally faithful to the conception of equal protection outlined in his *Harper* dissent. He normally refused to join the Court in subjecting nonracial voting classifications to strict scrutiny. Instead, he either dissented from the majority's application of strict standards,[169] voted to invalidate challenged regulations on rational-basis grounds,[170] or wrote or joined majority opinions which applied traditional standards or obscured the degree of scrutiny to which a challenged law was subjected.[171] Neither would he agree to add illegitimacy[172] or poverty[173] to the list of constitutional "suspects," nor welfare benefits[174] to the category of "fundamental rights" deserving of meaningful judicial protection.

Even so, Black's stance in equal protection cases was not entirely consistent with his *Harper* formula. Indeed, while in *Harper* he initially voted in conference to uphold the poll tax at issue there—the stance he would ultimately assume in the case—at one point he voted to overturn the challenged tax and even drafted an opinion which, although not resorting to strict scrutiny rhetoric, did characterize "the equal right of all to vote in elections" as "basic and precious."[175] His position in reapportionment cases also seemed more consistent with his original *Harper* stance—and the "new" equal protection—than with his *Harper* dissent. During conference discussion of *Colegrove* v. *Green*,[176] the Court's 1946 confrontation with the issue of congressional malapportionment, he initially expressed doubt whether such claims satisfied case-or-controversy requirements and whether courts had power to provide relief. He also indicated, however, that while he opposed judicial control of national and state elections, he thought the appellants had established a clear constitutional violation if judicial intervention were appropriate.[177] Ultimately, moreover, he dissented from a four-to-three decision to deny relief, arguing that malapportioned congressional districts conflicted with equal protection and with the requirement of Article I, Section 2, that congressmen "shall be chosen . . . by the People of the several States." Sixteen years later he joined the holding of the majority in *Baker* v. *Carr*[178] that state legislative malapportionment posed justiciable questions under the Fourteenth Amendment equal protection guarantee. In 1964 he held for the Court in *Wesberry* v. *Sanders*[179] that, under Article I, Section 2, "as nearly as practicable one man's vote in a congressional election is to be worth as much as another's."[180] Later, he joined opinions extending the "one person, one vote" principle to both houses of state legislatures[181] and to local governments.[182] And in 1970 he held for the Court in *Hadley* v. *Junior College District*[183] that, "as a general rule,"[184] the principle was applicable to any governmental body whose members are elected by district.

Nor was his application of strict scrutiny standards in nonracial contexts limited to the reapportionment arena. His willingness to author or join opinions forbidding systematic racial discrimination in jury selection[185] is consistent, of course, with his *Harper* dissent. But he also voted on due process and equal protection grounds to overturn "blue ribbon" juries,[186] to require states to provide indigent defendants with free trial transcripts or "find other means of affording [them] adequate and effective appellate review,"[187] to extend indigents a right of appointed counsel on appeal,[188] to exempt them from appellate and collateral filing fees,[189] and to invalidate provisions under which the poor could be imprisoned if unable to pay fines assessed in criminal cases.[190]

As I have attempted to demonstrate in greater depth elsewhere,[191] it is possible to reconcile Black's stance in such cases with his broader jurisprudence. His strict scrutiny of legislative malapportionment reflected, as suggested in Chapter Two, elements of a doctrine of popular sovereignty he considered implicit in the Constitution and the general history surrounding its adoption—a doctrine under which deviations from "one person, one vote" would be viewed as "irrational." Whatever the accuracy of his interpretation of Article I, Section 2, moreover, his position regarding malapportioned congressional districts was compatible with his conception of the clause's historic purposes. And for a judge committed to clear, precise legal standards, "one person, one vote" would appear clearly preferable to an approach requiring merely that apportionment schemes be "rational" in the usual meaning of that term and prevent "the systematic frustration" of the principle of majority rule.[192]

Just as Black's reapportionment stance is compatible with the political theory he found implicit in the Constitution as well as with his preference for clearcut legal standards, the Justice's strict scrutiny of nonracial discrimination in criminal procedure contexts arguably is consistent with his "law of the land" conception of due process and with the special emphasis given criminal procedure in the Constitution's text. In his opinion for the Court in *Griffin v. Illinois*,[193] which required free transcripts or comparable assistance for indigent defendants seeking to appeal their convictions, he relied as much on due process as on equal protection. And while later cases of the *Griffin* variety relegated due process to the background, then discarded it entirely as a basis for the Court's decisions, Black's conception of due process probably continued to provide the key to his position in such cases. For Black, it will be recalled, due process guaranteed to "all Americans, whoever they are and wherever they happen to be, the right to be tried by independent and unprejudiced courts using established and nondiscriminatory procedures and applying valid pre-existing laws."[194] Under such an interpretation of due process, discriminatory criminal procedures would arguably be subjected to stricter scrutiny than that required by the deferential formula Black normally embraced in nonracial contexts. The emphasis given procedural safeguards generally in the Constitution also convinced him that discrimination in the criminal process should be closely scrutinized. During his last term, for example, he observed:

> With all of these protections safeguarding defendants charged by government with crime, we quite naturally and quite properly held in *Griffin* that the Due Process and Equal Protection Clauses both barred any discrimination in criminal trials against poor defendants who are unable to defend themselves against the State. Had we not so held we would have been unfaithful to the explicit

commands of the Bill of Rights, designed to wrap the protections of the Constitution around all defendants upon whom the mighty powers of government are hurled to punish for crime.[195]

While Justice Black's strict review of certain nonracial classifications can thus be squared with his broader jurisprudence, it is difficult to reconcile his position in such cases with his "normal" stance in equal protection cases, the position he set forth most extensively in *Harper*. Even so, this element of his jurisprudence has been given little critical attention. Instead, his critics have focused on two areas in which, in their view, the Justice gave equal protection and the judicial role in eliminating racial discrimination an unduly restrictive reading. One continuing area of concern, of course, has been his reaction to sanctions imposed on Japanese-Americans and to the prosecution of enemy aliens during World War II. The other relates to elements of his stance during the Court's consideration of *Brown* v. *Board of Education*.[196]

The Japanese Cases. Justice Black's opinion for the Court in the *Korematsu* case upheld the conviction of an American citizen who violated a military order excluding persons of Japanese descent from certain "military areas" on the West Coast. The previous year he had joined a unanimous Court in *Hirabayashi* v. *United States*,[197] which upheld an order imposing a curfew on Japanese-Americans residing in such areas. On the same day *Korematsu* was decided, he again joined a unanimous Court in freeing a Japanese-American of established loyalty from a relocation center, but on the narrow, nonconstitutional ground that the detention was authorized by neither statute nor executive order.[198] And while, over the primary objection of Justice Owen Roberts, the Court avoided a ruling on the constitutionality of detention centers to which large numbers of Japanese-Americans were confined, Black found it "unjustifiable" in *Korematsu* "to call them concentration camps with all the ugly connotations that term implies."[199] In *In Re Yamashita*[200] and other cases involving military prosecution of enemy soldiers, he was equally deferential to executive authority, joining the Court in affirming the power of such tribunals over the eloquent "fair trial" contentions of Justices Murphy and Rutledge.

Korematsu and company are considered a significant element in the darker side of the modern Court's civil liberties record. In his *Korematsu* dissent Justice Murphy charged that the Court's position amounted to a "legalization of racism."[201] He also made a convincing case against blanket evacuation, contending, among other things, that the first exclusion order was not issued until four months after Pearl Harbor, that the separation of loyal from disloyal persons of German and Italian ancestry was being handled through individualized procedures, that military and civilian authorities had "the espionage and sabotage situation well in hand," and that "not one person of Japanese ancestry was accused or convicted of espionage or sabotage after Pearl Harbor while they were still free."[202] By the time *Korematsu* was decided, moreover, earlier fears of widespread treachery had proved groundless. By 1948 President Truman's Commission on Civil Rights had characterized the evacuation program as "the most striking mass interference since slavery with the right to physical freedom,"[203] and Congress had voted partial compensation for property losses suffered under the program. Yet the Court had upheld sanctions against Japanese-Americans, most of whom, Black assumed for the *Korematsu* Court, "no doubt were loyal."[204]

Arguably, however, Black's position in *Korematsu* and *Hirabayashi* is consistent with both his traditional distaste for racial discrimination and his broader jurisprudence. He never held that race was an absolutely forbidden basis for classification. When the Court upheld a lower court decision invalidating a statute which required racial segregation in Alabama's prisons, for example, he asserted in a brief concurrence joined by Justices Harlan and Stewart that "prison authorities [had] the right, acting in good faith and in particularized circumstances, to take into account racial tensions in maintaining security, discipline, and good order in prisons and jails."[205] In *Korematsu* he had assumed a similar stance, rejecting the contention that an admittedly race-based sanction was a per se reflection of racial hostility and insisting instead that the challenged action was bottomed on legitimate and "pressing" security concerns. To Murphy's claim that the Court was legalizing racism, he responded:

> Korematsu was not excluded from the Military Area because of hostility to him or his race. He was excluded because we are at war with the Japanese Empire, because the properly constituted military authorities feared an invasion of our West Coast and felt constrained to take proper security measures, because they decided that the military urgency of the situation demanded that all cit-

izens of Japanese ancestry be segregated from the West Coast temporarily, and finally, because Congress, reposing its confidence in this time of war in our military leaders—as inevitably it must—determined that they should have the power to do just this. There was evidence of disloyalty on the part of some, the military authorities considered that the need for action was great, and time was short. We cannot—by availing ourselves of the calm perspective of hindsight—now say that at the time these actions were unjustified.[206]

Black's perception of the situation has considerable merit. Heightened racial antagonism is an inevitable consequence of warfare between people of different racial characteristics. The World War II sanctions were obviously influenced to some degree by the racial identity of Japanese-Americans with a hated enemy. But they simply cannot be dismissed as mere reflections of racism. However sweeping their reach, they were, in part at least, a racially neutral response to a very real military crisis and based upon a wholly reasonable fear that some undetermined number of Japanese-Americans had maintained their loyalty to the Empire and might resort to sabotage. That such fears may later have proved largely groundless is irrelevant. The Court evaluated the sanctions in the context within which they were imposed—the months following Pearl Harbor—and not, as Black pointedly noted, in "the calm perspective of hindsight."

Nor is it surprising that a Hugo Black would be reluctant to substitute the Court's judgment for that of military authorities and executive officials. Unless required by what he considered the commands of the Constitution's language and history, he was consistently reluctant to evaluate the "reasonableness," "fairness," or "utility" of governmental action. His stance in *Korematsu* and *Hirabayashi* clearly reflects that reluctance. Indeed, he declined to join Chief Justice Stone's opinion for the *Hirabayashi* Court until Stone inserted the following passage: "Where, as they did here, the conditions call for the exercise of judgment and discretion and for the choice of means by those branches of the Government on which the Constitution has placed the responsibility of war-making, it is not for any court to sit in review of the wisdom of their action or substitute its judgment for theirs."[207]

An opinion Black drafted in the *Yamashita* case, but never circulated, indicates, moreover, that his willingness to allow military trials of enemy soldiers, even after cessation of hostilities and without the due process safeguards extended civilians, was consistent with his conception of due process and the Bill of Rights' reach.[208] He agreed in the draft that military prosecutions of enemy soldiers must conform to statutory and treaty restrictions, though none were applicable to General Yamashita's case. He emphasized, moreover, that the military had no power "to supercede the civil laws in [U.S.] territory, and to set up military tribunals there to try, convict, and punish civilians for all sorts of civil offenses." But he found nothing in the Constitution which authorized courts "to annul or modify" proceedings involving enemy soldiers. "Our civil laws," he asserted,

> do not make provision for punishment of enemy soldiers who wage war against us in violation of the standards of warfare declared by military agencies. These standards are not "laws" within the meaning in which that term is used with reference to civilian conduct and for this reason, among others, military tribunals set up to punish enemy violators of military rules are not courts and not a part of our judicial system.

It was not surprising, therefore, that Black rejected any assumption on the Court's part that the Fifth Amendment due process clause was applicable to such proceedings. Nor did the practical implications of such an assumption escape him. In his view, remember, due process required government to proceed according to the "law of the land" in taking away a person's life, liberty, or property, and that "law of the land" included all the guarantees of the Bill of Rights. While the Court might be willing to extend some flexible notion of due process to military prosecutions of enemy soldiers, it would obviously be unwilling to accord them the whole panoply of procedural safeguards guaranteed in the Bill of Rights, just as it had rejected their extension to state prosecutions of civilian defendants. Instead, the Court would suggest merely that enemy soldiers were entitled to "fair" proceedings. "To accomplish [such a] purpose," Black declared in his *Yamashita* draft,

> the Court drastically limits the meaning, thereby narrowing the scope of protection implicit in "due process of law." It bodily lifts from that great Constitutional safeguard of liberty a major part of its content, leaving it a mere shadow of what the founding fathers made it. As a consequence a proceeding in which a man's life is

forfeited has been placed on the same level with [what the Court has required for] an administrative action.

Black wanted no part of such an effort "to transplant [that] natural law concept into a new field." Yamashita had been sentenced to death "without a pretense of compliance with most" Bill of Rights safeguards. Had Black agreed that "the due process of 'law' clause applied to such proceedings," he could not have acquiesced in the Court's judgment. In his view, however, those guarantees were inapplicable to the trials of enemy soldiers accused of violating the laws of war.

The Segregation Cases. Questions have also arisen regarding Justice Black's stance in *Brown* v. *Board of Education*—specifically, questions relating to the degree of the Justice's commitment to the Court's conclusion that segregated public schools violate the Constitution and questions regarding the pace of desegregation Black favored. In 1970 political scientist S. Sidney Ulmer wrote Black, asking permission to quote from a letter written by the Justice that Ulmer had found in the papers of Justice Harold Burton at the Library of Congress.[209] "Since my letter is part of the inner workings of the Court," Black soon responded, "I would prefer that it not be published at all. In fact, I do not recall the letter." Although stressing the scholar's "obligation to try and understand the 'inner workings of the Court,' " Ulmer acceded to the Justice's preference. Later, Ulmer completed a conference paper on the Justice's "Parabolic Support for Civil Liberties, 1937–1967," also drawn partly from the Burton papers, and sent Black a copy.[210] "I am not able to find much support for the proposition that you have undergone some sort of fundamental change in recent years," he acknowledged in an accompanying letter, then added, "My data do suggest, however, that your support for civil liberties claims has declined as compared with past years." Black again responded, thanking Ulmer for the paper, gently chiding him about its "enigmatic" title, assuring Ulmer of his "belief that it is a fair representation of your views, extracted from information that I would not consider wholly reliable," and reiterating his opposition to scholarly or other uses of conference notes. "For some years," he wrote Ulmer, "my own view has been that probably the Justices would serve history better if they would not leave for comment and inferences the necessarily short notes they must take about statements made in conference by the Court members."

By this point Black's concerns with Ulmer's use of the Burton papers were general. Then, Ulmer mailed the Justice a copy of another conference paper. His latest effort examined Chief Justice Warren's role in *Brown*,[211] but concluded, again based on Burton's notes, that Black "was prepared to say that segregation by race violated the amendment (unless a long line of decisions prevented him from doing so)," adding: "In the event that a majority voted otherwise regarding segregation, then Black retained the option of changing his position." Ulmer also had "Black indicat[ing] that he would probably go with the majority in spite of his beliefs." After reading pertinent portions of the Burton papers himself, Black wrote Ulmer that, "without any comment on any other part of your article," the last passage quoted above "is not correct and I now doubt if Justice Burton's reports . . . justify any such inference."

But Ulmer was not dissuaded. The statement, he soon wrote Black, had been drawn from Justice Burton's record of the Justices' December 13, 1952, conference in the *Brown* case.

> While Burton states your view that segregation violated the 14th Amendment, he also records you as saying you would so decide— "unless long line of decision prevents. Didn't go all the way that was intended in old cases. Will vote that way—if majority other way as to segregation, then should be leeway for change." It was from this passage that I inferred that while you wished to outlaw segregation, should the majority not agree, you retained the option to change your vote.

Ulmer found his a "fair inference," but urged Black to respond "[i]f you could provide a more logical reading of this passage than mine."

By now the Justice was becoming impatient with the scholar. "Of course I do not intend to 'provide a more logical reading' of the passage on which you rely," he rejoined, adding, "I think your interpretation does a gross injustice to Justice Burton." When Ulmer wrote to indicate that he was removing the passage, yet continued to press Black for "an accurate reflection of your own view," the Justice obliged: "if you are saying that under any circumstances I would have voted to continue to hold that segregation was constitutional then your statement is not correct." When Ulmer "acknowledge[d]" that Black's statement of his position was "consistent with [the Justice's] philosophy as I understand that philosophy," but indicated that he might wish to correspond further with Black regarding his manuscript research, Black assured Ulmer that "it will not be necessary for you to correspond further about [such material] except to know that I believe your use or the use by any other historian of such articles may frequently leave a false impression of history." He hoped Ulmer would understand, however, "that there [was] no earthly reason why you and I should think less of one another because we happen to disagree. Disagreements are the life of progress."

While it did not enter into his exchanges with the Justice, Professor Ulmer's reading of the Burton papers, as well as those of Justice Frankfurter, also convinced him that Black believed that "the Court should move slowly in [the desegregation] area—like a glacier."[212] And Ulmer has not been alone in that conclusion. In his published reminiscences of his father,[213] Hugo Black, Jr., recalled the Justice's opposition to the Court's decision in *Brown* II, announcing its approach to desegregation, to declare that public schools be desegregated "with all deliberate speed"—a phrase drawn from an opinion of Justice Holmes[214] and pressed upon the *Brown* Court by Black's jurisprudential antagonist Justice Frankfurter. "It tells the enemies of the decision," Hugo Jr. remembers his father remarking at the time, "that for the present the status quo will do and gives them time to contrive devices to stall off [de]segregation."[215] In his fine biography of Chief Justice Warren, Bernard Schwartz found such a statement inconsistent with Black's remarks during an April 16, 1955, conference of the Justices regarding the proper decree to issue in the school segregation cases. "The Alabamian then had indicated that the Court should not try to settle the segregation issue too rapidly. If it attempted to do so, its decree 'would be like Prohibition.' Black, in fact, was the one Justice who predicted that the movement toward desegregation in the South would, at best, be only 'glacial.' "[216]

To assess both sets of concerns, it is perhaps best to begin with a detailed summary of the conference notes on which they are primarily based.[217] At the December 13, 1952, conference, Justice Burton records Black as having made the following observations: He was "not at all sure that Congress is [subject to the] same [constitutional] limitations as are the states," but he could see "the anomalous results of permitting [segregation in the District of Columbia] and not elsewhere," and he realized that all the parties seemed to have agreed that each level of government was subject to the same limitations. He believed that "serious incidents" might arise from school desegregation, that its effect would be "serious and drastic," that the "mixture of races [was] thought very dangerous" in the South, "weaken[ing] the white race," and that South Carolina "might abolish [its] public school system" if forced to desegregate. In his view "one of [the] worst features" of the case was that courts would be "on the battle front," and he opposed "law by judges." At the same time he was "compelled to say" for himself "that the reason for [segregation] is the belief that Negroes are inferior," that the Fourteenth Amendment's purpose was protection against "discrimination concerning color," and that the case could not "go contrary to [the] truth that [the] purpose [of segregation] is to discriminate on account of color." He would "have to say," he added, that segregation "in itself violates" the Constitution "unless [a] long line of decisions prevents" such a ruling, and that the Court had not gone "all the way that was intended in old cases." He would vote "that way—if majority the other way—to segregate, then should be leeway for change."

At the April 16, 1955, decree conference, Black, according to Burton's notes, made the following additional remarks: He was "not sure that [he had] any definite views" regarding the appropriate decree to be fashioned, but that if "humanly possible," he "intend[ed] to go along for unanimous action," presumably with any decree the majority approved. He did think that "the less we say the better off we are," and he favored "a careful statement that [segregation was] unconstitutional." He was "not fond of class action suits," since "many [members of a class] don't want to be included," and he would have preferred to treat the desegregation cases "as individual cases." Southerners were "just now beginning to feel some respect for [federal] officials," and race was at the "root" of that hostility. His law clerk did "not think that in this generation Negroes and whites would go to school together" in the South, and while the Court should not condone southern attitudes, it could not "ignore them." Whites in south Alabama counties would "never be a party to allowing whites and Negroes [to] go to school together," no southern federal judge favored desegregation, and there was "no more chance to enforce [desegregation] in [the deep South] than prohibition in [New York City]." To "issue orders which can't be enforced would [do] the greatest damage," and it was "futile to think that in these cases [the Court could] settle [the segregation issue] in [the] South." Justice Frankfurter's notes on the April 16 conference are similar to Justice Burton's. At one point, moreover, Frankfurter recorded on a separate line of his summary of Black's remarks the words "Glacial movement"—the words which apparently prompted Ulmer and Schwartz to conclude that Black favored a glacier-like approach to desegregation.

Assuming the complete accuracy of the Burton and Frankfurter notes, their version of Black's *Brown* conference stance is largely compatible with the strict scrutiny to which the Justice subjected racial classifications, as well as with his broader constitutional and judicial philosophy. At another juncture in the *Brown* deliberations, Black expressed "doubt if it would be possible to isolate the [Fourteenth Amendment's] framers' views about segregation in the primary schools."[218] Burton's notes suggest no doubt on Black's part, however, that the amendment was intended to abolish racial discrimination, that segregation was based on a belief in the inherent inferiority of blacks, and that segregation violated the Constitution. He did say that he would vote to strike down segregation unless a "long line of decisions" prevented such a decision. But this abstract nod to precedent was the closest he came to an expression of ambivalence on the constitutionality of segregation. Not once does he even hint at uncertainty in his personal resolve. His doubt whether the Fifth Amendment due process clause required an end to segregation in the District of Columbia schools is consistent, moreover, with his emphasis on literalism and historical intent in constitutional interpretation, for the status of racial discrimination was not nearly so clear under the Fifth Amendment as it was under the Fourteenth Amendment's language and history. His concern about judges being on the "battle front" in the desegregation controversy reflected his traditional aversion to judicial policy making, as did his opposition to class suits. (According to Justice Jackson's conference notes, it should be noted, Black also contended that it was the framers' intent that Congress should play the major role in enforcing the Fourteenth Amendment, and he lamented the Congress's continuing failure to attack racial discrimination.)[219] His suggestion that "the less we say [in a decree] the better off we are" can also be viewed in that light and as evidence not that he favored a weak decree, but that he feared—prophetically, as it turned out—that an elaborate one might furnish fuel to the opposition. Finally, his remarks about southern racial attitudes, the likely intensity of southern opposition, and southern hostility to the federal government appear more the reflections of a perceptive student of the South than a brief for racial gradualism.

If we go beyond Burton's and Frankfurter's notes, moreover, the inferences Ulmer and Schwartz have drawn from them seem even more questionable. In suggesting that Black might have gone in either direction on the segregation issue, Ulmer relied most heavily on the following passage from what Richard Kluger has termed Burton's "sometimes indecipherable and quite often cryptic notes":[220] "Will vote that way [to end segregation]—if majority the other way—to segregate, then should be leeway for change." In his notes for the same conference, however, Justice Jackson records Black as making the following observation: "Segregation itself violates amendment—unless can say decisions & stare decisis prevents. Vote to end segregation. If equal & separate prevails give weight to findings in each state."[221] Thus, while Justice Burton has Black making the enigmatic observation that, if segregation were upheld, "then should be leeway for change," Jackson records him making a statement consistent with his traditional reluctance to second-guess complex value judgments of trial courts and local officials—the sorts of judgments application of the separate-but-equal doctrine would require. Jackson also records Black as agreeing that segregation was based on a belief in black inferiority and adding—in an obvious slap at the psychological and sociological studies the Court was later to cite in *Brown* I's controversial Footnote Eleven—that he did "not need books" to reach that conclusion.

The reminiscences of Hugo Black, Jr., also dispute the notion that Black was ambivalent on segregation. While the school segregation cases were pending, Hugo Jr. telephoned his father with news of his plans to seek an Alabama congressional seat. Apparently assuming that the senior Black would be elated by such news, he was "surprised and a little alarmed" when his father seemed subdued by his son's announcement and asked him to fly to Washington for an important talk. When Hugo Jr. arrived there later in the day, his father swore him to secrecy, then told him that he agreed "with old Justice Harlan's dissent in *Plessy* v. *Ferguson*," adding, "I don't believe segregation is constitutional." Justice Black was deeply concerned about the disastrous effect his decision was bound to have on his son's political future, but told Hugo Jr., "You understand, son. I've got to do it even though it's going to mess up your plans." Hugo Jr. returned to Alabama and told reporters he was "not ready" to run.[222]

Hugo Jr.'s reminiscences are, of course, those of a son about his father. They are, however, unusually candid and at times harshly so regarding their subject. And the account of the senior Black's commitment to desegregation—like Hugo Jr.'s recollections of his father's doubts about "all deliberate speed"—has the ring of truth.

Nor should Black's early stance in *Briggs* v. *Elliott*, South Carolina's *Brown* counterpart and the first of the school cases to reach the Court, be ignored. After a three-judge district court upheld the separate-but-equal doctrine in *Briggs*, the Supreme Court dismissed an early appeal in order that the trial court could consider a state report on efforts to upgrade South Carolina's black schools. Black and Douglas dissented, arguing that the state report was "wholly irrelevant" to the per se challenge to segregation raised in the case and recommending that it be scheduled for argument.[223] Such a stance is hardly suggestive of uncertainty about segregation's constitutional status.

Black's *Briggs* dissent also seems inconsistent with assertions he favored a glacier-like approach to desegregation or, as one critic privately put it, "didn't want to offend his southern colleagues." So, too, do other elements of Black's school desegregation record. When the Court rebuffed the efforts of Governor Faubus and other Arkansas officials to obstruct desegregation of Little Rock's Central High School in *Cooper* v. *Aaron*,[224] Black contributed the first, forceful paragraph of the Court's opinion—a paragraph concluding with the assertion that the state's "contentions call for clear answers here and now." He also proposed that a sentence be added indicating that the obligation to desegregate "applies to every school system maintained from the public purse." When such a passage was added to the Court's opinion, "[c]ritics were quick to point out," Bernard Schwartz reminds us, "that the issue of public support of private segregated schools had not been present in the case and that the Court was gratuitously prejudging an issue, in violation of its own taboo against advisory opinions."[225] True enough. Whatever its consistency with judicial tradition, however, Black's suggestion seems surprising coming from one who, in the view of Schwartz and Ulmer, favored a go-slow approach to school desegregation. When Justice Frankfurter registered a *Cooper* concurrence, it might be added, Black and Justice Brennan, who was principally responsible for writing the Court's opinion, drafted, but never filed, a statement urging that the Frankfurter contribution "not be accepted as any dilution" of the Court's position.[226] That statement appears equally incompatible with Black's alleged preference for a glacier-like desegregation process, as does a passage from Justice Harlan's conference notes in the case.

"H. L. B.," Harlan wrote, "wants 'end date' for any [desegregation] plan."[227]

In later years, moreover, Black publicly voiced doubts about the Court's use of "all deliberate speed" in *Brown* II and became increasingly impatient with any delay in the progress of school desegregation. During his 1968 network television interview, he remarked of "all deliberate speed,"

> Looking back at it now, it seems to me that it's delayed the process of outlawing segregation. It seems to me, probably, with all due deference to the opinion and my brethren, all of them, that it would have been better—maybe, I don't say positively—not to have that sentence. To treat that case as an ordinary lawsuit and force that judgment on the counties it affected that minute.[228]

Sitting as a circuit justice the following year in *Alexander* v. *Holmes County Board of Education*,[229] a Mississippi desegregation case, he affirmed a stay of a lower court's desegregation order pending review by the full Supreme Court. He made it clear, however, that were he alone to make the Court's final judgment, he would allow no more delay. "I am of the opinion," he asserted, "that so long as that phrase [all deliberate speed] is a relevant factor [segregated schools] will never be eliminated. 'All deliberate speed' has turned out to be only a soft euphemism for delay."[230] And when the full Court seemed inclined to permit additional delay, he drafted a vehement dissent,[231] calling *Brown* II's "reference to delay in enforcement of cherished constitutional rights . . . an unfortunate one." The district court in the Mississippi case had decided that "immediate desegregation" might lead to "disastrous educational consequences." In Black's judgment "there [could] be no more disastrous educational consequence than the continuance for one more day of an unconstitutional dual school system." Ultimately, he had his way. On October 29, 1969, the Court affirmed "the obligation of every school district . . . to terminate dual school systems at once and to operate now and hereafter only unitary schools."[232]

Naturally, it can be argued that since *Cooper* v. *Aaron* came down three years after *Brown* II, and *Alexander* v. *Holmes County Board of Education* fourteen years, the impatience with delay in school desegregation that Black expressed there in no way refutes the thesis that he initially favored a glacier-like approach to the issue. Coming from a Sidney Ulmer, who argues that Black's support for civil liberties declined rather than grew in his last years, such a contention is not without irony. When Black's stance in *Cooper* and *Alexander* is combined, moreover, with his early impatience with the Court's approval of delay in the *Briggs* case, with his son's recollections of the senior Black's distaste for "all deliberate speed," and with the Justice's nationally televised disavowal of that phrase at a time when other *Brown* contemporaries were still living, it is difficult to accept the Ulmer-Schwartz position. In his conference notes regarding a decree to be fashioned in the school cases,[233] Chief Justice Warren records Black as remarking, "There will be [a] deliberate effort to circumvent the decree," then observing, "It becomes desirable to write as narrowly as possible," adding that he did "not believe that enumeration of principles would be helpful," and concluding, after expressing concern about class suits, that he would favor a decree indicating that segregation "is unconstitutional and that they must be admitted." Professors Ulmer and Schwartz read Black's preference for a "narrow" decree to mean that he believed that the Court should move very slowly in implementing school desegregation. Chief Justice Warren's notes indicate, however, that Black would have ordered the admission of students—an approach the Court shrank from adopting. Particularly in light of Black's overall racial record, it appears likely that his preference for a "narrow" *Brown* decree which would not "enumerat[e] principles," such as "all deliberate speed," reflected not a desire for a glacier-like approach to implementation, but a wish, as he told his son, to avoid giving ammunition to the opposition in what he knew was to be a protracted struggle.

Obviously, there were limits beyond which Justice Black was unwilling to go in attacking segregated public schools. During his last year on the bench he initially objected to portions of the Court's decision and opinion in *Swann v. Charlotte-Mecklenburg Board of Education*,[234] its most expansive statement to date of judicial authority in the field of school desegregation. In correspondence with Chief Justice Burger and a draft concurring and dissenting opinion, Black objected to language in the Chief Justice's opinion for the Court empowering judges to order "racial balance," placing a burden on school systems to prove that racially imbalanced schools were nondiscriminatory, and "compel[ling] a State and its taxpayers to buy millions of dollars worth of busses to haul students miles away from their neighborhood schools and their homes," thereby "unconstitutionally requiring the States to spend money." Only after negotiation and compromise was he persuaded to acquiesce silently in the Court's decision and opinion.[235] The available evidence simply does not support the notion, however, that he initially wavered on the constitutional status of segregation or favored a go-slow approach to its dismantling. He obviously appeared to realize that the progress of desegregation would be "glacial." But that does not mean that he favored a judicial strategy designed to fulfill that prophecy.

State Action

Just as Black saw limits to judicial power in the field of school desegregation, he also refused to give the "state" action which the Constitution controls an unduly expansive scope in racial and other contexts. During his career he wrote or joined a number of opinions holding that ostensibly private activity constitutes state action for constitutional purposes. Speaking for the Court in *Marsh* v. *Alabama*,[236] a 1946 case, he employed a "public forum" or "public function" rationale to subject a company town to First–Fourteenth Amendment requirements and overturn the trespass conviction of a Jehovah's Witness who had attempted to distribute religious literature on the town's streets. While he initially indicated in conference that Texas's white primary involved no impermissible state action,[237] he also ultimately voted to strike down the Texas scheme,[238] as well as later variations on that arrangement.[239] In *Shelley* v. *Kraemer* (1948),[240] moreover, he voted to strike down state judicial enforcement of racially restrictive housing covenants. He joined, too, decisions suggesting that a variety of factors tying the state to ostensibly private activities triggered pertinent constitutional safeguards.[241]

There were clearly limits, however, to the Justice's conception of state action. Certain language in his opinion for the *Marsh* Court suggested a flexible conception of the "public forum" doctrine. At one point, for example, he had observed: "Ownership [of property] does not always mean absolute dominion. The more an owner, for his advantage, opens up his property for use by the public in general, the more do his rights become circumscribed by the statutory and constitutional rights of those who use it."[242] In conference discussion of the case, however, he had termed Chickasaw, Alabama, the company town in question, "a political subdivision,"[243] and in his opinion for the Court he had enlarged upon that proposition, indicating that Chickasaw possessed "all the characteristics of any other American town."[244] When the Court in

1968 extended the *Marsh* decision to a shopping center in the *Logan Valley* case, Black vigorously dissented, emphasizing the differences between a shopping center and a town and concluding: "this [shopping center] sounds like a very strange 'town' to me."[245] Under *Marsh*, he maintained, private property could be treated as public for First Amendment purposes only when the former possessed all the characteristics of the latter. Failure to so limit the "public forum" doctrine, he warned, would subvert "the concept of private ownership of property" which the Constitution also recognized.[246] In other areas he was equally adamant in refusing to join what he considered an unduly broad reading of the doctrine to forbid racial discrimination by restaurants and the real estate industry, among other institutions.

In a number of sit-in cases growing out of the civil rights protests of the sixties, Black was also unwilling to give *Shelley* v. *Kraemer* an expansive reading.[247] *Shelley* held that a state court could not constitutionally invoke its injunctive power against a homeowner who wished to violate the terms of a racially restrictive covenant. In the sit-in cases petitioners argued that *Shelley* forbade use of state trespass laws to enforce the segregation or whites-only policies of privately operated lunch counters and related facilities. In certain of the sit-in cases Black joined decisions overturning breach-of-peace convictions of sit-in participants on the ground that no evidence supported the charge.[248] When he agreed that a decision to prosecute was permeated with significant state involvement, he also concurred in the Court's reversal of trespass convictions.[249] In *Bell* v. *Maryland*,[250] however, he vigorously rejected the claim that "the Fourteenth Amendment, of itself, forbids a State to enforce its trespass laws to convict a person who comes into a privately owned restaurant, is told that because of his color he will not be served, and over the owner's protest refuses to leave."[251] The *Shelley* case, he asserted, involved a property right recognized by federal law. More significantly, both the seller and the blacks who wished to buy the seller's home had been willing parties. Except for the active participation of the state court, a property transaction would have been completed and a racially restricted covenant partially overcome. Use of trespass laws against sit-in participants was, in his judgment, an entirely different matter. There, the decision to discriminate was not forced upon the property owner by the state; instead, it originated with the owner. The trespass law and the state's involvement were thus racially neutral and beyond the Fourteenth Amendment's reach. "The

Amendment does not forbid a State to prosecute for crimes committed against a person or his property, however prejudiced or narrow the victim's views may be. Nor can whatever prejudices and bigotry the victims of a crime may have be automatically attributed to the State that prosecutes. . . . The worst citizen no less than the best is entitled to equal protection of the laws."[252] A conclusion to the contrary, Black contended, would not only conflict with the principle of the "rule of law"; it would also infringe upon rights of private property. Nor, in his judgment, did enforcement of a trespass statute against sit-in participants violate First–Fourteenth Amendment guarantees. "The right to freedom of expression," he insisted, as he would on many subsequent occasions, "is a right to express views—not a right to force other people to supply a platform or a pulpit."[253]

In still other cases the Justice agreed that state action was present but was either insufficiently related to the discrimination at issue or not a violation of equal protection. He dissented, for example, when the Court struck down a California constitutional amendment granting people an "absolute discretion" in the sale or rental of housing.[254] The majority reasoned that in the context of its history, wording, and immediate impact, the amendment amounted to an "encouragement" of private discrimination. Black, however, joined Justice Harlan who argued in dissent that the amendment merely placed the state in a neutral position in the field of housing discrimination, complained that the majority's stance severely restricted a state's freedom to repeal fair housing controls, and warned that the Court's decision could threaten the prospects for future legislation in that controversial field. Speaking for the Court in *Evans* v. *Abney*,[255] Black also upheld the reversion of a city park to the heirs of an estate which had willed the property to the city for use by whites only. Even "assuming *arguendo* that the closing of" a city park to avoid court-ordered desegregation would violate equal protection, he wrote, such a "case would be clearly distinguishable from [*Evans*] because it is the State and not a private party which is injecting the racially discriminatory motivation."[256] Finally, in *Palmer* v. *Thompson*[257] he again spoke for the Court in upholding Jackson, Mississippi's closing of municipal swimming pools it had been ordered to desegregate, even though the YMCA had reopened one of the pools on a segregated basis. He found no constitutional provision or congressional statute requiring a state "to begin to operate or to continue to operate swimming pools"[258] and insisted that it would be improper for the Court to inquire into the psychological motives underlying the decision of city officials to cease operations.

Nor was the type facility involved of consequence to him. As the Court's spokesman in *Griffin v. County School Board* (1964),[259] he had maintained that "[w]hatever non-racial grounds might support a State's allowing a county to abandon its public schools, the object must be a constitutional one, and grounds of race and opposition to desegregation do not qualify as constitutional."[260] In *Bush v. Orleans Parish School Board*,[261] moreover, he joined the Court in affirming a lower court decision which had struck down laws empowering Louisiana's governor to close the state's public schools if any were ordered to integrate. And in *Palmer* he pointed out that *Bush* "did not involve swimming pools but rather public schools, an enterprise we have described as 'perhaps the most important function of state and local governments.' "[262] As he also indicated in *Palmer*, however, the "laws struck down in *Bush* were part of an elaborate package of legislation through which Louisiana sought to maintain public education on a segregated basis, not to end public education. . . . Of course there was no serious problem of probing the motives of a legislature in *Bush* because most of the Louisiana statutes explicitly stated they were designed to forestall integrated schools."[263] *Griffin* involved state funding of "private" schools. And personally, if not as the Court's spokesman, Black had no doubt of the state's general power to close its schools or any other public facility. When Justice Harry Blackmun raised the matter with him during deliberations over *Palmer*,[264] Black responded:

> I joined in [the *Bush*] affirmance and I can assure you that if I had ever entertained an idea that any part of the decision in that case would stand for the principle that the United States compels a State to tax its citizens to run public schools, I would never have voted to affirm the judgment. I cannot believe, for instance, that if the State of Minnesota should decide for any reason, good or bad, that the State no longer wanted to run public schools but depend on some other method of educating its people, that you or I would hold that a majority of the lifetime judges of this Court could compel the State to operate public schools. And certainly the same rule would apply with more force to a situation where for any reason a State through its legislature decided not to tax its people to operate

swimming pools. There is no closeness or troublesomeness what- ever in this case for me because I agree with the counsel who answered your question [during oral argument in *Palmer*] that if the judgment here is reversed the city will be "locked in" and must continue to operate swimming pools so long as a majority of our Court declines to let them free themselves from that burden.[265]

A number of commentators have contended, of course, that the Court has been unduly concerned with the state action issue. In a critical analysis of Justice Black's position in the *Bell* case, published in 1965,[266] William Van Alstyne concluded that sufficient state involve- ment to warrant judicial review exists "in every case where conflicting [private] claims of right are mediated by state law."[267] The Court's "*ad hoc . . . rulettes*" for distinguishing reviewable from nonreviewable action were, in Van Alstyne's judgment, so "numerous and unruly that no one [could] confidently predict what the Court may or may not do in a given case," yet their application had "sometimes resulted in a know- ing or unknowing abdication of the Court's clear responsibility of consti- tutional review."[268] Van Alstyne recommended that the Court abandon "the mythological 'no-reviewable state action' " formula and proceed in each case to a review of the merits.[269] Such an approach, he assured the reader, would not mean an inevitable victory for those challenging a particular private activity; only those activities found to be "fundamen- tally unfair or arbitrary" would be invalidated. The Court could find in its various rules of self-restraint, moreover, "ample means of avoiding unwelcome cases."[270]

Acceptance of Van Alstyne's proposal would have required funda- mental alterations in the Court's approach to racial classifications— and perhaps to other regulations as well. While the modern Court has indicated its willingness to uphold racial classifications found neces- sary to promote legitimate and compelling governmental interests, only the sanction at issue in the *Korematsu* case has withstood application of that standard. In practice, the Court has erected a virtually impenetra- ble barrier to such classifications. Were Van Alstyne's proposition to prevail, the Court would naturally be obliged to embrace a more flex- ible formula, actually balancing competing interests and giving serious weight to associational and other claims routinely rejected in the past as justifications for segregation laws and other state-imposed forms of racial discrimination. Such a formula might prove workable. There is a danger, however, that it might work to weaken precedents sculpted in cases attacking state-imposed classifications.

A Justice Black would have other fundamental objections to Van Alstyne's recommendation. If accepted, such an approach would abolish distinctions between state and private action long recognized in a variety of constitutional contexts, opening the way for federal courts to resolve all sorts of private conflicts traditionally considered beyond the Constitution's reach. It would be clearly incompatible with Black's emphasis on constitutional text and would also enlarge, to an unprecedented degree, judicial discretion to rule on the "reasonableness" of challenged practices—an expansion of judicial authority the Justice would no doubt have viewed with alarm. Nor would Van Alstyne's remedy for "unwelcome cases" have appeal for one of Black's jurisprudential persuasion. He never mustered much enthusiasm for the judge-made "passive virtues" many consider adequate safeguards against the abuse of judicial authority. Black readily agreed that the state action concept defied "mechanical application," but he apparently believed that the Constitution's text required courts to make such evaluations.

Van Alstyne did not merely challenge the efforts of Black and others to distinguish reviewable and nonreviewable state action, however. He also claimed that the Justice's stance in *Bell* v. *Maryland* was inconsistent with the position he had assumed in three other cases: *New York Times* v. *Sullivan*,[271] *AFL* v. *Swing*,[272] and *Black* v. *Cutter Labs*.[273] In each of those cases, Van Alstyne contended, the Court was asked to mediate competing private interests and the degree of state involvement was no greater than in *Bell*. Yet Black apparently had no difficulty finding sufficient state action to warrant a constitutional ruling.

Van Alstyne was certainly correct in his assertion that the quantity of state action in *Bell* was essentially the same as that in *New York Times*, *Swing*, and *Cutter Labs*. In each case a court did mediate private claims. In my judgment, however, Van Alstyne misperceived the nature of the threshold question in such litigation. The issue is not the amount of state involvement but its character or, more specifically, the degree to which the state is tied to or responsible for action alleged to be unconstitutional. The question, in short, is not whether there is state action, or "sufficient" state action, to use Van Alstyne's term, but whether there is "reviewable" state action. And in that sense there are significant factors distinguishing the state involvement at issue in *New York Times*,

Swing, and *Cutter Labs* from *Bell*. The trespass statute invoked in *Bell* was clearly constitutional on its face, and neither Black nor a majority of the Court agreed that lunch counters were quasi-state agencies which cannot discriminate on the basis of race, or that people have a First Amendment right to use such facilities for purposes of expression. The state's only role in the case, therefore, was application of a racially neutral and constitutional law. In *New York Times*, on the other hand, a private party sought relief under a state libel law which the Court held was itself unconstitutional. The state was thus not acting simply as a neutral third party enforcing a valid law; instead, it had also provided an impermissible legal weapon for private parties, as well as an arena in which that weapon could be wielded.

Swing and *Cutter Labs* are similarly distinguishable from *Bell*. *Swing* struck down a state common law policy limiting peaceful labor union picketing to cases in which the controversy was between an employer and his employees. An employer had the option, of course, to use or not use the policy to prevent nonemployee picketing of his business, but the ultimate authority for his refusal to allow such picketing was a state-mandated discriminatory restraint on picketing—a restraint which was itself unconstitutional.

In *Cutter Labs* Black dissented when the Court dismissed a writ of certiorari in a case involving a woman discharged from a company for active membership in the Communist party and falsification of her employment application. An arbitration board set up under a collective bargaining agreement which authorized discharge of workers only for "just cause" agreed that the woman was an active Communist and had falsified her employment application. But the board ordered her reinstated on the ground that the company had waived its right to assert those reasons for her discharge by failing to act promptly on them, and the board also concluded that she had actually been discharged for her union activities. In upholding her discharge and overturning the board's decision, the California Supreme Court found that the board had violated the "public policy" of the state by invoking the waiver doctrine in a case involving the discharge of a Communist. That court also agreed that Communist membership constituted "just cause" for discharge and devoted eleven pages of its twenty-one page opinion to a discussion of the tactics and dangers of Communists in employment. Since the California high court's decision rested on a finding regarding state "public policy," a policy based on the character of constitutionally protected associations, Justice Black's stance in *Cutter Labs* seems clearly distinguishable from the position he assumed in *Bell*.

Congressional Power

While Justice Black limited the substantive reach of constitutional provisions to state action, he also subscribed to the view that Congress can regulate private interferences with Fourteenth Amendment rights under its Section Five power to enforce the amendment through "appropriate legislation," and he apparently took the same position regarding the Fifteenth Amendment's enforcement provision. At one point in his *Bell* dissent he suggested his acceptance of such a stance by stating that the equal protection clause and other provisions of the Fourteenth Amendment's first section, "unlike other sections,"[274] were a restraint only upon state action, then quoting Section Five in a footnote.[275] In *United States* v. *Guest* (1966),[276] a civil rights prosecution growing out of the murder of a black motorist on a highway in Georgia, he joined Justice Clark in a brief concurrence recognizing congressional power over private conspiracies to interfere with Fourteenth Amendment rights. As part of efforts to produce a majority opinion in the *Guest* case, moreover, Justice Stewart deleted two passages which "caused difficulties" for Black and Justice Brennan. One of the passages indicated that Section Five "empower[ed] Congress to effectuate and implement only those rights the Amendment itself confers"[277]—rights protected by the amendment's language only against "state" action. During conference discussion of *United States* v. *Price*,[278] which involved challenges to the federal prosecution of police and private individuals accused of murdering three civil rights workers in Mississippi, Black agreed that, "if necessary," he would vote to overrule the *Civil Rights Cases*,[279] the 1883 decision holding that Congress could regulate only state interferences with Fourteenth Amendment rights.[280] Shortly before his death he indicated, too, though unfortunately without elaboration, that he agreed with the first Justice Harlan's dissent in the *Civil Rights Cases*.[281] Finally, in *Daniel* v. *Paul*[282] he dissented when the Court upheld the 1964 Civil Rights Act's ban on discrimination by places of public accommodation, as applied to a remote recreational facility. But he made it clear that his dissent was based purely on his belief that the law was not intended to reach the facility in question and that he would have joined the majority had he agreed that the public accommodations provision was based on congressional authority to enforce the Fourteenth Amendment.

Indeed, the Justice's conception of congressional power under the Fourteenth and Fifteenth Amendments was even more expansive than his *Guest* and *Price* stances would suggest. He agreed that congressional as well as judicial constructions of the substantive meaning of constitutional guarantees were governed by their text and the history surrounding their adoption. Accordingly, when Congress attempted to impose a statutory minimum age for voting in state elections, he voted in *Oregon v. Mitchell*[283] to uphold the requirement only as applied to federal elections, and that on non-Fourteenth Amendment grounds. Tying the amendment's scope largely to the racial context within which it was adopted, he rejected the claim that it limited the state's long-recognized power to set a minimum age for state elections. More fundamentally, he refused to accept Justice Brennan's contention that the amendment, whether in congressional or judicial hands, is "a broadly worded injunction capable of being interpreted by future generations in accordance with the vision and needs of those generations."[284] He did believe, however, that Congress could enlarge upon judicial interpretations of equal protection and other Fourteenth and Fifteenth Amendment guarantees over which it had been given enforcement powers. He joined the Court, for example, in affirming selective congressional bans on literacy tests as a means of eliminating racial discrimination in voter registration, even though he had earlier joined an opinion approving fairly administered tests.[285] And he persisted in that position even in the absence of evidence that a particular voter requirement had been employed in a racially discriminatory manner.[286]

Given the necessary and proper clause and the enforcement provisions of the Fourteenth Amendment, Black's deference to congressional enactments expanding upon judicial interpretations of the amendment's substantive meaning is understandable. As Justice Harlan forcefully argued in dissenting from Black's—and the Court's—position,[287] *Marbury v. Madison*[288] and its progeny do give courts the final power to interpret the Constitution's meaning. That does not mean, however, that Congress has no authority to impose a general ban on a practice which the Court has been willing to uphold under a particular set of circumstances. Congress can simply conclude that the practice at issue, while amenable to constitutional application in particular cases, is generally inconsistent with the Constitution's commands and should be prohibited. In short, Congress acting under its specific lawmaking powers and the necessary and proper clause can paint with a broader brush than the courts. At least since *McCulloch* v. *Maryland*,[289] after all, the Court has upheld congressional regulations reasonably related to an enumerated power of the national government, including Congress's authority to enforce the Fourteenth Amendment through "appropriate" legislation. And a Justice Black, of course, would have been especially reluctant to second-guess the judgment of Congress regarding the relationship of a law to one of Congress's enumerated powers—reluctant, at least, where he was convinced that the end pursued was within those powers, as determined by the Constitution's text and the history underlying adoption of its provisions.

Black's conclusion that Congress can reach private interferences with Fourteenth and Fifteenth Amendment rights is a different matter. In an opinion registered for *Terry* v. *Adams*,[290] striking down a further attempt to maintain the white primary in private hands, he strongly suggested that state inaction was the root of the offense at issue, concluding: "It violates the Fifteenth Amendment for a state, by such circumvention, to permit within its borders the use of any device that produces an equivalent of the prohibited election."[291] Since he termed the scheme at issue in *Terry* the "equivalent" of "precisely the kind of election that the Fifteenth Amendment seeks to prevent,"[292] however, his position there appeared to be based primarily on the "public function" rationale under which ostensibly private activities that serve an essentially "public" or governmental function are held to constitute state action for constitutional purposes. Among passages he had Justice Stewart delete from the Court's opinion in the *Guest* case on the ground that they might "cause confusion," moreover, was the following observation: "It has also been suggested that a State can violate the Equal Protection Clause by abdication as well as by affirmative action, and that the default or neglect of a State to accord the equal protection of the law to its inhabitants might be a predicate for congressional action under the Equal Protection Clause and [Section] 5 of the Fourteenth Amendment."[293] It thus seems doubtful that he subscribed to the potentially limitless state inaction thesis as a basis for congressional control of private interferences with Fourteenth and Fifteenth Amendment rights. Presumably, the key to his position lies instead in the broad discretion he extended to governments generally in areas over which they had been given regulatory power—a deference traditionally considered especially appropriate, given the necessary and proper clause, when extended to Congress. He may have agreed, too, with those who believe that the Fourteenth Amendment's framers intended to confer on Congress power to reach private interferences with rights the amendment guarantees. Even so, Black's stance is difficult to square entirely with the amendment's language and his usual emphasis on text in constitutional interpretation.

In the main, however, the Justice's treatment of the Constitution's flexible clauses—like his interpretation of criminal procedure guarantees calling, in his judgment, for absolutist constructions—was compatible with his broader jurisprudence. The Fourth Amendment's language forbids only the "unreasonable" search and seizure. Accordingly, he refused to agree that warrantless searches or arrests were presumptively invalid. Since the language of the amendment's first clause reaches only "persons, houses, papers, and effects," and its second clause demands that warrants "particularly" describe the things to be seized, he rejected the Amendment's extension to eavesdropping. Since its language does not specify the officers who are to issue warrants and requires only "probable cause" for their issuance, he was reluctant to second-guess the judgments of government officials and trial courts regarding such matters. And the failure of the amendment's language or history to provide a basis for recognition of an exclusionary rule was a constant source of frustration. Since, on the other hand, the Fourteenth Amendment's equal protection clause defies literal construction, he confined that guarantee's meaningful application largely, though not entirely, to the core racial context of its enactment. His Fourth Amendment and equal protection jurisprudence were thus further reflections of his emphasis on constitutional text, where text provided a basis for clear-cut construction, and on the historical record, where text offered little or no guidance.

Epilogue

WHATEVER the controversy his thinking generated, Justice Black's influence on modern trends in civil liberties law has been considerable. No more than three Justices ever joined his campaign for total incorporation of the Bill of Rights into the Fourteenth Amendment's meaning.[1] During his last decade on the bench, however, he had the satisfaction of joining his brethren in applying most of the safeguards of the first eight amendments to the states.[2] No other Justice concurred entirely with his rejection of libel, slander, and obscenity controls. But in *New York Times* v. *Sullivan*[3] and its progeny,[4] the Court did make it arguably difficult to penalize libelous comment about public officials and public figures. During Black's tenure government's power to punish the distribution and possession of obscenity was also dramatically curtailed.[5] Moreover, the Court's 1969 decision in *Brandenburg* v. *Ohio*,[6] limiting criminal punishment of speech to incitements of imminent lawless action actually likely to provoke such action, largely eliminated the imminent-danger test—a standard Black had long attacked—as a tool for the suppression of speech not closely brigaded with illegal conduct. When the Court banned state-guided prayer and Bible reading in the public schools, Black wrote the first of the Court's historic opinions.[7] His opinion for the Court in *Wesberry* v. *Sanders*,[8] extending "one person, one vote" to congressional districting, largely tracked his 1946 *Colegrove* dissent from the Court's denial of relief to the victims of malapportionment.[9] And his majority opinion for *Afroyim* v. *Rusk*,[10] rejecting any congressional power to strip bona fide citizens of their U.S. citizenship, represented the triumph of another constitutional position he had long urged the Court to adopt.[11]

Nor has Justice Black's influence been confined to his years on the high bench. On one occasion since his death the Court did approve a double standard for the application of a Bill of Rights safeguard in federal and state cases.[12] Otherwise, the Court apparently still adheres to the position, most vigorously advanced by Black, that such guarantees should have an identical force in all cases. A majority also ultimately embraced Black's dissent in *Food Employees* v. *Logan Valley Plaza*.[13] In 1972 Justice Lewis Powell relied heavily on the Black dissent in limiting the reach of the *Logan Valley* majority's conclusion that shopping centers, like company towns and municipalities, have First Amendment obligations.[14] Then in 1976 the Court rejected *Logan Valley* entirely.[15] The Court has reiterated and expanded, moreover, Justice Black's conclusion for the *Younger* v. *Harris*[16] majority that federal district courts should ordinarily deny petitions for their intervention in state judicial proceedings.[17] And the grave misgivings about facial review of challenged statutes which Black raised in his *Younger* opinion may have played a role in the Burger Court's drastic curtailment of such review and insistence that a statute claimed to impinge on First Amendment freedoms can be invalidated on its face only if its overbreadth is "substantial."[18]

The post-Black Court's reaction to claims of constitutional protection for privacy and related rights not specifically mentioned in the document's text may also reflect, to some degree, the continued presence of Black's influence on the high bench. *Roe* v. *Wade*,[19] bottoming a woman's right to abort an unwanted pregnancy on the due process guarantee, was hardly consistent with his total rejection of substantive due process doctrine—a stance even the *Roe* dissenters declined to embrace. But *Roe* and its progeny have proved to be exceptional cases. In general, the Burger and Rehnquist Courts have been reluctant to read new guarantees into the scope of due process. During the decade after Justice Black's death, for example, a majority rejected meaningful protection for asserted rights of personal appearance[20] and reputation;[21] and more recently the Court has refused to include homosexual sodomy among protected privacy relationships.[22] Along similar lines it has rejected the suggestions of certain Warren era decisions that the equal protection guarantee was a reservoir for rights not guaranteed elsewhere in the Constitution[23]—suggestions which prompted Black to accuse his brethren of seeking to convert equal protection into the same sort of "natural law" tool he had long condemned in the due process field.[24]

Nor has the *Tinker* decision,[25] from which Black registered one of his most caustic dissents, proved a harbinger for expansive judicial constructions of the scope of First Amendment rights in schools and other public property dedicated to special purposes. The Court has not specifically rejected the *Tinker* majority's conclusion that teachers and students enjoy First Amendment rights on school property, subject only to reasonable regulations necessary to maintain discipline and prevent substantial interferences with the educational process. Recent decisions reflect considerably greater deference to school officials, however, than the *Tinker* majority seemed willing to extend. They also make clear that the First Amendment rights to which students are entitled on school property are hardly "coextensive," as the Court has put it, "with the rights of adults in other settings"[26]—that, indeed, First Amendment rights in the school environment are much more comparable to "rights" guaranteed under a lenient substantive due process formula than under modern First Amendment precedents. In a 1986 case, for example, the Court voted seven to two to uphold sanctions imposed by a school against a student who employed sexual innuendo in a student government campaign speech, Chief Justice Burger observing for the Court, "Surely it is a highly appropriate function of public school education to prohibit the use of vulgar and offensive terms in public discourse."[27] In *Hazelwood School Dist.* v. *Kuhlmeier*,[28] moreover, a majority approved a principal's authority to excise from an issue of a student newspaper tastefully written articles on teenage pregnancy and the impact of divorce on children. "Educators," asserted Justice White for the majority, "do not offend the First Amendment by exercising editorial control over the style and content of student speech in school-sponsored expressive activities so long as their actions are reasonably related to legitimate pedagogical concerns."[29]

Although Justice Black's general impact on modern constitutional law is thus undoubted, few, if any, jurists and legal scholars have fully embraced major elements of his jurisprudence. Not only have his total incorporation construction of the Fourteenth Amendment and absolutist conception of the First won few adherents,[30] his interpretivist-positivist approach to the Constitution's meaning and efforts to ascribe relatively fixed constructions to due process and other potentially open-ended guarantees, thereby limiting the scope of judicial choice in constitutional cases, have proved equally controversial.[31] Judges and scholars have subjected his thinking to rigorous scrutiny, with some critics contending that the language and history of the open-ended safeguards foredoom attempts to give them fixed meanings uncolored by contemporary values, while others have charged that Black's interpretivism led to "arbitrary" choices among protected and unprotected activities— choices which prompted him to extend absolute constitutional protection, for example, to obscenity, libel, and other "undeserving" forms of expression, while according little protection for the much more "worthy" speech of the modern protest movements.[32]

As I have attempted to demonstrate in this book, however, such contentions are themselves vulnerable to criticism. John Hart Ely and others who have argued that the expansive language and history of due process and the Constitution's other open-ended guarantees virtually demand their noninterpretivist construction[33] arguably proceed from a dubious premise. They seem to assume that the linguistic and historical evidence Black marshaled in support of the relatively fixed constructions he assigned such clauses must be free from criticism and challenge from alternative approaches, or discarded. Since such clauses' language and the history underlying their adoption can be construed to call for their noninterpretivist construction, critics conclude, Black's clause-bound and relatively fixed interpretations must be rejected, or at least partially so, despite the fact that noninterpretivist approaches to the Constitution's open-ended guarantees obviously threaten majoritarian institutions which the document clearly recognizes.

In my judgment, however, such an approach imposes an unduly rigorous burden of proof on the Justice's jurisprudence. Given the inherent tension between judicial review and democratic principles, those assessing the feasibility rather than the desirability of Black's interpretations of the Constitution's open-ended clauses—interpretations limiting the scope of judicial discretion and thus reflecting the document's democratic as well as constitutional character—arguably should ask not whether Black's constructions are free from doubt, but whether his positions were based on highly plausible readings of text and history.

Black's constructions of the open-ended clauses clearly met that standard. The substantive due process formula, as Professor Corwin reminded us years ago,[34] flies in the face of the due process clause's very language, and the "law of the land" interpretation of the guarantee to which Black subscribed is compatible with both its original meaning in Anglo-American law and its actual application, if not semantic explication, by the Supreme Court in procedural contexts well into this century.[35] Moreover, not only has the Supreme Court never used the Ninth Amendment as a basis for the judicial recognition of rights not stated elsewhere in the Constitution; it is entirely plausible to construe that enigmatic provision, as Black did, to mean only that the national government is limited to delegated powers and that laws which go beyond those powers, yet interfere with no express liberty, violate other rights "retained by the people." Black's conclusion that the broad language of the Fourteenth Amendment's first section was intended by its framers to incorporate the Bill of Rights may not have been consistent with the findings of Professors Fairman and Morrison. His thesis does square, however, with the findings of most scholars who have studied the issue, including Michael Kent Curtis, whose research is the most extensive to appear to date. And the Justice's refusal either to limit the amendment's privileges or immunities clause to the Bill of Rights or to give it a substantive due process construction also is arguably consistent with the amendment's text and history. For, as Curtis has indicated, certain of the amendment's sponsors did believe that the privileges of national citizenship would include within their scope other guarantees than the specifics of the Bill of Rights. But the sponsors had no clear idea what those rights were, and they gave no hint that the clause would clothe courts with general power to "recognize" rights not then in existence or rule on the reasonableness of laws and procedures.[36] Finally, Black's decision to limit the meaningful reach of equal protection largely to racial classifications comports with the core racial context of its adoption and the inherent futility of efforts to assign the guarantee a literal construction.

Those who dismiss Black's efforts as a simplistic, quixotic attempt to find clarity and precision in imprecise constitutional language and an ambiguous historical record seriously misperceive what the Justice was about. As he undoubtedly realized, his fixed constructions of the Constitution's open-ended clauses were linguistically and historically flawed. But he was not seeking perfection. Instead, he was striving for constitutional constructions which were compatible with plausible readings of language and history, and thus consistent with his conception of judicial review, yet restrictive of judicial choice, and thus compatible with democratic principles. In my judgment, he largely succeeded. Taken together with his total incorporation thesis and literal, generally liberal readings of specific Bill of Rights safeguards, his constructions of due process and the other open-ended clauses formed a jurisprudence which arguably struck a workable, if imperfect, balance between the Constitution's critical role as a meaningful restraint on governmental power and the equally important majoritarian institutions the document also embodies.

Nor were the "arbitrary" distinctions between constitutionally protected and unprotected behavior which his jurisprudence was claimed to produce extreme departures from the mainstream of American constitutional law. In the protest cases of the sixties a majority did suggest that the First Amendment provides some degree of direct protection for demonstrative speech[37] and a limited right of access to public property for purposes of expression.[38] But while Black's absolutism rejected both these elements of the modern Court's thinking, his acceptance of the vagueness doctrine in such cases, like his insistence that controls over expression on public property generally open to the public be nondiscriminatory,[39] meant that his differences with the majority were often more conceptual than disagreements over the proper decision to be reached in a particular case. In *Brown* v. *Louisiana*,[40] the library sit-in case, he was among dissenting rather than majority Justices only because Justice White concluded that the breach-of-peace prosecutions at issue there were racially motivated. In *Adderley* v. *Florida*,[41] decided several months later, White found no racial taint in state trespass prosecutions of jail ground demonstrators and joined Black in upholding state power to deny individuals all use of certain public property for purposes of expression. And in *Edwards* v. *South Carolina*,[42] *Cox* v. *Louisiana*,[43] and most related cases, Black joined the vote, if not entirely the rationale, of the majority or registered only partial dissents.

In the *Tinker* case, of course, he did stand alone in challenging the Court's assumption that students and teachers take their First Amendment rights onto school property. As noted earlier, however, *Tinker* has been narrowly construed in subsequent cases.[44] So, too, has the symbolic speech concept it embraced.[45] Nor were Black's vigorous dissents in *Bell* v. *Maryland*[46] and *Logan Valley Plaza* deviations from established precedent. In *Bell*, after all, the majority simply concluded that passage of a state public accommodations law required abatement of the trespass prosecutions at issue there; no majority of the Court has ever agreed with the contention that restaurants and related facilities are quasi-governmental bodies subject to constitutional restrictions on state action, or that the First Amendment grants a right of access to private property. And Black's refusal to hold in *Logan Valley* that shopping centers are subject to such requirements has since become, of course, the prevailing position on the Court. Certainly, moreover, the Court is unlikely ever to accept William Van Alstyne's blurring of traditionally recognized distinctions between reviewable and non-reviewable state action on which Black's *Bell* dissent was essentially based.[47]

Of course, the charges of critics that Black's jurisprudence led him to "arbitrary" conclusions regarding the Constitution's meaning arguably are based primarily not on disagreements with the Justice's reading of text and history, or on the degree to which his voting patterns conflicted with those of his colleagues. Instead, they are bottomed on assertions that his jurisprudence denied judges the opportunity to give weight to "values" his critics deem important. During his historic 1968 television interview the Justice discussed the single thread he saw running through critical letters he had received over the years: "[T]heir idea is all the same. You can trace it to the same thing, doesn't make any difference what it is, what their experience is, or why they're mad with the Court. It's all because each one of them believes that the Constitution prohibits that which they think should be prohibited, and permits that which they think should be permitted."[48]

Black's reference, presumably, was to crank mail. But it also captures the essence, I believe, of much of the scholarly criticism directed at his judicial and constitutional philosophy. In attacking Black's literal interpretation of the Fourth Amendment, Jacob Landynski faults the Justice's uncharacteristic failure to heed the teachings of the history underlying the amendment's adoption—a history demonstrating, in Landynski's judgment, that the amendment's framers intended it to incorporate broad privacy values rather than literal commands. Arguably, however, Landynski's thesis, and the intensity with which he advances it, rests much less on direct historical evidence—which is scant at best—than on his belief that eavesdropping and other police investigative tactics pose a serious threat to individual liberty and thus *should be* subject to broad constitutional restraint.[49] Criticisms of Black's First Amendment jurisprudence are permeated with the same concerns, as are attacks on the desirability of his relatively fixed constructions of due process and the Constitution's other potentially open-ended provisions. Essentially the same conclusion seems in order whether Black's critics accuse the Justice of reading too much or too little into the document's meaning.

The urge to read into the Constitution policies one finds desirable is not confined, of course, to Black's critics. As Abram Chayes has reminded us, "the American legal tradition has always acknowledged the importance of substantive results for the legitimacy and accountability of judicial action."[50] People expect courts to secure "justice," and justice, like beauty, is in the eye of its beholder. In such a society the jurisprudence of a Hugo Black is unlikely ever to prevail.

Nor is the recent tendency to equate interpretivism with conservative political dogma likely to enhance the appeal of Black's thinking. A jurisprudence based on text and history is "conservative," of course, in the sense that it largely rejects any authority for judges to draw on values not bottomed on those guides to the Constitution's meaning. Accordingly, Black refused to read a general right of privacy into the document, disputed claims that a Fourth Amendment which protects against the unreasonable search of "persons, houses, papers, and effects" should also be extended to words, and rejected constructions of due process, equal protection, and other general constitutional provisions which would clothe judges with power to rule on the "reasonableness" of laws or the "fairness" of governmental procedures. But his reading of the Constitution's text and history also led him in decidedly liberal directions, prompting him, for example, not merely to support complete application of the Bill of Rights to the states and to reject all direct restrictions on what he considered the First Amendment's express language, but also to give equally absolutist interpretations to the Fifth Amendment guarantee against compulsory self-incrimination and to the Sixth Amendment's assurance of procedural safeguards in "all criminal prosecutions," among other constitutional provisions.

In recent years, however, Reagan administration officials, among others, have invoked Black's name in defending a jurisprudence of "original intent" which appears to lead its adherents almost invariably in politically conservative directions. Attorney General Edwin Meese III in particular sought to wrap the administration's professed devotion to "text as illuminated by intention" in whatever aura Justice Black's memory may offer. Praising the Justice's "dedication to the Constitution rather than to judicial musings," Meese cited Black's record as evidence that a "jurisprudence of original intention is not some recent conservative ideological creation," though adding, in classic understatement, "This is not to say that there is not room for disagreement among those of us who, like Justice Black, endeavor to root constitutional interpretation in the solid ground of text illuminated by intention."[51]

Indeed, there is room for disagreement. Meese alluded only to the administration's opposition to application of the Bill of Rights to the states via incorporation—a major element of Black's jurisprudence. But he also could have mentioned the administration's school prayer and pornography stances, and one suspects that there is much more in the Reagan administration's constitutional philosophy with which Justice Black would vehemently disagree.[52] Even so, the administration's resort to interpretivism as a tool for promoting its conservative political agenda—and its attempt to invoke the name of Black in the cause—is unlikely to enhance the appeal of the Justice's jurisprudence among those who, like the Justice himself actually, favor a liberal reading of the Constitution's commands.

Justice Black's efforts, however, were not in vain. His opinions are an enduring brief for the proposition that a jurisprudence rooted in text and history may provide a firmer mooring for individual rights than appeals to shifting values. For Justice Black, as Kenneth Karst once observed,[53] the guarantees of the Constitution had a "ceiling" as well as a "floor." And the Justice's opinions are a constant reminder that while a jurisprudence based on "fundamental values" can raise that ceiling to limitless heights, it also can destroy the floor.

Notes

Preface

1. New York Times Co. v. United States, 403 U.S. 713, 714–15 (1971) (Black, J., concurring).
2. 401 U.S. 37 (1971).
3. James v. Valtierra, 402 U.S. 137 (1971).
4. Labine v. Vincent, 401 U.S. 532 (1971).
5. Palmer v. Thompson, 403 U.S. 217 (1971).
6. Oregon v. Mitchell, 400 U.S. 112 (1970).
7. William J. Brennan Papers, Box 417, Library of Congress. The occasion was discussion of United States v. Vuitch.
8. Boddie v. Connecticut, 401 U.S. 371, 389 (1971).
9. Bivens v. Six Unknown Named Agents, 403 U.S. 388, 427 (1971).
10. Cohen v. California, 403 U.S. 15, 27 (1971) (Blackmun, J., joined by Black, J., dissenting).
11. 401 U.S. 1201 (1971).
12. Ibid., 1202–3.
13. Justice Black's most extensive summary of his judicial and constitutional philosophy is to be found in his *A Constitutional Faith* (New York: Knopf, 1969), the published version of his James S. Carpentier lectures, delivered at Columbia University School of Law in March of 1968.
14. Sylvia Snowiss, "The Legacy of Justice Black," *Supreme Court Review* 1973: 249.

One The Critics

1. A copy of the flyer circulated by the group, known as the Independent Young Americans, is on file in the Harlan Fiske Stone Papers, Box 73, Library of Congress. Justice Black's Klan ties are discussed in Gerald T. Dunne, *Hugo Black and the Judicial Revolution* (New York: Simon and Schuster, 1977), pp. 62–63, 105–6, 113–14, and Virginia Van Der Veer Hamilton, *Hugo Black: The Alabama Years* (Baton Rouge: Louisiana State University Press, 1972), pp. 98–100, 119–20, 136–38, 283–300.

2. The incident occurred during Black's defense of Edwin R. Stephenson for the murder of a Catholic priest who married Stephenson's daughter to a Puerto Rican paper-hanger and gave the young woman instruction in Catholic doctrine. It is thoroughly discussed in Hamilton, *Hugo Black*, pp. 85–93.

3. Black's investigations of corruption in the awarding of mail contracts and the activities of utility lobbyists, and the controversy they aroused, are discussed in ibid., pp. 235–59.

4. 323 U.S. 214 (1944).

5. *New York Times*, September 26, 1971.

6. *Southwestern University Law Review* 9 (1977): 1127, 1130, 1136.

7. Ibid., p. 1137.

8. Ibid.

9. For his summary of his jurisprudence, see his *A Constitutional Faith*.

10. Mark Silverstein, *Constitutional Faiths: Felix Frankfurter, Hugo Black, and the Process of Judicial Decision Making* (Ithaca, N.Y., and London: Cornell University Press, 1984), is an excellent analysis of the Black-Frankfurter jurisprudential relationship.

11. Memorandum for the Court, undated, Wiley B. Rutledge Papers, Box 8. I examined the Rutledge Papers at the Yale law library before they were placed in the Library of Congress. Box references are to the Yale collection.

12. "F.F" to "Brethren," August 30, 1945, ibid., Box 12.

13. Robert H. Jackson to Black, September 10, 1937, Robert H. Jackson Papers, Box 9, Library of Congress.

14. For an analysis of the leadership problems confronting the Supreme Court during Stone's tenure as Chief Justice, see David J. Danelski, "The Influence of the Chief Justice in the Decisional Process," in *Courts, Judges, and Politics: An Introduction to the Judicial Process*, 4th ed., Walter F. Murphy and C. Herman Pritchett (eds.) (New York: Random House, 1986), pp. 568–77.

15. Jewell Ridge Corp. v. Local, 325 U.S. 161 (1945).

16. Ibid., 176–78.

17. Note to members of the conference, May 5, 1945, Harlan Fiske Stone Papers, Box 71, Library of Congress.

18. Black to Harlan Fiske Stone, June 11, 1945, ibid.

19. Harlan Fiske Stone to Felix Frankfurter, June 15, 1945, ibid.

20. Jewell Ridge Coal Corporation v. Local, 325 U.S. 897 (1945).

21. Felix Frankfurter to Black, June 9, 1945, Stone Papers, Box 71.

22. *Washington Star*, May 16, 1946.

23. The text of the cablegram is reprinted in *New York Times*, June 11, 1946.

24. "John" to Black, June 11, 1946, Hugo L. Black Papers, Box 61, Library of Congress. John Frank apparently authored the telegram.

25. *New York Times*, June 11, 1946.

26. *New York Times*, June 13, 1946.

27. *New York Times*, June 15, 1946.

28. The memorandum is on file in the Jackson Papers, Box 26.

29. The "cheap" article to which Jackson referred had appeared in the *Commentator* and was authored by Yale law professor Fred Rodell.

30. The memorandum is also on file in the Jackson Papers, Box 26.
31. "Gordon" to Robert H. Jackson, November 25, 1949, ibid.
32. Dunne, *Hugo Black*, p. 248.
33. Felix Frankfurter to Black, September 30, 1950, Black Papers, Box 60. The book in question was Robert S. Allen and William Shannon, *The Truman Merry-Go-Round* (New York: Vanguard Press, 1950).
34. Black to Felix Frankfurter, October 2, 1950, Black Papers, Box 60.
35. "Eddie" to Felix Frankfurter, April 12, 1945, Felix Frankfurter Papers, Box 25, Library of Congress.
36. The memorandum is on file in ibid. The case was Vernon v. Wilson, 313 U.S. 547 (1941).
37. 309 U.S. 227 (1940).
38. The memorandum is on file in the Frankfurter Papers, Box 25.
39. Felix Frankfurter to Black, May 7, 1963, Black Papers, Box 60.
40. 378 U.S. 226 (1964); 379 U.S. 306 (1964); Felix Frankfurter to Black, December 15, 1964, ibid.
41. Black to Felix Frankfurter, December 22, 1964, ibid.
42. ICC v. Inland Waterways Corp., 319 U.S. 671, 692 (1943).
43. Ibid.
44. The draft is on file in the Frankfurter Papers, Box 25.
45. A copy of the letter is on file in ibid.
46. A copy of the letter is on file in ibid.
47. The draft opinion in Cicenia v. LaGay is on file in the John Marshall Harlan Papers, Box 533, Seeley G. Mudd Library, Princeton University.
48. 316 U.S. 455 (1942).
49. 357 U.S. 449 (1958).
50. The draft is on file in the Harlan Papers, Box 533.
51. Felix Frankfurter to John Marshall Harlan, April 23, 1958, ibid.
52. Felix Frankfurter to John Marshall Harlan, April 24, 1958, ibid.
53. Ibid.
54. John Marshall Harlan to Felix Frankfurter, April 24, 1958, ibid.
55. Black to John Marshall Harlan, May 2, 1958, ibid.
56. After one trip to a cemetery where the original Alabama Harlans were buried, Black excitedly reported to Harlan that while he and his colleague were related only by marriage, "the Alabama Harlans and their descendants are a part of your Harlan family." Black to John Marshall Harlan, ibid. When Black's niece Hazel Black Davis published *Uncle Hugo: An Intimate Portrait of Mr. Justice Black* in 1965, she inscribed her copy to Harlan, "For Mr. Justice John Marshall Harlan, Because he is one of our relatives." Ibid.
57. Although Harlan's law degree was from New York Law School rather than Harvard, Frankfurter's alma mater, Harlan received his undergraduate education at Princeton and studied at Oxford on a Rhodes scholarship, while Justice Black's combined college and law school training was limited to the University of Alabama's law school of two faculty members. The book on jurisdiction and procedure Frankfurter presented to Black was probably Felix Frankfurter and Harry Shulman (eds.), *Cases and Other Authorities on Federal Jurisdiction and Procedure* (Chicago: Callaghan,

1937). Frankfurter's spelling admonition to Black appeared on Frankfurter's copy of Black's draft dissent in Yates v. United States, Black Papers, Box 334. For cases reflecting a growing Black-Harlan voting, if not jurisprudential, alliance on certain issues during their last years on the bench, see, for example, Harper v. Virginia State Bd. of Elections, 366 U.S. 663 (1966), on equal protection; Reitman v. Mulkey, 387 U.S. 369 (1967), on state action; and Brown v. Louisiana, 383 U.S. 131 (1966), on the First Amendment.

58. Charles Fairman, "Does the Fourteenth Amendment Incorporate the Bill of Rights? The Original Understanding," *Stanford Law Review* 2 (1949): 5; Stanley Morrison, "Does the Fourteenth Amendment Incorporate the Bill of Rights? The Judicial Interpretation," *Stanford Law Review* 2 (1949): 140.

59. Wallace Mendelson to Felix Frankfurter, October 31, 1952, Frankfurter Papers, Box 83.

60. *Justices Black and Frankfurter: Conflict in the Court* (Chicago: University of Chicago Press, 1961, 1966).

61. See, for example, "Hugo Black and Judicial Discretion," *Political Science Quarterly* 85 (1970): 17; "Mr. Justice Black's Fourteenth Amendment," *Minnesota Law Review* 53 (1969): 711.

62. Mendelson, *Justices Black and Frankfurter*, p. 134.

63. 381 U.S. 479 (1965).

64. Mendelson, *Justices Black and Frankfurter*, p. 134.

65. Charles Reich, "Mr. Justice Black and the Living Constitution," *Harvard Law Review* 76 (1983): 673.

66. A. E. Dick Howard, "Mr. Justice Black: The Negro Movement and the Rule of Law," *Virginia Law Review* 50 (1967): 1030.

67. Mendelson, *Justices Black and Frankfurter*, p. 148.

68. Glendon Schubert, *The Constitutional Polity* (Boston: Boston University Press, 1970), pp. 118, 120.

69. Ibid., pp. 124, 127.

70. Ibid., p. 129.

71. Ibid., p. 127.

72. Ibid., p. 122.

73. Ibid., p. 124.

74. Dunne, *Hugo Black*, p. 419.

75. S. Sidney Ulmer, "The Longitudinal Behavior of Hugo Lafayette Black: Parabolic Support for Civil Liberties, 1937–1971," *Florida State University Law Review* 1 (1973): 152.

76. Ibid.

77. Burton M. Atkins and Terry Sloope, "The 'New' Hugo Black and the Warren Court," *Polity* 19 (1986): 621, 635.

78. John Hart Ely, *Democracy and Distrust: A Theory of Judicial Review* (Cambridge, Mass.: Harvard University Press, 1980), pp. 11–42.

79. James J. Magee, *Mr. Justice Black: Absolutist on the Court* (Charlottesville: University Press of Virginia, 1980).

80. Snowiss, "The Legacy of Justice Black," p. 187.

81. Jacob W. Landynski, "In Search of Justice Black's Fourth Amendment," *Fordham Law Review* 45 (1976): 453.
82. Patrick McBride, "Mr. Justice Black and his Qualified Absolutes," *Loyola University* [Los Angeles] *Law Review* 2 (1969): 37.
83. William Van Alstyne, "Mr. Justice Black, Constitutional Review, and the Talisman of State Action," *Duke Law Journal* 1965: 219.

Two **A Constitutional Faith**

1. Black, *A Constitutional Faith*, p. 66.
2. Paul A. Freund, "Mr. Justice Black and the Judicial Function," *UCLA Law Review* 14 (1967): 473.
3. Tinsley E. Yarbrough, "Mr. Justice Black and Legal Positivism," *Virginia Law Review* 57 (1971): 375.
4. Black to author, October 13, 1970, author's files and Black Papers, Box 55.
5. For a collection of writings illustrating these schools of jurisprudence, see M. P. Golding (ed.), *The Nature of Law: Readings in Legal Philosophy* (New York: Random House, 1966). See also Edgar Bodenheimer, *Jurisprudence* (Cambridge, Mass.: Harvard University Press, 1961), Part I.
6. Benjamin N. Cardozo, *The Nature of the Judicial Process* (New Haven, Conn.: Yale University Press, 1921), p. 66.
7. Mendelson, *Justices Black and Frankfurter*, p. 121.
8. Charlotte Williams, *Hugo L. Black: A Study in the Judicial Process* (Baltimore: Johns Hopkins University Press, 1950), p. 189.
9. John P. Frank, *Mr. Justice Black: The Man and His Opinions* (New York: Knopf, 1949), p. 139.
10. Reich, "Mr. Justice Black and the Living Constitution," p. 747.
11. Ibid.
12. 309 U.S. 227 (1940).
13. Ibid., p. 241.
14. "Justice Black and the Bill of Rights" (transcript of 1968 CBS News television interview), *Southwestern University Law Review* 9 (1977): 950 (hereinafter cited as CBS interview).
15. Griswold v. Connecticut, 381 U.S. 479, 522 (1965).
16. General summaries of the views of representative legal positivists are provided in Bodenheimer, *Jurisprudence*, ch. 7, and W. G. Friedmann, *Legal Theory* (New York: Columbia University Press, 1967), chs. 21–24. Major works of modern positivists include Hans Kelsen, *General Theory of Law and State* (New York: Russell and Russell, 1961), and H. L. A. Hart, *The Concept of Law* (London: Oxford University Press, 1961). Samuel Shuman's *Legal Positivism: Its Scope and Limitations* (Detroit: Wayne State University Press, 1963) is a critical analysis of positivist thinking.
17. See W. L. Morison, "Some Myths about Positivism," *Yale Law Journal* 68 (1958): 217.
18. John Chipman Gray, *The Nature and Sources of the Law*, 2d ed. (Boston: Beacon Press, 1963), p. 125.

19. See H. L. A. Hart, "Positivism and the Separation of Law and Morals," *Harvard Law Review* 71 (1958): 598–99.
20. Roscoe Pound, *Law and Morals*, 2d ed. (Chapel Hill: University of North Carolina Press, 1926), p. 44.
21. Bodenheimer, *Jurisprudence*, p. 224.
22. See, for example, John Austin, *Lectures on Jurisprudence*, 4th ed. rev. and edited by Robert Campbell (London: John Murray, 1873), I, p. 221.
23. Friedman, *Legal Theory*, p. 257.
24. Edward McWinney, "English Legal Philosophy and Canadian Legal Philosophy," *McGill Law Journal* 4 (1958): 218.
25. Morison, "Some Myths about Positivism," p. 214.
26. Austin, *Lectures*, II, p. 683.
27. Hart, *The Concept of Law*, pp. 73–74.
28. See Morison, "Some Myths about Positivism," p. 217.
29. Austin, *Lectures*, II, pp. 1023–24.
30. Hart, "Positivism and the Separation of Law and Morals," p. 615.
31. Austin, *Lectures*, II, pp. 674, 677.
32. Charles A. Reich, "Foreward: Mr. Justice Black as One Who Saw the Future," *Southwestern University Law Review* 4 (1977): 849.
33. Interviews with Hugo L. Black, Washington, D.C., August 31, 1970, July 6, 1971 (hereinafter cited as Black interviews).
34. Linkletter v. Walker, 381 U.S. 618, 642 (1965) (Black, J., dissenting).
35. Black interviews.
36. Ibid.
37. Raymond G. Decker, "Justice Hugo L. Black: The Balancer of Absolutes," *California Law Review* 59 (1971): 1351.
38. Shuman, *Legal Positivism*, pp. 195–99.
39. See, for example, Austin, *Lectures*, I, p. 221.
40. Black interviews.
41. Ibid. See also, for example, Brown v. Louisiana, 383 U.S. 131, 164–68 (1966) (Black, J., dissenting); Bell v. Maryland, 378 U.S. 226, 327–28 (1964) (Black, J., dissenting).
42. Howard, "Mr. Justice Black," p. 1086.
43. Black, *A Constitutional Faith*, pp. 10–11.
44. Hugo L. Black, "Reminiscences," *Alabama Law Review* 18 (1965): 10.
45. 400 U.S. 1031, 1035 (1971) (Black, J., dissenting). See also his dissents at 383 U.S. 1032 (1966); 374 U.S. 865 (1963); 368 U.S. 1012 (1961).
46. Reich, "Mr. Justice Black and the Living Constitution," pp. 725–26.
47. Boys Market, Inc. v. Retail Clerk's Union, 398 U.S. 235, 257–58 (1970) (Black, J., dissenting).
48. 303 U.S. 77 (1938).
49. Ibid., p. 85.
50. Ibid., p. 88.
51. Ibid., p. 89.
52. Ibid., p. 90.
53. See Marquis W. Childs, "The Supreme Court Today," *Harper's Magazine*, May 1938, pp. 581–88; Alpheus T. Mason, *Harlan Fiske Stone: Pillar of the Law* (New York:

Viking Press, 1956), ch. 29. He apparently stuck with his position, however. See Wheeling Steel Corp. v. Glander, 337 U.S. 562, 576 (1949) (Douglas, J., joined by Black, J., dissenting).

54. 319 U.S. 372 (1943).
55. Ibid., p. 396.
56. Ibid., p. 407.
57. Felix Frankfurter to Wiley Rutledge, May 20, 1943, Rutledge Papers, Box 2.
58. 325 U.S. 226 (1945). The Court's first decision is reported at 317 U.S. 287 (1942).
59. Ibid., p. 265.
60. Ibid., p. 268.
61. See, for example, Fletcher v. Peck, 6 Cr. 87 (1817).
62. 290 U.S. 398.
63. Ibid., p. 428.
64. City of El Paso v. Simmons, 379 U.S. 497 (1965).
65. Ibid., p. 516.
66. Ibid., p. 517.
67. Ibid., p. 521. For an example of his literal interpretation of the Fifth Amendment provision forbidding government to take private property without just compensation, see United States v. Causby, 328 U.S. 256 (1946).
68. Linkletter v. Walker, 381 U.S. 618, 640 (1965) (Black, J., dissenting).
69. "Justice Black and First Amendment 'Absolutes': A Public Interview," *New York University Law Review* 37 (1962): 562.
70. Black interviews.
71. Howard, "Mr. Justice Black," p. 1051.
72. Truman M. Hobbs, "Justice Black: Qualities of Greatness," *Alabama Law Review* 24 (1971): 11.
73. "Confessions of the Law Clerks," unpublished reminiscences prepared on the occasion of Justice Black's eightieth birthday.
74. 321 U.S. 158 (1944); Rutledge Papers, Box 104.
75. Webb Rice to Black, January 31, 1938, Black Papers, Box 252.
76. For historical discussions of congressional and Supreme Court policies regarding federal judicial intervention in state court proceedings, see, for example, Frank L. Maraist, "Federal Injunctive Relief against State Court Proceedings," *Texas Law Review* 48 (1970): 535; Telford Taylor and Everett L. Willis, "The Power of Federal Courts to Enjoin Proceedings in State Courts," *Yale Law Review* 42 (1933): 1169; Charles Warren, "Federal and State Court Interference," *Harvard Law Review* 43 (1930): 345. For a general analysis of Burger Court treatment of the issue, see Tinsley E. Yarbrough, "Litigant Access Doctrine and the Burger Court," *Vanderbilt Law Review* 31 (1978): 56–69.
77. 380 U.S. 479 (1965).
78. 401 U.S. 37 (1971).
79. Brandenburg v. Ohio, 395 U.S. 444 (1969).
80. Byrne v. Karalexis, 401 U.S. 216 (1971); Dyson v. Stein, 401 U.S. 200 (1971); Perez v. Ledesma, 401 U.S. 82 (1971); Boyle v. Landry, 401 U.S. 77 (1971); Samuels v. Mackell, 401 U.S. 66 (1971).
81. See files for Younger v. Harris, et al., Black Papers, Boxes 438–39.

82. 401 U.S. at 44.
83. Ibid.
84. Ibid., p. 50.
85. Ibid., pp. 52–53.
86. See 42 U.S.C. sec. 1983, for codification of the 1871 law.
87. South Carolina v. Katzenbach, 383 U.S. 301 (1966).
88. Ibid., p. 356.
89. Ibid., p. 357.
90. Ibid., p. 358–60.
91. Allen v. State Board of Elections, 398 U.S. 544, 596 (1969) (Black, J., dissenting).
92. Black interview.
93. See, for example, Harper v. Virginia State Board of Elections, 366 U.S. 663, 673 (1966) (Black, J., dissenting).
94. 376 U.S. 1 (1964).
95. See, for example, Hadley v. Junior College District, 379 U.S. 50 (1970).
96. 328 U.S. 549, 566 (1946).
97. Black interviews.
98. For a statement of the Stewart-Clark position on reapportionment, see Lucas v. Colo. Gen. Assembly, 377 U.S. 713, 753 (1964) (Stewart, J., joined by Clark, J., dissenting). For a discerning critique of Justice Black's interpretation of Article I, Section 2, see Justice Harlan's dissent in Wesberry v. Sanders, 376 U.S. at 20.
99. See generally Max Farrand (ed.), *The Records of the Federal Convention of 1787* (New Haven, Conn.: Yale University Press, 1911), and Max Farrand, *The Framing of the Constitution of the United States* (New Haven, Conn.: Yale University Press, 1926), pp. 156–57, 202.
100. 351 U.S. 536 (1956).
101. Harlan Papers, Box 484.
102. New York Times Co. v. United States, 403 U.S. 713, 718–19 (1971) (Black, J., concurring).
103. Youngstown Co. v. Sawyer, 343 U.S. 579 (1952).
104. For example, Dennis v. United States, 341 U.S. 494 (1951).
105. This discussion is based on Justice Jackson's conference notes in the case, Jackson Papers, Box 176.
106. 343 U.S. at 585.
107. Ibid., p. 587.
108. Ibid., pp. 587–88.
109. Ibid., pp. 588–89.
110. Ibid., p. 589.
111. 356 U.S. 44 (1958).
112. Trop v. Dulles, 356 U.S. 86 (1958).
113. For example, Schneider v. Rusk, 377 U.S. 162 (1964); Kennedy v. Mendoza-Martinez, 372 U.S. 144 (1963).
114. 387 U.S. 253 (1967).
115. Ibid., p. 267.
116. Quoted in ibid., p. 257.
117. Ibid.

118. 401 U.S. 815 (1971).
119. Ibid., p. 840.
120. Ibid., p. 844.
121. 387 U.S. at 269.
122. 12 How. 299 (1852).
123. Bernard Schwartz, *A Commentary on the Constitution of the United States, Part I: The Powers of Government* (New York: Macmillan, 1963), I, pp. 246, 247–48. For a thorough survey of burden-on-commerce case law, see ibid., ch. 7.
124. William O. Douglas, *We the Judges* (Garden City, N.Y.: Doubleday, 1956), p. 254.
125. 312 U.S. 52 (1941).
126. Gwin, White & Prince, Inc. v. Henneford, 305 U.S. 434, 454–55 (1939) (Black, J., dissenting) (footnote omitted). For another early expression of his position, see McCarroll v. Dixie Lines, 309 U.S. 176, 183 (Black, J., dissenting).
127. 303 U.S. 177 (1938).
128. Harlan F. Stone to Black, February 11, 1938, Stone Papers, Box 63. The precedent cited was Sproles v. Binford, 286 U.S. 374 (1932).
129. 325 U.S. 761 (1945).
130. Ibid., p. 788, n. 4.
131. Ibid., p. 789.
132. Ibid., p. 794.
133. 328 U.S. 373 (1946).
134. Ibid., p. 387.
135. See, for example, Hood & Sons v. DuMond, 336 U.S. 525, 545 (1949) (Black, J., dissenting); Dean Milk Co. v. City of Madison, 340 U.S. 349, 357 (1951) (Black, J., dissenting).
136. Hood & Sons v. DuMond, 336 U.S. at 561–62.
137. Ibid.
138. Chandler v. Judicial Council, 398 U.S. 74, 141–43 (1970) (Black, J., dissenting).
139. The guarantee appeared in Chapter 39 of the Magna Carta, 25 Edw. 1, c. 39 (1297). For a discussion of the document by a former Black law clerk, see A. E. Dick Howard, *Magna Carta: Text and Commentary* (Charlottesville: University Press of Virginia, 1964).
140. 13 N.Y. 378 (1856).
141. See, for example, Slaughter-House Cases, 16 Wall. 36 (1873); Munn vs. Illinois, 94 U.S. 113 (1877).
142. 198 U.S. 45 (1905).
143. U.S., *Congressional Record* 81 (1937): 1294.
144. Ibid., pp. 306–7.
145. Bartels v. Iowa, 262 U.S. 404, 412 (1923) (Holmes, J., dissenting).
146. U.S., *Congressional Record* 81 (1937): 2828.
147. United Gas Public Serv. Co. v. Texas, 303 U.S. 123, 146 (1938).
148. 304 U.S. 144 (1938).
149. Black to Harlan F. Stone, April 21, 1938, Stone Papers, Box 63.
150. Harlan F. Stone to Black, April 22, 1938, ibid.; United States v. Carolene Products, 304 U.S. at 155 (Black, J., concurring and dissenting).
151. United States v. Darby Lumber Co., 312 U.S. 100 (1941).

152. Black notation on *Darby Lumber Co.* draft, Stone Papers, Box 66.
153. Mercoid Corp. v. Mid-Continent Co., 320 U.S. 661, 673 (Black, J., concurring).
154. Federal Power Commission v. Natural Gas Pipeline Co., 315 U.S. 575, 608 (1942) (Black, J., concurring).
155. Federal Power Commission v. Hope Natural Gas Co., 320 U.S. 591, 619–20 (1944) (Black, J., concurring). Frankfurter's citation was to Chicago, M. & St. P. Ry. Co. v. Minnesota, 134 U.S. 418 (1890).
156. Morey v. Doud, 354 U.S. 439 (1957); City of New Orleans v. Dukes, 472 U.S. 297 (1976).
157. Lincoln Federal Labor Union v. Northwestern Iron & Metal Co., 335 U.S. 525, 536–37 (1949).
158. 372 U.S. 726 (1963).
159. Ibid., pp. 731–32.
160. Arthur J. Goldberg to Black, April 18, 1963, Black Papers, Box 372.
161. See ibid.
162. See, for example, Adamson v. California, 332 U.S. 46, 68 (1947) (Black, J., dissenting).
163. 262 U.S. 390 (1923).
164. 268 U.S. 510 (1925).
165. See, for example, Gitlow v. New York, 268 U.S. 652 (1925); Near v. Minnesota, 283 U.S. 697 (1931).
166. See, for example, Cantwell v. Connecticut, 310 U.S. 296 (1940); Everson v. Bd. of Education, 330 U.S. 1 (1947).
167. 316 U.S. 535 (1942).
168. 378 U.S. 500 (1964).
169. 381 U.S. 479 (1965).
170. 378 U.S. at 518.
171. Ibid.
172. 367 U.S. 497 (1961).
173. Ibid., p. 517.
174. Ibid., pp. 517–18.
175. Ibid., p. 521.
176. William J. Brennan to William O. Douglas, April 24, 1965, Brennan Papers, Box 130.
177. 381 U.S. at 482.
178. Ibid., p. 484.
179. Ibid., pp. 482–83.
180. Ibid., p. 486.
181. Ibid.
182. The substantive due process basis for the *Meyer* and *Pierce* rulings is not only clear from the opinions in those cases. When the Court later cited them in striking down federal territorial regulations applicable to private schools, Farrington v. Tokushige, 273 U.S. 284 (1927), it held that the Fourteenth Amendment rights guaranteed under *Meyer* and *Pierce* were applicable to the federal government by virtue of the Fifth Amendment due process clause, not the First Amendment.
183. 381 U.S. at 508–10.
184. Ibid., p. 500.

185. Ibid., p. 511.
186. Ibid., p. 522.
187. Ibid., p. 520.
188. 410 U.S. 113 (1973).
189. Brennan Papers, Box 417, conference discussion of United States v. Vuitch.
190. United States v. Vuitch, 402 U.S. 62 (1971).
191. 300 U.S. 123 (1938).
192. 96 U.S. 97, 105 (1877).
193. 309 U.S. 227 (1940).
194. Ibid., pp. 236–37.
195. See, for example, In Re Murchison, 349 U.S. 133, 136 (1955); In Re Oliver, 333 U.S. 257, 278 (1948).
196. Ibid.; Rideau v. Louisiana, 373 U.S. 723 (1963); Irvin v. Dowd, 366 U.S. 717 (1961). See also United States ex rel. Smith v. Baldi, 344 U.S. 561 (1953).
197. See, for example, Edelman v. California, 344 U.S. 357 (1953) (Black, J., dissenting); Lanzetta v. New Jersey, 306 U.S. 451 (1939). See also Shull v. Virginia ex rel. Comm. on Law Reform and Racial Activities, 359 U.S. 344 (1959) (Black, J.).
198. See, for example, Thompson v. City of Louisville, 362 U.S. 199 (1960) (Black, J.).
199. See, for example, Pyle v. Kansas, 317 U.S. 213 (1942); Hysler v. Florida, 315 U.S. 411 (1942).
200. See, for example, Alcorta v. Texas, 355 U.S. 28 (1957).
201. See, for example, Miller v. Pate, 386 U.S. 1 (1967).
202. Sniadach v. Family Finance Corp., 395 U.S. 337, 350–51 (1969) (Black, J., dissenting).
203. Goldberg v. Kelly, 397 U.S. 254, 276–77 (1970) (Black, J., dissenting).
204. Boddie v. Connecticut, 401 U.S. 371, 391 (1971) (Black, J., dissenting).
205. 397 U.S. 358 (1970).
206. Ibid., p. 359.
207. Brinegar v. United States, 338 U.S. 160 (1949); Holland v. United States, 348 U.S. 121 (1954); Speiser v. Randall, 357 U.S. 513 (1958). See also Leland v. Oregon, 343 U.S. 790, 802 (1952) (Frankfurter, J., joined by Black, J., dissenting).
208. 397 U.S. at 382.
209. Ibid., pp. 383–84. For an excellent analysis of Black's due process views, see also Roger Haigh, "Defining Due Process of Law: The Case of Mr. Justice Hugo L. Black," *South Dakota Law Review* 17 (1971): 1.
210. Griswold v. Connecticut, 381 U.S. 479, 501 (1945) (Harlan, J., concurring).
211. Ronald Dworkin, *Taking Rights Seriously* (Cambridge, Mass.: Harvard University Press, 1977), p. 134.
212. See, for example, John Hart Ely, *Democracy and Distrust: A Theory of Judicial Review* (Cambridge, Mass.: Harvard University Press, 1980), ch. 2.
213. Michael J. Perry, *The Constitution, the Courts, and Human Rights: An Inquiry into the Legitimacy of Constitutional Policymaking by the Judiciary* (New Haven, Conn.: Yale University Press, 1982).
214. Thomas C. Grey, "Do We Have an Unwritten Constitution?" *Stanford Law Review* 27 (1975): 706, 713.
215. Snowiss, "The Legacy of Justice Black," p. 248.

216. Ibid., pp. 248–49.
217. Ibid., pp. 249–50.
218. Ibid., p. 250.
219. Griswold v. Connecticut, 381 U.S. at 511, n. 4.
220. Rochin v. California, 342 U.S. 165, 173 (1952) (Frankfurter, J.).
221. Snyder v. Massachusetts, 291 U.S. 97, 105 (1934).
222. Malinski v. New York, 324 U.S. 401, 47 (1945) (Frankfurter, J., concurring).
223. Black, *A Constitutional Faith*, p. 35.
224. See generally his *Democracy and Distrust*.
225. See generally his *The Constitution, the Courts, and Human Rights*.
226. Edward S. Corwin, "The Doctrine of Due Process of Law before the Civil War," *Harvard Law Review* 24 (1911): 467–68.
227. Ibid., pp. 474–75.
228. 18 How. 272, 276–77.
229. 211 U.S. 78 (1908).
230. Ibid., p. 101.
231. Ibid., p. 110.
232. For example, In Re Oliver, 333 U.S. 257 (1948).
233. For example, Thompson v. City of Louisville, 362 U.S. 199 (1960).
234. For example, In Re Gault, 387 U.S. 1 (1967).
235. 314 F. Supp. 1217, 1221 (N.D. Texas, 1970).
236. See, for example, Bennett B. Patterson, *The Forgotten Ninth Amendment* (Indianapolis: Bobbs-Merrill, 1955).
237. See, for example, Ely, *Democracy and Distrust*, p. 35.
238. Griswold v. Connecticut, 381 U.S. at 519–20.
239. Gaillard Hunt (ed.), *Writings of James Madison*, Vol. 5 (New York: Putnam, 1900–1910), pp. 271–72.
240. U.S., *Annals of Congress* 1: 439.
241. See, for example, United States v. Darby Lumber Co., 312 U.S. 100 (1941).
242. Ely, *Democracy and Distrust*, p. 28.
243. Colgate v. Harvey, 296 U.S. 404 (1935).
244. Madden v. Kentucky, 309 U.S. 83 (1940).
245. 314 U.S. 160 (1941).
246. See, for example, Duncan v. Louisiana 391 U.S. 145, 166–67 (1968) (Black, J., concurring). Black's conference discussion of *Edwards* is drawn from the Frank Murphy Papers, Michigan Historical Collection, University of Michigan, Box 62.
247. Slaughter-House Cases, 16 Wall. 36, 79 (1873).
248. See, for example, Ely, *Democracy and Distrust*, pp. 22–30.
249. Howard cited Justice Bushrod Washington's circuit court opinion in Corfield v. Coryell, 6 Fed. Cases 3230 (1823), which gave the clause such an interpretation; U.S., *Congressional Globe*, 39th Cong., 1st Sess. 2765–66 (1866).
250. Ely, *Democracy and Distrust*, p. 28.
251. Michael Kent Curtis, *No State Shall Abridge: The Fourteenth Amendment and the Bill of Rights* (Durham, N.C.: Duke University Press, 1986), p. 82.
252. 383 U.S. 663 (1966).
253. For example, Kotch v. Pilot Comm'ns, 330 U.S. 552 (1947) (Black, J.).

254. 383 U.S. at 673–74.
255. Ibid., p. 674.
256. Ibid.
257. Ibid.
258. See, for example, Ely, *Democracy and Distrust*, pp. 30–32.
259. Lief H. Carter, *Contemporary Constitutional Lawmaking: The Supreme Court and the Art of Politics* (New York: Pergamon Press, 1985), pp. 45–46.

Three **The Bill of Rights and the States**

1. 332 U.S. 46 (1947); Black interviews.
2. 16 Wall. 36 (1873).
3. See, for example, Crandall v. Nevada, 6 Wall. 35 (1868).
4. See Hurtado v. California, 110 U.S. 516 (1884).
5. 211 U.S. 78 (1908).
6. Ibid., p. 113.
7. Ibid., p. 101.
8. Ibid., p. 113.
9. Chicago B. & Q. RR. v. Chicago, 166 U.S. 226 (1897).
10. 268 U.S. 652 (1925).
11. 287 U.S. 45 (1932).
12. 268 U.S. at 672.
13. 302 U.S. 319.
14. Ibid., p. 323.
15. Ibid., p. 325.
16. Ibid., p. 326 n. 4, quoting 211 U.S. at 99.
17. Ibid., p. 328.
18. Jerome Cooper, "Mr. Justice Hugo L. Black: Footnotes to a Great Case," *Alabama Law Review* 24 (1971): 1, 4.
19. John Frank, "The New Court and the New Deal," in Stephen P. Strickland (ed.), *Hugo Black and the Supreme Court* (New York: Bobbs-Merrill, 1967), pp. 281–82 n. 29.
20. Black interviews.
21. See, for example, Adamson v. California, 332 U.S. at 89; Duncan v. Louisiana, 391 U.S. 145, 163–64 (1968) (Black, J., concurring).
22. 304 U.S. at 152 n. 4.
23. 307 U.S. 496 (1939).
24. Frankfurter Papers, Box 25.
25. See, for example, Adamson v. California, 332 U.S. at 64–65 (Frankfurter, J., concurring).
26. J. Woodford Howard, *Mr. Justice Murphy: A Political Biography* (Princeton, N.J.: Princeton University Press, 1968), p. 428 n. c.
27. 309 U.S. 227 (1940).
28. On this point see the exchange of letters between Senator George W. Norris, February 29, 1940, and NAACP Secretary Walter White, March 4, 1940, in Black Papers, Box 259. After their acquittals following retrial, the petitioners wrote Justice Black,

extending "to the Supreme Court of the United States and to you in particular, our most humble thanks for making it possible for us to be living today." Ibid., Box 266.

29. Black interviews.
30. 309 U.S. at 236–37.
31. Ibid., p. 241.
32. Ibid., p. 236.
33. Ibid.
34. Ibid., p. 237.
35. Ibid., n. 10.
36. Ibid., p. 236 n. 8.
37. 314 U.S. 252 (1941).
38. Ibid., p. 263 n. 6.
39. Adamson v. California, 332 U.S. at 85.
40. 314 U.S. at 268.
41. Felix Frankfurter to John Marshall Harlan, May 19, 1961, Frankfurter Papers, Box 66.
42. 314 U.S. at 280–81.
43. 316 U.S. 455 (1942).
44. 304 U.S. 458 (1938).
45. 316 U.S. at 462.
46. Ibid.
47. Ibid., p. 472.
48. Murphy Papers, Box 63.
49. 316 U.S. at 474.
50. Ibid., n. 1.
51. Ibid., p. 474.
52. Ibid., pp. 476–77.
53. John R. Green, "The Bill of Rights, the Fourteenth Amendment and the Supreme Court," *Michigan Law Review* 46 (1948): 884–94, discusses these cases and Black's stance in them.
54. 324 U.S. 401 (1945).
55. Ibid., p. 414.
56. Ibid., pp. 414–15.
57. Ibid., pp. 414–17.
58. Fowler Harper, *Justice Rutledge and the Bright Constellation* (New York: Bobbs-Merrill, 1965), p. 214.
59. 329 U.S. 459 (1947).
60. Ibid., p. 462.
61. The drafts are on file in the Rutledge Papers, Box 17.
62. Ibid. See also Frankfurter's concurrence in the case, 329 U.S. at 466.
63. 332 U.S. at 53.
64. Murphy Papers, Box 69.
65. 332 U.S. at 67.
66. Murphy Papers, Box 69.
67. 332 U.S. at 71–72.
68. Ibid., p. 72.

69. Ibid.
70. Ibid., p. 73.
71. 171 U.S. 581 (1900).
72. Ibid., p. 601–2.
73. William D. Guthrie, *The Fourteenth Amendment to the Constitution* (Boston: Little, Brown, 1898).
74. 332 U.S. at 74.
75. Ibid., quoting 211 U.S. at 96, 113.
76. Ibid.
77. Ibid., p. 75.
78. Ibid., pp. 75–76.
79. Ibid., p. 77.
80. Ibid., p. 81.
81. Ibid., p. 92.
82. Ibid., p. 89.
83. Ibid., p. 84.
84. Ibid., p. 85.
85. Ibid., p. 85–86.
86. Ibid., p. 86.
87. Ibid., p. 87.
88. Ibid., p. 86.
89. Ibid., p. 66.
90. Ibid., p. 90.
91. Ibid.
92. Ibid.
93. See Black Papers, Box 252.
94. 332 U.S. at 89.
95. Ibid., p. 75.
96. Including Justice Frankfurter in ibid., p. 64.
97. Memorandum of May 28, 1947, Rutledge Papers, Box 17.
98. Memorandum of March 27, 1947, ibid.
99. William O. Douglas to Black, May 21, 1947, Black Papers, Box 284.
100. Memorandum of May 28, 1947.
101. Ibid.
102. Memorandum of May 29, 1947, Rutledge Papers, Box 17.
103. Undated memorandum, ibid.
104. Frank Murphy to Black, undated, Black Papers, Box 284.
105. 332 U.S. at 124.
106. Black to Frank Murphy, June 19, 1947, Murphy Papers, Box 68.
107. 110 U.S. 516 (1884).
108. 333 U.S. 257 (1948).
109. Ibid., p. 278.
110. 372 U.S. 335 (1963).
111. 380 U.S. 400 (1965).
112. Ibid., p. 403.
113. Robinson v. California, 370 U.S. 660 (1962); Malloy v. Hogan, 378 U.S. 1 (1964);

Washington v. Texas, 388 U.S. 14 (1967); Klopfer v. North Carolina, 386 U.S. 213 (1967); Duncan v. Louisiana, 391 U.S. 145 (1968); Benton v. Maryland, 395 U.S. 784 (1969).

114. Duncan v. Louisiana, 391 U.S. at 164.
115. Apodaca v. Oregon, 406 U.S. 404 (1972).
116. Gideon v. Wainwright, 372 U.S. at 346–47.
117. Douglas's note to Justice Black and Black's notes to his secretary and Justice Brennan are in the Black Papers, Box 372.
118. 338 U.S. 25 (1949).
119. Ibid., pp. 27–28.
120. Weeks v. United States, 232 U.S. 383 (1914).
121. 338 U.S. at 26.
122. Ibid., p. 27.
123. Ibid., p. 39.
124. 342 U.S. 165 (1952).
125. Ibid., pp. 175–77.
126. 391 U.S. 145 (1968).
127. 364 U.S. 263 (1960).
128. Ibid., p. 275.
129. Duncan v. Louisiana, 391 U.S. at 149.
130. Ibid., p. 176.
131. Ibid., p. 174.
132. Ibid., p. 175 n. 9.
133. Ibid., pp. 166–67.
134. 397 U.S. 358 (1970).
135. 366 U.S. 117 (1961).
136. Ibid., p. 136.
137. 362 U.S. 199 (1960).
138. John Marshall Harlan to Black, March 17, 1960, Harlan Papers, Box 86.
139. See, for example, Justice Frankfurter's *Adamson* concurrence, 332 U.S. at 62–64.
140. 391 U.S. at 177.
141. Felix Frankfurter to William Brennan, April 16, 1959, Harlan Papers, Box 533.
142. Adamson v. California, 332 U.S. at 71.
143. 391 U.S. at 166 n. 1.
144. 332 U.S. at 61.
145. See, for example, Mendelson, "Mr. Justice Black's Fourteenth Amendment," p. 715.
146. Ibid.
147. 314 U.S. 160 (1961).
148. Murphy Papers, Box 62. The California law at issue in *Edwards* made it a crime for a resident to knowingly bring an indigent into the state. According to Murphy's notes, Justice Black remarked in conference that poverty could not justify a state in preventing "a citizen from moving from one state to another," but added: "We have a different situation when aliens are involved."
149. Green, "The Bill of Rights," p. 904.
150. 381 U.S. 479 (1965).
151. Ibid., p. 501.

152. 332 U.S. at 67–68.
153. Ibid., p. 67.
154. Williams v. Florida, 399 U.S. 78, 133 (1970) (Harlan, J., concurring and dissenting).
155. Ibid.
156. See Justice Harlan's summary in ibid., pp. 126–28.
157. Ibid., p. 118.
158. Ibid., p. 130.
159. 332 U.S. at 67.
160. 381 U.S. at 499–500.
161. 332 U.S. at 90.
162. For example, United States v. Leon, 468 U.S. 897 (1984).
163. 399 U.S. 66 (1970).
164. Ibid., p. 74.
165. Ibid., p. 75.
166. Fairman, "Does the Fourteenth Amendment Incorporate the Bill of Rights? The Original Understanding," p. 5.
167. Ibid., pp. 34–36.
168. Ibid., p. 134.
169. Ibid., p. 137.
170. Ibid., p. 138.
171. Ibid., p. 139.
172. Ibid.
173. Morrison, "Does the Fourteenth Amendment Incorporate the Bill of Rights? The Judicial Interpretation," p. 5.
174. Ibid., pp. 159, 150 (footnote omitted).
175. Ibid., p. 162.
176. Ibid., p. 167.
177. A recent listing is to be found in Curtis, *No State Shall Abridge*, p. 222 n. 19.
178. Raoul Berger, *Government by Judiciary: The Transformation of the Fourteenth Amendment* (Cambridge, Mass.: Harvard University Press, 1977).
179. "Justice Black, the Fourteenth Amendment, and Incorporation," *University of Miami Law Review* 30 (1976): 231.
180. See, for example, 332 U.S. at 94–95, 104.
181. 391 U.S. at 165.
182. Especially in the *Civil Rights Cases*, 109 U.S. 3 (1883).
183. 211 U.S. at 98, 96.
184. 7 Wall. 321 (1869).
185. 9 Wall. 274 (1869).
186. 7 Wall. at 325.
187. Mendelson, "Mr. Justice Black's Fourteenth Amendment," p. 721.
188. In Spies v. Illinois, 123 U.S. 131 (1887).
189. For example, Presser v. Illinois, 116 U.S. 252 (1886); Hurtado v. California, 110 U.S. 516 (1884); Walker v. Sauvinet, 92 U.S. 90 (1876).
190. Durham, N.C.: Duke University Press, 1986.
191. See, for example, ibid., pp. 41–56, 61.
192. Ibid., pp. 58–64.

193. Ibid., pp. 34–35.
194. Ibid., p. 72. The provision quoted is now codified at 42 U.S.C. sec. 1981.
195. Ibid., p. 91.
196. Ibid., p. 112.
197. Ibid., p. 152.
198. Ibid., p. 154–56.
199. Ibid., p. 105.
200. Ibid., p. 82.
201. "The *Adamson* Case: A Study in Constitutional Technique," *Yale Law Journal* 58 (1949): 274.
202. Curtis, *No State Shall Abridge*, p. 82.

Four **Black's First Amendment**

1. 314 U.S. 252 (1941).
2. Ibid., p. 263. Black's concern for safeguarding First Amendment rights did not begin, of course, with his appointment to the Court. While in the Senate, he moved to repeal legislation enacted in 1935 which provided that appropriations for Washington, D.C., schools could not be used to pay the salaries of "any person teaching or advocating communism." U.S., *Congressional Record* 81: 1282.
3. Felix Frankfurter to John Marshall Harlan, May 19, 1961, Frankfurter Papers, Box 66.
4. For a balanced discussion of Frankfurter's First Amendment jurisprudence relative to Black's, see Silverstein, *Constitutional Faiths*, ch. 5.
5. Felix Frankfurter to Zechariah Chafee, October 25, 1955, Frankfurter Papers, Box 42.
6. Felix Frankfurter to John Marshall Harlan, May 19, 1961, ibid. The cases were Scales v. United States, 367 U.S. 203 (1961), and Noto v. United States, 362 U.S. 290 (1961).
7. New York Times v. United States, 403 U.S. 713 (1971).
8. Ibid., p. 718.
9. 370 U.S. 421 (1962).
10. A copy of the lecture, delivered at the University of Utah Law School, is on file in the Harlan Papers, Box 148.
11. Hugo L. Black, "The Bill of Rights," *New York University Law Review* 35 (1960): 867.
12. "Justice Black and First Amendment 'Absolutes,' " p. 582.
13. Book Review, *University of Chicago Law Review* 39 (1962): 191.
14. Sidney Hook, " 'Lord Monboddo' and the Supreme Court," *New Leader*, May 13, 1963, p. 11. This piece was a review of Irving Dilliard's tribute to Justice Black, *One Man's Stand for Freedom* (New York: Knopf, 1963).
15. Ibid.
16. Ibid.
17. For example, Cox v. Louisiana, 379 U.S. 536, 575 (1965) (Black, J., concurring and dissenting); Brown v. Louisiana, 383 U.S. 131, 151 (Black, J., dissenting); Adderley v. Florida, 385 U.S. 38 (1966) (Black, J.); Gregory v. City of Chicago, 394 U.S. 111,

113 (1969) (Black, J., concurring); Tinker v. Des Moines School Dist., 393 U.S. 503, 515 (1969) (Black, J., dissenting).

18. Snowiss, "The Legacy of Justice Black," p. 239.
19. Ibid., quoting Black's opinion in Chambers v. Florida, 309 U.S. 227, 238 (1940).
20. Magee, *Mr. Justice Black*, p. 156.
21. For example, Milk Wagon Drivers Union v. Meadowmoor Dairies, 312 U.S. 287, 299 (1941) (Black, J., dissenting); Carpenters Union v. Ritter's Cafe, 315 U.S. 722, 729 (1942) (Black, J., dissenting); Giboney v. Empire Storage & Ice Co., 336 U.S. 490 (1949) (Black, J.); Martin v. Struthers, 319 U.S. 141 (1943) (Black, J.).
22. Magee, *Mr. Justice Black*, p. 183.
23. Ibid., p. 155.
24. 339 U.S. 382 (1950).
25. Ibid., p. 448 (Black, J., dissenting).
26. 341 U.S. 494 (1951).
27. Ibid., p. 580 (Black, J., dissenting).
28. Ibid., p. 581.
29. 342 U.S. 524 (1952).
30. Ibid., p. 555 (Black, J., dissenting).
31. 343 U.S. 250 (1952).
32. Ibid., p. 263.
33. Ibid., pp. 274–75.
34. Ibid., p. 275.
35. 360 U.S. 109 (1959).
36. Ibid., p. 143. For opinions rejecting the clear and present danger doctrine, see, for example, his dissent in Dennis v. United States, 341 U.S. 494, 579 (1951), and concurrence in Brandenburg v. Ohio, 395 U.S. 444, 449 (1969).
37. See, for example, Communist Party v. Subversive Activities Control Board, 367 U.S. 1, 137 (1961) (Black, J., dissenting).
38. See, for example, Barenblatt v. United States, 360 U.S. at 143 (Black, J., dissenting), quoting U.S., *Annals of Congress* 1 (1789): 439.
39. "Justice Black and First Amendment 'Absolutes,'" p. 553.
40. Ibid., p. 557. See also Black, "The Bill of Rights," p. 867.
41. See generally Alexander Meiklejohn, *Free Speech and its Relation to Self-Government* (New York: Harper and Row, 1948).
42. Black, *A Constitutional Faith*, p. 46.
43. Black interviews.
44. 376 U.S. 254 (1964).
45. For example, Garrison v. Louisiana, 379 U.S. 64 (1964); Curtis Publishing Co. v. Butts, 388 U.S. 130 (1967).
46. 376 U.S. at 293.
47. Ibid., p. 297 (footnote omitted).
48. Smith v. California, 361 U.S. 147, 155 (1959) (Black, J., concurring). Earlier, he had joined Justice Douglas's dissent in Roth v. United States, 354 U.S. 476, 508 (1957).
49. Ginsberg v. New York, 390 U.S. 629 (1968).
50. 394 U.S. 557 (1969).
51. See, for example, United States v. Thirty-seven Photographs, 402 U.S. 363 (1971).

52. Ibid., p. 382.

53. 376 U.S. at 293.

54. Curtis Publishing Co. v. Butts, 388 U.S. at 171.

55. Ginzburg v. United States, 383 U.S. 463 (1966).

56. 383 U.S. 413 (1966).

57. 383 U.S. at 480.

58. Ginzburg v. United States, 383 U.S. 463 (1966).

59. Ibid., p. 477.

60. Smith v. California, 361 U.S. at 160.

61. CBS interview.

62. Black interviews.

63. Black to John Marshall Harlan, December 10, 1969, Harlan Papers, Box 533.

64. Smith v. California, 361 U.S. at 157.

65. NLRB v. Fruit Packers Local 760, 377 U.S. 58, 77 (1964) (Black, J., concurring).

66. Gregory v. City of Chicago, 394 U.S. 111, 124 (1969) (Black, J., concurring).

67. 393 U.S. 503.

68. Ibid., p. 505.

69. Ibid., p. 517.

70. Ibid., citing Giboney v. Empire Storage & Ice Co., 336 U.S. 490 (1949).

71. 394 U.S. 576 (1969).

72. Ibid., p. 610 (emphasis in original).

73. 398 U.S. 58 (1970).

74. Ibid., pp. 62–63 (emphasis added).

75. Black, *A Constitutional Faith*, p. 58.

76. CBS interview.

77. 372 U.S. 229 (1963).

78. Ibid., p. 237.

79. 394 U.S. 111 (1969).

80. Ibid., pp. 118–19.

81. See, for example, Cox v. Louisiana, 379 U.S. 536, 580–81 (1965) (Black, J., concurring and dissenting). See also Black, *A Constitutional Faith*, p. 60.

82. Konigsberg v. State Bar, 366 U.S. 36, 68 (1961) (Black, J., dissenting). See also, for example, Black, *A Constitutional Faith*, p. 60. Early cases in which this sort of balancing was developed include Schneider v. Irvington, 308 U.S. 147 (1939), and Cox v. New Hampshire, 312 U.S. 569 (1941).

83. Ibid., pp. 68–69 (footnotes omitted).

84. Ibid., p. 69.

85. 336 U.S. at 498.

86. Ibid., p. 502.

87. 361 U.S. 52 (1942).

88. William O. Douglas to Felix Frankfurter, November 22, 1958, Frankfurter Papers.

89. Pittsburgh Press Co. v. Human Relations Commission, 413 U.S. 376 (1973). For an analysis of Justice Black's possible reaction to First Amendment issues confronting the Burger Court after his death, see Tinsley E. Yarbrough, "Justice Black, the First Amendment, and the Burger Court" *Mississippi Law Journal* 46 (1975): 203.

90. Giboney v. Empire Storage & Ice Co., 336 U.S. at 502.

91. 326 U.S. 1 (1945).
92. Ibid., p. 20.
93. Ibid., p. 7.
94. 395 U.S. 367 (1969).
95. Ibid., p. 375.
96. Ibid., p. 389.
97. FCC v. Pacifica Foundation, 438 U.S. 726 (1978).
98. 379 U.S. 536, 559 (1965).
99. 383 U.S. 131 (1966).
100. 385 U.S. 38 (1966).
101. Tinker v. Des Moines School Dist., 393 U.S. 503 (1969).
102. 379 U.S. at 577.
103. Ibid., p. 581.
104. Ibid.
105. Ibid., p. 578 (emphasis in original).
106. Brennan Papers, Box 411.
107. 379 U.S. at 582–83.
108. Ibid., p. 583.
109. Ibid., pp. 583–84.
110. 383 U.S. 131 (1966).
111. Ibid., p. 142 (footnote omitted).
112. Ibid., pp. 150–51.
113. John Marshall Harlan to Black, January 12, 1966, Black Papers, Box 387.
114. Ibid., p. 142.
115. The draft is on file in the Brennan Papers, Box 137.
116. 383 U.S. at 160.
117. Ibid., p. 157.
118. Pertinent portions of the statute are quoted at ibid., p. 143.
119. Ibid., p. 157.
120. Ibid., p. 162.
121. Ibid., pp. 162, 157.
122. Ibid., p. 162.
123. Ibid., p. 164.
124. Ibid., p. 166.
125. Ibid., pp. 167–68.
126. 385 U.S. 39 (1966).
127. Ibid., p. 49.
128. Ibid., p. 56 (footnote omitted).
129. Ibid.
130. Ibid., p. 41.
131. Ibid., p. 48.
132. Ibid., p. 47.
133. Ibid., p. 48.
134. 393 U.S. 503 (1969).
135. Ibid., p. 506.
136. Ibid., p. 513.

137. Ibid., p. 508.
138. Ibid., p. 510.
139. Ibid., pp. 510–11.
140. Ibid., p. 526.
141. 383 U.S. at 165.
142. 262 U.S. 390 (1923).
143. 262 U.S. 404 (1923).
144. 393 U.S. at 526.
145. Ibid., p. 524.
146. Black to Charles Alan Wright, August 27, 1969, Black Papers, Box 409.
147. NAACP v. Alabama, 357 U.S. 449 (1958).
148. See, for example, Magee, *Mr. Justice Black*, p. 184.
149. "Justice Black and First Amendment 'Absolutes,'" p. 559 (emphasis deleted).
150. Black, *A Constitutional Faith*, p. 45.
151. Ibid., pp. 55–56.
152. 98 U.S. 145 (1878).
153. Black, *A Constitutional Faith*, p. 56. Little has been written regarding Black's interpretation of the religion clauses. But see Donald Meiklejohn, "Religion in the Burger Court: The Heritage of Mr. Justice Black," *Indiana Law Review* 10 (1977): 645.
154. Braunfeld v. Brown, 366 U.S. 599 (1961).
155. Sherbert v. Verner, 374 U.S. 398 (1963).
156. 319 U.S. 624 (1943).
157. Minersville School District v. Gobitis, 310 U.S. 586 (1940). Black first publicly indicated his doubt about his *Gobitis* stance in Jones v. Opelika, 316 U.S. 584, 623 (1942).
158. 319 U.S. at 643, 644.
159. The Court first specifically articulated these standards in School District of Abington Township v. Schempp, 374 U.S. 203 (1963). Chief Justice Burger added a prohibition against "excessive entanglements" of church and state in Walz v. Tax Commission, 397 U.S. 664 (1970). And the Court embraced this trilogy of guidelines in Lemon v. Kurtzman, 403 U.S. 602 (1971).
160. See, for example, Martin v. City of Struthers, 319 U.S. 141 (1943); Marsh v. Alabama, 326 U.S. 501 (1946).
161. 370 U.S. 421 (1962). Black also joined, of course, the *Schempp* decision invalidating state-sponsored Bible reading and recitation of the Lord's Prayer in the public schools.
162. Torasco v. Watkins, 367 U.S. 488 (1961).
163. 330 U.S. 1 (1947).
164. Ibid., pp. 15–16.
165. Ibid., p. 16.
166. Ibid., p. 17.
167. Ibid., p. 18.
168. Ibid.
169. Ibid., p. 20.
170. Ibid., p. 21.

171. Ibid., pp. 25–26.
172. Ibid., p. 60.
173. Ibid., p. 62 (footnotes omitted).
174. Ibid., p. 20.
175. 333 U.S. 203 (1948).
176. Memorandum for the Conference, February 11, 1948, Rutledge Papers, Box 21.
177. 333 U.S. at 211.
178. Ibid., p. 212.
179. 343 U.S. 306 (1952).
180. Ibid., pp. 317–18.
181. Ibid., p. 313.
182. Ibid., p. 315.
183. Ibid., p. 316.
184. Engel v. Vitale, 370 U.S. 421, 443–44 (1962) (Douglas, J., concurring).
185. Walz v. Tax Commission, 397 U.S. 664 (1970), upholding tax exemptions for church property; McGowan v. Maryland, 366 U.S. 420 (1961), upholding modern Sunday closing laws against establishment challenge.
186. See, for example, Lemon v. Kurtzman, 403 U.S. 602, 625 (1971) (Douglas, J., joined by Black, J., concurring).
187. Board of Education v. Allen, 392 U.S. 236, 252–53 (1968) (Black, J., dissenting).
188. 380 U.S. 163 (1965).
189. Ibid., p. 176.
190. 398 U.S. 333 (1970).
191. Ibid., p. 341.
192. Brennan Papers, Box 411.
193. The draft is on file in the Black Papers, Box 385.
194. 393 U.S. 97 (1968).
195. Ibid., p. 112.
196. Ibid., p. 113.
197. Ibid., p. 111.
198. Ibid., p. 113.
199. Ibid., pp. 113–14.
200. Ibid., p. 114.

Five **Black's First Amendment Critics**

1. Magee, *Mr. Justice Black.*
2. Felix Frankfurter to John Marshall Harlan, May 19, 1961, Frankfurter Papers, Box 66.
3. 314 U.S. at 263 (footnote omitted).
4. See, for example, Dennis v. United States, 341 U.S. at 580.
5. The draft is on file in the Black Papers, Box 258.
6. Silverstein, *Constitutional Faiths*, p. 183.
7. Magee, *Mr. Justice Black*, pp. 83–86; Pennekamp v. Florida, 328 U.S. 331 (1946); Craig v. Harney, 331 U.S. 367 (1947).
8. Elizabeth S. Black, "Hugo Black: A Memorial Portrait," in *Yearbook 1982: Supreme*

Court Historical Society (Washington, D.C.: Supreme Court Historical Society, 1982), p. 91 n. 24.

9. 323 U.S. 214 (1944).
10. Magee, *Mr. Justice Black*, p. 70.
11. CBS interview.
12. 387 U.S. 253 (1967).
13. 401 U.S. 815 (1971).
14. Ibid., p. 844.
15. 328 U.S. 654 (1946).
16. Magee, *Mr. Justice Black*, pp. 75–76.
17. 328 U.S. at 674–75.
18. Magee, *Mr. Justice Black*, pp. 76–77.
19. Ibid., p. 77.
20. The provision, Section 338(a) of the Nationality Act of 1940, is quoted at 328 U.S. at 656 n. 1.
21. Ibid., p. 674.
22. See, for example, Magee, *Mr. Justice Black*, pp. 95–98.
23. 315 U.S. 568 (1942).
24. Ibid., pp. 571–72 (footnote omitted).
25. The draft is on file in the Murphy Papers, Box 61.
26. The draft is on file in ibid.
27. Black interviews.
28. 403 U.S. 15 (1971).
29. Magee, *Mr. Justice Black*, p. 96 (footnote omitted).
30. Hannegan v. Esquire, 327 U.S. 146 (1946).
31. Winters v. New York, 333 U.S. 507 (1948).
32. 328 U.S. 331 (1946).
33. 343 U.S. at 267.
34. For example, Roth v. United States, 354 U.S. at 502 (Douglas, J., joined by Black, J., dissenting).
35. Dennis v. United States, 341 U.S. at 579.
36. 320 U.S. 790 (1943).
37. Magee, *Mr. Justice Black*, pp. 105–6 (footnote omitted).
38. William O. Douglas, *The Court Years* (New York: Random House, 1980), p. 94.
39. 333 U.S. 178 (1948).
40. 361 U.S. 52 (1942); Magee, *Mr. Justice Black*, p. 96.
41. 333 U.S. at 180.
42. Ibid., p. 191.
43. Black to Fred M. Vinson, October 31, 1947, Rutledge Papers, Box 21.
44. Magee, *Mr. Justice Black*, pp. 96–97.
45. Ibid., p. 183.
46. Ibid., p. 183; Tinsley E. Yarbrough, "Mr. Justice Black and his Critics on Speech-Plus and Symbolic Speech," *Texas Law Review* 52 (1974): 257.
47. Yarbrough, "Mr. Justice Black and His Critics," p. 273.
48. Ibid., p. 275.
49. 310 U.S. 88 (1940).

50. J. Woodford Howard, *Mr. Justice Murphy: A Political Biography* (Princeton, N.J.: Princeton University Press, 1968), p. 247.
51. See, for example, Giboney v. Empire Storage & Ice Co., 336 U.S. 490, 498–99 (Black, J.).
52. The draft is on file in the Murphy Papers, Box 60.
53. 315 U.S. 722.
54. Ibid., p. 731.
55. Ibid., p. 729.
56. Murphy Papers, Box 62.
57. 315 U.S. at 731.
58. 312 U.S. 287 (1941).
59. Ibid., p. 309–10.
60. Ibid., p. 313.
61. Ibid., p. 317.
62. Ibid.
63. 315 U.S. 769 (1942).
64. Murphy Papers, Box 62.
65. 315 U.S. at 776–77.
66. 312 U.S. 569 (1941).
67. The draft is on file in the Black Papers, Box 262.
68. Black to Charles Evans Hughes, March 27, 1941, ibid.
69. Charles Evans Hughes to Black, March 28, 1941, ibid.
70. Felix Frankfurter to Charles Evans Hughes, March 28, 1941, Frankfurter Papers, Box 68.
71. 308 U.S. 147 (1939).
72. Ibid., p. 163. See also, for example, Lovell v. Griffin, 303 U.S. 444 (1938).
73. 319 U.S. 141 (1943).
74. Ibid., p. 146.
75. 318 U.S. 413 (1943).
76. Ibid., p. 415.
77. Ibid., p. 416.
78. A copy is on file in the Murphy Papers, Box 63.
79. 307 U.S. 496 (1939).
80. Ibid., p. 515.
81. A copy is contained in the *Hague* file in the Black Papers, Box 256.
82. Cox v. Louisiana, 379 U.S. at 581.
83. 336 U.S. 490 (1949) (Black, J.).
84. Ibid., p. 494.
85. Ibid., p. 501.
86. Ibid., p. 502.
87. Ibid., p. 498.
88. Ibid., p. 502.
89. The draft is on file in the Black Papers, Box 299.
90. Magee, *Mr. Justice Black*, p. 164.
91. Ibid., p. 165.
92. Ibid., pp. 165–66.

93. See Justice Rutledge's conference notes, Rutledge Papers, Box 24.

94. 340 U.S. 315 (1951).

95. 336 U.S. 77 (1949).

96. McBride, "Mr. Justice Black and His Qualified Absolutes," p. 63, n. 97.

97. 340 U.S. at 326 (emphasis added).

98. 336 U.S. at 98–99.

99. Ibid., p. 102.

100. Ibid., p. 103.

101. Ibid., p. 104.

102. Snowiss, "The Legacy of Justice Black," p. 234.

103. Ibid., p. 236.

104. Ibid.

105. Ibid., p. 237.

106. Ibid., p. 240.

107. Ibid., p. 245.

108. Ibid., p. 237.

109. George Gallup (ed.), *The Gallup Poll*, vol. 3 (New York: Random House, 1972), pp. 1723–24, 1828, 1884, 1836, 1970, 2225.

110. See, for example, McBride, "Mr. Justice Black and His Qualified Absolutes," p. 47.

111. Michael Ash, "The Growth of Justice Black's Philosophy on Freedom of Speech," *Wisconsin Law Review* 1967: 853.

112. Harry Kalven, "The Concept of the Public Forum: *Cox* v. *Louisiana*," *Supreme Court Review* 1965: 23.

113. 402 U.S. 611, 616 (1971).

114. Ash, "The Growth of Justice Black's Philosophy," p. 853. Justice Black dissented on overbreadth and vagueness grounds from the Court's decision in United Public Workers v. Mitchell, 330 U.S. 75, 105 (1947), upholding Hatch Act provisions which forbade federal employees to "take any active part in political management or in political campaigns." Since the act allows employees "to express their opinions on all political subjects and candidates," Professor Magee views it as an attempt by Congress "to draw the line between speech and conduct" and notes that the early Black considered the product of Congress's effort "hopelessly contradictory and undesirable." Magee, *Mr. Justice Black*, p. 167. No doubt, Black would reply that Congress had simply done a poor job in drawing that line. As he pointed out in his dissent, the law prohibited the public expression of political views at a political gathering for or against any partisan candidate or cause, participation in a (lawful) parade, and the writing for publication or publication of any letter or article, signed or unsigned, in favor of or against any political party, candidate, or faction, among other activities squarely within the scope of the Justice's First Amendment. He simply found a "hopeless contradiction," and thus unconstitutional vagueness and overbreadth, between the law's recognition of a right to "express . . . opinions" and "prohibition[s] against . . . talking" of the sort cited above. 330 U.S. at 108.

115. Freund, "Mr. Justice Black," p. 472.

116. McBride, "Mr. Justice Black and His Qualified Absolutes," p. 51.

117. Ibid., p. 52.

118. For expressions of their conceptions of the issue, see, for example, their opinions in

Konigsberg v. State Bar, 366 U.S. 36 (1961); Barenblatt v. United States, 360 U.S. 109 (1959); Dennis v. United States, 341 U.S. 494 (1951).

119. Konigsberg v. State Bar, 366 U.S. at 69 (Black, J., dissenting) (emphasis added).

120. See, for example, Palmer v. Thompson, 403 U.S. 217, 225 (1971) (Black, J.); Epperson v. Arkansas, 393 U.S. 97, 112–13 (1968) (Black, J., concurring).

121. Cox v. Louisiana, 379 U.S. at 581.

122. 385 U.S. 39 (1967) (Black, J.).

123. Konigsberg v. State Bar, 366 U.S. at 68.

124. McBride, "Mr. Justice Black and His Qualified Absolutes," p. 65.

125. Along these lines, consider the following passage from Black's opinion in Cameron v. Johnson, 381 U.S. 741, 742–43 (1965) (Black, J., dissenting):

> [T]he Court [has failed] properly to enlighten state or federal courts or the people who deserve to know what are the rights of the people, the rights of affected groups, the rights of the Federal Government, and the rights of the States in this field of activities which encompasses some of the most burning, pressing and important issues of our time. . . . These issues are of such great importance that I am of the opinion that before the Court relegates the States to the position of mere onlookers in struggles over their streets and the accesses to their public buildings, this Court should at least write an opinion making clear to the States and interested people the boundaries between what they can do in this field and what they cannot.

126. Adderley v. Florida, 385 U.S. at 47.

127. Cox v. Louisiana, 379 U.S. at 581.

128. Magee, Mr. Justice Black, pp. 178, 181.

129. Kalven, "Public Forum," p. 30.

130. Black interviews.

131. For example, Zechariah Chafee, *Free Speech in the United States* (Cambridge, Mass.: Harvard University Press, 1941); Edward S. Corwin, "Freedom of Speech and Press under the First Amendment: A Résumé, " *Yale Law Journal* 30 (1920): 48.

132. Magee, *Mr. Justice Black*, p. 50.

133. Ibid., p. 59.

134. Quoted in New York Times Co. v. United States, 403 U.S. at 718. Wallace Mendelson's most thorough critique of Black's First Amendment jurisprudence is *Justices Black and Frankfurter*, pp. 42–64.

135. Felix Frankfurter to John Marshall Harlan, February 29, 1960, Frankfurter Papers, Box 66.

136. Magee, *Mr. Justice Black*, p. 22.

137. Schenck v. United States, 249 U.S. 47, 52 (1919).

138. McBride, "Mr. Justice Black and His Qualified Absolutes," p. 69.

139. Snowiss, "The Legacy of Justice Black," pp. 247–48.

140. 360 U.S. 109 (1959).

141. Ibid., p. 143.

142. Hook, " 'Lord Monboddo,' " p. 11.

143. For opposing views on the value of libel actions, see David M. Hunsaker, "Freedom and Responsibility in First Amendment Theory: Defamation Law and Media Cred-

ibility," *Quarterly Journal of Speech* 65 (1929); 25; Franklyn S. Haiman, *Speech and Law in a Free Society* (Chicago: University of Chicago Press, 1981), pp. 48–54.

144. 384 U.S. 333 (1966).
145. Magee, *Mr. Justice Black*, p. 188.
146. See, for example, Irvin v. Dowd, 366 U.S. 717 (1961), in which nearly 90 percent of prospective jurors entertained some opinion as to the defendant's guilt, and eight of twelve jurors impaneled to hear the case thought the defendant was guilty; Rideau v. Louisiana, 373 U.S. 723 (1963), in which film of the defendant's detailed confession to a sheriff and state troopers was telecast on several occasions prior to trial, yet the trial judge denied a change of venue though authorized by state law.

Six **The Flexible Clauses**

1. See especially his *Search and Seizure and the Supreme Court: A Study in Constitutional Interpretation* (Baltimore: Johns Hopkins University Press, 1966).
2. Landynski, "In Search of Justice Black's Fourth Amendment," p. 453.
3. See, for example, "The Longitudinal Behavior of Hugo Lafayette Black," p. 131.
4. Black interviews.
5. Van Alstyne, "Mr. Justice Black," p. 219.
6. See Joseph W. Bishop, Jr., *Justice Under Fire: A Study of Military Law* (New York: Charterhouse, 1974), ch. 4.
7. Wade v. Hunter, 336 U.S. 684, 688 (1949).
8. Toth v. Quarles, 350 U.S. 11 (1955).
9. Reid v. Covert, 354 U.S. 1 (1957).
10. O'Callahan v. Parker, 395 U.S. 258 (1969).
11. Toth v. Quarles, 350 U.S. at 22.
12. Green v. United States, 356 U.S. 165, 197 (1958).
13. Illinois v. Allen, 397 U.S. 337 (1970).
14. Sacher v. United States, 343 U.S. 1, 22 (1952) (Black, J., dissenting).
15. Mayberry v. Pennsylvania, 400 U.S. 455, 463 (1971).
16. Black to William O. Douglas, January 18, 1971, Harlan Papers, Box 484.
17. 400 U.S. at 466.
18. Green v. United States, 356 U.S. at 198.
19. Baldwin v. New York, 399 U.S. 66, 74 (1970) (Black, J., concurring).
20. In re Gault, 387 U.S. 1, 61 (1967) (Black, J., concurring).
21. 399 U.S. 1 (1970).
22. A copy of the dissent is on file in the Black Papers, Box 415.
23. Ibid.
24. Black to Warren E. Burger, April 17, 1970, ibid.
25. Black to Warren E. Burger, April 24, 1970, ibid.
26. Warren E. Burger to Black, April 28, 1970, ibid.
27. Coleman v. Alabama, 399 U.S. at 12. Black considered all other post-arrest, pretrial procedures part of the "criminal prosecution" and subject to the counsel requirement as well. See, for example, United States v. Wade, 388 U.S. 218, 243 (1967) (Black, J., dissenting), involving lineup identifications.
28. See, for example, Ashcraft v. Tennessee, 322 U.S. 143 (1944).

29. Orozco v. Texas, 394 U.S. 324 (1969).
30. This summary is drawn from Chief Justice Warren's *Miranda* conference notes, Earl Warren Papers, Box 381, Library of Congress.
31. Schmerber v. California, 384 U.S. 757, 773 (1966) (Black, J., dissenting).
32. Gilbert v. California, 308 U.S. 263, 277 (1967) (Black, J., dissenting).
33. United States v. Wade, 388 U.S. 218, 243 (1967) (Black, J., concurring and dissenting).
34. Ibid.
35. Rogers v. United States, 340 U.S. 367, 375–76 (1951) (Black, J., dissenting).
36. Ibid., pp. 377–78.
37. 322 U.S. 487 (1944).
38. Ibid., p. 497.
39. 350 U.S. 422 (1956).
40. Kastigar v. United States, 406 U.S. 441 (1972).
41. 350 U.S. at 443.
42. Ibid., p. 440.
43. 359 U.S. 121 (1959).
44. Ibid., p. 155.
45. Waller v. Florida, 397 U.S. 387 (1970).
46. Wade v. Hunter, 336 U.S. 684 (1949).
47. 395 U.S. 711 (1969).
48. Ibid., p. 738.
49. Ibid.
50. Ibid., p. 742.
51. Ibid., p. 741.
52. Duncan v. Louisiana, 391 U.S. at 162.
53. Baldwin v. New York, 399 U.S. at 74.
54. Williams v. Florida, 399 U.S. at 106.
55. Apodaca v. Oregon, 406 U.S. 404 (1972).
56. Galloway v. United States, 319 U.S. at 407.
57. 378 U.S. 368 (1964).
58. Ibid., p. 405.
59. Ibid., p. 402.
60. For an interesting exchange between Black and the author of the Court's opinion in Jackson v. Denno, see Black to Byron R. White, February 21, 1964, and Byron R. White to Black, February 22, 1964, Black Papers, Box 379.
61. Groppi v. Wisconsin, 400 U.S. 505, 515 (1971) (Black, J., dissenting).
62. 373 U.S. 723 (1963).
63. 370 U.S. 660 (1962).
64. Brennan Papers, Box 408.
65. A copy of the dissent is on file in the Black Papers, Box 401.
66. 389 U.S. 810 (1968).
67. McGautha v. California, 402 U.S. 183, 226 (1971) (Black, J., separate opinion).
68. Black to John Marshall Harlan, May 28, 1969, Harlan Papers, Box 484.
69. Furman v. Georgia, 408 U.S. 238 (1972).
70. McGautha v. California, 402 U.S. at 225.

71. Witherspoon v. Illinois, 391 U.S. 510, 532 (1968) (Black, J., dissenting).
72. 399 U.S. 30 (1970).
73. 395 U.S. 752 (1969).
74. 399 U.S. at 40.
75. Ibid., p. 39.
76. Ibid., p. 38.
77. Ibid., p. 35.
78. Ibid., p. 40.
79. 378 U.S. 108 (1964).
80. A copy is on file in the Black Papers, Box 376.
81. Coolidge v. New Hampshire, 403 U.S. 443 (1971).
82. 393 U.S. 410 (1969).
83. Ibid., pp. 433–34.
84. 403 U.S. 443 (1971).
85. Ibid., p. 501.
86. 316 U.S. 129 (1942).
87. 277 U.S. 438 (1928).
88. 388 U.S. 41 (1967).
89. 389 U.S. 346 (1967).
90. Ibid., p. 364.
91. Ibid., p. 365.
92. Ibid.
93. Ibid., pp. 365–66.
94. Ibid., p. 374.
95. Bivens v. Six Unknown Fed. Narcotics Agents, 403 U.S. 388, 428 (1971) (Black, J., dissenting).
96. 334 U.S. 699 (1948).
97. United States v. Rabinowitz, 339 U.S. 56, 66 (1950) (Black, J., dissenting).
98. United States v. Wallace & Tiernan Co., 336 U.S. 793 (1949).
99. 338 U.S. 25 (1949).
100. 232 U.S. 383 (1914).
101. Ibid., p. 40.
102. 342 U.S. 165 (1952).
103. For example, Irvine v. California, 347 U.S. 128 (1954).
104. 367 U.S. 643 (1961).
105. 116 U.S. 616 (1886).
106. 367 U.S. at 662.
107. Ibid., p. 666.
108. 342 U.S. at 175.
109. 367 U.S. at 665.
110. Coolidge v. New Hampshire, 403 U.S. at 498.
111. Linkletter v. Walker, 381 U.S. 618, 640 (1965) (Black, J., dissenting).
112. 367 U.S. at 662.
113. See, for example, Chapman v. California 386 U.S. 18 (1967) (Black, J.).
114. Ibid., p. 23, n. 8.
115. Kaufman v. United States, 394 U.S. 217, 231 (1969) (Black, J., dissenting).

116. For a generally well-based discussion of such inconsistencies, see Landynski, "In Search of Justice Black's Fourth Amendment," pp. 463–79.
117. Ibid., p. 462.
118. Ibid.
119. Ibid., p. 458.
120. Ibid., p. 457.
121. Landynski, *Search and Seizure*, p. 45.
122. Landynski, "In Search of Justice Black's Fourth Amendment," p. 461.
123. Black, "The Bill of Rights," p. 873.
124. Katz v. United States, 389 U.S. at 366.
125. Landynski, "In Search of Justice Black's Fourth Amendment," p. 488.
126. 359 U.S. 360 (1959).
127. Camara v. Municipal Court, 387 U.S. 523 (1967); See v. Seattle, 387 U.S. 541 (1967).
128. Landynski, "In Search of Justice Black's Fourth Amendment," p. 490.
129. Ibid.
130. 359 U.S. at 374.
131. Ibid., p. 376.
132. 381 U.S. 479 (1965).
133. Landynski, "In Search of Justice Black's Fourth Amendment," p. 490.
134. 389 U.S. at 365 (emphasis added).
135. Landynski, "In Search of Justice Black's Fourth Amendment," p. 472.
136. See, for example, Bumper v. North Carolina, 391 U.S. 543, 558–59 (1968) (Black, J., dissenting).
137. 402 U.S. 424 (1971).
138. Ibid., p. 463.
139. 391 U.S. 543 (1968).
140. Landynski, "In Search of Justice Black's Fourth Amendment," p. 472.
141. 391 U.S. at 556.
142. Ibid., p. 557.
143. Landynski, "In Search of Justice Black's Fourth Amendment," p. 477 (footnote omitted).
144. Reich, "Mr. Justice Black and the Living Constitution," pp. 735–36.
145. See, for example, Carlson v. Landon, 342 U.S. 524, 556 (1952) (Black, J., dissenting).
146. Landynski, "In Search of Justice Black's Fourth Amendment," p. 491.
147. Ibid., p. 496 (footnote omitted).
148. Ibid., p. 493.
149. Ibid., p. 495.
150. For a more detailed descriptive analysis of Black's equal protection jurisprudence than that presented here, see Tinsley E. Yarbrough, "Justice Black and Equal Protection," *Southwestern University Law Review* 4 (1978): 899.
151. 336 U.S. 220 (1949).
152. The draft is on file in the Murphy Papers, Box 70.
153. Morey v. Doud, 354 U.S. 457 (1957).
154. Martin v. Walton, 368 U.S. 25 (1961).
155. 330 U.S. 552 (1947).
156. Black interviews.

157. 330 U.S. at 565–66.
158. 316 U.S. 535 (1942).
159. Ibid., p. 541.
160. Korematsu v. United States, 323 U.S. 214, 216 (1944).
161. Takahashi v. Fish & Game Comm'n, 334 U.S. 410 (1948) (Black, J.); Oyama v. California 332 U.S. 633, 647 (1948) (Black, J., concurring); Graham v. Richardson, 403 U.S. 365 (1971).
162. 393 U.S. 23 (1968).
163. Ibid., pp. 30–31.
164. Black interviews.
165. The *Korematsu* draft is on file in the Rutledge Papers, Box 116, in the current Library of Congress collection; the *Williams* draft is on file in the Black Papers, Box 411.
166. 366 U.S. at 670.
167. Ibid., p. 677, n. 7.
168. Ibid., p. 674.
169. Kramer v. Union Free School Dist., 395 U.S. 621, 634 (1969) (Stewart, J., joined by Black, J., dissenting).
170. Cipriano v. City of Houma, 395 U.S. 701 (1969).
171. City of Phoenix v. Kolodziejski, 399 U.S. 204, 215 (1970) (Black, J., concurring); Evans v. Cornman, 398 U.S. 419 (1970); McDonald v. Board of Election, 394 U.S. 802 (1969); Fortson v. Morris, 385 U.S. 231 (1966); Carrington v. Rash, 380 U.S. 89 (1965); Abate v. Mundt, 403 U.S. 182 (1971); Whitcomb v. Chavis, 403 U.S. 124 (1971); Jenness v. Fortson, 403 U.S. 431 (1971).
172. Labine v. Vincent, 401 U.S. 532 (1971) (Black, J.); Levy v. Louisiana, 391 U.S. 68 (1968); Glona v. American Guaranty & Liability Ins. Co., 391 U.S. 73 (1968).
173. James v. Valtierra, 402 U.S. 137 (1971) (Black, J.).
174. Dandridge v. Williams, 397 U.S. 471 (1970).
175. The draft concurrence is on file in the Black Papers, Box 388; his conference position is indicated in Justice Brennan's *Harper* conference notes, Brennan Papers, Box 412.
176. 328 U.S. 549 (1946).
177. Murphy Papers, Box 67.
178. 369 U.S. 186 (1962).
179. 376 U.S. 1 (1964) (Black, J.).
180. Ibid., pp. 7–8.
181. Reynolds v. Sims, 377 U.S. 533 (1964).
182. Avery v. Midland County, 390 U.S. 474 (1968).
183. 397 U.S. 50 (1970).
184. Ibid., p. 56.
185. For example, Avery v. Georgia, 345 U.S. 559 (1953). It should be noted, however, that in Carter v. Jury Comm'n, 396 U.S. 320, 341 (1970) (Black, J., concurring) he rejected any implication in the Court's opinion "that this Court has the power to vacate a state governor's appointment of jury commissioners or the power to compel the governor of a State to appoint Negroes or any other persons to the office of jury commissioner." And in Swain v. Alabama, 380 U.S. 202, 228 (1965) he concurred in the result without opinion when the majority rejected jury discrimi-

nation claims but suggested that a prosecutor's consistent use of peremptory challenges to exclude blacks from jury service would be unconstitutional.

186. Fay v. New York, 332 U.S. 261 (1947); Moore v. New York, 333 U.S. 565 (1948).

187. Griffin v. Illinois, 351 U.S. 12, 20 (1956) (Black, J.).

188. Douglas v. California, 372 U.S. 353 (1963).

189. Burns v. Ohio, 360 U.S. 252 (1959); Smith v. Bennett, 365 U.S. 708 (1961).

190. Tate v. Short, 401 U.S. 395 (1971); Williams v. Illinois, 399 U.S. 235 (1970).

191. Yarbrough, "Justice Black and Equal Protection," pp. 908–18.

192. Lucas v. Colo. Gen. Assembly, 377 U.S. 713, 753 (1964) (Stewart, J., joined by Clark, J., dissenting).

193. 351 U.S. 12 (1956).

194. Black, *A Constitutional Faith*, p. 33.

195. Boddie v. Connecticut, 401 U.S. 371, 390–91 (1971) (Black, J., dissenting).

196. 347 U.S. 483 (1954); 349 U.S. 294 (1955).

197. 320 U.S. 81 (1943).

198. *Ex Parte* Endo, 323 U.S. 283 (1944).

199. Korematsu v. United States, 323 U.S. at 223.

200. 327 U.S. 1 (1946).

201. 323 U.S. at 242.

202. Ibid., p. 241.

203. Quoted in C. Herman Pritchett, *The American Constitution*, 3d ed. (New York: McGraw-Hill, 1977), p. 284.

204. 323 U.S. at 219.

205. Lee v. Washington, 390 U.S. 333, 334 (1968).

206. 323 U.S. at 223–24.

207. Harlan Fiske Stone, Memorandum for the Conference, Black Papers, Box 270.

208. The draft is on file in ibid., Box 283.

209. This discussion is drawn largely from correspondence in ibid., Box 53.

210. For a published version of the paper, see Ulmer, "The Longitudinal Behavior of Hugo Lafayette Black: Parabolic Support for Civil Liberties."

211. For a published version, see S. Sidney Ulmer, "Earl Warren and the *Brown* Decision," *Journal of Politics* 33 (1971): 689.

212. S. Sidney Ulmer, "Bricolage and Assorted Thoughts on Working in the Papers of Supreme Court Justices," *Journal of Politics* 35 (1973): 286, 306.

213. Hugo Black, Jr., *My Father: A Remembrance* (New York: Random House, 1975), pp. 208–9.

214. West Virginia v. Virginia, 222 U.S. 17 (1911).

215. Black, Jr., *My Father*, p. 209.

216. Bernard Schwartz, *Super Chief* (New York: New York University Press, 1983), p. 123.

217. Justice Burton's *Brown* conference notes are in the Harold H. Burton Papers, Library of Congress, Box 337; Frankfurter's notes are in the Frankfurter Papers, Box 219.

218. Schwartz, *Super Chief*, p. 80.

219. Jackson Papers, Box 184.

220. Richard Kluger, *Simple Justice* (New York: Random House, Vintage Books, 1977), p. 594.

221. Jackson Papers, Box 184.

222. Black, Jr., *My Father*, pp. 207–8.

223. Briggs v. Elliott, 342 U.S. 350, 352 (1952).

224. 385 U.S. 1 (1958).

225. Schwartz, *Super Chief*, p. 297.

226. Brennan Papers, Box 14.

227. Harlan Papers, Box 57.

228. CBS interview.

229. 396 U.S. 1218 (1969).

230. Ibid., p. 1219.

231. The draft is on file in the Black Papers, Box 429.

232. 396 U.S. 19 (1969).

233. On file in the Warren Papers, Box 574.

234. 403 U.S. 1 (1971).

235. Black to Warren Burger, March 25, 1971, Black Papers, Box 436; Burger, Memorandum to the Conference, April 8, 1971, ibid. The draft opinion is also on file in ibid.

236. 326 U.S. 501 (1946).

237. Conference notes for Smith v. Allwright, Murphy Papers, Box 64.

238. 321 U.S. 649 (1944).

239. Terry v. Adams, 345 U.S. 461 (1953) (Black, J., announcing judgment of the Court).

240. 334 U.S. 1 (1948).

241. For example, Burton v. Wilmington Parking Authority, 365 U.S. 715 (1961).

242. 326 U.S. at 506.

243. Murphy Papers, Box 67.

244. 326 U.S. at 502.

245. Food Employees Local 590 v. Logan Valley Plaza, 391 U.S. 308 (1968).

246. Ibid., p. 330.

247. For a thorough discussion of Black's position in such cases, written by a law clerk of the period in which the cases arose, see A. E. Dick Howard, "Mr. Justice Black: The Negro Protest Movement and the Rule of Law," *Virginia Law Review* 53 (1967): 1030. While serving as Justice Black's clerk, Howard and another clerk prepared a detailed summary of the Court's deliberations in the cases, now on file in the Black Papers, Box 376.

248. For example, Barr v. City of Columbia, 378 U.S. 199 (1964); Garner v. Louisiana, 368 U.S. 157 (1961).

249. Robinson v. Florida, 378 U.S. 153 (1964); Lombard v. Louisiana, 373 U.S. 267 (1963); Peterson v. City of Greenville, 373 U.S. 244 (1963).

250. 378 U.S. 226 (1964).

251. Ibid., p. 318.

252. Ibid., pp. 327–28.

253. Ibid., p. 345.

254. Reitman v. Mulkey, 387 U.S. 369 (1967).

255. 396 U.S. 435 (1970).

256. Ibid., p. 445. See also his dissent in Evans v. Newton, 382 U.S. 296, 312 (1966), an earlier decision arising from the same litigation.

257. 403 U.S. 217 (1971).

258. Ibid., p. 220.
259. 377 U.S. 218 (1964).
260. Ibid., p. 231 (footnote omitted).
261. 365 U.S. 569 (1961).
262. 403 U.S. at 221, n. 6.
263. Ibid.
264. Harry Blackmun to Black, February 12, 1971, Harlan Papers, Box 484.
265. Black to Harry Blackmun, February 16, 1971, ibid.
266. William Van Alstyne, "Mr. Justice Black, Constitutional Review, and the Talisman of State Action," p. 219.
267. Ibid., p. 231.
268. Ibid., pp. 245–47.
269. Ibid., p. 246.
270. Ibid., p. 245, n. 53.
271. 376 U.S. 254 (1964).
272. 312 U.S. 321 (1941).
273. 351 U.S. 292 (1956).
274. 378 U.S. at 326 (footnote omitted).
275. Ibid., n. 11.
276. 383 U.S. 745 (1966).
277. Potter Stewart, Memorandum to the Conference, February 21, 1966, Harlan Papers, Box 252.
278. 383 U.S. 87 (1966).
279. 109 U.S. 3 (1883).
280. The observation is based on Justice Harlan's conference notes in *Price*, Harlan Papers, Box 412.
281. Black interviews.
282. 395 U.S. 298 (1969).
283. 400 U.S. 112 (1970).
284. Ibid., p. 278 (Brennan, J., concurring and dissenting).
285. South Carolina v. Katzenbach, 383 U.S. 301 (1966); Lassiter v. Northampton Co. Bd. of Elections, 360 U.S. 45 (1959).
286. Katzenbach v. Morgan, 384 U.S. 641 (1966).
287. Ibid.
288. I Cr. 137 (1803).
289. 4 Wheat. 316 (1819).
290. 345 U.S. 461 (1953).
291. Ibid., p. 469.
292. Ibid.
293. Harlan Papers, Box 252.

Epilogue

1. Justices Douglas, Murphy, and Rutledge in Adamson v. California, 332 U.S. 46 (1947).
2. See, for example, Robinson v. California, 370 U.S. 660 (1962); Gideon v. Wainwright, 372 U.S. 335 (1963); Duncan v. Louisiana, 391 U.S. 145 (1968).

3. 376 U.S. 254 (1964).

4. For example, Associated Press v. Walker, 388 U.S. 130 (1967).

5. Roth v. United States, 354 U.S. 476 (1957); Memoirs v. Massachusetts, 383 U.S. 413 (1966).

6. 395 U.S. 444 (1969).

7. 370 U.S. 421 (1962).

8. 376 U.S. 1 (1964).

9. Colegrove v. Green, 328 U.S. 549 (1946).

10. 387 U.S. 253 (1967).

11. Perez v. Brownell, 356 U.S. 44 (1958).

12. Apodaca v. Oregon, 406 U.S. 404 (1972).

13. 391 U.S. 308 (1968).

14. Lloyd Corporation v. Tanner, 407 U.S. 551 (1972).

15. Hudgens v. NLRB, 424 U.S. 507 (1976).

16. 401 U.S. 37 (1971).

17. See, for example, Yarbrough, "Litigant Access Doctrine and the Burger Court," pp. 56–69.

18. See, for example, Broadrick v. Oklahoma, 413 U.S. 601 (1973).

19. 410 U.S. 113 (1973).

20. Kelley v. Johnson, 425 U.S. 238 (1976).

21. Paul v. Davis, 424 U.S. 693 (1976).

22. Bowers v. Hardwick, 106 S.Ct. 2841 (1986).

23. See especially San Antonio Indep. School Dist. v. Rodriguez, 411 U.S. 1 (1973).

24. In, for example, his dissent in Harper v. Virginia State Bd. of Elections, 366 U.S. 663, 673 (1966).

25. Tinker v. Des Moines School Dist., 393 U.S. 503 (1969).

26. Bethel School Dist. v. Fraser, 106 S.Ct. 3159, 3164 (1986).

27. Ibid., p. 3165.

28. 108 S.Ct. 562 (1988).

29. Ibid., p. 571.

30. See generally ch. 3.

31. See generally ch. 2, especially the text accompanying notes 210–59.

32. For such criticisms in the First Amendment field, see ch. 5, especially the text accompanying notes 138–46.

33. See ch. 2, text accompanying notes 210–59.

34. Corwin, "The Doctrine of Due Process of Law before the Civil War," pp. 467–68.

35. See ch. 2, text accompanying notes 228–33.

36. See ch. 3, text accompanying notes 166–202, and ch. 2, text accompanying notes 248–51.

37. For example, Cox v. Louisiana, 319 U.S. 536 (1965).

38. For example, Brown v. Louisiana, 383 U.S. 131 (1966).

39. See ch. 4, text accompanying notes 77–84.

40. 383 U.S. 131 (1966).

41. 385 U.S. 39 (1966).

42. 372 U.S. 229 (1963).

43. 379 U.S. 536 (1965).

44. For example, Hazelwood School Dist. v. Kuhlmeier, 108 S.Ct. 562 (1988); Bethel School Dist. v. Fraser, 106 S. Ct. 3159, 3164 (1986).
45. In Spence v. Washington, 418 U.S. 405 (1974), for example, the Court reversed the conviction of an antiwar protester who displayed his flag with a peace symbol attached. But the Court's decision was closely limited to the facts of the case. When antiwar demonstrators were prosecuted for flag burning, it refused to review their convictions. Sutherland v. Illinois, 425 U.S. 947 (1976).
46. 378 U.S. 226 (1964).
47. See ch. 6, text accompanying notes 266–73.
48. CBS interview.
49. See ch. 6, text accompanying notes 116–49.
50. Abram Chayes, "The Role of the Judge in Public Law Litigation," *Harvard Law Review* 89 (1976): 1281.
51. Edwin Meese III, Address, School of Law, St. Louis University, February 12, 1986. I am grateful to Gary L. McDowell for copies of this and related Meese addresses.
52. For a survey of administration positions in a variety of civil liberties fields, see Tinsley E. Yarbrough (ed.), *The Reagan Administration and Human Rights* (New York: Praeger, 1985).
53. Kenneth Karst, "Invidious Discrimination: Justice Douglas and the Return of the 'Natural-Law-Due-Process Formula,'" *UCLA Law Review* 16 (1969): 716, 726.

Bibliographical Note

Shortly before his death, Justice Black prepared the following memorandum for his faithful secretary Frances Lamb:

> As I have indicated to you on several occasions, I do not believe that my personal notes on and for Court conferences should be left in the official files or made public. I have decided that the best thing to do is to burn them, as Justice Roberts did. Nobody can get any history out of them that is worthwhile. Please burn them at your earliest convenience and advise me that you have done so.
>
> If you have any questions about what are conference notes to be burned and what are not, and you are not able to consult with me, Hugo, Jr., will tell you what to do, which is to destroy them all.

The Justice's instructions were honored. Even so, the Hugo Lafayette Black Papers at the Library of Congress are an extensive and extremely valuable collection of correspondence, unfiled opinions, annotated drafts of opinions later published, and Court memoranda. The Library of Congress papers of Chief Justices Harlan Fiske Stone and Earl Warren, as well as those of Justices William J. Brennan, Harold H. Burton, William O. Douglas, and Robert H. Jackson, were also very helpful, as were the papers of Wiley Rutledge, which I examined at the Yale Law School before their addition to the Library of Congress's manuscript collections, and those of Frank Murphy, on file in the Michigan Historical Collection at the University of Michigan, and John Marshall Harlan, in the Seeley G. Mudd Manuscript Library at Princeton University.

Perhaps of even more value than those major primary sources, however, were my August 31, 1970, and July 6, 1971, interviews with the Justice, as well as, of course, his published opinions, citations to all of which are available in Roger W. Haigh, "The Judicial Opinions of Mr. Justice Hugo L. Black," *Southwestern University Law Review* 9 (1977): 1069, and the Justice's public statements of his judicial and constitutional philosophy in *A Constitutional Faith* (New York: Knopf, 1968); "The Bill of Rights," *New York University Law Review* 35 (1960): 865; "Justice Black and First Amendment 'Absolutes': A Public

Interview," *New York University Law Review* 37 (1962): 562; and his 1968 network television interview, a transcript of which is available in *Southwestern University Law Review* 9 (1977): 950.

Excellent general bibliographies of research on Justice Black abound. Among the more extensive are those to be found in Gerald T. Dunne, *Hugo Black and the Judicial Revolution* (New York: Simon and Schuster, 1977), pp. 469–78; Virginia Van der Veer Hamilton, *Hugo Black: The Alabama Years* (Baton Rouge: Louisiana State University Press, 1972), pp. 309–18; James J. Magee, *Mr. Justice Black: Absolutist on the Court* (Charlottesville: University Press of Virginia, 1980), pp. 197–202; and Mark Silverstein, *Constitutional Faiths: Felix Frankfurter, Hugo Black, and the Process of Judicial Decision Making* (Ithaca, N.Y.: Cornell University Press, 1984), pp. 223–30. Anthologies of Black research are also plentiful. They include Stephen P. Strickland (ed.), *Hugo Black and the Supreme Court: A Symposium* (New York: Bobbs-Merrill, 1967); "Justice Hugo L. Black: A Symposium," *Southwestern University Law Review* 9 (1977): 845; and "Mr. Justice Black: A Symposium," *Yale Law Journal* 65 (1956): 499. General analyses of his judicial and constitutional philosophy, in addition to those cited above, include Howard Ball, *The Vision and the Dream of Justice Hugo L. Black: An Examination of a Judicial Philosophy* (University: University of Alabama Press, 1975); Charles Reich, "Mr. Justice Black and the Living Constitution," *Harvard Law Review* 76 (1963): 673; John P. Frank, *Mr. Justice Black: The Man and His Opinions* (New York: Knopf, 1949); and Charlotte Williams, *Hugo L. Black: A Study in the Judicial Process* (Baltimore: Johns Hopkins University Press, 1950). And my own earlier research on the Justice includes "Mr. Justice Black and Legal Positivism," *Virginia Law Review* 57 (1971): 375; "Justices Black and Douglas: The Judicial Function and the Scope of Constitutional Liberties," *Duke Law Journal* 1973: 441; "Justice Black and his Critics on Speech-Plus and Symbolic Speech," *Texas Law Review* 52 (1974): 257; "Justice Black, the First Amendment, and the Burger Court," *Mississippi Law Journal* 46 (1975): 203; and "Justice Black, the Fourteenth Amendment, and Incorporation," *University of Miami Law Review* 30 (1976): 231.

Not surprisingly, given the nature of his jurisprudence, much research on Justice Black has been highly critical. This study focuses primarily, however, on critical assessments of the Justice's thinking in the writings of his colleagues and in John Hart Ely, *Democracy and Distrust: A Theory of Judicial Review* (Cambridge, Mass.: Harvard University Press, 1979); Charles Fairman, "Does the Fourteenth Amendment Incorporate the Bill of Rights? The Original Understanding," *Stanford Law Review* 2 (1949): 5; Stanley Morrison, "Does the Fourteenth Amendment Incorporate the Bill of Rights? The Judicial Interpretation," *Stanford Law Review* 2 (1949): 140; Magee, *Mr. Justice Black*; Sylvia Snowiss, "The Legacy of Justice Black," *Supreme Court Review* 1973: 249; Patrick McBride, "Mr. Justice Black and His Qualified Absolutes," *Loyola University* [Los Angeles] *Law Review* 2 (1969): 37; Jacob Landynski, "In Search of Justice Black's Fourth Amendment," *Fordham Law Review* 45 (1976): 453; S. Sidney Ulmer, "The Longitudinal Behavior of Hugo Lafayette Black: Parabolic Support for Civil Liberties, 1937–1971," *Florida State University Law Review* 1 (1973):

152, and "Earl Warren and the *Brown* Decision," *Journal of Politics* 33 (1971): 689; William Van Alstyne, "Mr. Justice Black, Constitutional Review, and the Talisman of State Action," *Duke Law Journal* 1965: 219; and the extensive research of Wallace Mendelson, especially *Justices Black and Frankfurter: Conflict in the Court* (Chicago: University of Chicago Press, 1961, 1966), "Hugo Black and Judicial Discretion," *Political Science Quarterly* 85 (1970): 17, and "Mr. Justice Black's Fourteenth Amendment," *Minnesota Law Review* 53 (1969): 711.

Index

36; final term of, ix–x; First Amendment interpretation by, 149–50 (*see also* Absolutism in First Amendment interpretation; First Amendment, Black interpretation of; Religion clauses of First Amendment); first day on Supreme Court, 1; on flag burning, 136; on Fourteenth Amendment (*see* Fourteenth Amendment); on Fourth Amendment, 198–99, 210–26; on Frankfurter due process definition, 95; on freedom of assembly, 137–40, 142–49; on handbill cases, 190; Harlan, relationship with, 15–16; on housing restrictions, 245, 246, 247; incorporation thesis of (*see* Incorporation thesis); increasing conservatism of, 17–18; influence of, on post-Black Court decisions, 256–58; influence of, summary of, 256–64; on insanity defense, 209; on interpretations based on legislative intent, 52–53; interpretivist jurisprudence of, 63–78; on interstate commerce affected by state laws, 44–48; on Japanese-Americans' sanctions, 232–36; on judges' personal attitudes affecting decisions, 51–52; on judicial councils, 49; on judicial legislation, 12–13, 26–27; on judicial precedents, 27–28; on judicial review, 77–78; on jury trials, 206–8; on juvenile offenders, 201–2; Ku Klux Klan affiliation of, 1, 84; language use by, 32–33; later opinions of, 185; on "law of the land," 63, 85, 99, 105–6; leftist positions of, 7–8; legal education of, 27; on libel, 134, 168; liberal image of, 120; literalist interpretation by, 27, 28, 66, 67–69; on malapportioned governmental bodies, 37–38; 231; on marital right to privacy, 22–23; on military courts, 200, 232, 234–36; on minimum wage regulation, 52; natural law and, 21–22, 26, 95, 97; on Ninth Amendment, 72–73; on obscenity, 134–36, 141, 166; on parades, 189–91; on passport denial, 55–56; on personal attitudes of

judges affecting decisions, 66; on picketing, 136, 140, 169–74, 178–81, 190, 251; on poll tax, 229; positivist characteristics of, 21–33, 35–36, 38, 39–48; on presidential policymaking authority, 39–42; on private property treated as public property, 245–47; on privileges and immunities clause, 74–75, 122–23; on privileges or immunities clause, 73–74, 108–10; on probable cause in issuing warrants, 212–13; on protest cases, 26, 188–91, 261–62; on racial discrimination in jury selection, 230, 231; on racial discrimination in prison, 233; on railroad rates, 11; on reapportionment of governmental bodies, 231; on religious freedom clauses, 150–58; on retrial, 206; on retroactivity of rulings, 32; on Roberts retirement letter, 2–3; on scheduled conferences during holiday, 9; on school hair code, x; on school-religion issues, 152–58; on school segregation, 236–45; on self-incrimination waiver, 203; as senator, 1–2, 4, 50–52; on sit-in cases, 10–11; on slander, 134; sociological jurisprudence elements in, 21–22; speech/conduct dichotomy of, 142–49, 185–88; on speech-related conduct, 141; on stare decisis, 28, 117; on state action cases, 245–52; on state marriage laws, 30–31; on steel seizure litigation, 39–42; on sterilization of criminals, 228; substantive due process doctrine rejected by, 69; on Sunday closing laws, 151; television interview of 1968, 137–38, 243, 262; on train length regulation, 46–47; on trespass cases, 244–47; on truck size regulation, 46; on verbal assault (*Chaplinsky* case), 164, 165–66; on voting age minimum, 253; on voting rights, 228–29, 254–55; on Voting Rights Act of 1965, 36–37; "wall of separation" doctrine of, 152–53; on warrants, 210–14
Black, Justice Hugo L. (court cases):
Adair-Coppage line of cases, 53–54; *Ad-*

Douglas, Justice William O. (*continued*)
v. *Price*, 104; on *Perez* v. *Brownell*, 42;
on self-incrimination waiver, 204; on
Skinner v. *Oklahoma*, 228; on *Ullmann*
v. *United States*, 204–5; on *Valentine* v.
Chrestensen, 140; on *Zorach* v. *Clauson*,
155
Due process: Black interpretation of, 48–
63, 69, 71, 84–85, 108–11; Cardozo interpretation of, 116–17; in *Chambers* v.
Florida, 84–85; before Civil War, 69;
economic legislation and, 48–54; Frankfurter interpretation of, 90, 107–8, 112;
Harlan interpretation of, 107–8; incorporation thesis and (*see* Incorporation
thesis); in Magna Carta, 49–50; in
NAACP v. *Alabama*, 14; nature of, 48–
63; property interests protected by, 80;
Roberts interpretation of, 87; Webster
interpretation of, 106. *See also* "Law of
the land"; Substantive due process
Duncan v. *Louisiana* (1968), 104–6, 107–8,
108–9, 113, 119
Dunne, Gerald, on Schubert's criticism of
Black, 18
Dunne v. *United States* (1943), 166
Dworkin, Ronald, on noninterpretivism,
63, 66

Eavesdropping, 198–99, 214–15, 220–22
Economic cases, equal protection applied
to, 227–28
Economic legislation, Court jurisdiction
over, 48–54
Education. *See* Schools
Edwards v. *California* (1941), 74, 110
Edwards v. *South Carolina* (1963), 138
Eighth Amendment, cruel and unusual
punishment provisions in, 208–9
Elections. *See* Voting; Voting rights
Electronic surveillance, 220–21
Ely, John Hart, as Black critic, 19; on
Fourteenth Amendment, 73–74; on in-

terpretivism, 259; on Ninth Amendment, 71, 72; on noninterpretivism, 63–
64, 68, 75
Engel v. *Vitale* (1962), 127, 152
Epperson v. *Arkansas* (1968), 157–58
Equal protection, 76–77, 162, 226–45; application of, to corporations, 29; Black
frustration with, 226; Black interpretation of, 198–99; in desegregation cases,
236–45; in economic cases, 227–28; governmental body apportionment and,
37–38; historical approach to interpretation of, 227; in Japanese cases, 1–
2, 232–36
Equitable relief, denial of, 34
Evans v. *Abney* (1970), 247
Everson v. *Board of Education* (1947),
152–55
Evolution, teaching in schools, 157–58
Exclusionary rule, 103–4, 215–18, 222–24
Execution: failed, as cruel and unusual
punishment (*Francis* case), 90–92; stay
of, in *Chambers* v. *Florida*, 8–9. *See also*
Capital punishment
Executive power, 39–42
Expatriation, provisions for, 42–44

Facial review, Black opposition to, 35–36
Fair Labor Standards Act, coal mine
travel time and, 3–7
Fairman, Charles, as Black critic, on in-
corporation thesis, 16, 115–19, 123–24
Fairness doctrine in broadcasting, 141
Federal courts, interference of, in state
court proceedings, 33–36
Federalism: incorporation accommodated
to, 113, 114, 115. *See also* "Our Federal-
ism" policy
Feiner v. *New York* (1951), 181
Feldman v. *United States* (1944), 204
Ferguson v. *Skrupa* (1963), 54
Field, Justice Stephen J., on incorporation
thesis, 117

114; on *Marbury v. Madison*, 253–54; on noninterpretivism, 63; on racial discrimination in prison, 233; on *Thompson v. City of Louisville*, 106; on *Tinker v. Des Moines Independent Community School District*, 148; on *Torasco v. Watkins* (religious oaths), 152; on *Williams v. Florida*, 113
Harper v. Virginia State Board of Elections (1966), 76, 229
Harris, Crampton, as Black law partner, 4
Hart, H. L. A.: on law interpretation, 25; on legislation, 24
Hazelwood School District v. Kuhlmeier (1988), 258
Hines v. Davidowitz (1941), 45–46
Hirabayashi v. United States (1943), 232, 233, 234
Hitler, Adolf, judicial law and, 13
Holmes, Justice Oliver Wendell: on due process, 51; on judicial legislation, 25
Home Building & Loan Assn. v. Blaisdell (1934), 31–32
Hook, Sidney, as Black critic, on absolutism, 129, 195
Housing, racial restrictions on, 245, 246–47
Howard, A. E. Dick, on rule of law, 17
Howard, J. Woodford, on *Chambers v. Florida*, 84
Howard, Senator Jacob, as Fourteenth Amendment sponsor, 74–75, 94, 98, 116, 118, 119–20
Hughes, Justice Charles E., on *Cox v. New Hampshire*, 174–75
Hurtado v. California (1884), 101

Immunity statutes: incriminating statements obtained under, 204–6. *See also* Privileges and immunity clause
Impeachment of judges, 49
Incorporation thesis, 79–125; accommodated to federalism principles, 113, 114, 115; Black commitment to total incorporation, 98–99, 102; criticism of, 16,

82, 99–101, 104–5, 106–25; early history of, 79–90; effects on states' rights, 96–97; versus flexible conception of due process, 95; historical aspects of, 93–95, 97–98, 115–25; *Louisiana ex rel. Francis v. Rewesber* as potential forum for, 90–92; nonacceptance of, after Black term, 258; policy criticisms of, 112–15; previous decisions compared with, 95–96; refinements of, 101–6; Republican view of, 122–23, 124; selective language used in, 102–3; selective versus total, 98; semantic criticisms of, 107–12; total, 98–101, 102. *See also Adamson v. California*
Insanity defense, 209
Interpretivism, 63–78; Black Fourth Amendment position and, 225–26; conservative politics and, 263–64; in criminal procedure cases, 199; difficulty in implementation of, 66; negative consequences of, 65; nonacceptance of, after Black tenure, 258–59; versus noninterpretivism, 63–66, 68–69
Interstate commerce, state laws affecting, 44–48
Interstate Commerce Commission, railroad rates case of, 11

Jackson, Justice Robert H.: on *Betts v. Brady*, 88; on Black as senator, 7; on Black position on desegregation, 241; on Black's appointment to Court, 3, 7; on *Chaplinsky v. New Hampshire*, 165; on *Everson v. Board of Education*, 153–54; on executive power, 40; on *Jackson v. Denno*, 207; on *Jewell Ridge Corp. v. Local 325*, 3–7; on losing Chief Justiceship, 5–6, 8; on *McCollum v. Board of Education*, 155; as Nuremberg prosecutor, 4; on *Zorach v. Clauson*, 155
Jackson v. Denno (1964), 207
Jail. *See* Prisons
Jamison v. Texas (1943), 176
Japanese-Americans, civil rights of, in World War II, 1–2, 162, 228–29, 232–36

About the Author. Tinsley E. Yarbrough is professor of political science at East Carolina University. In addition to publishing numerous articles in scholarly journals, he is the author of *Judge Frank Johnson and Human Rights in Alabama* (1981) and *A Passion for Justice: J. Waties Waring and Civil Rights* (1987). He is also editor of *The Reagan Administration and Human Rights* (1985). His biography of Judge Johnson was awarded the American Bar Association Silver Gravel award in 1982.

Library of Congress Cataloging-in-Publication Data
Yarbrough, Tinsley E. 1941–
Mr. Justice Black and his critics / Tinsley E. Yarbrough.
p.   cm.
Bibliography: p.
Includes index.
ISBN 0-8223-0866-5
1. Freedom of the press—United States—History. 2. Freedom of speech—United States—History. 3. United States—Constitutional history. 4. Black, Hugo LaFayette, 1886–1971. I. Title.
KF4770.Y37 1989
342.73'0853—dc19
[347.302853]   88-16184

DATE DUE
